Brainerd Kellogg

A Text-book on English Literature

With Copious Extracts from the Leading Authors, English and American.

Brainerd Kellogg

A Text-book on English Literature
With Copious Extracts from the Leading Authors, English and American.

ISBN/EAN: 9783744772884

Printed in Europe, USA, Canada, Australia, Japan

Cover: Foto ©Thomas Meinert / pixelio.de

More available books at **www.hansebooks.com**

A,

TEXT-BOOK

ON

English Literature,

With Copious Extracts from the Leading Authors,
English and American,

WITH FULL INSTRUCTIONS AS TO THE METHOD IN WHICH THESE ARE
TO BE STUDIED,

ADAPTED FOR USE IN COLLEGES, HIGH SCHOOLS AND
ACADEMIES,

BY

BRAINERD KELLOGG, A.M.,

Professor of the English Language and Literature in the Brooklyn Collegiate
and Polytechnic Institute, Author of a " Text-Book on Rhetoric," and one of
the Authors of Reed & Kellogg's " Graded Lessons in English," and
" Higher Lessons in English."

NEW YORK:

CLARK & MAYNARD, PUBLISHERS,

734 BROADWAY.

1884.

PREFACE.

May we not hope and expect that our children are to be taught English literature better than their parents were ? The intelligent teacher is now brushing aside the text-book that keeps pupil and authors apart, and he and they are allowed to meet face to face. How we could ever have thought that the study of what some one had said about literature or its authors was a study of literature itself excites our wonder now; we wonder that as pupils we did not detect the usurper, and rise against him in indignant revolt. Some of us have learned—what our teachers did not seem to know—that grievous wrong is done a pupil in furnishing him a mass of second-hand knowledge concerning authors, and in substituting the study of this mass for the study of the authors themselves.

Indeed, is it not to utter an educational truism now to say that no greater harm can be inflicted upon a pupil in *any* study than doing for him in it what he can do for himself? Such help takes from him the keen relish which the discovery of a fact or the conquest of a principle gives; it robs him of the pleasure which such conquest or discovery yields; it deprives him of the inestimable discipline which such labor compels; and it weakens his hold upon the fact or the principle, which slips from a grasp that would have been tenacious had he made the attainment unaided. Better far than the whole prepared for him and communicated to him by text-book or teacher would be the half or the tenth found out by himself—better that among his possessions, independently acquired, there should be some error than that through fear of error he should be kept from making any self-relying effort.

But we have not said, and do not say, that a text-book in English literature is not needed by the pupil; we say only that it should not assume functions which do not belong to it. A text-book, we think, is needed. It is needed to furnish the pupil that which he cannot help himself to. It may group the authors so that their places in the line and their relations to each other can be seen by the pupil; it may throw light upon the authors' times and surroundings, and note the great influences at work helping to make their writings what they are; it may point out such of these as should be studied, and may present extracts from them full of the author's real flavor; it may teach the pupil how these are to be studied, soliciting and exacting his judgment at every step of the way which leads from the author's diction up through his style and thought to the author himself; it may present critical estimates of the leading writers, by those competent to make them, provided it requires the pupil to accept these judgments only as he finds them borne out by the passages quoted or the writings referred to;—in all these ways and in other ways it may place the pupil on the best possible footing with those whose acquaintance it is his business as well as his pleasure to make. Such functions as these, discharged by a text-book, would justify its use; and such a text-book we have tried to make the one we now present.

The Primer of English Literature by Stopford Brooke, admirably adapted for our purpose, has been chosen as the basis, or nucleus, of our work. The excellence of the Primer is our only apology for its appropriation. Great liberties have been taken with the text. Many passages have been eliminated —specially those criticised by Matthew Arnold in his review of the work. The Primer has been rearranged to suit our purpose, and has been cut up into Lessons. All the matter taken from Mr. Brooke has been enclosed in quotation marks. We have added a Biographical and Topical Index, which contains much valuable information concerning authors that is not to be found in the body of the work.

The Eight Periods in which Mr. Brooke places English literature, and into which it seems naturally to fall, have, with slight changes, been retained. . Each Period is preceded by a Lesson containing a brief résumé of the great historical events that have had somewhat to do in shaping or in coloring the literature of that Period. The pupil, it is hoped, will be able to see the better in the light thus shed.

We have inserted short estimates of the leading authors, made by the best English and American critics. These criticisms are to be used as indicated above, and as pointed out in the Introductory Lesson. They are not to take the place of the pupil's work, but are themselves to be judged by him, and ratified or amended according to his findings in the study of the authors themselves.

Extracts, as many and as ample as the limits of a text-book would allow, have been made from the principal writers of each Period. We have tried to find such as contain the characteristic traits of their authors both in thought and in expression. But few of these extracts have, so far as we know, ever seen the light in books of selections—anthologies of poetry or prose. None of them, we may say, have been worn threadbare by use, or have lost their freshness by the pupil's familiarity with them in school-readers. There is less need than formerly of such extracts, now that short classics, full of good things from the best authors, and admirably annotated, can be easily and cheaply procured. We heartily commend for use in the class-room the list of short *English Classics*, already quite extensive, published by Clark & Maynard, and the list entitled *American Classics for Schools*, issued by Houghton, Mifflin & Co., Boston.

We have prepared a Bibliography for the most eminent

authors. This will be of service to such teachers and pupils
as have access to public libraries, and who care to correct
or supplement their knowledge by reading the opinions of
others. We had for a long time been making these Bib-
liographies, when we found the work already largely done for
us in the catalogue of the Brooklyn Library. Since then the
catalogue has been freely used. It will be seen that the
greater part of the references are to Magazine articles, and
that these are recent. Whatever may be claimed for the
critics of the generations gone, it will be allowed that never
has criticism been more discriminating, delicate, just, and
appreciative than it is now.

In the Introductory Lesson we have indicated how we wish
the book to be studied. The method there detailed has
grown up out of a long experience with classes in literature.
It is that, also, up to which the work in Reed and Kellogg's
Grammars and in Kellogg's Rhetoric has led the pupil; it
completes such work, and applies it to the study of authors.
We beg teachers to examine the method carefully, and test it
by trial before rejecting it.

We wish here to express our grateful acknowledgments to
Messrs. Houghton, Mifflin & Co., to G. P. Putnam's Sons,
and to Messrs. Appleton & Co. for the generous use they have
allowed us of the sterling works published by them. It is
through their kindness that we have been enabled to supplement our historical account and critical estimate of American
literature with more than sixty pages of choice extracts from
the best American authors.

POLYTECHNIC INSTITUTE, Brooklyn, N. Y.,

CONTENTS.

PERIOD I.

PERIOD II.

PERIOD VIII.

PERIODS OF ENGLISH LITERATURE.

ENGLISH LITERATURE.

LESSON 1.

INTRODUCTORY.

REQUISITES FOR THE STUDY OF ENGLISH LITERATURE.—To teach one English literature is to acquaint him with the writings which constitute it. It is to put him in the way of getting at the characteristics of those who in a memorable degree have contributed to it; and to lead him along this way until the traits peculiar to each are distinctly seen by him, and in some measure of intimacy the desired acquaintance with them is reached. To such a study it is evident that the student should come prepared; he should bring to it respectable attainments, and a respectable discipline acquired in making these attainments. What rhetoric can teach him of thought and its invention, of words and the handling of them, of sentences in their myriad variety, of the cardinal qualities of style, of the great classes of literary productions, and all that this instruction can do in developing his power to discriminate and to classify he should bring to this work. Some knowledge of what goes to the making of literature and so of what he is to seek in it, some standard of excellence by which to judge the writings he is to study, and a faculty to compare, to estimate, and to decide are desirable, may we not say needful, at the outset.

THE TEXT-BOOK.—The text-book can aid the pupil in his work—it will be something if it aids without hindering him. Instead of coming in between the pupil and the author to keep them apart with matter of its own, it should come only to introduce the one to the other, and to put the one on the best possible footing with the other. It has no right to substitute, for what the author has written, something which another has said about his writings, and call the study of this the study of English literature. It has no right to tax the memory of the pupil in the learning of this, and omit calling his judgment into vigorous exercise by a careful study of the authors themselves.

The text-book may map out literature by dividing it into the periods into which it naturally falls; some account of the great events which have helped to shape the literature of each period may be given; the continuity of the literary stream through all these changes in its channel may be traced ; the influence of his surroundings upon an author and his reaction upon them may be indicated ; the productions of each writer should be named ; a more ample description of this and that great representative of his period may be given ; and even a critical estimate of some works may be made that the pupil through the glasses thus furnished may see what his unaided vision could not detect : but all this, be it remembered, the book should offer the pupil, not as the end of his study, but only as a means to place him in a better attitude for forming his own opinions, and to enable him to judge more accurately because of the light thus added. Let this also be remembered—that what the author of the text-book or the critics whom he quotes may say of these writings is not to be received and retailed without question, but is to be passed upon by the pupil himself, and ratified or amended according to his findings in the extracts given or the works referred to for study in the preparation of his lesson, and for reading in the class-room. Only by making the pupils witnesses to give the evidence, advocates to arrange and present it, and the jury to weigh it and decide upon it, will the study be made interesting

and profitable in the highest degree. Only thus can a cultivated taste and a sound judgment be formed to guide pupils in
their after-reading, and a key be placed in their hands to
unlock the treasures of literature—the study of which will be
to most of them the best, perhaps the only, means with which
to continue the life-long work of education.

HOW THIS WORK IS TO BE STUDIED.—We wish here to point
out more in detail how this work should be studied—to younger
teachers the experience of an elder may be useful. The questions below are framed for all except the eight historical
Lessons, which introduce the periods of our literature. Some
of these questions may seem trifling, others may be too difficult. The teacher will take into account the age and ability
of his class, and the rank of the author under discussion. He
will take counsel from his experience and from his use of
methods—David could not fight in the armor of another.
Remembering that he cannot shift from himself the responsibility for his work, he will use his best discretion in conducting
it. But if the line here traced is followed, we ask that these
questions shall not be put in detail. They are grouped under
headings, such as *classification* and *diction*. Let each pupil
take the heading assigned him, and answer the questions under
it without interrogation from the teacher or interruption from
any one. The recitation is his work and his only. The
direction of the whole, correction of what is amiss, and expan-
sion of what is only suggested will give the teacher all needed
occupation. If any heading is too comprehensive for a single
pupil, he may share it with another, with others. The questions under *classification* relate to the text; those under the
heads which follow relate to the author's writings. Insist that
the pupil, in answering these, shall put his finger upon the
words or passages from which he claims to derive his opinion.
His answers, when he has ended, will provoke question and
objection, and furnish matter for profitable debate.

I. CLASSIFICATION.—In what period is the writer placed? What great men are representative of it, and what is their exact date? Who were his contemporaries? To what class* of prose writers or of poets does he belong? What are his works? What is said of him? Of them? Have his productions become classic?

II. DICTION.—As a whole, are his words long or short? Simple or abstruse? Native in origin or foreign? Does he use words with precision, or is he careless of their exact meanings? Does he handle them with ease? Has he a copious vocabulary? Judged by our standard, is he always grammatically correct?

III. SENTENCES.—Does he affect long sentences or short? Are they diffuse or epigrammatic? Are they sonorous, or are they written with slight regard to the ear? Are they mainly simple? Compound? Complex? Are his complex sentences involved and intricate, or is the connection of clauses obvious? In the arrangement of parts, does he incline to the natural order or to the transposed? Are any of his sentences climaxes, the parts growing in importance as the sentence proceeds? Are any periods, keeping the meaning in suspense till the close? Are any loose sentences, containing each at least one point before the end at which the sense is complete, the part following not making complete sense? Does he abound in parentheses? Is he happy in grouping his sentences into paragraphs?

IV. STYLE. 1. PERSPICUITY.—Is the author always clear? If so, to what is his perspicuity owing? If not, is his obscurity due to imperfect mastery of his subject? To an inexact use of words? To the use of strange words—technical, obsolete, foreign, or newly-coined? To excess of words—tautology or verbosity? To the omission of needed words? To expression too condensed? To a careless use of personal pronouns? To a faulty arrangement of words, phrases, or clauses? To an overloading of the sentence that destroys unity?

2. IMAGERY.—Does he use imagery? Does he use an excess of it? Is his imagery helpful to the thought? Are any of his figures of speech used only for ornament? What class of figures does he prefer? Do his figures contain allusions? From what sources are his figures drawn? Are any faulty?

3. ENERGY.—Is the writer distinguished for strength? If so, is it due to vigor of thought? To strong feeling? To the use of specific words? To conciseness of expression? To the transposed order of arrangement? To rapidity of movement? To striking imagery? To idiomatic expression? To apt quotations? To the use of the climax? To the use of

---

* For explanation of this and of other points in this Lesson, see Kellogg's Rhetoric.

the period? To variety in the structure of his sentences? To variety in the kinds of sentences used?

4 and 5. WIT AND PATHOS.—Is the author witty? If so, does he prefer wit with malice in it? Or that without hostility—humor? Has he pathetic passages?

6. ELEGANCE.—Is the production remarkable for beauty? If so, is the beauty in the thought? Is it secured by the choice of euphonious words? By beautiful imagery? By long and flowing sentences? By sentences harmonious and symmetrical, with parts nicely balanced?

For what quality of style is the author chiefly distinguished? Is the style as a whole attractive to you? Would further study of it be profitable to you? Is it adapted to the thought? Does it lend value to the thought? Does the author show a mastery of the art of expression? Are you curious to see more of his writings?

V. THOUGHT.—Is the author's grasp of his thought firm? Is the selection crowded with thought? Does he make fine distinctions in his thinking? Is his thought profound or superficial? Original or commonplace? True or erroneous? Does he deal with facts only, or is he highly imaginative? Is he dogmatic? Is he controversial? What is the topic of the extract, and what is the gist of his thought upon it? Is he didactic? Is he aiming mainly to please? Is he persuasive? Had he observed much? Had he read widely? Was he a man of great learning? Had he digested and assimilated his knowledge? If argumentative, is his reasoning easily followed? Does he cling closely to his subject, or does he digress? Is his reasoning open to any criticism? Do his paragraphs develop each a topic or sub-topic of the subject? Is the transition from one paragraph to another easy and natural? Is the connection between them close?

VI. FEELING.—Is the author's heart in his writings or only his intellect? If the writing is colored by sentiment, what feelings of the reader are principally appealed to? What in a subordinate degree? Does the thought predominate over the feeling, or the feeling over the thought? Is the author hopeful and inspiring? Is he genial and delightful? If so, because of what? Is he in love with his kind, or is he cynical? Is he in love with external nature? If so, with what phase or department of it? Is he sincere or affected? What else would you infer of his disposition and character? Do you feel after reading him that you know him? Does further acquaintance with him seem desirable?

The questions asked above apply to **Prose.** But, omitting those under the headings **Sentences** and **Energy**, some of those under **Perspicuity**, and those under **Thought** which relate to argumentative writing, they apply to **Poetry** also. Make much of **Feeling** in relation to poetry. A few questions, peculiar to poetry, may be set down under the head of

FORM. 1. RHYTHM.—What foot prevails in the poem? Is it dissyllabic or trisyllabic? What other feet, if any, are substituted for this, and where? In the scansion, is elision, or slurring, anywhere resorted to? Can you scan the poem?

2. METRE.—How many feet are there in the standard, or prevailing, line? And so, in what metre is the poem written? What is the metre of those lines varying from the standard?

3. RHYME.—Do the lines rhyme, or is the poem in blank-verse?

FURTHER REMARKS.—On some productions, questions, in addition to those above, will be asked, or suggestions will be made. Characteristic specimens from only the principal authors, and not from all of these, can, in a work of this kind, be given or referred to for study. How many authors shall be studied in this way and how long they shall be studied are questions difficult to answer. Much depends upon the attainments and maturity of the class, and much upon the time allowed for the work. There are those who insist that but a few even of the best should be taken up, and that the pupil should tarry with these until his acquaintance has ripened into real intimacy. But such intimacy with a few, even if attainable when the material for comparison and contrast is scanty, must be paid for by total ignorance of literature as a whole. There is danger, too, that it would nourish in the pupil that "conceit of knowledge" which "is the arrest of progress." It would not cultivate breadth of view or catholicity of taste. It is at issue with the aim of all other education in the preparatory school and in college, which is to open up to the pupil many departments of study and to enter him a little way in each, without attempting to make him a proficient in any. Better a taste of the characteristic flavor of many authors, a taste that will crave feeding when school days are over, than a long and relishable feast upon a few which shall leave the pupil without appetite for more food of the same, or of a different, kind. The man of many books may well heed the warning, Beware of the man of one book; not, however, because of this home-bred wit's superior knowledge, but rather because of his intolerable bigotry and one-sidedness.

There are those, too, who in this study disallow all such methods as the one we have been unfolding, who even discourage the reading of extracts by the pupils, except under the teacher's supervision and with his explanation in the classroom, where he and they are jointly to commune with the author. Communion with the author is, of course, the one thing desired. Everything in the study should lead up to it as the goal. But how is this goal of communion, joint communion if you please, to be reached except by a start at some definite point, and by an orderly progress from it. The writer's thought is in his expression, the one can be got at only by and through the other. He is in both, both are his —may we not say both are he. Shakespeare's thought, saturated with feeling,—could it be divorced, as it cannot, from Shakespeare's diction and style, would lose its charm and its power; could it be reached by the pupil, as it cannot, without approaching it through his diction and style, the *whole* of the dramatist would not be seen—the pupil would not then stand in the presence of Shakespeare himself.

But we unite with all who disparage methods that divert the pupil's attention from what we have seen is its proper object, and concentrate it upon a prolonged examination of the author's words in their etymology and history, making this a study of linguistics and not of literature.

Differ, however, as we may in other respects, in this one thing all will agree—that by the study of English literature the pupil is to be put in the way of deriving intellectual culture and intense enjoyment from books; that any method of study by which he secures these is good; and that that method is the best by which he secures them in the largest measure.

PERIOD I.

BEFORE THE NORMAN CONQUEST,
670–1066.

LESSON 2.

Brief Historical Sketch.—Britain, at the beginning of the historic period, was inhabited by Celts. This race occupied Gaul, a part of Spain, the north of Italy, and some provinces of Central Europe, also. They belong to the great Indo-European family, the other members of which are the peoples using or having used (1) the Indian languages, notably the Sanskrit, of Northern Hindostan, (2) the Iranian of ancient and modern Persia, (3) the Hellenic of ancient Greece and the modern Greek, (4) the Slavonic, of which the Russian is chief, (5) the Italic, of which the Latin is the great representative, and (6) the Teutonic, subdivisible into the Gothic, the Scandinavian, the High Germanic, and the Low Germanic. The Celts of Britain were independent tribes, rarely uniting against a common foe. They lived in huts hollowed out of hills, sides vaulted and roofs thatched, or in circular houses with low stone walls and conical roofs—ten or twelve families under one roof. Practiced polyandry. Lived on the products of the chase, on fruits, milk, and flesh, and in the South on grain bruised and baked. Wore tunics and short trowsers and cloaks; wove, made earthenware and the implements of war, and tattooed their bodies. Religion Druidism; the priests, called Druids, were somewhat educated, decided all disputes public and private, were exempt from taxes and all public duties, and offered sacrifices, even human. The Celts held the soul to be immortal, believed in transmigration, and burned their dead, or buried them doubled up in cists or lying straight in canoe-shaped coffins. Irish teachers visit Britain and make converts to Christianity before 400 A.D. Cæsar disclosed Britain to the Romans, 55 and 54 B.C. Agricola pushed its conquest to the Friths of Forth and of Clyde, 78–84 A.D. The Romans held Britain by fortified posts—Eboricum (York) the central one—connected by broad military roads passing straight over hills, and crossing morasses on piles. Romans exacted tribute, and afterward taxes on arable and on pasture land, and customs at the ports, proscribed Druidism, abolished tattooing, made cremation general, quickened agriculture, and exported corn. By 420 A.D., the Roman legions are recalled to defend Rome against the northern hordes. Angles, Saxons, and Jutes of the Teutonic race, dwelling about the mouths of the Elbe, begin the conquest of Britain by 450, complete it by 607. Celts exterminated or driven to the moun· tains. Few Celtic words, dating from this period, in our language. Their names given to the rivers survive. Sovereignty of the Anglo-Saxons at first in the hands of the people. War gives birth to mon-archy, the king chosen from the leaders in battle. Houses of stone or timber, sometimes with an upper story, mead hall the principal room, no chimneys. Had chairs, stools, and benches, used carpets and cush-ions, glass drinking cups, few plates and knives, no forks, and a board on trestles for a table. Ate animal food, fish, and grain ground by hand or in water mills and baked in ovens. Weapons were the sword, battle axe, bow and arrow, dagger, spear, wooden shield with iron boss, and mail of leather. Prisoners taken in battle, debtors surrendering themselves, and criminals were made slaves. Land was divided into marks, each occupied by a community of related families. In time, marks unite to form shires (32 in Ælfred's reign, 871–901), each with its own organization legal, political, and religious. Shires (now counties) unite to form a kingdom. Wives practically bought at first, polygamy forbidden, voluntary separation allowed, and children could be sold or possibly put to death by the parent. Religion Scandinavian, names of the gods seen in the names of some of our days of the week. Names of demons and water sprites survive in *Old Scratch, Old Nick,* and *Deuce.* This religion drove Christianity out of Britain. Right of private re-venge claimed at first, afterward crimes and injuries could be expiated with money. In Ælfred's time, death was the punishment for murder and for some other crimes. Christianity introduced from Rome, 597 A.D., by Augustine, who became first Archbishop of Canterbury. From 607 onward, the Anglo-Saxons were fighting each other, until in 827 the seven or eight kingdoms were united under Egbert, king of Wessex, who now styled himself "King of the English." The glorious period of A. S. history is the reign of Ælfred the Great. Frequent Danish in-vasions from 832–1011. Danish kings on the throne, 1018–1042. Did not materially change the institutions or the language, which was the Anglo-Saxon, the mother-tongue of the English of to-day. Anglo-Saxon dynasty restored by Edward the Confessor, 1042. Conquest of the country by William the Conqueror, Duke of Normandy, 1066.

To THE TEACHER.—Make as much as the hour will allow of each historical Lesson. Develop points that are only suggested. Emphasize especially those events that account for any feature or phase of the literature.

LESSON 3.

THE HISTORY OF ENGLISH LITERATURE.—" This is the story of what great English men and women thought and felt, and then wrote down in good prose or beautiful poetry in the English language. The story is a long one. It begins about the year 670, and it is still going on in the year 1882. Into this book, then, is to be put the story of 1,200 years. English men and women have good reason to be proud of the work done by their forefathers in prose and poetry. Every one who can write a good book or a good song may say to himself, 'I belong to a great company which has been teaching and delighting the world for more than 1,000 years.' And that is a fact in which those who write and those who read ought to feel a noble pride.

THE ENGLISH AND THE WELSH.—This literature is written in English, the tongue of our fathers. They lived, while England was still called Britain, in Sleswick, Jutland, and Holstein; but, either because they were pressed from the inland or for pure love of adventure, they took to the sea, and, landing at various parts of Britain at various times, drove back, after 150 years of hard fighting, the Britons, whom they called Welsh, to the land now called Wales, and to Cornwall. It is well for those who study English literature to remember that in these two places the Britons remained as a distinct race with a distinct literature of their own, because the stories and the poetry of the Britons crept afterwards into English literature and had a great influence upon it. The whole tale of King Arthur, of which English poetry and even English prose is so full, was a British tale.

THE ENGLISH * TONGUE.—Of the language in which our

---

* " There is no good reason for rejecting the term *Anglo-Saxon*, and, as has been proposed, employing *English* as the name of the language from the earliest date to the present day. A change of nomenclature like this would expose us to the inconvenience not merely of embracing within one designation objects which have been literature is written we can say little here. Of course it has changed its look very much since it began to be written. The earliest form of our English tongue is very different from modern English in form, pronunciation, and appearance, and one must learn it almost as if it were a foreign tongue; but still the language written in the year 700 is the same as that in which the prose of the Bible is written, just as much as the tree planted a hundred years ago is the same tree to-day. It is this sameness of language, as well as the sameness of national spirit, which makes the literature one literature for 1200 years.

THE FIRST ENGLISH POETRY.—When the English came to Britain, they were great warriors and great sea pirates—'sea wolves' as a Roman poet calls them; and all English poetry down to the present day is full of war, and still more of the sea. No other nation has ever written so much sea-poetry. It was in the blood of these men, who chanted their sea war-songs as they sailed. But they were more than mere warriors. They were a home-loving people when settled either in Sleswick or in England, and all English literature from the first writings to the last is full of domestic love, the dearness of home, and the ties of kinsfolk. They were a religious people, even as heathen,

---

conventionally separated but of confounding things logically distinct; for, though our modern English is built upon, and mainly derived from, the Anglo-Saxon, the two dialects are now so discrepant that the fullest knowledge of one would not alone suffice to render the other intelligible to either the eye or the ear. They are too unlike in vocabulary and in inflectional character to be still considered as one speech."—*George P. Marsh.*

These reasons are equally conclusive against calling our earliest *literature* English. Wherever, then, in this Lesson and in the three or four following, Mr. Brooke uses *English* to designate either the language or the literature before 1066 or even 1150, we suggest that *Anglo-Saxon* be substituted for it by the teacher and the pupil.

This distribution of our language and our literature, adopted by some of our latest and best authorities, seems to us excellent:—

I. **Anglo-Saxon**		450—1150
II. **Early English** { **Semi-Saxon** .... 1150—1250 { **Old English** .... 1250—1350		1150—1350
III. **Middle English**		1350—1550
IV. **Modern English**		1550——.

still more so when they became Christian; and their poetry is as much tinged with religion as with war. Whenever literature died down in England, it rose again in poetry; and the first poetry at each recovery was religious, or linked to religion. We shall soon see that the first poems were of war and religion.

English Poetry was different then from what it is now. It was not written in rhyme, nor were its syllables counted. The lines are short; the beat of the verse depends on the emphasis given by the use of the same letter, except in the case of vowels, at the beginning of words; and the emphasis of the words depends on the thought. The lines are written in pairs; and in the best work the two chief words in the first and the one chief word in the second usually begin with the same letter. Here is one example from a war-song:—

| ‘ *W*igu *w*intrum geong
 *W*ordum mælde.’ | ‘ *W*arrior of *w*inters young
 With *w*ords spake.’ |

After the Norman Conquest there gradually crept in a French system of rhymes and of metres, which we find full-grown in Chaucer's works. But unrhymed and alliterative verse lasted in poetry to the reign of John, and alliteration was blended with rhyme up to the sixteenth century. The latest form of it occurs in Scotland.

. **The greatest early Poems** remaining are two—*Beowulf* and *Cædmon's Paraphrase of the Bible*. The first is on the whole a war story, the second is religious; and on these two subjects of war and religion English poetry for the most part speaks till the Conquest. *Beowulf* was brought into England from the Continent, and was rewritten in parts by a Christian Englishman of Northumbria. It is a story of the great deeds and death of a hero named Beowulf. Its social interest lies in what it tells us of the manners and customs of these people before they came to the island; its poetical interest lies in its descriptions of wild nature, of the lives and feelings of the

men of that time, and of the way in which the Nature-worship
of these men made dreadful and savage places seem dwelt in
—as if the places had a spirit—by monstrous beings. For it
was thus that all that half-natural, half-spiritual world began
in English poetry which, when men grew gentler and the country more cultivated, became so beautiful as faeryland.   Here is
the description (taken from Thorpe's edition of the poem) of
the dwelling-place of the Grendel, a man-fiend that devoured
men, and whom Beowulf overcomes in battle:—

' Hie dygel lond
warigeað wulf-hleóðu,
windige næssas,
frecne fen-gelâd,
ðær fyrgen-streâm,
under næssa genipu,
niþer gewiteð,
flôd under foldan.
Nis þæt feor heonon,
mil gemearces,
þæt se mere standeð,
ofer þǽm hongiað
hrinde-bearwas .

They *that* secret land
inhabit, *the* wolf's retreats,
windy nesses,
the dangerous fen-path,
where *the* mountain-stream,
under *the* nesses' mists,
downward flows,
the flood under *the* earth.
It is not far thence,
a mile's distance,
that *the* mere stands,
over which hang
barky groves ,

Feþa eal gesæt ;
gesawon þá æfter wætere
wyrm-cynnes fela,
sêllíce sǽ-dracan,
sund cunnian ;
swylce on nǽs-hleoþum
nicras licgean,
ða on undern mæl
oft bewitigað
sorhfulne sið
on segl-ráde,
wyrmas and wildeór :

The band all sat ;
they saw along *the* water
of *the* worm-kind many,
strange sea dragons,
tempting *the* deep ;
also in *the* headland-clefts
nickers lying,
which at morning time
oft keep
their sorrowful course
on *the* sail-road,
worms and wild beasts'.

"The love of wild nature in English poetry, and the peopling of it with wild, half-human things begin in work like this. After the fight Beowulf returns to his own land, where he rules well for many years, till a Fire-drake, who guards a treasure, comes down to harry his people. The old king goes out then to fight his last fight, slays the dragon, but dies of its flaming breath, and his body is burned high up on a sea-washed Ness, or headland."

"Similes are very rare in A. S. poetry. The whole romance of Beowulf contains only five, and these are of the simplest kind; the vessel gliding swiftly over the waves is compared to a bird; the Grendel's eyes to fire; his nails to steel; the light which Beowulf finds in the Grendel's dwelling, under the waters, resembles the serene light of the sun; and the sword which has been bathed in the monster's blood melts immediately like ice."—*Wright.*

BIBLIOGRAPHY. ANGLO-SAXON LITERATURE AND THE ANGLO-SAXON WRITERS.— Turner's *Hist. of Manners, Poetry, and Lit. of the Anglo-Saxons;* H. Corson's *Hand-book of A. S. and Early Eng.;* H. Morley's *Eng. Writers;* T. Wright's *Biographia Britannica Literaria;* Guest's *Hist. Eng. Rhythms;* Taine's *Eng. Lit.;* Craik's *Eng. Lit.;* J. J. Conybeare's *Illust. of A. S. Poetry;* G. P. Marsh's *Origin and Hist. of Eng. Lang.;* Prof. Ten Brink's *Hist. Eng. Lit.;* H. Sweet's *Hist. of A. S. Poetry; A. S. Lit.* in Encyclo. Britannica; in Johnson's Cyclo.; in Appleton's, and in others.

LESSON 4.

CÆDMON.– "The poem of Beowulf has the grave Teutonic power, but it is not native to English soil. It is not the first true English poem. That is the work of CÆDMON, and is also from Northumbria. The story of it, as told by Bæda, proves that the making of songs was common at the time. Cædmon was a servant to the monastery of Hild, an abbess of royal blood, at Whitby in Yorkshire. He was somewhat aged when the gift of song came to him, and he knew nothing of the art of verse, so that at the feasts, when for the sake of mirth all sang

in turn, he left the table. One night, having done so and gone
to the stables, for he had care of the cattle, he fell asleep, and
One came to him in vision and said, ' Cædmon, sing me some
song.' And he answered, ' I cannot sing; for this cause I left
the feast and came hither.' Then said the other, ' However,
you shall sing.' ' What shall I sing?' he replied. ' Sing
the beginning of created things,' answered the other. Whereupon he began to sing verses to the praise of God, and, awaking, remembered what he had sung, and added more in verse
worthy of God. In the morning he came to the steward, and
told him of the gift he had received, and, being brought to
Hild, was ordered to tell his dream before learned men that
they might give judgment whence his verses came. And,
when they had heard, they all said that heavenly grace had
been conferred on him by our Lord.

Cædmon's poem, written about 670, is for us the beginning
of English poetry, and the story of its origin ought to be loved
by us. Nor should we fail to reverence the place where it
began. Above the small and land-locked harbor of Whitby
rises and juts out towards the sea the dark cliff where Hild's
monastery stood, looking out over the German Ocean. It is
a wild, wind-swept upland, and the sea beats furiously beneath, and standing there one feels that it is a fitting birthplace
for the poetry of the sea-ruling nation. Nor is the verse of
the first poet without the stormy note of the scenery among
which it was written. In it also the old, fierce, war element is
felt when Cædmon comes to sing the wrath of the rebel angels
with God and the overthrow of Pharaoh's host, and the lines,
repeating, as was the old English way, the thought a second
time, fall like stroke on stroke in battle. But the poem is
religious throughout—Christianity speaks in it simply, sternly,
with fire, and brings with it a new world of spiritual romance
and feeling. The subjects of the poem were taken from the
Bible, in fact Cædmon paraphrased the history of the Old and
the New Testament. He sang the creation of the world, the

history of Israel, the book of Daniel, the whole story of the
life of Christ, future judgment, purgatory, hell, and heaven.
All who heard it thought it divinely given. 'Others after
him,' says Bæda, 'tried to make religious poems, but none
could vie with him, for he did not learn the art of poetry from
men, nor of men, but from God.' It was thus that English
song began in religion. The most famous passage of the poem
not only illustrates the dark sadness, the fierce love of freedom,
and the power of painting distinct characters which has always
marked English poetry, but it is also famous for its likeness to
a parallel passage in Milton. It is when Cædmon describes the
proud and angry cry of Satan against God from his bed of
chains in hell. The two great English poets may be brought
together over a space of a thousand years in another way, for
both died in such peace that those who watched beside them
knew not when they died.

LESSER OLD ENGLISH POEMS.—Of the poetry that came after Cædmon we have few remains. But we have many things
said which show us that his poem, like all great works, gave
birth to a number of similar ones. The increase of monasteries,
where men of letters lived, naturally made the written poetry
religious. But an immense quantity of secular poetry was
sung about the country. ALDHELM, a young man when Cædmon died, and afterwards Abbot of Malmesbury, united the
song-maker to the religious poet. He was a skilled musician,
and it is said that he had not his equal in the making or singing of English verse. His songs were popular in King Ælfred's
time, and a pretty story tells that, when the traders came into
the town on the Sunday, he, in the character of a gleeman,
stood on the bridge and sang them songs, with which he mixed
up Scripture text and teaching. Of all this wide-spread poetry
we have now only the few poems brought together in a book
preserved at Exeter, in another found at Vercelli, and in a
few leaflets of manuscripts. The poems in the *Vercelli book*
are all religious—legends of saints and addresses to the soul;

those in the *Exeter book* are hymns and sacred poems. The famous *Traveller's Song* and the *Lament of Deor* inserted in it are of the older and pagan time. In both there are poems by CYNEWULF, whose work is remarkably fine. They are all Christian in tone. The few touches of love of nature in them dwell on gentle, not on savage, scenery. They are sorrowful when they speak of the life of men, tender when they touch on the love of home, as tender as this little bit which still lives for us out of that old world: 'Dear is the welcome guest to the Frisian wife when the vessel strands; his ship is come, and her husband to his house, her own provider. And she welcomes him in, washes his weedy garment, and clothes him anew. It is pleasant on shore to him whom his love awaits.' Of the scattered pieces the finest are two fragments, one long, on the story of *Judith,* and another short, in which Death speaks to Man, and describes 'the low and hateful and door-less house,' of which he keeps the key. But stern as the fragment is, with its English manner of looking dreadful things in the face, and with its English pathos, the religi-ous poetry of this time always went with faith beyond the grave. Thus we are told that King Eadgar, in the ode on his death in the *Anglo-Saxon Chronicle,* 'chose for himself another light, beautiful and pleasant, and left this feeble life.'

The war poetry of England at this time was probably as plentiful as the religious. But it was not likely to be written down by the writers who lived in religious houses. It was sung from feast to feast and in the halls of kings, and it naturally decayed when the English were trodden down by the Normans. But we have two examples of what kind it was, and how fine it was, in the *Battle Song of Brunanburh,* 937, and in the *Song of the Fight at Maldon,* 991. A still earlier fragment exists in a short account of the *Battle of Finnesburg,* probably of the same time and belonging to as long a story as the story of Beowulf. Two short odes on the victories of King Eadmund and on the coronation of King Eadgar, inserted in the *Anglo-Saxon Chronicle*, complete the list of war poems.

The Songs of Brunanburh and Maldon are fine war odes, the fitting sources, both in their short and rapid lines and in their almost Homeric simplicity and force, of such war-songs as the ' Battle of the Baltic' and the ' Charge of the Light Brigade.' The first describes the fight of King Æthelstan with Anlaf the Dane. From morn till night they fought till they were 'weary of red battle' in the 'hard hand play,' till five young kings and seven earls of Anlaf's host lay in that fighting place 'quieted by swords,' and the Northmen fled, and only ' the screamers of war were left behind, the black raven and the eagle to feast on the white flesh, and the greedy battle-hawk, and the grey beast the wolf in the wood.' The second is the story of the death of Brihtnoth, an ealdorman of Northumbria, in battle against the Danes. It contains 690 lines. In the speeches of heralds and warriors before the fight, in the speeches and single combats of the chiefs, in the loud laugh and mock which follow a good death-stroke, in the rapid rush of the verse when the battle is joined, the poem, though broken, as Homer's verse is not, is Homeric. In the rude chivalry which disdains to take vantage ground of the Danes, in the way in which the friends and churls of Brihtnoth die, one by one, avenging their lord, keeping faithful the tie of kinship and clanship, in the cry not to yield a foot's breadth of earth, in the loving sadness with which home is spoken of, the poem is English to the core. And in the midst of it all, like a song from another land, but a song heard often in English fights from then till now, is the last prayer of the great earl, when, dying, he commends his soul with thankfulness to God.''

LESSON 5.

OLD ENGLISH PROSE.—"It is pleasant to think that I may not unfairly make English prose begin with BÆDA. He was born about A.D. 673, and was, like Cædmon, a Northumbrian. From 683 he spent his life at Jarrow, in the same monastery, he says, 'and while attentive to the rule of mine order, and the service of the Church, my constant pleasure lay in learning or teaching or writing.' He long enjoyed that pleasure, for his quiet life was long, and from boyhood till his very last hour his toil was unceasing. Forty-five works prove his industry, and their fame over the whole of learned Europe during his time proves their value. His learning was as various as it was great. All that the world then knew of science, music, rhetoric, medicine, arithmetic, astronomy, and physics was brought together by him ; and his life was as gentle and himself as loved as his work was great. His books were written in Latin, and with these we have nothing to do, but his was the first effort to make English prose a literary language, for his last work was a *Translation of the Gospel of St. John,* as almost his last words were in English verse. In the story of his death, told by his disciple, CUTHBERT is the first record of English prose writing. When the last day came, the dying man called his scholars to him that he might dictate more of his translation. 'There is still a chapter wanting,' said the scribe, 'and it is hard for thee to question thyself longer.' 'It is easily done,' said Bæda, 'take thy pen and write quickly.' Through the day they wrote, and when evening fell, 'There is yet one sentence unwritten, dear master,' said the youth. 'Write it quickly,' said the master. 'It is finished now.' 'Thou sayest truth,' was the reply, 'all is finished now.' He sang the 'Glory to God,' and died. It is to that scene that English prose looks back as its sacred source, as it is in the greatness and variety of

Bæda's Latin work that English literature strikes its key-note.

ÆLFRED'S WORK.—When Bæda died, Northumbria was the home of English literature. Though as yet written mostly in Latin, it was a wide-spread literature. Wilfrid of York and Benedict Biscop had founded libraries and established monastic schools far and wide. Six hundred scholars gathered round Bæda ere he died. But towards the end of his life, this northern literature began to decay, and after 866 it was, we may say, blotted out by the Danes. The long battle with these invaders was lost in Northumbria, but it was gained for a time by Ælfred the Great in Wessex; and with ÆLFRED'S literary work learning changed its seat from the north to the south. But he made it by his writings an English, not a Latin, literature; and in his translations he, since Bæda's work is lost, is the true father of English prose.

As Whitby is the cradle of English poetry, so is Winchester of English prose. At Winchester Ælfred took the English tongue and made it the tongue in which history, philosophy, law, and religion spoke to the English people. No work was ever done more eagerly or more practically. He brought scholars from different parts of the world. He set up schools in his monasteries. He presided over a school in his own court. He made himself master of a literary English style, and he did this that he might teach his people. He translated the popular manuals of the time into English, but he edited them with large additions of his own, needful, as he thought, for English use. He gave his nation moral philosophy in Boethius's *Consolation of Philosophy;* a universal history, with geographical chapters of his own, in the *History of Orosius;* a history of England in *Bæda's History,* giving to some details a West Saxon form; and a religious hand-book in the *Pastoral Rule* of Pope Gregory. We do not quite know whether he worked himself at the *English,* or *Anglo - Saxon, Chronicle,* but at least it was in his reign that it rose out of meagre lists into a full narrative of events. To him, then, we look back as the father of English literature."

"With the Peace of Wedmore in 878 began a work even more noble than this deliverance of Wessex from the Dane. 'So long as I have lived,' wrote Ælfred in later days, 'I have striven to live worthily.' He longed, when death overtook him, ' to leave to the men that come after a remembrance of me in good works.' The aim has been more than fulfilled. The memory of the life and doings of the noblest of English rulers has come down to us living and distinct through the mists of exaggeration and legend that gathered round it. He really lived for the good of his people. He is the first instance, in the history of Christendom, of the Christian King, of a ruler who put aside every personal aim or ambition to devote himself to the welfare of those whom he ruled. The defence of his realm provided for, he devoted himself to its good government. His work was of a simple and practical order. He was wanting in the imaginative qualities which mark the higher statesman, nor can we trace in his acts any sign of the creative faculty or any perception of new ideas. In politics as in war, or in his after dealings with letters, he simply took what was closest at hand, and made the best of it. The laws of Ini and Offa were codified and amended, justice was more rigidly administered, corporal punishment was substituted in most cases for the old blood-wite, or money-fine, and the right of private revenge was curtailed.

The strong moral bent of Ælfred's mind was seen in some of the novelties of his legislation. The Ten Commandments and a portion of the Law of Moses were prefixed to his code, and thus became part of the law of the land. Labor on Sundays and holy days was made criminal, and heavy punishments were exacted for sacrilege, perjury, and the seduction of nuns. The spirit of adventure that made him in youth the first huntsman of his day, and the reckless daring of his early manhood took later and graver form in the activity that found time amidst the cares of state for the daily duties of religion, for converse with strangers, for study and translation, for learning poems by heart, for planning buildings and instructing craftsmen in gold-work, for teaching even falconers and dog-keepers their business. Restless as he was, his activity was the activity of a mind strictly practical. Ælfred was pre-eminently a man of business, careful of detail, laborious, and methodical. He carried in his bosom a little hand-book, in which he jotted down things as they struck him—now a bit of family genealogy, now a prayer, and now a story, such as that of Bishop Ealdhelm's singing sacred songs on the bridge.   Each hour of the king's day had its peculiar task ; there was the same order in the division of his revenue and in the arrangement of his court.   But, active and busy as he was, his temper remained simple and kindly.

Neither the wars nor the legislation of Ælfred was destined to leave such lasting traces upon England as the impulse he gave to its literature. His end indeed even in this was practical rather than literary.   What he aimed at was simply the education of his people.   As yet Wessex was the most ignorant of the English kingdoms.   'When I began to reign,' said Ælfred, 'I cannot remember one south of Thames who could explain his service-book in English.'   To remedy this ignorance Ælfred desired that at least every free-born youth who possessed the means should ' abide at his book till he can well understand English writing.' "— *J. R. Green.*

THE LATER OLD ENGLISH PROSE.—"The impulse Ælfred gave soon fell away, but it was revived under King Eadgar, when Æthelwald, Bishop of Winchester, made it his constant work to keep up English schools and to translate Latin works into English, and when Archbishop Dunstan took up the same pursuits with eagerness.   Æthelwald's school sent out from it a scholar and abbot named. Ælfric.   He takes rank as the first large translator of the Bible, turning into English the first seven books and part of Job.   We owe to him a series of *Homilies* and his *Colloquy,* afterwards edited by another Ælfric, may be called the first English-Latin dictionary.   But this revival had no sooner begun to take root than the Northmen came again in force upon the land and conquered it. During the long interweaving of Danes and English together under Danish kings from 1013 to 1042, no English literature arose.   It was not till the quiet reign of Edward the Confessor that it again began to live.   But no sooner was it born than the Norman invasion repressed, but did not quench, its life.

THE ENGLISH CHRONICLE.—One great monument, however, of old English prose lasts beyond the Conquest.   It is the *English Chronicle,* and in it the literature is continuous from Ælfred to Stephen.   At first it was nothing but a record of the births and deaths of bishops and kings, and was probably a West Saxon Chronicle. Ælfred edited it from various sources, added largely to it from Bæda, and raised it to the dignity of a national history. After his reign, and that of his son Eadward, 901–925, it becomes scanty, but songs and odes are inserted in it. In the reign of Æthelred and during the Danish kings, its fulness returns, and, growing by additions from various quarters, it continues to be the great contemporary authority in English history till 1154, when it abruptly closes with the death of Stephen. 'It is the first history of any Teutonic people in their own language; it is the earliest and the most venerable monument of English prose.' In it old English poetry sang its last song, in its death old English prose dies. It is not till the reign of John that English poetry in any extended form appears again in the *Brut* of Layamon. It is not till the reign of Edward the Third that original English prose again begins."

"Taking the Chronicle as a whole, I know not where else to find a series of annals so barren of all human interest, and for all purposes of real history so worthless."—*Geo. P. Marsh.*

SCHEME FOR REVIEW.

PERIOD II.

From the Conquest to the Death of Chaucer, 1066–1400.

LESSON 6.

Brief Historical Sketch.—At the time of the Norman Conquest, the Anglo-Saxons and their literature were languishing. The Conquest did not cause, only hastened, the downfall of the Saxon Commonwealth. It infused new life into the exhausted race. Rescued it from sinking into utter barbarism. Feudalism introduced by William. King the feudal lord and source of all jurisdiction. Crown vassals, afterward called Barons, greater and lesser, held fiefs directly from the king. Thanes were feudatories of vassals. During the 12th and 13th centuries, the larger towns secure by charter the right of self-taxation, the control of their trade, and self-government; serfs the right to buy their freedom; and villeins the right to commute labor-service by the payment of money. Art of weaving woollen cloth introduced by the Flemings about 1110. Trial by jury begins, 1166. Partial conquest of Ireland by Strongbow, under Hen. II., 1170. Richard's Crusade, 1190–94. Loss of Normandy, 1204. John grants Magna Charta, 1215. First summons of burgesses to Parliament, 1265. The independence of Scotland from the overlordship of England, secured by Wallace and Bruce, recognized by Treaty of Northampton, 1328. With the battle of Cressy, 1346, Edward III. begins the Hundred Years' War for the recovery of the English possessions in France, acquired by the marriage of Hen. II., the first of the Plantagenet kings, with Eleanor of Acquitaine. This war and that with Scotland developed the spirit of English nationality. First use of gunpowder and of artillery at this battle of Cressy. Gunpowder makes war a profession, undermines feudalism, destroying military service, the tenure by which land under it was held, and advances civilization. Treaty of Bretigny, by which Gascony, Guienne, Poitou, Santoigne, and Calais came into the full possession of the English, and Edward's claim to the Crown of France and to Normandy was waived, 1360. Dress and diet of each class fixed by statute, 1363. Peasant's Revolt under Wat Tyler, 1381. Rich. II. invades Ireland, 1894 and 1399. Four visitations of the Black Death, sweeping off 2,500,000 people, one half of the population of England, 1348-9, 1361-2, 1369, and 1375-6. Population of London in Chaucer's time about 35,000 (now 4,000,000). First royal proclamation in the English language, 1258. Pleadings in law-courts required to be in English by act of Parliament, 1362. Instruction in the schools was in English after 1349. The eight Crusades for the recovery of Jerusalem between 1095 and 1272. The Norman Conquest (1) stripped the native speech of grammatical inflections, (2) abolished a large number of its formative suffixes and prefixes, (3) destroyed its power of forming self-explaining compounds, (4) caused the loss of vast numbers of its words—from one third to one half of all it possessed, (5) brought in a multitude of French words and opened the door for the Latin (the two now forming three tenths of our vocabulary), added (6) prefixes and suffixes and (7) the comparison of adjectives by the use of adverbs, (8) generalized the use of *s* as a plural termination of nouns, (9) introduced the custom of indicating the possessive relation by a preposition, *of*, and (10) helped to bring in or to extend the use of *to* before the infinitive. In the admixture of races, humor, lightness, imagination, and sensibility to beauty were added to the plain and solid, but obtuse, Saxon mind.

LESSON 7.

GENERAL OUTLINE.—"The invasion of Britain by the English made the island, its speech, and its literature English. The invasion of England by the Danes left the speech and literature still English. The Danes were of same stock and tongue as the people invaded, and were absorbed by them. The invasion of England by the Normans seemed likely to crush the English people, to root out their literature, and even to threaten their speech. But that which happened to the Danes happened to the Normans also, and for the same reason. They were originally of like blood with the English, and of like speech; and, though during their settlement in Normandy they had become French in manner and language, and their literature French, yet the old blood prevailed in the end. The Norman felt his kindred with the English tongue and spirit, became an Englishman, and left the French

tongue to speak and write in English. He, too, was absorbed,
and into English literature and speech were taken some
French elements he had brought with him. It was a process slower in literature than it was in the political history,
but it began from the political struggle. Up to the time of
Henry II. the Norman troubled himself but little about the
English tongue. But when French foreigners came pouring
into the land in the train of Henry and his sons, the Norman
allied himself with the Englishman against these foreigners,
and the English tongue began to rise into importance. Its
literature grew slowly, but as quickly as most of the literatures of Europe, and it never ceased to grow. There are
English sermons of the same century, and now, early in the
next century, at the central time of this struggle, after the
death of Richard the First, the *Brut* of Layamon and the *Ormulum* come forth within ten years of each other to prove
the continuity, the survival, and the victory of the English
tongue. When the patriotic struggle closed in the reign of
Edward I., English literature had risen again through the
song, the sermon, and the poem, into importance, and was
written by a people made up of Norman and Englishman
welded into one by the fight against the foreigner. But,
though the foreigner was driven out, his literature influenced
and continued to influence the new English poetry. The
poetry, we say, for in this revival the literature was only poetical. All prose, with the exception of a few sermons and some
religious works from the French, was written in Latin.

RELIGIOUS POETRY AND STORY-TELLING POETRY.—These are
the two main streams into which this poetical literature divides
itself. The religious poetry is entirely English in spirit and a
poetry of the people, from the *Ormulum* of Ormin, 1215, to the
Vision of Piers the Plowman, in which poem the distinctly English poetry reached its truest expression in 1362. The story-
telling poetry is English at its beginning but becomes more
and more influenced by the romantic poetry of France, and in

the end grows in Chaucer's hands into a poetry of the court and of high society, a literary in contrast with a popular, poetry. But even in this the spirit of the poetry is English, though the manner is French. Chaucer becomes less French and even less Italian, till at last we find him entirely national in the *Canterbury Tales,* the best example of English story-telling we possess. The struggle, then, of England, against the foreigner, to become and remain England finds its parallel in the struggle of English poetry, against the influence of foreign poetry, to become and remain English. Both struggles were long and wearisome, but in both England was triumphant. She became a nation, and she won a national literature. It is the steps of this struggle we have now to trace along the two lines already laid down—the poetry of religion and the poetry of story-telling; but to do so we must begin in both instances with the Norman Conquest.

THE RELIGIOUS POETRY.—The religious revival of the 11th century was strongly felt in Normandy, and both the knights and the Churchmen who came to England with William the Conqueror and during his son's reign were founders of abbeys whence the country was civilized. In Henry I.'s reign the religion of England was further quickened by missionary monks sent by Bernard of Clairvaux. London was stirred to rebuild St. Paul's, and abbeys rose in all the well-watered valleys of the North. The English citizens of London and the English peasants in the country received a new religious life from the foreign noble and the foreign monk, and both were drawn together through a common worship. When this took place, a desire arose for religious hand-books in the English tongue. ORMIN'S *Ormulum* is a type of these. We may date it, though not precisely, at 1215, the date of the Great Charter. It is entirely English, not five French words are to be found in it. It is a metrical version of the service of each day with the addition of a sermon in verse. The book was called *Ormulum,* 'for this that Orm it wrought,' *Orm* being a con-

traction for *Ormin*.   It marks the rise of English religious
literature, and its religion is simple and rustic.   Orm's ideal
monk is to be 'a very pure man, and altogether without property, except that he shall be found in simple meat and
clothes.'   He will have 'a hard and stiff and rough and
heavy life to lead.   All his heart and desire ought to be aye
toward heaven, and his Master well to serve.'   This was
English religion in the country at this date.

LITERATURE AND THE FRIARS.—There was little religion in
the towns, but this was soon changed.   In 1221 the Mendicant
Friars came to England, and they chose the towns for their
work.   Their influence was great, and they drew Norman
and English more closely together on the ground of religion.
In 1303 ROBERT OF BRUNNE translated a French poem, the
Manual of Sins (written thirty years earlier by William of
Waddington), under the title of *Handlyng Sinne*.   WILLIAM
OF SHOREHAM translated the whole of the Psalter into English prose about 1327, and wrote religious poems.   The *Cur-
sor Mundi*, written about 1320, and thought 'the best book
of all' by men of that time, was a metrical version of the Old
and the New Testament, interspersed, as was the *Handlyng
Sinne*, with legends of saints.   Some scattered Sermons, and
in 1340 the *Ayenbite of Inwyt* (Remorse of Conscience),
translated from the French, mark how *English prose* was
rising through religion.   About the same year RICHARD
ROLLE OF HAMPOLE wrote in Latin, and in Northumbrian
English for the 'unlearned,' a poem called the *Pricke of
Conscience*, and some prose treatises.   The poem marks the
close of the religious influence of the Friars.

In the *Vision of Piers the Plowman*, the protest its writer
makes for purity of life is also a protest against the foul life
and the hypocrisy of the Friars.   In this poem, the whole of
the popular English religion of the time of Chaucer is represented.   In it also the natural, unliterary, country English is
best represented.   Its author, WILLIAM LANGLAND, though we

arc not certain of his Christian name, was born about 1332, at Cleobury Mortimer, in Shropshire. His *Vision* begins with a description of his sleeping on the Malvern Hills, and the first text of it was probably written in the country in 1362. At the accession of Richard II., 1377, he was in London. The great popularity of his poem made him in that year, and again in the year 1393, send forth two more texts of his poem. In these texts he added to the original *Vision* the poems of *Do Wel, Do Bet,* and *Do Best.* In 1399 he wrote at Bristol his last poem, *The Deposition of Richard II.,* and then died, probably in 1400.

He paints his portrait as he was when he lived in Cornhill, a tall, gaunt figure, whom men called Long Will; clothed in the black robes in which he sung for a few pence at the funerals of the rich; hating to take his cap off his shaven head to bow to the lords and ladies that rode by in silver and furs as he stalked in observant moodiness along the Strand. It is this figure which in indignant sorrow walks through the whole poem.

HIS VISION.—The dream of the 'field full of folk,' with which it begins, brings together nearly as many typical characters as the Tales of Chaucer do. In the first part, the Truth sought for is *righteous dealing* in Church and Law and State. In the second part, the Truth sought for is that of *righteous life.* None of those who wish to find Truth know the way till Piers the Plowman, who at last enters the poem, directs them aright. The search for a righteous life is a search to *Do Well,* to *Do Better,* to *Do Best,* the three titles of the poems which were added afterwards. In a series of dreams and a highly-wrought allegory, *Do Well, Do Better,* and *Do Best* are identified with Jesus Christ, who appears at last as Love, in the dress of Piers the Plowman. The second of these poems describes Christ's death, his struggle with sin, his resurrection, and the victory over Death and the Devil. And the dreamer wakes in a transport of joy, with the Easter chimes pealing in his ears. But as Langland looked round on the world, the victory did not seem real, and the stern dreamer passed out of triumph into the dark sorrow in which he lived. He dreams again in *Do Best*, and sees, as Christ leaves the earth, the reign of Antichrist. Evils attack the Church and mankind. Envy, Pride, and Sloth, helped by the Friars, besiege Conscience. Conscience cries on Contrition to help him, but Contrition is asleep, and Conscience, all but despairing, grasps his pilgrim staff and sets out to wander over the world, praying for luck and health, ' till he have Piers the Plowman,' till he find the Saviour.

This is the poem which wrought so strongly in men's minds that its influence was almost as great as Wyclif's in the revolt which had now begun against Latin Christianity. Its fame was so great that it produced imitators. About 1394 another alliterative poem was set forth by an unknown author, with the title of *Pierce the Plowman's Crede*, and the *Plowman's Tale*, wrongly attributed to Chaucer, is another witness to the popularity of Langland."

BIBLIOGRAPHY. ORMULUM AND PIERS PLOWMAN.—G. P. Marsh's *Lectures on Eng. Lang.*, Lectures V., VI., XIX., and XXIV.; Marsh's *Or. and Hist. Eng. Lang.*, Lectures IV. and VII. Also many works referred to at the end of Lesson 3.

LESSON 8.

ENGLISH STORY-TELLING POETRY.—"This grew out of historical literature. There was a Welsh priest at the court of Henry I., called GEOFFREY OF MONMOUTH, who took upon himself to write history. He had been given, he said, an ancient Welsh book to translate, which told in verse the history of Britain from the days when Brut, the great grandson of Æneas, landed on its shores, through the whole history of King Arthur and his Round Table down to Cadwallo, a Welsh king who died in 689.. The Latin translation he made of this he called a history. The real historians were angry at the fiction, and declared that throughout the whole of it 'he had lied saucily and shamelessly.' It was indeed only a clever putting together of a number of Welsh legends, but it was *the beginning of story-telling* in England. Every one who read it was delighted with it; it made, as we should say, a sensation, and as much on the Continent as in England. In it the Welsh had in some sort their revenge, for in its stories they invaded English literature, and their tales have never since ceased to live in it. They charm us as much in Tennyson's *Idylls of the King* as they charmed the people in the days of Henry I. But the stories Geoffrey of Monmouth told were in the Latin tongue. They were put first into French verse by Geoffrey Gaimar. They got afterwards to France and, added to from Breton legends, were made into a poem and decked out with the ornaments of French romance. In that form they returned to England as the work of *Wace*, a Norman trouveur, who called his poem the *Brut*, and completed it in 1155, shortly after the accession of Henry II.

LAYAMON'S BRUT.—In this French form the story drifted through England, and at last falling into the hands of an English priest in Worcestershire, he resolved to tell it in English verse to his countrymen, and doing so became the author of the first English poem after the Conquest. We may roughly say that its date is 1205, ten years or so before the *Ormulum* was written, ten years before the Great Charter. It is plain that its composition, though it told a Welsh story, was looked on as a patriotic work by the writer. 'There was a priest in the land,' he writes of himself, 'whose name was Layamon; he was son of Leovenath: may the Lord be gracious unto him! He dwelt at Earnley, a noble church on the bank of Severn, near Radstone, where he read books. It came in mind to him and in his chiefest thought that he would tell the noble deeds of England, what the men were named, and whence they came who first had English land.' And it was truly of great importance. The poem opened to the imagination of the English people an immense past for the history of the island they dwelt in, and made a common bond of interest between Norman and Englishman. Though chiefly rendered from the French, there are not fifty Norman words in its more than 30,000 lines. The old English alliterative metre is kept up with a few rare rhymes. As we read the short, quick lines in which the battles are described, as we listen to the simple metaphors, and feel the strong, rude character of the poem, it is as if we were reading Cædmon; and what Cædmon was to early English poetry, Layamon is to English poetry after the Conquest. He is the first of the new singers.

STORY-TELLING GROWS FRENCH IN FORM.—After an interval, the desire for story-telling increased in England. The story of *Genesis and Exodus* was versified about 1250, and in it and some others about the same date, rhymes are used. Many tales of Arthur's knights, and other tales which had an English origin, such as the lays of *Havelok the Dane* and of *King Horn* (about 1280), were translated from the French; ROBERT OF GLOUCESTER wrote his *Riming Chronicle*, 1298; and the *Romance of King Alexander*, about 1280, originally a Greek work, was adapted from the French into English. As the dates grow nearer to 1300, seven years before the death of Edward I., the amount of French words increases, and the French romantic manner of telling stories is more and more marked. In the *Lay of Havelok*, the spirit and descriptions of the poem still resemble old English work; in the *Romance of Alexander*, on the other hand, the natural landscape, the conventional introductions to the parts, the gorgeous descriptions of pomps and armor and cities, the magic wonders, the manners, and feasts, and battles of chivalry, the love passages are all steeped in the colors of French romantic poetry. Now this romance was adapted by a Frenchman in the year 1200.(?) It took, therefore, nearly a century before the French romantic manner of poetry could be naturalized in English; and it was naturalized, curious to say, at the very time when England as a nation had lost its French elements and become entirely English. Finally, the influence of this French school in England is seen in the earlier poems of Chaucer, and in poems, such as the *Court of Love*, attributed to him. It came to its height and died in the translation of the *Romaunt of the Rose*, the last and crowning effort also of French romance. After that time the story-telling of England sought its subjects in another country than France. It turned to Italy.

JOHN GOWER belongs to a school older than Chaucer, inasmuch as he is never touched by the Italian, only by the French, influence. He belongs to a different school even as an artist; for his tales are not pure story-telling like Chaucer's, but tales with a special moral. Partly the religious and social reformer and partly the story-teller, he represents a transition, and fills up the intellectual space between Langland and Chaucer. In the church of St. Saviour, at Southwark, his head is still seen resting on his three great works, the *Speculum Meditantis*, the *Vox Clamantis*, and the *Confessio Amantis*, 1393. It marks the unsettled state of the literary language that each of these was written in a different tongue, the first in French and the second in Latin.

The third is his English work.   In 30,000 lines or more, he mingles up allegory, morality, the sciences, the philosophy of Aristotle, all the studies of the day with comic or tragic tales as illustrations.   We have seen that Robert de Brunne was the first to do this; Gower was the second.   The tales are wearisome and long, and the smoothness of the verse makes them more wearisome.   Gower was a careful writer of English; and in his satire of evils and in his grave reproof of the follies of Richard II., he rises into his best strain.   The king himself, even though reproved, was a patron of the poet. It was as Gower was rowing on the Thames that the royal barge drew near, and he was called to the king's side.   'Book some new thing,' said the king, 'in the way you are used, into which book I myself may often look;' and the request was the origin of the *Confessio Amantis*, the *Confession of a Lover.*"

"Of original imaginative power the poem shows not the slightest trace, and its principal merit lies in the sententious passages which are here and there interspersed, and which, whether borrowed or original, are often pithy and striking."—*G. P. Marsh.*

" Gower has positively raised tediousness to the precision of science; he has made dulness an heirloom for the students of our literary his-tory.   It matters not where you try him, whether his story be Christian or pagan, borrowed from history or fable, you cannot escape him.   Dip in at the middle or at the end, dodge back to the beginning, the patient old man is there to take you by the button and go on with his imperturbable narrative.   His tediousness is omnipresent, and, like Dogberry, he could find it in his heart to bestow it all on your worship.   The word *lengthy* has been charged to our American account, but it must have been invented by the first reader of Gower's works—the only inspiration of which they were ever capable.   Our literature had to lie by and recruit for . more than four centuries ere it could give us an equal vacuity in Tupper, so persistent a uniformity of commonplace in the *Recreations of a Country Parson.*"—*J. R. Lowell.*

ENGLISH LYRICS.—" In the midst of all this story-telling, like prophecies of what should afterwards be so lovely in Eng-lish poetry, rose, no one can tell how, some lyric poems, country idylls, love songs, and, later on, some war songs. The English ballad, sung from town to town by wandering gleemen,* had never altogether died. A number of rude ballads collected round the legendary *Robin Hood*, and the kind of poetic literature which sung of the outlaw and the forest, and afterwards so fully of the wild border life, gradually took form. About 1280 a beautiful little idyll, called *The Owl and the Nightingale*, was written in Dorsetshire, in which the author, Nicholas of Guildford, judges between the rival birds. In 1300 we meet with a few lyric poems, full of charm. They sing of springtime with its blossoms, of the woods ringing with the thrush and nightingale, of the flowers and the seemly sun, of country work, of the woes and joy of love, and many other delightful things. They are tinged with the color of French romance, but they have an English background. We read nothing like them, except in Scotland, till we come to the Elizabethan time. After this, in 1352, the war lyrics of Laurence Minot sing the great deeds and battles of Edward III."

Bibliography. Layamon and Gower.—Marsh's *Or. and Hist. Eng. Lang.*, Lects. IV. and IX.; R. Pauli's *Ed. of Confessio Amantis;* F. J. Child's *Lang. of Ch. and Gow.* in A. J. Ellis' *Early Eng. Pronunciation;* Littell, v. 2, 1858; Fraser's *Mag.*, v. 50. Also some of the works referred to in Less. 3.

*"The minstrel, or gleeman, was held in high esteem among the Saxons. His genius obtained for him everywhere the respect and protection of the great and powerful. His place was in the hall of princes, where he never failed to earn admiration and applause, attended generally with advantages of a more substantial nature. He was sometimes a household retainer of the chief whom he served, sometimes he wandered through different countries, visiting the courts of various princes. It was the minstrel's duty not only to tell the mythic history of the earlier ages but to relate contemporary events, and to clothe in poetry the deeds which fell under his eye, to turn into derision the coward or the vanquished enemy, and to laud and exalt the conduct of his patrons. At times the bard raised his song to higher themes, and laid open the sacred story of the cosmogony and the beginning of all things.

These minstrel-poets had by degrees composed a large mass of national poetry, which formed collectively one grand mythic cycle. Their education consisted chiefly in committing this poetry to memory, and it was thus preserved from age to age. They rehearsed such portions of it as might be asked for by the hearers, or as the circumstances of the moment might require. In their passage from one minstrel to another, these poems underwent successive changes."—*Wright*.

LESSON 9.

HISTORY.—"The Normans carried a historical taste with them to England, and created a most valuable historical literature. It was written in Latin, and we have nothing to do with it till story-telling grew out of it in the time of the Great Charter. But it was in itself of such importance that a few things must be said about it.

1. **The men who wrote it** were called CHRONICLERS. At first they were mere annalists—that is, they jotted down the events of year after year without any attempt to bind them together into a connected whole. But afterwards, from the time of Henry I., another class of men arose, who wrote, not in scattered monasteries, but in the Court. Living at the centre of political life, their histories were written in a philosophic spirit, and wove into a whole the growth of law and national life and the story of affairs abroad. They are our great authorities for the history of these times. They begin with WILLIAM OF MALMESBURY, whose book ends in 1142, and die out after MATTHEW PARIS, 1235–73. Historical literature in England is represented after the death of Henry III. only by a few dry Latin annalists till it rose again in modern English prose in 1513, when Sir Thomas More's *Life of Edward V. and Richard III.* is said to have been written.

2. **A distinct English feeling** soon sprang up among these Norman historians. English patriotism was far from having died among the English themselves. The *Sayings of Ælfred*, about 1200, were written in English by the English. These and some ballads, as well as the early English war songs, interested the Norman historians and were collected by them. William of Malmesbury, who was born of English and Norman parents, has sympathies with both peoples, and his history marks how both were becoming one nation. The same welding together of the conquered and the conquerors

Is seen in the others till we come to Matthew Paris, whose view of history is entirely that of an Englishman. When he wrote, Norman noble and English yeoman, Norman abbot and English priest, were, and are in his pages, one in blood and one in interests.

MANDEVILLE.—He is called the 'first writer in formed English.' Chaucer himself, however, wrote some things, and especially one of his Tales, in rhythmical prose, and John of Trevisa translated into English prose, 1387, Higden's *Polychronicon*. MANDEVILLE wrote his *Travels* first in Latin, then in French, and finally put them into the English tongue about 1356, 'that every man of the nation might understand them.' His quaint delight in telling his 'traveller's tales,' and sometimes the grace with which he tells them rank him among the story-tellers of England.

WYCLIF.—At the time the *Vision* of Langland was being read all over England, JOHN WYCLIF, about 1380, began his work in the English tongue with a nearly complete *translation of the Bible*, and in it did as much probably to fix the language as Chaucer did in his Tales. But he did much more than this for the English tongue. He made it the popular language of religious thought and feeling. In 1381 he was in full battle with the Church on the doctrine of transubstantiation, and was condemned to silence. He replied by appealing to the whole of England in the speech of the people. He sent forth tract after tract, sermon after sermon, couched not in the dry, philosophic style of the schoolmen, but in short, sharp, stinging sentences, full of the homely words used in his own Bible, denying one by one almost all the doctrines, and denouncing the practices, of the Church of Rome. He was the first Protestant. It was a new literary vein to open, the vein of the pamphleteer.

RELIGIOUS LITERATURE IN LANGLAND AND WYCLIF.—We have traced the work of 'transition English,' as it has been called, along the lines of popular religion and story-telling.

The first of these, in the realm of poetry, reaches its goal in the work of William Langland; in the realm of prose it reaches its goal in Wyclif. In both these writers, the work differs from any that went before it by its extraordinary power, and by the depth of its religious feeling. It is plain that it represented a society much more strongly moved by religion than that of the beginning of the fourteenth century. In Wyclif, the voice comes from the university, and it went all over the land in the body of preachers whom, like Wesley, he sent forth. In Langland's *Vision*, we have a voice from the centre of the people themselves; his poem is written in a rude English dialect, in alliterative English verse, and in the old English manner. The very ploughboy could understand it. It became the book of those who desired social and Church reform. It was as eagerly read by the free laborers and fugitive serfs who collected round John Ball and Wat Tyler.

CAUSES OF THE RELIGIOUS REVIVAL.—This was originally due to the preaching of the Friars in the last century and to the noble example they set of devotion to the poor. When the Friars, however, became rich, though pretending to be poor, and impure of life, though pretending to goodness, the religious feeling they had stirred turned against themselves, and its two strongest cries, both on the Continent and in England, were for Truth and for Purity in life and in the Church.

Another cause, common to the Continent and to England in this century, was the movement for the equal rights of man against the class system of the middle ages. It was made a religious movement when men said that they were equal before God, and that goodness in his eyes was the only nobility. And it brought with it a religious protest against the oppression of the people by the class of the nobles.

There were two other causes, however, special to England at this time. *One* was the utter misery of the people owing to the French wars. Heavy taxation fell upon them, and

they were ground down by severe laws, which prevented their
bettering themselves. They felt this all the more because so
many of them had bought their freedom, and began to feel
the delight of freedom. It was then that in their misery they
turned to religion, not only as their sole refuge, but as sup-
plying them with reasons for a social revolution. The *other*
cause was the Black Death, the great Plague which, in 1349,
'62, and '69, swept over England. Grass grew in the towns;
whole villages were left uninhabited; a wild panic fell upon
the people, which was added to by a terrible tempest in 1362
that to men's minds told of the wrath of God. In their
terror then, as well as in their pain, they fled to religion.

THE KING'S ENGLISH.—We have thus traced the rise of
English literature to the time of Chaucer. We must now
complete the sketch by a word or two on the language in
which it was written. The literary English language seemed
at first to be destroyed by the Conquest. It lingered till
Stephen's death in the English Chronicle; a few traces of it are
still found about the time of Henry III.'s death in the *Brut* of
Layamon. But, practically speaking, from the 12th century
till the middle of the 14th, there was no standard of English.
The language, spoken only by the people, fell back into that
broken state of anarchy in which each part of the country has
its own dialect, and each writer uses the dialect of his own
dwelling-place. All the poems, then, of which we have
spoken were written in dialects of English, not in a fixed
English common to all writers. French or Latin was the
language of literature and of the literary class. But towards
the middle of Edward the Third's reign, English got the
better of French. After the Black Death in 1349, French
was less used; in 1362 English was made the language of the
courts of law. At the same time a standard English language
was born. It did not overthrow the dialects, for the *Vision
of Piers the Plowman* and Wyclif's *Translation of the Bible*
are both in a dialect: but it stood forth as the literary lan-

guage in which all future English literature had to be written. It had been growing up in Robert of Brunne's work,
and in the *Romance of King Alexander;* but it was fixed into
clear form by Chaucer and Gower. It was, in fact, the English
language talked in the Court and in the Court society to which
these poets belonged. It was the King's English, and the
fact that it was the tongue of the best and most cultivated
society, as well as the great excellence of the works written in
it by these poets made it at once the tongue of literature."

BIBLIOGRAPHY. WYCLIF.—F. Myers' *Lectures;* R. Vaughan's *Life and Opinions*
of; W. Hanna's *Wyclif and the Huguenots;* N. Br. Rev., v. 20, 1853–4; Quar. Rev.,
v. 104, 1858; West. Rev., v. 62, 1854; Green's *Hist. England*, and other histories of
Eng.

LESSON 10.

CHAUCER. HIS FRENCH PERIOD.—"GEOFFREY CHAUCER
was the son of a vintner, of Thames Street, London, and was
born, it is now believed, in 1340. He lived almost all his life
in London, in the centre of its work and society. When he
was sixteen, he became page to the wife of Lionel, Duke of
Clarence, and continued at the Court till he joined the
army in France in 1359. He was taken prisoner, but was
ransomed before the treaty of Bretigny in 1360. We then
know nothing of his life for six years; but, from items in the
Exchequer Rolls, we find that he was again connected with
the Court from 1366 to 1372. It was during this time that
he began to write. His first poem may have been the A, B,
C, a prayer Englished from the French at the request of the
Duchess Blanche. The translation of the *Romaunt of the
Rose* has been attributed to him, but the best critics are
doubtful of, or deny, his authorship of it. They are sure of
only two poems, the *Compleynte to Pity* in 1368, and in the
next year the *Dethe of Blaunche the Duchesse*, whose husband,
John of Gaunt, was Chaucer's patron. These, written under
the influence of French poetry, are classed under the name
of Chaucer's first period. There are lines in them which seem

to speak of a luckless love affair, and in this broken love it has been supposed that we find the key to Chaucer's early life.

CHAUCER'S ITALIAN PERIOD.—Chaucer's second poetic period may be called the period of Italian influence, from 1372 to 1384. During these years he went for the king on no less than seven diplomatic missions. Three of these, in 1372, '74, and '78, were to Italy. At that time the great Italian literature which inspired then, and still inspires, European literature, had reached full growth, and it opened to Chaucer a new world of art. If he read the *Vita Nuova*, and the *Divina Commedia* of Dante, he knew for the first time the power and range of poetry. He read the Sonnets of Petrarca, and he learnt what is meant by ' form ' in poetry. He read the tales of Boccaccio, who made Italian prose, and in them he first saw how to tell a story exquisitely. Petrarca and Boccaccio he may even have met, for they died in 1374 and 1375, but he never saw Dante, who died at Ravenna in 1321. When he came back from these journeys, he was a new man. He threw aside the romantic poetry of France, and laughed at it in his gay and kindly manner in the *Rime of Sir Thopas*, afterwards made one of the *Canterbury Tales*.

His chief work of this time bears witness to the influence of Italy. It was *Troylus and Creseide*, 1382 (?), which is a translation, with many changes and additions, of the *Filostrato* of Boccaccio. The additions (and he nearly doubled the poem) are stamped with his own peculiar tenderness, vividness, and simplicity. His changes from the original are all towards the side of purity, good taste, and piety. We meet the further influence of Boccaccio in the birth of some of the *Canterbury Tales*, and of Petrarca in the Tales themselves. To this time is now referred the tale of the Second Nun, that of the Doctor, the Man of Law, the Clerk, the Prioress, the Squire, the Franklin, Sir Thopas, and the first draft of the Knight's Tale, borrowed, with much freedom, from the *Teseide* of Boccaccio.

The other poems of this period were the *Parlament of Foules*, the *Compleynt of Mars, Anelida and Arcite, Boece*, and the *Former Age*, all between 1374 and '76, the *Lines to Adam Scrivener*, 1383, and the *Hous of Fame*, 1384 (?). In the passion with which Chaucer describes the ruined love of Troilus and Anelida, some have traced the lingering sorrow of his early love affair. But if this be true, it was now passing away, for, in the creation of Pandarus in the *Troilus* and in the delightful fun of the *Parlament of Foules*, a new Chaucer appears, the humorous poet of the *Canterbury Tales*. In the active business life he led during this period, he was likely to grow out of mere sentiment, for he was not only employed on service abroad but also at home. In 1374 he was Comptroller of the Wool Customs, in 1382 of the Petty Customs, and in 1386 Member of Parliament for Kent.

CHAUCER'S ENGLISH PERIOD.—It is in the next period, from 1384 to 1390, that he left behind Italian influence as he had left French, and became entirely himself, entirely English. The comparative poverty in which he now lived, and the loss of his offices, for in John of Gaunt's absence he lost Court favor, may have given him more time for study and the retired life of a poet. At least in his *Legende of Good Women*, the prologue to which was written in 1385, we find him a closer student than ever of books and of nature. His appointment as Clerk of the Works in 1389 brought him again into contact with men. He superintended the repairs and building at the Palace of Westminster, the Tower, and St. George's Chapel, Windsor, till July, 1391, when he was superseded, and lived on pensions allotted to him by Richard and by Henry IV., after he had sent the King in 1399 his *Compleint to his Purse*. Before 1390, however, he had added to his great work the tales of the Miller, the Reeve, the Cook, the Wife of Bath, the Merchant, the Friar, the Nun's Priest, the Pardoner, and perhaps the Sompnour. The Prologue was probably written in 1388. In the humor of these, in their vividness of por-

traiture, in their ease of narration, and in the variety of their
characters, Chaucer shines supreme. A few smaller poems
belong to this best time, such as *Truth* and the *Moder of
God*.

During his last ten years, he wrote some small poems, and
along with the *Compleynte of Venus* and a prose treatise on
the Astrolabe, four more tales, the Canon's-yeoman's, the
Manciple's, the Monk's, and the Parsone's. The last was
written the year of his death, 1400. Having done this work,
he died in a house under the shadow of the Abbey of Westminster. Within the walls of the Abbey Church, the first of
the poets who lie there, that ' sacred and happy spirit ' sleeps.

CHAUCER'S CHARACTER.—Born of the tradesman class,
Chaucer was in every sense of the word one of the finest of
gentlemen: tender, graceful in thought, glad of heart, humorous, and satirical without unkindness; sensitive to every change
of feeling in himself and others, and therefore full of sympathy; brave in misfortune, even to mirth, and doing well and
with careful honesty all he undertook. His first and great
delight was in human nature, and he makes us love the noble
characters in his poems and feel with kindliness towards the
baser and ruder sort. He never sneers, for he had a wide
charity, and we can always smile in his pages at the follies and
forgive the sins of men. He had a true and chivalrous regard
for women, and his wife and he must have been very happy if
they fulfilled the ideal he had of marriage. He lived in aristocratic society, and yet he thought him the greatest gentleman
who was 'most vertuous alway, privé, and pert (open), and
most entendeth aye to do the gentil dedës that he can.' He
lived frankly among men, and, as we have seen, saw many
different types of men, and in his own time filled many parts
as a man of the world and of business.

Yet, with all this active and observant life, he was commonly
very quiet and kept much to himself. The Host in the Tales
japes at him for his lonely, abstracted air. ' Thou lookest as

thou wouldest find a hare, And ever on the ground I see thee stare.' Being a good scholar, he read morning and night alone, and he says that after his (office) work he would go home and sit at another book as dumb as a stone, till his look was dazed. While at study and when he was making of songs and ditties, 'nothing else that God had made' had any interest for him. There was but one thing that roused him then, and that too he liked to enjoy alone. It was the beauty of the morning, and the fields, the woods, and streams, and flowers, and the singing of the little birds. This made his heart full of revel and solace, and, when spring came after winter, he rose with the lark and cried, 'Farewell my book and my devotion.' He was the first who made the love of nature a distinct element in English poetry. He was the first who, in spending the whole day gazing alone on the daisy, set going that lonely delight in natural scenery which is so special a mark of the later poets. He lived thus a double life, in and out of the world, but never a gloomy one. For he was fond of mirth and good-living, and, when he grew towards age, was portly of waist, ' no poppet to embrace.' But he kept to the end his elvish countenance, the shy, deli- -cate, half-mischievous face which looked on men from its grey hair and forked beard, and was set off by his dark-colored dress and hood. A knife and an inkhorn hung on his dress, we see a rosary in his hand, and, when he was alone, he walked swiftly.

THE CANTERBURY TALES.—Of his work it is not easy to speak briefly, because of its great variety. Enough has been said of it, with the exception of his most complete creation, the *Canterbury Tales*. It will be seen from the dates given above that they were not written at one time. They are not and cannot be looked on as a whole. Many were written independently, and then fitted into the framework of the Prologue in 1388. At that time a number more were written, and the rest added at intervals till his death. In fact, the whole thing was done much in the same way as Mr. Tennyson has written his *Idylls of the King*. The manner in which he knitted them together was very simple and likely to please English people. The holiday excursions of the time were the pilgrimages, and the most famous and the pleasantest pilgrimage to go, especially for Londoners, was the three or four days' journey to see the shrine of St. Thomas at Canterbury. Persons of all ranks in life met and travelled together, starting from a London inn. Chaucer seized on this as the frame in which to set his pictures of life. He grouped around the jovial host of the Tabard Inn men and women of every class of society in England, set them on horseback to ride to Canterbury, and made each of them tell a tale.

No one could hit off a character better, and in his Prologue, and in the prologues to the several Tales, the whole of the new, vigorous English society which had grown up since Edward I. is painted with astonishing vividness. 'I see all the pilgrims in the Canterbury Tales,' says Dryden, 'their humors, their features, and the very dress as distinctly as if I had supped with them at the Tabard in Southwark.' The Tales themselves take in the whole range of the poetry of the middle ages—the legend of the saint, the romance of the knight, the wonderful fables of the traveller, the coarse tale of common life, the love story, the allegory, the satirical lay, and the apologue. And they are pure tales. He has been said to have had dramatic power, but he has none. He is simply the greatest English story-teller in verse. All the best tales are told easily, sincerely, with great grace, and yet with so much homeliness that a child can understand them. Sometimes his humor is broad, sometimes sly, sometimes gay, sometimes he brings tears into our eyes, and he can make us smile or be sad as he pleases.

He had a very fine ear for the music of verse, and the tale and the verse go together like voice and music. Indeed, so softly flowing and bright are they that to read them is like listening in a meadow full of sunshine to a clear stream rippling over its bed of pebbles. The English in which they are written is almost the English of our time; and it is literary

English. Chaucer made our tongue into a true means of poetry. He did more, he welded together the French and English elements in the language and made them into one English tool for the use of literature, and all prose writers and poets in English since his day derive their tongue from the language of the *Canterbury Tales*. They give him honor for this, but still more for that he was the first English artist. Poetry is an art, and the artist in poetry is one who writes for pure pleasure, and for nothing else, and who desires to give to others the same fine pleasure by his poems which he had in writing them. The thing he most cares about is that the form in which he puts his thoughts or feelings may be perfectly fitting to the subject, and as beautiful as possible—but for this he cares very greatly; and in this Chaucer stands apart from the other poets of his time. Gower wrote with a moral object, and nothing can be duller than the form in which he puts his tales. The author of *Piers the Plowman* wrote with the object of reform in social and ecclesiastical affairs, and his form is uncouth and harsh. Chaucer wrote because he was full of emotion and joy in his own thoughts, and thought that others would weep and be glad with him, and the only time he ever moralizes is in the tales of the Yeoman and the Manciple. He has, then, the best right to the poet's name. He is the first English artist."

" The English writers of the fourteenth century had an advantage which was altogether peculiar to their age and country. At all previous periods, the two languages had co-existed, in a great degree independently of each other, with little tendency to intermix; but in the earlier part of that century, they began to coalesce, and this process was going on with a rapidity that threatened a predominance of the French, if not a total extinction of the Saxon element. That the syntax should be English national feeling demanded; but French was so familiar and habitual to all who were able to read that probably the scholarship of the day would scarcely have been able to determine, with respect to a large proportion of the words in common use, from which of the two great wells of speech they had proceeded.

Happily, a great arbiter arose at the critical moment to determine what share of the contributions of France should be permanently annexed to the linguistic inheritance of Englishmen. Chaucer did not introduce into our language words which it had rejected as aliens before, but out of those which had been already received he invested the better portion with the rights of citizenship, and stamped them with the mint-mark of English coinage. In this way he formed a vocabulary which, with few exceptions, the taste of succeeding generations has approved. He is eminently the creator of our literary dialect, the introducer, if not the inventor, of some of our finest poetical forms; and so essential were his labors in the founding of our national literature that, without Chaucer, the seventeenth century could have produced no Milton, the nineteenth no Keats."—*Geo. P. Marsh.*

" Chaucer was the first great poet who really loved outward nature as the source of conscious pleasurable emotion. Chaucer took a true delight in the new green of the leaves and the return of singing birds—a delight as simple as that of Robin Hood. He has never so much as heard of the 'burthen and the mystery of all this unintelligible world.' He himself sings more like a bird than any other poet, because it never occurred to him that he ought to do so. He pours himself out in sincere joy and thankfulness. The pleasure which Chaucer takes in telling his stories has in itself the effect of consummate skill, and makes us follow all the windings of his fancy with sympathetic interest. His best tales run on like one of our inland rivers, sometimes hastening a little and turning upon itself in eddies that dimple, without retarding, the current; sometimes loitering smoothly, while here and there a quiet thought, a tender feeling, a pleasant image, or a golden-hearted verse opens quietly as a water-lily, to float on the surface without breaking it into ripple.

But it is in his characters, especially, that his manner is large and free; for he is painting history, though with the fidelity of portrait. He brings out strongly the essential traits characteristic of the genus rather than of the individual. The Merchant who keeps so steady a counte nance that 'There wist no wight that he was e'er in debt,' the Sergeant at Law, 'who seemed busier than he was,' the Doctor of Medicine whose 'study was but little on the Bible'—in all these cases it is the type and not the personage that fixes the attention. In his outside accessories, it is true he sometimes seems as minute as if he were illuminating a missal. Nothing escapes his eye for the picturesque—the cut of the beard, the soil of armor on the buff jerkin, the rust on the sword, the expression of the eye. But in this he has an artistic purpose. It is here that he individualizes, and, while every touch harmonizes with and seems to complete the moral features of the character, makes us feel that we are among living men and not the abstracted images of men."—*J. R. Lowell.*

BIBLIOGRAPHY. CHAUCER.—*Chaucer Society's Publications*; Clar. Press Ed. of *Canterbury Tales*; Prof. Lounsbury's *Parlament of Foules*; *English Men of Letters* Series; Minto's *Characteristics of Eng. Poets*; J. R. Lowell's *My Study Windows*; Ward's *Anthology*; Ecl. Mag., 1849, and Dec., 1866; Fort. Rev., v. 6, 1866; Quar. Rev., Jan., 1873; West. Rev., Oct., 1871.

LESSON 11.

From Chaucer's *Prologue to Canterbury Tales.* *

BYFEL[1] that, in that sesoun on a day,
In Southwerk at the Tabard,[2] as I lay
Redy to wenden on my pilgrimage
To Caunterbury with ful devout corage,
At night was come into that hostelrie
Wel[3] nyne and twenty in a companye
Of soundry folk, by aventure i-falle[4]
In felaweschipe, and pilgryms were thei alle,
That toward Caunterbury wolden ryde;
The chambres and the stables weren wyde,
And wel we weren esed atte beste.[5]
And schortly, whan the sonnë was to reste,
So hadde I spoken with hem everychon[6]
That I was of here[7] felaweschipe anon,
And madë forward[8] erly for to ryse
To take our wey ther as I yow devyse.
But natheles,[9] whil I have tyme and space,
Or[10] that I forther in this talë pace,[11]
Me thinketh it acordaunt to resoun,
To tellë yow al the condicioun
Of eche of hem, so as it semede me,
And whiche[12] they weren and of what degre.[13]

. . . . . .

A Clerk[14] ther was of Oxenford[15] also,
That unto logik haddë longe i-go.[16]

---

* Syllables containing *e* with a diæresis (ë) are to be pronounced in reading and scanning.
[1] It chanced. [2] An inn in Southwark. [3] Full. [4] Fallen by chance. [5] Entertained in the best manner. [6] Them, everyone. [7] Their. [8] Agreement. [9] Nevertheless. [10] Ere. [11] Pass on. [12] Who. [13] Rank. [14] Student. [15] Oxford. [16] Had long given himself—*i* a prefix used to indicate the past participle, the *ge* of the A.S. and the German, and the *y* in *yclept* and *ychained.*

As lenĕ was his hors as is a rake,
And he was not right fat, I undertake;
But lokede holwe,[1] and therto[2] soberly.
Ful thredbare was his overeste courtepy,[3]
For he hadde geten him yit no benefice,
Ne was so worldly for to have office.[4]
For him was leverc[5] have at his beddes heede
Twenty bookĕs, clad in blak or reede,
Of Aristotle and his philosophie,
Then robĕs riche or fithele[6] or gay sawtrie.[7]
But al be[8] that he was a philosophre,
Yet haddĕ he but litel gold in cofre;
But al that he mighte of his frendĕs hente[9]
On bookĕs and on lernyng he it spente,
And busily gan for the soulĕs preye
Of hem that gaf him wherwith to scoleye.[10]
Of studie took he most cure[11] and most heede.
Not oo word spak he morĕ than was neede,
And that was seid in forme and reverence
And schort and quyk and ful of high sentence.[12]
Sownynge in[13] moral vertu was his speche,
And gladly wolde he lerne and gladly teche.

. . . . . . ,

A good man was ther of religioun,
And was a pourĕ Persoun[14] of a toun;
But riche he was of holy thought ánd werk.
He was also a lerned man, a clerk
That Cristĕs gospel trewely woldĕ preche;
His parischens[15] devoutly wolde he teche.
Benigne he was and wonder diligent,
And in adversité ful pacient;
And such he was i-provĕd oftĕ sithes.[16]
Ful loth were him to cursĕ for his tythes,[17]
But rather wolde he geven out of dowte
Unto his pourĕ parisschens aboute
Of his offryngĕ[18] and eek of his substaunce.
He cowde in litel thing han suffisaunce.

---

[1] H·llow. [2] Also. [3] Uppermost short cloak. [4] Secular calling. [5] Rather. [6] Fiddle. [7] Harp. [8] Although—philosophers were thought to be able to transmute the baser metals into gold. [9] Get. [10] Attend school. [11] Care. [12] Meaning. [13] Tending to. [14] Parson, priest. [15] Parishioners. [16] Often-times. [17] Excommunicate for failing to pay what was due him. [18] Contributions from his people.

Wyd was his parische, and houses fer asonder,
But he ne lafte[1] not for reyne ne thonder,
In siknesse nor in meschief[2] to visite
The ferreste in his parissche, moche and lite,[3]
Uppon his feet, and in his hond a staf.
This noble ensample to his scheep he gaf,
That first he wroughte, and afterward he taught.
Out of the gospel he tho wordes caughte,
And this figure he addede eek therto
⸤That if gold ruste, what schal yren doo?⸥
Wel oughte a prest ensample for to give
By his clennesse how that his scheep schulde lyve.
   He sette not his benefice to hyre,
And leet[4] his scheep encombred in the myre,
And ran to Londone, unto seynte Poules,
To seeken him a chaunterie[5] for soules,
Or with a bretherhede to ben withholde;[6]
But dwelte at hoom, and kepte wel his folde,
So that the wolf ne made it not myscarye;
He was a schepherde and no mercenarie.
And though he holy were and vertuous,
He was to sinful man nought despitous,[7]
Ne of his speche daungerous ne digne,[8]
But in his teching discret and benigne.
To drawe folk to heven by fairnesse,
By good ensample, this was his busynesse.
But it were[9] eny persone obstinat,
What so he were, of high or lowe estat,
Him wolde he snybbe[10] scharply for the nones.[11]
A bettre preest I trowe ther nowher non is.
He waytede after no pompe and reverence
Ne makede him a spiced[12] conscience,
But Cristes lore[13] and his apostles twelve
He taughte, but first he folwede it himselve

---

[1] Ceased. [2] Misfortune. [3] Great and small. [4] Let, left. [5] An endowment for the payment of a priest to sing mass. [6] Supported. [7] Merciless. [8] Not affable, disdainful. [9] If there were. [10] Reprove. [11] Nonce. [12] Scrupulous. [13] Teaching.

From the *Nonne Prestēs*[1] *Tale.*

A pourĕ wydow somdel stopĕ[2] in age
Was whilom dwellyng in a narwe cotage
Bisyde a grovĕ, stondyng in a dale.
This wydwe of which I tellĕ yow my tale.
Syne thilkĕ[3] day that sche was last a wif
In pacience ladde a ful symple lyf,
For litel was hire catel[4] and hire rente.[5]
By housbondrye[6] of such as God hire sente, ~
Sche fond[7] hireself and eek hire doughtren tuo.[8]
Thre largĕ sowĕs hadde sche and no mo,
Thre kyn and eek a scheep thet hightĕ[9] Malle.
Ful sooty was hire bour[10] and eek hire halle,
In which she eet ful many a sclender meel.
Of poynaunt[11] sawce hire needede never a deel.[12]
No deynté morsel passede thurgh hire throte;
Hire dyeté was accordant to hire cote.[13]
Repleccioun ne made hire nevere sik;
Attemprĕ[14] dyete was al hire phisik
And exercise and hertĕs suffisaunce.[15]
The goutĕ lette[16] hire nothing for to daunce.
Hire bord[17] was servĕd most with whit and blak,
Milk and broun bred, in which sche fond no lak.
  A yerd[18] sche hadde, enclosĕd al aboute
With stikkĕs and a dryĕ dich withoute,
In which she hadde a cok, hightĕ Chauntecleer;
In al the lond, of crowyng nas[19] his peer.
His vois was merier than the merye orgon[20]
On masse dayĕs that in the chirchĕ goon.[21]
Wel sikerer[22] was his crowyng in his logge
Than is a clok or an abbay orlogge.[23]
By nature knew he ech ascencioun
Of equinoxial[24] in thilkĕ toun;
For whan degrees fyftenĕ were ascended,
Thanne crew[25] he that it mighte not ben amended.

---

[1] Nun's Priest. [2] Somewhat advanced. [3] Since that. [4] Wealth. [5] Income. [6] Economy. [7] Supported. [8] Two daughters. [9] Was called. [10] Inner room. [11] Pungent. [12] Never a whit. [13] Cottage. [14] Spare. [15] Contented mind. [16] Gout hindered. [17] Table. [18] Yard. [19] Was not. [20] Organ or organs. [21] Go, sounds or sound. [22] Much surer. [23] Abbey-clock, clock in the tower. [24] Knew each hour. [25] Then he crowed, that is, each hour, as the sun climbs 15° an hour.

His comb was redder than the fyn coral,
And bataylld [1] as it were a castel wal.
His bile[2] was blak, and as the geet [3] it schon;
Like asure[4] were his leggës and his ton;[5]
His naylës whitter than the lilye flour,[6]
And lik the burnischt gold was his colour.

    This gentil cok hadde in his governaunce
Scvene hennës for to don al his pleasaunce,
Whiche were his sustres and his paramoures,
And wonder[7] like to him as of coloures,
Of whiche the faireste hewëd [8] on hire throte
Was clepëd [9] fayre damoysele Pertelote.
Curteys[10] sche was, discret, and debonaire,[11]
And compainable,[12] and bar hire self ful faire
Syn thilkë day that sche was seven night old
That trewëly sche hath the herte in hold
Of Chauntecleer loken in every lith;[13]
He lovede hire so that wel him was therwith.
But such a joye was it to here hem synge,
Whan that the brightë sonnë gan to springe
In swete accord, "my lief is faren on londe."[14]
For thilkë tyme, as I have understonde,
Bestës and briddës cowdë speke and synge.

    And so byfel that in a dawenynge,
As Chauntecleer among his wyvës alle
Sat on his perchë, that was in the halle,
And next him sat this fairë Pertelote,
This Chauntecleer gan gronen in his throte
As man that in his dreem is dreechëd [15] sore.
And whan that Pertelote thus herde him rore,
Sche was agast,[16] and sayde, "O hertë deere,
What eyleth[17] you to grone in this manere?
Ye ben a verray sleper, fy, for schame!"
And he answerde and saydë thus, "Madame,
I praye you that ye take it nought agrief.
Me mette[18] how that I romede up and doun

---

[1] Indented, as a castle wall seems to be with its turrets. [2] Bill. [3] Jet. [4] Azure
[5] Toes. [6] Flower. [7] Wonderfully. [8] Colored. [9] Called. [10] Courteous. [11] Gracious. [12] Sociable. [13] Locked in every limb, bound to her in every muscle. [14] My beloved is gone away—from some popular song. [15] Troubled. [16] Afraid. [17] Ails.
[18] I dreamed.

Withinne oure yerde, wher as[1] I saugh a beest,
Was lik an hound, and wolde han maad areest[2]
Upon my body and wolde han had me deed.
His colour was bitwixe yelwe and reed;
And tippëd was his tail and bothe his ceres
With blak, unlik the remenaunt of his heres;
His snowtë smal, with glowyng eyen tweye.[3]
Yet of his look for feere almost I deye;
This causede me my gronyng douteles."
"Avoy!" quod[4] sche, "fy on yow herteles!
Allas!" quod sche, "for, by that God above,
Now han ye lost myn herte and al my love;
I can nought love a coward, by my feith.
For, certes,[5] what so eny womman seith,
We alle desiren, if it mightë be,
To han housbondës hardy, wise, and fre,
And secré,[6] and no nygard, ne no fool,
Ne him that is agast of every tool,[7]
Ne noon avauntour,[8] by that God above.
How dorste ye sayn for schame unto youre love
That any thing mighte makë yow aferd?
Han ye no mannës herte, and han a berd?"

.   .   .   .   .   .

Whan that the moneth in which the world bigan
That hightë[9] March, whan God first madë man,
Was complet, and y-passëd were also,
Syn March bygan, thritty dayës and tuo,
Byfel that Chauntecleer in al his pride,
His sevën wyvës walkyng him by syde,
Caste up his eyghen to the brightë sonne
That in the signe of Taurus hadde i-ronne
Twenty degrees and oon, and somewhat more;
He knew by kynde,[10] and by noon other lore,
That it was prime,[11] and crew with blisful stevene.[12]
"The sonne," he sayde, "is clomben up on hevene
Fourty degrees and oon, and more i-wis.[13]
Madamë Pertelote, my worldës blis,
Herkneth these blisful briddës how they synge,
And seth the fresschë flourës how they springe;

---

[1] Where. [2] Attack. [3] Two eyes. [4] Fie! said. [5] Certainly. [6] Secret. [7] Weapon. [8] Boaster. [9] Is called. [10] Nature. [11] Nine o'clock. [12] Voice. [13] Truly.

Ful is myn hert of revel and solaas."
But sodeinly him fel a sorweful cans;[1]
For evere the latter ende of joye is wo.
God wot[2] that worldly joye is soone ago.

   .   .   .   .   .   .

    A col[3]-fox, ful of sleigh iniquité,
That in the grove hadde wonëd[4] yerës thre,
By heigh ymaginacioun forncast,[5]
The samë nighte thurghout the heggës brast[6]
Into the yerd, ther[7] Chauntecleer the faire
Was wont, and eek his wyvës, to repaire;
And in a bed of wortës[8] stille he lay
Til it was passëd undern[9] of the day,
Waytyng his tyme on Chauntecleer to falle,
As gladly doon these homicidës alle.

   .   .   .   .   .   .

    This Chauntecleer, whan he gan him espye,
He wolde han fled, but that the fox anon
Saide, "Gentil sire, allas! wher wol ye goon?
Be ye affrayd of me that am youre freend?
Now, certes, I were worsë than a feend,
If I to yow wolde[10] harm or vileynye.
I am nought come youre counsail for tespye.
But trewëly the cause of my comynge
Was oonly for to herkne how that ye singe.
My lord, youre fader, (God his soulë blesse)
And eek youre moder of hire gentilesse
Han in myn hous i-been to my gret ese;
And, certes, sire, ful fayn wolde I yow plese.
But for men speke of syngyng, I wol saye,
So mot I broukë[11] wel myn eyen twaye,
Save you, I herdë nevere man so synge
As 'dede youre fader in the morwenynge.
Certes it was of herte al that he song.
And for to make his vois the morë strong,
He woldë so peyne him[12] that with bothe his eyen
He mostë wynke, so lowde he woldë crien,

---

[1] Mishap. [2] Knows. [3] Crafty. [4] Dwelt. [5] Preordained. [6] Burst. [7] Where.
[8] Herbs. [9] Time of the mid-day meal. [10] Wished, would do. [11] So may I enjoy.
[12] Take such pains.

And stonden on his typtoon[1] therwithal
And strecchë forth his nekkë, long and smal."

This Chauntecleer stood heighe upon his toos,
Strecching his nekke, and held his eyghen cloos,
And gan to crowë lowdë for the noones;
And daun Russel, the fox, sterte up at oones,
And by the garget[2] hentë Chauntecleer,
And on his bak toward the woode him beer.

Certes, such cry ne lamentacioun
Was nevere of ladies maad whan Ilioun
Was wonne, and Pirrus with his streite[3] swerd,
Whan he haddë hent kyng Priam by the berd
And slayn him (as saith us Eneydos),
As maden alle the hennës in the clos,
Whan they haddë seyn of Chauntecleer the sighte.
But soveraignly dame Pertelotë schrighte[4]
Ful lowder than dide Hasdrubalës wyf,
Whan that hire housbonde haddë lost his lyf.

Lo, how fortunë torneth sodeinly
The hope and pride eek of hire enemy!
This cok that lay upon the foxes bak
In all his drede, unto the fox he spak,
And saidë, "Sire, if that I were as ye,
Yet schulde I sayn (as wis[5] God helpë me),
'Turneth agein, ye proudë cherlës alle,
A verray pestilens upon yow falle!
Now am I come unto this woodës syde,
Maugre[6] youre heed, the cok schal heer abyde;
I wol him ete, in faith, and that anoon.'"
The fox answerede, "In faith, it schal be doon."
And as he spak that word, al sodeinly
This cok brak from his mouth delyverly,[7]
And heigh upon a tree he fleigh anoon.
And whan the fox seigh that he was i-goon,
"Allas!" quod he, "O Chauntecleer, allas!
I have to yow," quod he, "y-don trespas,
In-as-moche as I makede yow aferd,
Whan I yow hente, and broughte out of the yerd;

---

[1] Tip-toes. [2] Throat. [3] Drawn. [4] Shrieked. [5] As truly. [6] In spite of. [7] Quickly.

But, sire, I dedc it in no wikke entente.
Com doun, and I schal tclle yow what I mente.
I schal seye soth to yow, God help me so."
" Nay than," quod he, " I schrewe[1] us bothe tuo
And first I schrewe myself, bothe blood and boones,
If thou bigile me any ofter than oones.
Thou schalt no more, thurgh thy flaterye,
Do[2] me to synge, and wynke with myn eye.
For he that wynketh whan he scholde see,
Al wilfully, God let him never the[3]!"
" Nay," quod the fox, " but God give him meschaunce[4]
That is so undiscret of governaunce,
That jangleth whan he scholde holde his pees."
  Lo, such it is for to be reccheles[5]
And necgligent and truste on flaterie.
But ye that holden this tale a folye,
As of a fox or of a cok and hen,
Taketh the moralité therof, goode men.
For seint Poul saith that al that writen is
To oure doctrine[6] it is i·write i-wys.
Taketh the fruyt, and let the chaf be stille.
  Now goode God, if that it be thy wille
As saith my lord, so make us alle good men,
And bringe us to his heighe blisse. *Amen.*

FURTHER READING.—The remainder of the *Prologue*, *The Knightes Tale*, *The Tale of the Man of Lawe*, *The Squieres Tale*, *The Seconde Nonnes Tale*, and *The Clerkes Tale*, in the Clarendon Press Series, and *The Parlament of Foules*, edited by Prof. Lounsbury. Keep the pupils with Chaucer till they in some degree appreciate the ease, freshness, simplicity, sweetness, tenderness, good sense, good humor, and wholesomeness of his writings. For questions, see Lesson 1.

SCHEME FOR REVIEW.

[1] Curse. [2] Cause. [3] Prosper. [4] Misfortune. [5] Careless. [6] Instruction.

LESSON 12.

Brief Historical Sketch.—First English statute enacting religious blood-shed was that against the Lollards, followers of Wyclif, 1401. Battle of Agincourt, by which Normandy was reconquered, 1415. The Hundred Years' War ended and France delivered, 1451. Joan of Arc the French leader, 1422–31. Jack Cade's Revolt, 1450. House of Lancaster —Hen. IV., Hen. V., and Hen. VI.—1399–1461. House of York—Ed. IV., Ed. V., and Rich. III.—1461–1485. War of the Roses, in which the castles were battered down, and the nobility almost destroyed, 1452–1485. At its close on Bosworth Field, the Earl of Richmond, a Lancastrian, marries Eliz. of York, and becomes Hen. VII., the first Tudor king. At the taking of Constantinople by the Turks, 1453 (they had settled in Europe, 1356) the learned scholars studying the Greek manuscripts there fled principally to Italy. Disclosure of the stores of Greek literature wrought the Revival of Learning. Caxton set up the first printing-press in England, 1476. Only the gentry ate wheaten bread; poorer people ate bread made of barley or rye, sometimes of peas, beans, or oats. Plaster ceilings not yet used. Chimneys introduced about 1485. Discovery of America by Columbus, 1492. Grocyn and Colet the first to teach Greek in England, at Oxford, 1490–1500. Hen. VIII. succeeded Hen. VII., 1509. Erasmus professor of Greek at Cambridge, 1511. Hen. VIII. fought the battle of Flodden Field against the Scots, 1513. Magellan circumnavigated the earth, 1519. Hen. VIII. became head of the Eng. Church, 1531. First pavement in London, 1534. Sir Thomas More beheaded for refusing to take the Oath of Supremacy to Hen. VIII., 1535. Dissolution of monasteries in England, 1536–9. Rebellion in Ireland crushed, 1535, and in 1541 Hen. VIII. received the title "King of Ireland." During Ed. VI.'s reign, 1547–53, English prayer-book prepared by Cranmer. Under Mary, 1553–8, English Church again acknowledges the pope, and persecution of heresy is resumed.

LESSON 13.

THE FIFTEENTH CENTURY PROSE.—"'The last poems of
Chaucer and Langland bring our story up to the year 1400.
The century that followed is the most barren in the literature.
History sank down into a few Latin chroniclers, of whom
THOMAS WALSINGHAM is best known.   Two *Riming Chronicles* were written in Henry V.'s time by ANDREW OF WYNTOUN,
a Scotchman, and JOHN HARDING, an Englishman.   JOHN
CAPGRAVE wrote in English, in Edward IV.'s reign, a *Chronicle of England* which began with the Creation.   Political prose
is then represented by SIR JOHN FORTESCUE'S book on the
Difference between Absolute and Limited Monarchy.   It is the
second important book in the history of English prose.   The
religious war between the Lollards and the Church went on
during the reigns of Henry V. and VI., and, in the reign of the
latter, REGINALD PECOCK took it out of Latin into homely
English.   He fought the Lollards with their own weapons,
with sermons preached in English, and with tracts in English;
and after 1449, when Bishop of Chichester, he published his
work *The Repressor of overmuch Blaming of the Clergy*.   It
pleased neither party.   The Lollards disliked it, because it defended the customs and doctrines of the Church.   Churchmen
burnt it, because it agreed with the ' Bible-men ' that the
Bible is the only rule of faith.   Both abjured it, because it
said that doctrines were to be proved from the Bible by reason.
Pecock is the first of all the Church theologians who wrote in
English, and the book is a fine example of early prose.

GROWTH OF INTEREST IN LITERATURE.—Little creative work
was done in this century, and that little was poor.   There was
small learning in the monasteries, and few books were written.   But a good deal of interest in literature was scattered
about the country, and it increased as the century went on.
The Wars of the Roses stopped the writing, but not the read

ing, of books. We have in the *Paston Letters*, 1422–1505, the correspondence of a country family from Henry VI. to Henry VII., pleasantly, even correctly, written—passages which refer to translations of the classics, and to manuscripts' being sent to and fro for reading. Henry VI., Edward IV., and some of the great nobles were lovers of books. Men like Duke Humphrey of Gloucester made libraries, and brought over Italian scholars to England to translate Greek works. There were fine scholars in England, like John Lord Tiptoft, Earl of Worcester, who had won fame in the schools of Italy. Before 1474, when Caxton finished the first book said to have been printed in England, *The Game and Playe of the Chesse*, a number of French translations of the Latin authors were widely read. There was, therefore, in England, a general, though an uninformed, interest in the ancient writers.

FIRST INFLUENCE OF THE ITALIAN REVIVAL.—Such an interest was added to by the revival of letters which arose at this time in Italy, and the sixteenth century had not long begun before many Englishmen went to Italy to read and study the old Greek authors on whom the scholars driven from Constantinople, at its capture by the Turks in 1453, were lecturing in the schools of Florence. Printing enabled these men on their return to render the classic books they loved, into English for their own people. The English began to do their own work as translators ; and, from the time of Henry VIII. onwards, there is scarcely any literary fury equal to that with which the young scholars fell upon the ancient authors, and filled the land with English versions of them. It is, then, in the slow upgrowth, during this century, of interest in and study of the ancients that we are to see the gathering together at its source of•one of the streams which fed that great river of Elizabethan literature, which it is so great a mistake to think burst suddenly up through the earth.

INFLUENCE OF CAXTON'S WORK.—We find another of these sources in the work of our first printer, WILLIAM CAXTON.

The first book that bears the inscription, 'Imprynted by me, William Caxton, at Westmynstre,' is *The Dictes and Sayings of Philosophers*. Caxton did little or nothing for classical learning. His translation of the *Æneid* of Vergil is from a contemptible French romance. But he preserved for us Chaucer and Lydgate and Gower with zealous care. He printed the Chronicles of Brut and Higden ; he translated the *Golden Legend :* and the *Morte d'Arthur*, written by SIR THOMAS MALORY in the reign of Edward IV., one of the finest and simplest examples of early prose, was printed by him with all the care of one who loved the 'noble acts of chivalry.' He had a tradesman's interest in publishing the romances, for they were the reading of the day, but he could scarcely have done better for the interests of the coming literature. These books nourished the imagination of England, and supplied poet after poet with fine subjects for work or fine frames for their subjects. He had not a tradesman's, but a loving literary, interest in printing the old English poets ; and, in sending them out from his press, Caxton kept up the continuity of English poetry. The poets after him at once began on the models of Chaucer and Gower and Lydgate ; and the books themselves, being more widely read, not only made poets but a public that loved poetry. If classic literature, then, was one of the sources in this century of the Elizabethan literature, the recovery of old English poetry was another.

PROSE UNDER HENRY VIII.—With the exception of Caxton's work all the good prose of the fifteenth century was written before the death of Edward IV. The reigns of Richard III. and of Henry VII. produced no prose of any value, but the country awakened from its dulness with the accession of Henry VIII., 1509. A band of new scholars, who had studied in Italy, taught Greek in Oxford, Cambridge, and London. John Colet, Dean of St. Paul's, with John Lily, the grammarian, set on foot a school where the classics were taught in a new and practical way. Erasmus, who had all the enthusiasm which sets others on fire, taught in England, and with Grocyn, Linacre, Sir Thomas More, and Archbishop Warham formed a centre from which a liberal and wise theology was spread.

The new learning which had been born in Italy, and which these men represented in England, stirred and gave life to everything, and woke up English Prose from its sleep. Much of the new life of English Literature was due to the patronage of the young king. It was Henry VIII. who supported SIR THOMAS ELYOT, and encouraged him to write books in the vulgar tongue that he might delight his countrymen. It was the king who asked LORD BERNERS to translate Froissart, a book which ' made a landmark in our tongue,' and who made LELAND, our first English writer on antiquarian subjects, the ' King's Antiquary.' It was the king to whom ROGER ASCHAM dedicated his first work, and the king sent him abroad to pursue his studies. This book, the *Toxophilus*, or the *School of Shooting*, 1545, was written for the pleasure of the yeomen and gentlemen of England, in their own tongue. Ascham apologizes for this, and the apology marks the state of English prose. ' Everything has been done excellently in Greek and Latin, but in the English tongue so meanly that no man can do worse.' He has done his work well, and in quaint but charming English.

PROSE AND THE REFORMATION.—But the man who did best in English prose was SIR THOMAS MORE in the earliest English history, the *History of Edward V. and Richard III.* The simplicity of his genius showed itself in the style, and his wit in the picturesque method and the dramatic dialogue that graced the book. English prose grew larger and richer under his pen, and began that stately step which future historians followed. The work is said to have been written in 1513, but it was not printed till 1557. The most famous book More wrote, *The Utopia*, was not written in English. The most famous controversy he had was with WILLIAM TYNDALE, a man who in his *translation of the New Testament*, 1525,

'fixed our tongue once for all.' His style was as purely English as More's, and of what kind it was may be read in our
Bibles, for our authorized version is still in great part
his translation. In this work, Tyndale was assisted by
WILLIAM ROY, a runaway friar ; his friend ROGERS, the first
martyr in Mary's reign, added to it a translation of the
Apocrypha, and made up what was wanting in Tyndale's
translation from Chronicles to Malachi, out of COVERDALE's
translation.

It was this Bible which, revised by Coverdale and edited
and re-edited as *Cromwell's Bible*, 1539, and again as
Cranmer's Bible, 1540, was set up in every parish church
in England. It got north into Scotland and made the Lowland English more like the London English, and, after its
revisal in 1611, went with the Puritan fathers to New England,
and fixed the standard of English in America. There is no
other book which has had so great an influence on the style of
English literature. In Edward VI.'s reign CRANMER edited
the *English Prayer Book*, 1549–52. Its English is a good
deal mixed with Latin words, and its style is sometimes weak
and heavy, but, on the whole, it is a fine example of stately
prose. LATIMER, on the contrary, whose *Sermon on the
Ploughers* and other sermons were delivered in 1549 and in
1552, wrote in a plain, shrewd style, which by its humor and
rude directness made him the first preacher of his day."

BIBLIOGRAPHY. CAXTON AND MORE.—I. Disraeli's *Amenities of Lit.;* C. Knight's
Old Printer and Mod. Press ; Mackintosh's *Life of More ;* J. Campbell's *Lord
Chan. of Eng.;* F. Myers' *Lectures on Great Men ;* E. Lodge's *Portraits ;*
Froude's *Hist. of Eng.;* Fort. Rev., v. 9, 1868, and v. 14, 1870; N. Br. Rev., v. 30, 1859.

LESSON 14.

THE FIFTEENTH CENTURY POETRY.—" The only literature
which reached any strength was poetical, but even that is
almost wholly confined to the reign of Henry VI. The new
day of poetry still went on, but its noon in Chaucer was now
succeeded by the grey afternoon of Lydgate, and the dull

twilight of Occleve. JOHN LYDGATE, a monk of Bury, who was thirty years of age when Chaucer died, wrote nothing of importance till Henry VI.'s reign. Though a long-winded and third-rate poet, he was a delightful man ; fresh, natural, and happy even to his old age, when he recalls himself as a boy 'weeping for nought, and anon after glad.' There was scarcely any literary work he could not do. He rhymed history, ballads, and legends till the monastery was delighted. He made pageants for Henry VI., masks and May-games for aldermen, mummeries for the Lord Mayor, and satirical ballads on the follies of the day. Educated at Oxford, a traveller in France and Italy, he knew the literature of his time, and he even dabbled in the sciences. He enjoyed everything, but had not the power of adequately expressing his enjoyment. He was as much a lover of nature as was Chaucer, but he cannot make us feel the beauty of nature as Chaucer does. It is his story-telling which brings him closest to Chaucer.

His three chief poems are the *Falls of Princes, The Storie of Thebes,* and the *Troye Book.* The first is a translation of a book of Boccaccio's. It tells the tragic fates of great men from the time of Adam to the capture of King John of France, at Poitiers. There is a touch of the drama in the plan, which was suggested by the pageants of the time. The dead princes appear before Boccaccio pensive in his library, and each relates his downfall. The *Storie of Thebes* is an additional Canterbury Tale, and the *Troye Book* is a version from the French of the prose romance of Guido della Colonna, a Sicilian poet, if the book be not in truth originally French. The *Complaint of the Black Knight,* usually given to Chaucer, is stated to be Lydgate's by Shirley, the contemporary of him and of Chaucer. I should like to be able to call him the author of the pretty little poem called the *Cuckoo and the Nightingale,* included in Chaucer's works. But its authorship is unknown.

THOMAS OCCLEVE, who wrote chiefly in Henry V.'s reign,

about 1420, was nothing but a bad versifier. His one merit is
that he loved Chaucer. With his loss 'the whole land smart-
ith,' he says, and he breaks out into a kind of rapture once:—

> 'Thou wert acquainted with Chaucer! Pardie,
> God save his soul,
> The first finder of our faire langage.'

And it is in the MS. of his longest poem, *The Governail of
Princes*, that he caused to be drawn, with 'fond idolatry,' the
portrait of his master. With this long piece of verse we mark
the decay of the poetry of England. Romances and lays
were still translated ; there were verses written on such subjects as hunting and alchemy. Caxton himself produced a
poem ; but the only thing here worth noticing is, that at the
end of the century some of our ballads were printed.

Ballads, lays, and fragments of romances had been sung in
England from the earliest times, and popular tales and jokes
took form in short lyric pieces to be accompanied by music
and dancing. We have seen war celebrated in Minot's songs,
and the political ballad is represented by the lampoon made by
some follower of Simon de Montfort on the day of the battle
of Lewes, and by the *Elegy on Edward I.'s Death*. But the
ballad went over the whole land· among the people. The
trader, the apprentices, the poor of the cities, and the peasantry had their own songs. They tended to collect themselves round some legendary name, like Robin Hood, or some
historical character made legendary, like Randolf, Earl of
Chester. Sloth, in *Piers Plowman's Vision*, does not know
his paternoster, but he does know the rhymes of these heroes.

A crowd of minstrels sang them through city and village.
The very friar sang them, 'and made his Englissch swete
upon his tunge.' A collection of Robin Hood ballads was soon
printed under the title of *A Lytel Geste of Robin Hood*, by
Wynken de Worde. *The Nut Brown Maid, The Battle of
Otterburn*, and *Chevy Chase* may belong to the end of the

century, though probably not in the form we possess them. It was not, however, till much later that any collection of ballads was made ; and few, as we possess them, can be dated farther back than the reign of Elizabeth."

From *Chevy Chase.* (Prof. Child's edition.)

The Persè owt off Northombarlande,
   And a vowe to God mayd he,
That he wold hunte in the mountayns
   Off Chyviat, within days thre,
In the mauger[1] of doughtè Dogles,
   And all that ever with him be.

The fattiste hartes in all Cheviat
   He sayd he wold kill, and cary them away:
" Be my feth" sayd the dougheti[2] Doglas agayn,
   " I wyll let[3] that hontyng yf that I may."

Then the Persè owt of Banborowe cam,
   With him a myghteè meany;[4]
With fifteen hondrith archares bold off blood and bone,
   The wear chosen owt of shyars thre.

He sayd, "It was the Duglas promys
   This day to met me hear;
But I wyste[5] he wold faylle, verament:"[6]
   A great oth the Persè swear.

At the laste a squyar of Northombelonde
   Lokyde at his hand full ny;
He was war a[7] the doughetie Doglas comynge,
   With him a myghttè meany.

The dougheti Dogglas on a stede
   He rode att his men beforne;
His armor glytteryde as dyd a glede;[8]
   A bolder barne[9] was never born.

"Tell me whos men ye ar," he says,
   "Or whos men that ye be:
Who gave youe leave to hunte in this Chyviat chays,
   In the spyt of me?"

---

[1] Spite.   [2] Doughty, brave.   [3] Hinder.   [4] Company.   [5] Knew.
[6] Truly.   [7] Aware of.   [8] Live coal.   [9] Man.

The first mane that ever him an answear mayd,
    Yt was the good lord Persè:
"We wyll not tell the whoys men we ar," he says,
    "Nor whos men thet we be;
But we wyll hount hear in this chays,
    In the spyt of thyne and of the.[1]

The fattiste hartes in all Chyviat
    We have kyld, and cast[2] to carry them a-way:"
"Be my troth," sayd the doughtè Dogglas agayn,
    "Ther-for the ton[3] of us shall de[4] this day."

Then sayd the doughtè Doglas
    Unto the lord Persè:
"To kyll all thes giltles men,
    Alas, it wear great pittè!

But, Persè, thowe art a lord of lande,
    I am a yerle[5] callyd within my contrè;
Let all our men uppone a parti[6] stande,
    And do the battell off the and of me."

Then bespayke a squyar off Northombarlonde,
    Richard Wytharyngton was him nam;
"It shall never be told in Sothe-Ynglonde," he says,
    "To kyng Herry the fourth for sham.

I wat[7] youe byn great lordes twaw,
    I am a poor squyar of lande;
I wyll never se my captayne fyght on a fylde,
    And stande myselffe, and loocke on,
But whyll I may my weppone welde,
    I wyll not [fayl] both hart and hande."

    .   .   .   .   .   .

At last the Duglas and the Persè met,
    Lyk to captayns of myght and of mayne;
The swapte[8] togethar tyll the both swat,[9]
    With swordes that wear of fyn myllàn.[10]

---

[1] Thee.   [2] Propose.   [3] One.   [4] Die.   [5] Earl.   [6] Apart.   [7] Know.
      [8] They smote.   [9] Sweat.   [10] Milan steel.

With that ther cam an arrowe hastely,
   Forthe off a myghttè wane;[1]
Hit[2] hathe strekene the yerle Duglas
   In at the brest bane.

The Persè leanyde on his brande,
   And sawe the Duglas de;
He tooke the dede mane be the hande,
   And sayd, "Wo ys me for the!"

Off all that se a Skottishe knyght,
   Was callyd Sir Hewe the Monggonbyrry;[3]
He sawe the Duglas to the deth was dyght,[4]
   He spendyd[5] a spear, a trusti tre.[6]

He set uppone the lord Persè
   A dynte[7] that was full soare;
With a suar[8] spear of a myghttè tre
   Clean thorow the body he the Persè ber,[9]

A' the tothar[10] syde that a man myght se
   A large cloth yard and mare:
Towe better captayns wear nat in Cristiantè,[11]
   Then that day slain wear ther.

.   .   .   .   .   .

This battell begane in Chyviat
   An owar[12] before the none,
And when even-song bell was rang,
   The battell was not half done.

Of fifteen hondrith archars of Ynglonde
   Went away but fifti and thre;
Of twenty hondrith spear-men of Skotlonde
   But even five and fifti.

For Wetharryngton my harte was wo,
   Thet ever he slayne shulde be;
For when both his leggis wear hewyne in to,
   Yet he knyled and fought on hys kny.

---

[1] One, man. [2] It. [3] Montgomery. [4] Done. [5] Grasped. [6] Spear-shaft.
[7] Blow. [8] Sure. [9] Bare. [10] The other. [11] Christendom. [12] Hour.

LESSON 15.

SCOTTISH POETRY.—"This is poetry written in the English tongue by men living in Scotland. These men, though calling themselves Scotchmen, are of good English blood. But the blood, as I think, was mixed with an infusion of Celtic blood.

Old Northumbria extended from the Humber to the Firth of Forth, leaving, however, on its western border a line of unconquered land which took in Lancashire, Cumberland, and Westmoreland in England, and over the border most of the western country between the Clyde and Solway Firth. This unconquered country was the Welsh kingdom of Strathclyde, and it was dwelt in by the Celtic race. The present English part of it was soon conquered, and the Celts were driven out. But in the part to the north of the Solway Firth, the Celts were not driven out. They remained, lived with the Englishmen who were settled over the old Northumbria, intermarried with them, and became under Scot kings one mixed people. Literature in the Lowlands, then, would have Celtic elements in it; literature in England was purely Teutonic. The one sprang from a mixed, the other from an unmixed race. I draw attention to this, because it seems to me to account for certain peculiarities in Scottish poetry which color the whole of it, which rule over it, and are specially Celtic.

CELTIC ELEMENTS OF SCOTTISH POETRY.—The *first* of these is *the love of wild nature for its own sake.* There is a passionate, close, and poetical observation and description of natural scenery in Scotland, from the earliest times of its poetry, such as is not seen in English poetry till the time of Wordsworth. The *second* is *the love of color.* All early Scottish poetry differs from English in the extraordinary way in which color is insisted on, and at times in the lavish exag-

geration of it. The *third* is *the wittier, more rollicking humor*
in the Scottish poetry, which is distinctly Celtic in contrast
with that humor which has its root in sadness, and which
belongs to the Teutonic races. Few things are really more
different than the humor of Chaucer and the humor of Dunbar, than the humor of Cowper and that of Burns. These
are the special Celtic elements in the Lowland poetry.

Its **National Elements** came into it from the circumstances
under which Scotland rose into a separate kingdom. The
first of these is the strong, almost fierce, assertion of national
life. The English were as national as the Scots, and felt the
emotion of patriotism as strongly. But they had no need to
assert it; they were not oppressed. But for nearly forty years
the Scotch resisted for their very life the efforts of England to
conquer them. And the war of freedom left its traces on their
poetry from Barbour to Burns and Walter Scott in the almost
obtrusive way in which Scotland and Scottish liberty and
Scottish heroes are thrust forward in their verse.

Their passionate nationality appears in another form in
their descriptive poetry. The natural description of Chaucer,
Shakespeare, or even Milton is not distinctively English. But
in Scotland it is always the scenery of their own land that the
poets describe. Even when they are imitating Chaucer, they
do not imitate his conventional landscape. They put in a
Scotch landscape, and, in the work of such men as Gawin
Douglas, the love of Scotland and the love of nature mingle
their influences together to make him sit down, as it were, to
paint, with his eye on everything he paints, a series of Scotch
landscapes. It is done without any artistic composition; it
reads like a catalogue, but it is work which stands quite alone
at the time he wrote. There is nothing even resembling it
in England for centuries after.

ITS INDIVIDUAL ELEMENT.—There is one more special
element in early Scottish poetry which arose, I think, out of
its political circumstances. All through the struggle for free-

• dom, carried on, as it was at first, by small bands under separate leaders till they all came together under a leader like Bruce, a much greater amount of individuality and a greater habit of it were created among the Scotch than among the English. Men fought for their own land, and lived in their own way. Every little border chieftain, almost every border farmer was, or felt himself to be, his own master. The poets would be likely to share in this individual quality, and, in spite of the overpowering influence of Chaucer, to strike out new veins of poetic thought and new methods of poetic expression. And this is what happened. Long before forms of poetry like the short pastoral or the fable had appeared in England, the Scottish poets had started them. They were less docile imitators than the English, but their work in the new forms they started was not so good as the after English work in the same forms.

The first of the Scottish poets, omitting Thomas of Ercel- doune, is JOHN BARBOUR, Archdeacon of Aberdeen. His long poem of *The Bruce* represents the whole of the eager struggle for Scottish freedom against the English which closed at Bannockburn; and the national spirit, which I have mentioned, springs in it, full grown, into life. But it is temperate, it does not pass into the fury against England which is so plain in writers like BLIND HARRY, who, about 1461, composed a long poem in the heroic couplet of Chaucer, on the deeds of *William Wallace*. Barbour was often in Eng- land for the sake of study, and his patriotism, though strong, is tolerant of England. The date of his poem is 1375, 7; it never mentions Chaucer, and Barbour is the only early Scot- tish poet on whom Chaucer had no influence. In the next poet we find the influence of Chaucer, and it is hereafter con- tinuous till the Elizabethan time.

JAMES THE FIRST of Scotland was prisoner in England for nineteen years, till 1422. There he read Chaucer, and fell in love with Lady Jane Beaufort, niece of Henry the Fourth. The poem which he wrote, *The King's Quhair,* the quire, or book, is done in imitation of Chaucer, and in Chaucer's seven-lined stanza, which from James's use of it is called Rime Royal. In six cantos, sweeter, tenderer, and purer than any other verse till we come to Spenser, he describes the beginning of his love and its happy end. ' I must write,' he says, ' so much, because I have come so from Hell to Heaven.' Nor did the flower of his love and hers ever fade. She defended him in the last ghastly scene of murder when his kingly life ended. There is something especially pathetic in the lover of Chaucer, in the first poet of sentiment in Scotland's being slain so cruelly. He was no blind imitator of Chaucer. We are conscious at once of an original element in his work. The natural description is more varied, the color is more vivid, and there is a modern self-reflective quality, a touch of spiritual feeling, which does not belong to Chaucer at all. The poems of *The Kirk on the Green* and *Peebles to the Play* have been attributed to him. If they are his, he originated a new vein of poetry, which Burns afterwards carried out—the comic and satirical ballad poem. But they are more likely to be by James V.

ROBERT HENRYSON, who died before 1508, a school-master in Dunfermline, was also an imitator of Chaucer, and his *Testament of Cresseid* continues Chaucer's *Troilus.* But he set on foot two new forms of poetry. He made poems out of the *fables.* They differ entirely from the short, neat form in which Gay and La Fontaine treated the fable. They are long stories, full of pleasant dialogue, political allusions, and with elaborate morals attached to them. They have a peculiar Scottish tang, and are full of descriptions of Scotch scenery. He also began the short *pastoral* in his *Robin and Makyne.* It is a natural, prettily turned dialogue ; and a subtile Celtic wit, such as charms us in *Duncan Grey,* runs through it. The individuality which struck out two original lines of poetic work in these poems appears again in his sketch of the graces

of womanhood in the *Garment of Good Ladies ;* a poem of the
same type as those thoughtful lyrics which describe what is
best in certain phases of professions, or life, such as Sir H.
Wotton's *Character of a Happy Life*, or Wordsworth's *Happy
Warrior.*

But among lesser men, whom we need not mention, the
greatest is WILLIAM DUNBAR. He carries the influence of
Chaucer on to the end of the fifteenth century and into the sixteenth. Few have possessed a more masculine genius, and
his work was as varied in its range as it was original. He
followed the form and plan of Chaucer in his two poems of
The Thistle and the Rose, 1503, and *The Golden Terge*, 1508,
the first on the marriage of James IV. to Margaret Tudor,
the second an allegory of Love, Beauty, Reason, and the Poet.
In both, though they begin with Chaucer's conventional May
morning, the natural description becomes Scottish, and in
both the national enthusiasm of the poet is strongly marked.
But he soon ceased to imitate. The vigorous fun of the
satires and of the satirical ballads that he wrote is matched
only by their coarseness, a coarseness and a fun that descended
to Burns. Perhaps Dunbar's genius is still higher in a wild
poem in which he personifies the seven deadly sins, and
describes their dance, with a mixture of horror and humor
which makes the little thing unique.

A man almost as remarkable as Dunbar is GAWIN DOUG-
LAS, Bishop of Dunkeld, who died in 1522, at the Court of
Henry VIII., and was buried in the Savoy. He is the author
of the first metrical English translation from the original of
any Latin book. He translated Ovid's *Art of Love*, and afterwards, with truth and spirit, the *Æneid* of Vergil, 1513. To
each book of the *Æneid* he wrote a prologue of his own.
And it is chiefly by these that he takes rank among the Scottish poets. Three of them are descriptions of the country in
May, in autumn, and in winter. The scenery is altogether
Scotch, and the few Chaucerisms that appear seem absurdly

out of place in a picture of nature which is as close as if it had been done by Keats in his early time. The color is superb, the landscape is described with an excessive detail, but the poem is not composed by any art into a whole. Still it astonishes the reader, and it is only by bringing in the Celtic element of love of nature that we can account for the vast distance between work like this and contemporary work in England such as Skelton's. Of Douglas's other original work, one poem, *The Palace of Honour*, 1501, continues the influence of Chaucer.

There were a number of other Scottish poets belonging to this time who are all remembered and praised by SIR DAVID LYNDSAY, whom it is best to mention in this place, because he still connects Scottish poetry with Chaucer. He was born about 1490 and is the last of the old Scottish school, and the most popular. He is the most popular, because he is not only the Poet but also the Reformer. His poem, *The Dreme*, 1528, connects him with Chaucer. It is in the manner of the old poet. But its scenery is Scottish, and, instead of the May morning of Chaucer, it opens on a winter's day of wind and sleet. The place is a cave over the sea, whence Lyndsay sees the weltering of the waves. Chaucer goes to sleep over Ovid or Cicero, Lyndsay falls into dream as he thinks of the 'false world's instability' wavering like the sea waves. The difference marks not only the difference of the two countries, but the different natures of the men. Chaucer did not care much for the popular storms, and loved the Court more than the Commonweal. Lyndsay in the *Dreme*, and in two other poems—the *Complaint to the King*, and the *Testament of the King's Papyngo*—is absorbed in the evils and sorrows of the people, and in the desire to reform the abuses of the Church, of the Court, of party, of the nobility.

In 1539 his *Satire of the Three Estates*, a Morality interspersed with interludes, was represented before James V. at Linlithgow. It was first acted in 1535, and was a daring attack on the ignorance, profligacy, and exactions of the priesthood, on the vices and flattery of the favorites—'a mocking of abuses used in the country by diverse sorts of estate.' A still bolder poem, and one thought so even by himself, is the *Monarchie*, 1553, his last work. Reformer as he was, he was more a social and political than a religious one. He bears the same relation to Knox as Langland did to Wiclif. When he was sixty-five years old, he saw the fruits of his work. Ecclesiastical councils met to reform the Church. But the reform soon went beyond his temperate wishes. In 1557 the Reformation in Scotland was fairly launched when in December the Congregation signed the Bond of Association. Lyndsay had died three years before ; he is as much the reformer as he is the poet, of a transition time. 'Still his verse hath charms,' but it was neither sweet nor imaginative. He had genuine satire, great moral breadth, much preaching power in verse, coarse, broad humor in plenty, and more dramatic power and invention than the rest of his fellows, and he lived an active, bold, and brave life in a very stormy time."

LESSON 16.

POETRY IN THE SIXTEENTH CENTURY UNDER THE INFLUENCE OF CHAUCER.—" We shall speak in this and in the next two paragraphs only of the poets in England whose work was due to the publication of Chaucer, Gower, and Lydgate by Caxton. After a short revival that influence died, and a new one entered from Italy into English verse in the poems of Surrey and Wyatt. The transition period between the one influence and the other is of great interest. We see how the old poets had been neglected by the way in which the new poets speak of them as of something wonderful, and by the indignant reproach a man like Hawes makes when he says that people care for nothing but ballads, and will not read these old books. But the reproach was unwise. It is better for the interests of literature to make a new ballad than to read an old poem, and the ballads of England kept up the original vein of poetry. It is one of the signs of a new poetic life in a nation when it is fond of poetry which, like the ballad, has to do with the human interests of the present: and, when that kind of human poetry pleases the upper classes as well as the lower, a resurrection of poetry is at hand.

HAWES AND SKELTON.—At such a time we are likely to find imitators of the old work, and in the reign of Henry VII. STEPHEN HAWES recast a poem of Lydgate's (?) *The Temple of Glass*, and imitated Chaucer's work and the old allegory in his *Pastime of Pleasure*, 1506. We shall also find men who, while they still follow the old, leave it for an original line, because they are more moved by human life in the present than in the past. Their work will be popular, it may even resemble the form of the ballad. Such a man was JOHN SKELTON, who wrote in Henry VII.'s and in Henry VIII.'s reign, and died, 1529. His earliest poems were after the manner of Chaucer, but he soon took a manner of his own, and, being greatly excited by the cry of the people for Church reformation, wrote a bitter satire on Wolsey for his pride, and on the clergy for their luxury. His poem, *Why come ye not to Court?* was a fierce satire on the great Cardinal. That of *Colin Clout* was the cry of the country Colin, and of the Clout or mechanic of the town, against the corruption of the Church.

Both are written in short, 'rude, rayling rimes, pleasing only the popular ear,' and Skelton chose them for that purpose. Both have a rough, impetuous power; their language is coarse, full even of slang, but Skelton could use any language he pleased. He was an admirable scholar. Erasmus calls him the 'glory and light of English letters,' and Caxton says that he improved our language. *Colin Clout* represents the whole popular feeling of the time just before the movement of the Reformation took a new turn by the opposition of the Pope to Henry's divorce. It was not only in this satirical vein that Skelton wrote. We owe to him some pretty and new love lyrics; and the *Boke of Phyllyp Sparowe*, which tells the grief of a nun, called Jane Scrope, for the death of her sparrow, is one of the gayest and most inventive poems in the language. Skelton stands quite alone between the last flicker of the influence of Chaucer, whose last true imitator he was, and the <u>rise of a new Italian influence</u> in England in the poems of Surrey and Wyatt. In his own special work he was entirely original, and, standing thus between two periods of poetry, he is a kind of landmark in English literature. The *Ship of Fooles*, 1508, by BARCLAY, is of this time, but it has no value. It is a recast of a work published at Basel, and was popular because it attacked the follies and questions of the time. It was written in Chaucer's stanza.

ITALIAN INFLUENCE—WYATT AND SURREY.—While poetry under Skelton and Lyndsay became an instrument of reform, it revived as an art at the close of Henry VIII.'s reign in SIR THOMAS WYATT and the EARL OF SURREY. They were both Italian travellers, and, in taking back to England the inspiration they had gained from Petrarca, they re-made English poetry. They are the first really modern English poets; the first who have anything of the modern manner. Though Italian in sentiment, their language is more English than Chaucer's is, they use fewer romance words. They handed down this purity of English to the Elizabethan poets, to Sackville, Spenser, and Shakespeare. They introduced a new kind of poetry, the amourist poetry. The 'AMOURISTS,' as they are called, were poets who composed poems on the subject of love—sonnets mingled with lyrical pieces after the manner of Petrarca, and in accord with the love philosophy he built on Plato. The *Hundred Passions* of WATSON, the sonnets of Sidney, Shakespeare, Spenser, and Drummond are all poems of this kind, and the same impulse in a similar form appears in the sonnets of Rosetti and Mrs. Browning of our time.

The subjects of Wyatt and Surrey were chiefly lyrical, and the fact that they imitated the same model has made some likeness between them. Like their personal characters, however, the poetry of Wyatt is the more thoughtful and the more strongly felt, but Surrey's has a sweeter movement and a livelier fancy. Both did this great thing for English verse—they chose an exquisite model, and in imitating it 'corrected the ruggedness of English poetry.' ₁. Such verse as Skelton's became impossible. A new standard was made, below which the after poets could not fall. They also added new stanza measures to English verse, and enlarged 2. in this way the 'lyrical range.' Surrey was the first, in his *translation of Vergil's Æneid*, to use the ten-syllabled, unrhymed verse, which we now call BLANK-VERSE. In his hands it is not worthy of praise; it had neither the true form nor the harmony into which it grew afterwards. Sackville, Lord Buckhurst, introduced it into drama; Marlowe, in his *Tamburlaine*, made it the proper verse of the drama; and Shakespeare, Beaumont, and Massinger used it splendidly. In plays it has a special manner of its own; in poetry proper it was, we may say, not only created but perfected by Milton.

The new impulse thus given to poetry was all but arrested by the bigotry that prevailed during the reigns of Edward VI. and Mary, and all the work of the New Learning seemed to be useless. But THOMAS WILSON's book in English on *Rhetoric and Logic* in 1553, and the publication of THOS. TUSSER's *Pointes of Husbandrie* and of Tottel's *Miscellany of Uncertain Authors*, 1557, in the last years of Mary's reign, proved that something was stirring beneath the gloom. The latter book contained the poems of Surrey and Wyatt, and others by Grimald, by Lord Vaux, and Lord Berners. The date should be remembered, for it is the first printed book of modern English poetry. It proves that men cared now more for the new than for the old poets, that the time of imitating Chaucer was over, and that of original creation was begun. It ushers in the Elizabethan literature."

SCHEME FOR REVIEW.

PERIOD IV.

ELIZABETH'S REIGN,

1558–1603.

LESSON 17.

Brief Historical Sketch.—Elizabeth's first Parliament undid Mary's work, repealed the statutes of heresy, dissolved the refounded monasteries, and restored the Royal Supremacy. Manufactures of all kinds are stimulated, commerce is developed, and the diet of the common people improved; pewter plates replace wooden trenchers, and feather beds straw mattresses; carpets supersede rushes, glass windows become common, and houses are no longer built for defence, but for comfort, and of brick instead of wood. Members of the House of Commons no longer paid. The thirty-nine articles of faith enacted by Parliament, 1562. Hawkins begins Slave Trade with Africa, 1562. First penal statute against Catholics and first Poor Law, 1562. Puritans secede from English Church, 1566. The Revolt of the Netherlands against Philip II. assisted by Elizabeth, 1575 and on. Futile attempts to colonize America made by Gilbert, 1578, and by Raleigh, 1584, 6, and 7. Drake circumnavigated the earth, 1577. London supplied by water in pipes, 1582. Potatoes and tobacco introduced, 1586. Mary, Queen of Scots, executed by Elizabeth, 1587. Spanish Armada defeated, 1588. Episcopacy abolished in Scotland and Presbyterianism established as the state religion, 1596. Ruin of second Armada, 1597. Bodleian library founded at Oxford, 1598. East India Company chartered, 1600. Magnetism discovered same year. Earl of Essex executed, 1601. Tyrone's rebellion in Ireland crushed, 1603. Wonders of the New World powerfully influenced the literature of this period.

LESSON 18.

ELIZABETHAN LITERATURE.—"This may be said to begin with Surrey and Wyatt. But as their poems were published shortly before Elizabeth came to the throne, we date the be-

ginning of the *earlier* Elizabethan literature from the year of
her accession, 1558. The era of this earlier literature lasted
till 1579, and was followed by the great literary outburst, as
it has been called, of the days of Spenser and Shakespeare.
The apparent suddenness of this outburst has been an object
of wonder. Men have searched for its causes chiefly in those
which led to the revival of learning, and no doubt these bore
on England as they did on the whole of Europe. But we
shall best seek its nearest causes in the work done during the
early years of Elizabeth, and in doing so we shall find that
the outburst was not so sudden after all. It was preceded by
a various, plentiful, but inferior, literature, in which new
forms of poetry and prose-writing were tried, and new veins
of thought opened, which were afterwards wrought out fully
and splendidly. All the germs of the coming age are to be
found in these twenty years. The outburst of a plant into
flower seems sudden, but the whole growth of the plant has
caused it, and the flowering of Elizabethan literature was the
slow result of the growth of the previous literature and the
influences that bore upon it.

The Earlier Elizabethan Poetry, 1558–1579, is *first* represented by SACKVILLE, Lord Buckhurst. The *Mirror of
Magistrates*, 1559, for which he wrote the *Induction* and one
tale, is a poem on the model of Boccaccio's *Falls of Princes*,
already imitated by Lydgate. Seven poets, along with Sackville, contributed tales to it, but his poem is the only one of
any value. The *Induction* paints the poet's descent into
Avernus, and his meeting with Henry Stafford, Duke of
Buckingham, whose fate he tells with a grave and inventive
imagination. Being written in the manner and stanza of the
elder poets, this poem has been called the transition between
Lydgate and Spenser. But it does truly belong to the old time;
it is as modern as Spenser. GEORGE GASCOIGNE, whose satire,
the *Steele Glas*, 1576, is our first long satirical poem, is the
best among a crowd of lesser poets who came after Sackville.

They wrote legends, pieces on the wars and discoveries of the Englishmen of their day, epitaphs, epigrams, songs, sonnets, elegies, fables, and sets of love poems; and the best things they did were collected in a miscellany called the *Paradise of Dainty Devices*, in 1576. This book, with Tottel's, set on foot in the later years of Elizabeth a crowd of other miscellanies of poetry, which were of great use to the poets. Lyrical poetry and that which we may call ' occasional poetry ' were now fairly started.

2. The *masques, pageants, interludes*, and *plays* that were written at this time are scarcely to be counted. At every great ceremonial, whenever the queen made a progress or visited one of the great lords or a university, at the houses of the nobility, and at the court on all important days, some obscure versifier, or a young scholar at the Inns of Court, at Oxford, or at Cambridge produced a masque or a pageant, or wrote or translated a play. The habit of play-writing became common; a kind of school, one might almost say a manufacture, of plays arose, which partly accounts for the rapid production, the excellence, and the multitude of plays that we find after 1579. Represented all over England, these masques, pageants, and dramas were seen by the people, who were thus accustomed to take an interest, though of an uneducated kind, in the larger drama that was to follow. The literary men, on the other hand, ransacked, in order to find subjects and scenes for their pageants, ancient and mediæval and modern literature, and many of them in doing so became fine scholars. The imagination of England was quickened and educated in this way, and, as Biblical stories were also largely used, the images of oriental life were added to the materials of imagination.

3. *Frequent translations* were now made from the classical writers. We know the names of more than twelve men who did this work, and there must have been many more. Already in Henry VIII.'s and in Edward VI.'s time, ancient authors

had been made English; and before 1579, Vergil, Ovid, Cicero, Demosthenes, and many Greek and Latin plays were translated. In this way the best models were brought before the English people, and it is in the influence of the spirit of Greek and Roman literature on literary form and execution that we are to find one of the vital causes of the greatness of the later Elizabethan literature.

The Earlier Elizabethan Prose, 1558-1579, began with the *Scholemaster* of ASCHAM, published 1570. This book, which is on education, is the work of the scholar of the New Learning of the time of Henry VIII. who has lived on into another time. It is not, properly speaking, Elizabethan, it is like a stranger in a new land and among new manners.

2. *Theological reform* stirred men to literary work. A great number of satirical ballads and pamphlets and plays issued every year from obscure presses and filled the land. Writers, like George Gascoigne and, still more, BARNABY GOOGE, represent in their work the hatred the young men had of the old religious system. It was a spirit which did not do much for literature, but it quickened the habit of composition, and made it easier. The Bible also became common property, and its language glided into all theological writing and gave it a literary tone; while the publication of JOHN FOX's *Acts and Monuments*, or *Book of Martyrs*, 1563, gave to the people all over England a book which, by its simple style, the ease of its story-telling, and its popular charm, made the very peasants who heard it read feel what is meant by literature.

3. The *love of stories* again awoke. The old English tales and ballads were eagerly read and collected. Italian Tales by various authors were translated and sown so broadcast over London by William Painter, in his collection, *The Palace of Pleasure*, 1566, by George Turbervile and others, that it is said they were to be bought at every bookstall. A great number of subjects for prose and poetry were thus made ready for literary men, and fiction became possible in English literature.

Another influence of the same kind bore on literature. It was that given by the *stories of the voyagers*, who, in the new commercial activity of the country, penetrated into strange lands. Before 1579 books had been published on the north-west passage. Frobisher had made his voyages, and Drake had started, to return in 1580 to amaze all England with the story of his sail round the world, and of the riches of the Spanish main. We may trace everywhere in Elizabethan literature the impression made by the wonders told by the sailors and captains who explored and fought from the North Pole to the Southern Seas.

4. The *history* of the country and its manners was not neglected. A whole class of antiquarians wrote steadily, if with some dulness, on this subject. GRAFTON, STOW, HOLIN-SHED, and others at least supplied materials for the study and use of the historical drama.

5. Lastly, we have proof that there was a large number of *persons writing who did not publish their works.* It was considered at this time that to write for the public injured a man, and, unless he were driven by poverty, he kept his manuscript by him. But things were changed when a great genius like Spenser took the world by storm; when Lyly's *Euphues* enchanted the whole of court society; when a great gentleman, like Sir Philip Sidney, became a writer. Literature was made the fashion, and, the disgrace being taken from it, the production became enormous. Manuscripts written and laid by were at once sent forth; and, when the rush began, it grew by its own force. Those who had previously been kept from writing by its unpopularity now took it up eagerly, and those who had written before wrote twice as much now. The great improvement also in literary quality is easily accounted for by this—that men strove to equal such work as Sidney's or Spenser's, and that a wider and sharper criticism arose."   -

LESSON 19.

THE PROSE OF THE LATER ELIZABETHAN LITERATURE, 1579-1603.—"This begins with the publication of Lyly's *Euphues* in 1579, and with the writing of Sir Philip Sidney's *Arcadia* and his *Defence of Poetrie*, 1580–81. The *Euphues* and the *Arcadia* carried on the story-telling literature ; the *Defence of Poetrie* created a new form of literature, that of criticism.

The *Euphues* was the work of JOHN LYLY, poet and dramatist. It is in two parts, *Euphues* and *Euphues' England*. In six years it ran through five editions, so great was its popularity. Its prose style is too poetic, but it is admirable for its smoothness and charm, and its very faults were of use in softening the rudeness of previous prose. The story is long and is more a loose framework into which Lyly could fit his thoughts on love, friendship, education, and religion than a true story. The second part is made up of several stories in one, and is a picture of the Englishman abroad. It made its mark, because it fell in with all the fantastic and changeable life of the time. Its far-fetched conceits, its extravagance of gallantry, its endless metaphors from the classics and natural history, its curious and gorgeous descriptions of dress, and its pale imitation of chivalry were all reflected in the life and talk and dress of the court of Elizabeth. It became the fashion to talk 'Euphuism,' and, like the *Utopia* of More, Lyly's book has created an English word.

The *Arcadia* was the work of SIR PHILIP SIDNEY and, though written in 1580, did not appear till after his death. It is more poetic in style than the *Euphues*, and Sidney himself, as he wrote it under the trees of Wilton, would have called it a poem. It is less the image of the time than of the man. Most people know that bright and noble figure, the friend of Spenser, the lover of Stella, the last of the old knights, the poet, the critic, and the Christian, who, wounded to the death, gave up the cup of water to a dying soldier. We find his whole spirit in the story of the *Arcadia*, in the first two books and a part of the third, which alone were written by him. It is a romance mixed up with pastoral stories after the fashion of the Spanish romances. The characters are real, but the story is confused by endless digressions. The sentiment is too fine and delicate for the world. The descriptions are picturesque, and the sentences are made as perfect as possible. A quaint or poetic thought or an epigram appears in every line. There is no real art in it or in its prose. But it is so full of poetical thought that it became a mine into which poets dug for subjects.

Criticism began with Sidney's *Defence of Poetrie*. Its style shows us that he felt how faulty the prose of the *Arcadia* was. The book made a new step in the creation of a dignified English prose. It is still too flowery, but in it the fantastic prose of his own *Arcadia* and of the *Euphues* dies. As criticism it is chiefly concerned with poetry. It defends, against STEPHEN GOSSON's *School of Abuse*, in which poetry and plays were attacked from the Puritan point of view, the nobler uses of poetry. Sackville, Surrey, and Spenser are praised, and the other poets made little of in its pages. It was followed by WEBBE's *Discourse of English Poetrie*, written ' to stirre up some other of meet abilitie to bestow travell on the matter. Already the other was travailing, and the *Arte of English Poesie*, supposed to be written by GEORGE PUTTENHAM, was published in 1589. It is the most elaborate book on the whole subject in Elizabeth's reign, and it marks the strong interest now taken in poetry in the highest society that the author says he writes it ' to help the courtiers and the gentlewomen of the court to write good poetry, that the art may become vulgar for all Englishmen's use.'

LATER THEOLOGICAL LITERATURE.—Before we come to the Poetry we will give an account of the Prose into which the tendencies of the earlier years of Elizabeth grew. The first is

that of *theology*. For a long time it remained only a literature
of pamphlets. Puritanism, in its attack on the stage and in
the Martin Marprelate controversy upon episcopal government
in the Church, flooded England with small books. Lord
Bacon even joined in the latter controversy, and Nash, the
dramatist, made himself famous in the war by the vigor and
fierceness of his wit. Over this troubled sea rose at last the
stately work of RICHARD HOOKER. It was in 1594 that the
first four books of *The Laws of Ecclesiastical Polity*, a defence
of the Church against the Puritans, were given to the world.
Before his death he finished the other four. The book has
remained ever since a standard work. It is as much moral
and political as theological. Its style is grave, clear, and
often musical. He adorned it with the figures of poetry, but
he used them with temperance, and the grand and rolling
rhetoric with which he often concludes an argument is kept
for its right place. On the whole it is the first monument of
splendid literary prose that we possess."

"Hooker affords our first example of an elaborate, high-sounding,
'periodic style.' His sentences, in their general character, are long and
involved. With all their excellencies, they are not good models for
English periods. In writing our first elaborate theological treatise, his
fine ear was irresistibly caught by the rhythm of Latin models ; and,
while he learned from them a more even proportion of sentence, he
learned also to build an elaborate rhythm at the expense of native idiom.
Attention to clearness and simplicity in the structure of paragraphs was
a thing unknown in the age of Elizabeth, and Hooker was, in this respect, neither better nor worse than the good writers of his time."—
William Minto.

THE ESSAY.—" We may place alongside of it, as the other
great prose work of Elizabeth's later time, the development of
the Essay in LORD BACON'S *Essays,* 1597. Their highest
literary merit is their combination of charm and even of poetic
prose with conciseness of expression and fulness of thought.
The rest of Bacon's work belongs to the following reign. The
splendor of the form, and of the English prose of the *Advance-*

ment of Learning, afterwards written in the Latin language, and intended to be worked up by the addition of the *Novum Organum* and the *Sylva Sylvarum* into the treatise of the *Instauratio Magna*, which Bacon meant to be a philosophy of human knowledge, raises it into the realm of pure literature."

"The works of Bacon afford very little food for ordinary human feelings. All the pleasure we gain from them is founded upon their intellectual excellencies. Even the similitudes are intellectual rather than emotional, ingenious rather than touching or poetical. To adapt an image of Ben Jonson's, the wine of Bacon's writings is a dry wine. As we read, we experience the pleasure of surmounting obstacles; we are electrified by unexpected analogies, and the sudden revelations of new aspects in familiar things; and we sympathise more or less with the boundless exhilaration of a mind that pierces with ease and swiftness through barriers that reduce other minds to torpor and stagnancy. The opinions contained in his Essays, observations and precepts on man and society, are perhaps the most permanent evidence of his sagacity. In this field he was thoroughly at home; the study of mankind occupied the largest part of his time."—*William Minto.*

"JOHN FLORIO'S *translation of the Essays of Montaigne*, 1603, is also worth mentioning, because Shakespeare used the book and because we trace Montaigne's influence on English literature even before his retranslation by Charles Cotton.

History, except in the publication of the earlier Chronicles by Archbishop Parker, does not appear again in Elizabeth's reign; but in the next reign Camden, Spelman, and John Speed continued the antiquarian researches of Stow and Grafton. Bacon published a history of Henry VII., and SAMUEL DANIEL, the poet, in his *History of England to the Time of Edward III.*, 1613, 18, was one of the first to throw history into such a literary form as to make it popular. KNOLLES' *History of the Turks* and SIR WALTER RALEIGH'S vast sketch of the *History of the World* show how, for the first time, history spread itself beyond English interests. Raleigh's book, written in the peaceful evening of a stormy life, and in the quiet of his prison, is literary not only from the ease and vigor of its style but from its still spirit of melancholy thought.

The Literature of Travel was carried on by the publication in 1589 of HAKLUYT's *Navigation, Voyages, and Discoveries of the English Nation*, enlarged afterwards in 1625 by SAMUEL PURCHAS, who had himself written a book called *Purchas, his Pilgrimage; or The Relations and Religions of the World*. The influence of a compilation of this kind, containing the great deeds of the English on the seas, has been felt ever since in the literature of fiction and poetry.

In the Tales, which poured out like a flood from the dramatists, from such men as Peele and Lodge and Greene, we find the origin of English fiction and the subjects of many of our plays; while the fantastic attempt to revive the practices of chivalry, which we have seen in the *Arcadia*, found food in the translation of a new school of romances, such as *Amadis of Gaul, Palmerin of England*, and the *Seven Champions of Christendom.*"

BIBLIOGRAPHY. SIDNEY AND HOOKER.—Disraeli's *Amen. of Lit.*; R. Southey's *Fragment of Life* of; Marsh's *Orig. and Hist. Eng. Lit.*; E. P. Whipple's *Lit. of the Age of Eliz.*; Minto's *Man. of Eng. Prose Lit.*; Littell, v. 3, 1863; N. A. Rev., v. 88, 1859; Ecl. Mag., Apr., 1847; and Dec., 1855; N. Br. Rev., v. 26, 1856-7.

BACON.—*Essays* with *Annotations* by Whately; *Works* with *Life* by B. Montagu; Minto's *Man. of Eng. Prose Lit.*; Boyd's *Autumn Holidays*; Littell, 1863, v. 3; Nat. Quar. Rev., v. 6, 1863; Fraser's Mag., v. 55, 1857; N. Br. Rev., v. 27, 1857; Ecl. Mag., Oct., 1849; Feb., 1855; and Feb., 1857.

LESSON 20.

From Sidney's *Defence of Poetrie*.

Nowe therein of all Sciences is our Poet the Monarch. For he dooth not only show the way but giveth so sweete a prospect into the way as will intice any man to enter into it. Nay, he dooth, as if your journey should lie through a faire Vineyard, at the first give you a cluster of Grapes, that, full of that taste, you may long to passe further. He beginneth not with obscure definitions, which must blur the margent[1] with interpretations, and load the memory with doubtfulnesse; but hee

---

[1] Margin.

cometh to you with words set in delightfull proportion, either accompanied with, or prepared for, the well enchaunting skill of Musicke; and with a tale, forsooth, he cometh unto you—with a tale which holdeth children from play, and old men from the chimney corner. And, pretending no more, doth intende the winning of the mind from wickednesse to vertue; even as the childe is often brought to take most wholsom things, by hiding them in such other as have a pleasant tast; which, if one should beginne to tell them the nature of Aloes or Rubarb they shoulde receive, woulde sooner take their Phisicke at their eares then[1] at their mouth. So is it in men, (most of which are childish in the best things till they bee cradled in their graves) glad they will be to heare the tales of Hercules, Achilles, Cyrus, and Aeneas: and hearing them, must needs heare the right description of wisdom, valure,[2] and justice; which, if they had been barely, that is to say, philosophically set out, they would sweare they bee brought to schoole againe.

Sith,[3] then, Poetrie is of all humane[4] learning the most auncient, and of most fatherly antiquitie, as from whence other learnings have taken their beginnings; sith it is so universall, that no learned Nation dooth despise it, nor no barbarous Nation is without it; sith both Roman and Greek gave divine names unto it, the one of prophecying, the other of making; and that indeede that name of making is fit for him, considering that, where as other Arts retaine themselves within their subject and receive, as it were, their beeing from it, the Poet onely, bringeth his owne stuffe, and dooth not learne a conceite[5] out of a matter, but maketh matter for a conceite; sith neither his description nor his ende containeth any evill, the thing described cannot be evill; sith his effects be so good as to teach goodnes and to delight the learners; sith therein (namely in morrall doctrine, the chiefe of all knowledges,) hee dooth not onely farre passe the Historian, but for instructing is well nigh comparable to the Philosopher, and for moving leaves him behind him; sith the holy scripture (wherein there is no uncleannes) hath whole parts in it poeticall, and that even our Saviour Christ vouchsafed to use the flowers of it; sith all his[6] kindes are not onlie in their united formes but in their severed dissections fully commendable, I think (and think I thinke rightly) the Lawrell crowne appointed for triumphing Captaines, doth worthilie (of al other learnings) honor the Poets tryumph.

So that sith the ever-praiseworthy Poesie is full of vertue-breeding delightfulnes, and voyde of no gyfte that ought to be in the noble name of learning; sith the blames laid against it are either false or feeble; sith the

---

cause why it is not esteemed in Englande is the fault of Poet-apes not Poets; sith, lastly, our tongue is most fit to honor Poesie, and to bee honored by Poesie, I conjure you all that have had the evill lucke to reade this incke-wasting toy of mine, even in the name of the nyne Muses no more to scorne the sacred misteries of Poesie; no more to laugh at the name of Poets, as though they were next inheritours to Fooles; no more to jest at the reverent title of Rymer: but to beleeve with Aristotle that they were the auncient Treasurers of the Græcians Divinity; to beleeve with Bembus that they were first bringers in of all civilitie; to beleeve with Scaliger that no Philosophers precepts can sooner make you an honest man, then the reading of Virgill; to beleeve with Clauserus that it pleased the heavenly Deitie, by Hesiod and Homer, under the vayle of fables, to give us all knowledge, Logick, Rethorick, Philosophy, naturall and morall; to beleeve with me that there are many misteries contained in Poetrie, which of purpose were written darkely, lest by prophane wits it should bee abused; to beleeve with Landin¹ that they are so beloved of the Gods that whatsoever they write proceeds of a divine fury; lastly, to beleeve themselves when they tell you they will make you immortall by their verses.

Thus doing, your name shal florish in the Printers shoppes; thus doing, you shall bee of kinne to many a poeticall Preface; thus doing, you shall be most fayre, most ritch, most wise, most all, you shall dwell upon Superlatives; thus doing, though you be *Libertino patre natus*,¹ you shall suddenly grow *Hercules proles;*² thus doing, your soule shal be placed with Dantes Beatrix or Virgils Anchises. But if (fie of such a but) you be borne so neere the dull making Cataphract of Nilus³ that you cannot heare the Plannet-like Musick of Poetrie; if you have so earth-creeping a mind that it cannot lift it selfe up to looke to the sky of Poetry; or rather, by a certaine rusticall disdaine will become such a Mome⁴ as to be a Momus⁵ of Poetry; then, though I will not wish unto you the Asses eares of Midas,⁶ nor to bee driven by a Poets verses (as Bubonax was) to hang himselfe, nor to be rimed to death, as is sayd to be doone in Ireland; yet thus much curse I must send you in the behalfe of all Poets, that, while you live, you live in love and never get favour for lacking skill of a Sonnet; and when you die, your memory die from the earth for want of an Epitaph.

---

¹ Of a father who was a freedman. ² Of the race of Hercules (son of Jupiter).
³ There were three celebrated cataracts of the Nile. ⁴ A dolt. ⁵ God of raillery.
⁶ Ears lengthened for holding Pan's reed to be superior to Apollo's lyre.

From Hooker's *Ecclesiastical Polity.*

The stateliness of houses, the goodliness of trees, when we behold them, delighteth the eye; but that foundation which beareth up the one, that root which ministereth to the other nourishment and life are in the bosom of the earth concealed; and, if there be at any time occasion to search into it, such labor is then more necessary than pleasant both to them which undertake it and for the lookers on. In like manner, the use and benefit of good laws all that live under them may enjoy with delight and comfort; albeit the grounds and first original causes from which they have sprung be unknown, as to the greater part of men they are. But when they who withdraw their obedience pretend that the laws which they should obey are corrupt and vicious, for better examination of their quality it behoveth the very foundation and root, the highest well-spring and fountain of them, to be discovered.

All things that are have some operation not violent or casual. Neither doth anything ever begin to exercise the same without some fore-conceived end for which it worketh. And the end which it worketh for is not obtained unless the work be also fit to obtain it by. For unto every end every operation will not serve. That which doth assign unto each thing the kind, that which doth moderate the force and power, that which doth appoint the form and measure of working, the same we term a *Law*. So that no certain end could ever be obtained unless the actions whereby it is obtained were regular, that is to say, made suitable, fit, and correspondent with their end by some canon, rule, or law.

As it cometh to pass in a kingdom rightly ordered that after a law is once published it presently takes effect far and wide, all states framing themselves thereunto, even so let us think it fareth in the natural course of the world; since the time that God did first proclaim the edicts of his law upon it, heaven and earth have hearkened unto his voice, and their labor hath been to do his will. "He made a law for the rain; he gave his decree unto the sea, that the waters should not pass his commandment." Now, if nature should intermit her course, and leave altogether, though it were but for a while, the observation[1] of her own laws; if those principal and mother elements of the world, whereof all things in this lower world are made, should lose the qualities which now they have; if the frame of that heavenly arch erected over our heads should loosen and dissolve itself; if celestial spheres should forget their wonted motions, and by irregular volubilities[2] turn themselves any way as it might happen; if the prince of the lights of heaven, which now

---

[1] Observance.   [2] Turnings.

as a giant doth run his unwearied course, should, as it were through a languishing faintness, begin to stand and to rest himself; if the moon should wander from her beaten way; the times and seasons of the year blend themselves by disordered and confused mixture; the winds breathe out their last gasp; the clouds yield no rain; the earth be defeated of heavenly influence; the fruits of the earth pine away as children at the withered breasts of their mother, no longer able to yield them relief; what would become of man himself, whom these things now do all serve? See we not plainly that obedience of creatures[1] unto the law of nature is the stay of the whole world ?

Of Law there can be no less acknowledged than that her seat is the bosom of God, her voice the harmony of the world. All things in heaven and earth do her homage; the very least as feeling her care, and the greatest as not exempted from her power: both angels and men, and creatures of what condition soever, though each in different sort and manner, yet all with uniform consent, admiring her as the mother of their peace and joy.

From Bacon's Essays.

Of Great Place.—Men in great place are thrice servants—servants of the sovereign or state, servants of fame, and servants of business; so as[2] they have no freedom, neither in their persons nor in their actions nor in their times. It is a strange desire to seek power and to lose liberty, or to seek power over others and to lose power over a man's self. The rising unto place is laborious, and by pains men come to greater pains; and it is sometimes base, and by indignities men come to dignities. The standing is slippery, and the regress is either a downfall or at least an eclipse, which is a melancholy thing. Nay, men cannot retire when they would, neither will they when it were reason,[3] but are impatient of privateness, even in age and sickness, which require the shadow; like old townsmen that will be still sitting at their street door, though thereby they offer age to scorn. Certainly great persons had need to borrow other men's opinions to think themselves happy, for, if they judge by their own feeling, they cannot find it; but, if they think with themselves what other men think of them, and that other men would fain be as they are, then they are happy as it were by report, when, perhaps, they find the contrary within; for they are the first that find their own griefs, though they be the last that find their own faults.

---

[1] Created things.   [2] That.   [3] Reasonable.

Certainly men in great fortunes are strangers to themselves; and, while they are in the puzzle of business, they have no time to tend their health either of body or mind. In place there is license to do good and evil, whereof the latter is a curse; for, in evil, the best condition is not to will,[1] the second not to can.[2] But power to do good is the true and lawful end of aspiring; for good thoughts, though God accept them, yet towards men are little better than good dreams except they be put in act, and that cannot be without power and place as the vantage and commanding ground. Merit and good works are the end of man's motion, and conscience[3] of the same is the accomplishment of man's rest; for if a man can be partaker of God's theatre,[4] he shall likewise be partaker of God's rest.

Of Youth and Age.—Young men are fitter to invent than to judge, fitter for execution than for counsel, and fitter for new projects than for settled business; for the experience of age, in things that fall within the compass of it, directeth them, but in new things abuseth them. The errors of young men are the ruin of business, but the errors of aged men amount but to this—that more might have been done, or sooner. Young men, in the conduct and manage[5] of actions, embrace more than they can hold; stir more than they can quiet; fly to the end without consideration of the means and degrees; pursue some few principles which they have chanced upon, absurdly; care not[6] to innovate, which draws unknown inconveniences; use extreme remedies at first; and that, which doubleth all errors, will not acknowledge or retract them, like an unready horse that will neither stop nor turn.

Men of age object too much, consult too long, adventure too little, repent too soon, and seldom drive business home to the full period,[7] but content themselves with the mediocrity of success. Certainly it is good to compound employments of both; for that will be good for the present, because the virtues of either age may correct the defects of both;[8] and good for succession, that young men may be learners while men in age are actors; and, lastly, good for extern[9] accidents, because authority followeth old men, and favor and popularity youth; but, for the moral part, perhaps, youth will have the preeminence, as age hath for the politic. A certain rabbin, upon the text, "Your young men shall see visions, and your old men shall dream dreams," inferreth that young men are admitted nearer to God than old, because vision is a clearer revelation than a dream; and, certainly, the more a man drink-

---

[1] Desire.	[2] Be able.	[3] Consciousness.	[4] Work.	[5] Management.
[6] Are not cautious.		[7] Extent.		[8] The other.	[9] Outward.

eth of the world, the more it intoxicateth; and age doth profit rather in the powers of understanding than in the virtues of the will and affections.

From Bacon's *Advancement of Learning.*

For the conceit[1] that learning should dispose men to leisure and privateness[2] and make men slothful, it were a strange thing if that which accustometh the mind to a perpetual motion and agitation should induce slothfulness; whereas, contrariwise, it may be truly affirmed that no kind of men love business for itself but those that are learned; for other persons love it for profit, as an hireling, that loves the work for the wages; or for honor, as because it beareth them up in the eyes of men, and refresheth their reputation, which otherwise would wear; or because it putteth them in mind of their fortune, and giveth them occasion to pleasure or displeasure; or because it exerciseth some faculty wherein they take pride, and so entertaineth them in good humor and pleasing conceits toward themselves; or because it advanceth any other their ends.

So that as it is said of untrue valors, that some men's valors are in the eyes of them that look on; so such men's industries are in the eyes of others, or at least in regard of their own designments:[3] only learned men love business as an action according to nature, as agreeable to health of mind as exercise is to health of body, taking pleasure in the action itself and not in the purchase;[4] so that of all men they are the most indefatigable, if it be towards any business which can hold or detain their mind. And if any man be laborious in reading and study and yet idle in business and action, it groweth from some weakness of body or softness of spirit and not of learning. Well may it be that such a point of a man's nature may make him give himself to learning, but it is not learning that breedeth any such point in his nature.

And that learning should take up too much time or leisure, I answer, the most active or busy man that hath been or can be hath (no question) many vacant times of leisure, while he expecteth the tides and returns of business, and then the question is but how those spaces and times of leisure shall be filled and spent, whether in pleasures or in studies; as was well answered by Demosthenes to his adversary, Æschines, that was a man given to pleasure and told him that his orations did smell of the lamp. "Indeed," said Demosthenes, "there is a great difference between the things that you and I do by lamp-light." So as no man need doubt[5] that learning will expulse[6] business, but rather it will keep

---

[1] Conception.   [2] Privacy.   [3] Designs.   [4] Acquisition.   [5] Fear.   [6] Drive out.

and defend the possession of the mind against idleness and pleasure, which otherwise at unawares may enter to the prejudice of both.

Again, for that other conceit that learning should undermine the reverence of laws and government, it is assuredly a mere depravation[1] and calumny, without all shadow of truth. For to say that a blind custom of obedience should be a surer obligation than duty taught and understood—it is to affirm that a blind man may tread surer by a guide than a seeing man can by a light. And it is without all controversy that learning doth make the minds of men gentle, generous, maniable,[2] and pliant to government; whereas ignorance makes them churlish, thwart[3] and mutinous: and the evidence of time doth clear[4] this assertion, considering that the most barbarous, rude, and unlearned times have been most subject to tumults, seditions, and changes.

And as to the judgment of Cato the Censer, he was well punished for his blasphemy against learning, in the same kind wherein he offended; for, when he was past threescore years old, he was taken with an extreme desire to go to school again and to learn the Greek tongue, to the end to peruse the Greek authors; which doth well demonstrate that his former censure[5] of the Grecian learning was rather an affected gravity than according to the inward sense of his own opinion. And as for Virgil's verses, though it pleased him to brave the world in taking to the Romans the art of empire and leaving to others the arts of subjects; yet so much is manifest that the Romans never ascended to that height of empire till the time they had ascended to the height of other arts.

LESSON 21.

THE LATER POETRY OF THE ELIZABETHAN LITERATURE, 1579–1603. EDMUND SPENSER.— "The later Elizabethan poetry begins with the *Shepheardes Calender* of SPENSER. Spenser was born in London, 1552, and educated at Merchant Taylor's School and at Cambridge, which he left at the age of twenty-four. His early boyhood was passed in London, and he went frequently to an English home among the glens of Lancashire. He returned thither after he left Cambridge, and fell in love with a 'fair widowe's daughter of the glen,' whom

---

[1] Slander. [2] Manageable. [3] Perverse. [4] Make clear. [5] Opinion.

he called Rosalind.   His love was not returned, and her coldness drove him southward.

His college friend, Gabriel Harvey, made him known to
Leicester, and probably, since Harvey was 'Leicester's man,'
to Philip Sidney, Leicester's nephew; and it was at Sidney's
house of Penshurst that the *Shepheardes Calender* was made,
and the *Faerie Queen* begun. 'The publication of the former
work in 1579 at once made Spenser the first poet of the day,
and its literary freshness was such that men felt that, for the
first time since Chaucer, England had given birth to a great
poet.   It was a pastoral poem, divided into twelve eclogues,
one for each month of the year.   Shepherds and shepherd
life were mixed in its verse with complaints for his lost love,
with a desire for Church reform, with loyalty to the Queen.
It marks the strong love of old English poetry by its reference
to Chaucer, though it is in form imitated from the French
pastoral of Clément Marot.   The only tie it really has to
Chaucer is in the choice of disused English words and spelling, a practice of Spenser's which somewhat spoils the *Faerie
Queen*.   The Puritanism of the poem does not lie in any attack on the Episcopal theory, but in an attack on the sloth
and pomp of the clergy, and in a demand for a nobler moral
life.   It is the same in the *Faerie Queen*.

THE FAERIE QUEEN.—The twelve books of this poem were
to represent the twelve moral virtues, each in the person of a
knight who was to conquer all the separate sins and errors
which were at battle with the virtue he personified.   In
Arthur, the king of the company, the Magnificence of the
whole of virtue was to be represented, and he was at last to
arrive at union with the Faerie Queen, that divine glory of
God to which all human thought and act aspired.   This was
Spenser's Puritanism—the desire after a perfectly pure life for
State and Church and Man.   It was opposed in State and
Church, he held, by the power of Rome, which he paints as
Duessa, the falsehood which wears the garb of truth, and who

also serves to represent her in whom Catholicism most threatened England—Mary, Queen of Scots. Puritan in this sense, he is not Puritan in any other. He had nothing to do with the attack on Prelacy which was then raging, and the last canto of the Faerie Queen represents Calidore, the knight of courtesy, sent forth to bridle 'the blatant beast,' the many-tongued and noisy Presbyterian body which attacked the Church.

The poem, however, soars far above this region of debate into the calm and pure air of art. It is the poem of the human soul and all its powers struggling towards the perfect love, the love which is God. Filled full with christianized platonism, the ideas of truth, justice, temperance, courtesy do not remain ideas in Spenser's mind, as in Plato's, but become real personages, whose lives and battles he honors and tells in verse so delicate, so gliding, and so steeped in the finer life of poetry, that he has been called the poet's poet.

As the nobler Puritanism of the time is found in it, so also are the other influences of the time. It goes back, as men were doing then, to the old times for its framework, to the Celtic story of Arthur and his knights, which Geoffrey of Monmouth and Chaucer and Thomas Malory had loved. It represents the new love of chivalry, the new love of classical learning, the new delight in mystic theories of love and religion. It is full of those allegorical schemes in which doctrines and heresies, virtues and vices were contrasted and personified. It takes up and uses the popular legends of fairies, dwarfs, and giants, and mingles them with the savages and the wonders of the New World, of which the voyagers told in every company. Nearly the whole spirit of the English Renaissance under Elizabeth, except its coarser and baser elements, is in its pages. Of anything impure or ugly or violent, there is not a trace. Spenser walks through the whole of this woven world of faerie,

'With the moon's beauty and the moon's soft pace.'

The first three books were finished in Ireland, whither he
had gone as secretary to Lord Grey of Wilton in 1580.
Raleigh listened to them in 1589 at Kilcolman Castle, among
the alder shades of the river Mulla, that fed the lake below
the castle. Delighted with the poem, he took Spenser to
England. The books were published in 1590, and the Queen,
the Court, and the whole of England soon shared in Raleigh's
delight. It was the first great ideal poem that England had
produced, and it is the source of all our modern poetry. It has
never ceased to make poets, and it will not lose its power
while our language lasts."

"The interest in *The Faerie Queen* is twofold. There is the interest
of the moral picture which it presents, and there is the interest of it as a
work of poetical art.

The moral picture is of the ideal of noble manliness in Elizabeth's time.
Besides the writers and the thinkers, the statesmen and the plotters, the
traders and the commons, of that fruitful and vigorous age, there were
the men of action—the men who fought in France and the Netherlands
and Ireland; the men who created the English navy, and showed
how it could be used; the men who tried for the north-west passage with
Sir Humphrey Gilbert, and sailed round the world with Sir Francis
Drake, and planted colonies in America with Sir Walter Raleigh; the
men who chased the Armada to destruction, and dealt the return buffet
to Spanish pride in the harbor of Cadiz; men who treated the sea as the
rightful dominion of their mistress, and, seeking adventures on it far
and near, with or without her leave, reaped its rich harvests of plunder
from Spanish treasure-ships and West Indian islands, or from the exposed towns and churches of the Spanish coast. They were at once men
of daring enterprise, and sometimes very rough execution; and yet men
with all the cultivation and refinement of the time—courtiers, scholars,
penmen, poets These are the men whom Spenser had before his eyes
in drawing his knights—their ideas of loyalty, of gallantry, of the
worth and use of life,—their aims, their enthusiasm, their temptations,
their foes, their defeats, their triumphs.

As a work of art *The Faerie Queen* at once astonishes us by the wonderful fertility and richness of the writer's invention and imagination,
by the facility with which he finds or makes language for his needs,
and, above all, by the singular music and sweetness of his verse. The
main theme seldom varies: it is a noble knight, fighting, overcoming,
tempted, delivered; or a beautiful lady, plotted against, distressed, in

danger, rescued. The poet's affluence of fancy and speech gives a new turn and color to each adventure.

But, besides that under these conditions there must be monotony, the poet's art, admirable as it is, gives room for objections. Spenser's style is an imitation of the antique; and an imitation, however good, must want the master charm of naturalness, reality, simple truth. And in his system of work, with his brightness and quickness and fluency, he wanted self-restraint—the power of holding himself in, and of judging soundly of fitness and proportion. There was a looseness and careless-ness, partly belonging to his age, partly his own. In the use of mate-rials, nothing comes amiss to him. He had no scruples as a copyist. He took without ceremony any piece of old metal—word or story or image—which came to his hand, and threw it into the melting-pot of his imagination to come out fused with his own materials, often trans-formed, but often unchanged. The effect was sometimes happy, but not always so."—*R. W. Church.*

SPENSER'S MINOR POEMS.—"The next year, 1591, Spenser, being still in England, collected his smaller poems and pub-lished them. Among them *Mother Hubbard's Tale* is a bright imitation of Chaucer, and the *Tears of the Muses* supports my statement that literature was looked on coldly previous to 1580, by the complaint the Muses make in it of their subjects' being despised in England. Sidney had died in 1586, and three of these poems bemoan his death. The others are of slight importance, and the whole collection was entitled *Com-plaints.* Returning to Ireland, he gave an account of his visit in *Colin Clout's come Home again*, 1591, and at last, after more than a year's pursuit, won his second love for his wife, and found with her perfect happiness. A long series of *Son-nets* records the progress of his wooing, and the *Epithalamion,* his marriage hymn, is the most glorious love-song in the Eng-lish tongue. At the close of 1595 he carried to England, in a second visit, the last three books of the *Faerie Queen.* The next year he spent in London, and published these books with his other poems, the *Prothalamion* on the marriage of Lord Worcester's daughters, and his *Hymnes to Love and Beauty*, and to *Heavenly Love and Beauty*, in which the love philosophy of Petrarca is enshrined. The end of his life was sorrowful.   In 1598 the Irish rising took place, his castle was burnt, and he and his family fled for their lives to England. Broken-hearted, poor, but not forgotten, the poet died in a London tavern.   All his fellows went with his body to the grave where, close by Chaucer, he lies in Westminster Abbey. London, 'his most kindly nurse,' takes care also of his dust, and England keeps him in her love."

BIBLIOGRAPHY. SPENSER.—G. L. Craik's *Spenser and his Poetry*; *Eng. Men of Letters* Series; Ward's *Anthology*; Disraeli's *Amen. of Lit.*; Howitt's *Homes of the Brit. Poets*, vol. 1; Lowell's *Among my Books*, 2d Ser.; Whipple's *Lit. of the age of Eliz.*; *Clar. Press Ed.* of Faerie Queen; Minto's *Char. of Eng. Poets*; *Atlantic*, v. 2, 1858; West. Rev., v. 87, 1867; Allibon', v. 2.

From Spenser's *Faerie Queen.*

Thus being entred, they behold around
A large and spacious plaine, on every side
Strowed with pleasauns;[1] whose faire grassy ground
Mantled with greene, and goodly beautifide
With all the ornaments of Floraes pride,
Wherewith her mother Art, as halfe in scorne
Of niggard Nature, like a pompous bride
Did decke her, and too lavishly adorne,
When forth from virgin bowre she comes in th' early morne.

Thereto the hevens alwayes joviall
Lookt on them lovely, still in stedfast state,
Ne suffred storme nor frost on them to fall,
Their tender buds or leaves to violate:
Nor scorching heat, nor cold intemperate,
T'afflict the creatures which therein did dwell;
But the milde aire with season moderate
Gently attempred, and disposed so well
That still it breathed forth sweet spirit and holesome[2] smell:

More sweet and holesome then[3] the pleasaunt 1 ill
. Of Rhodope,[4] on which the nimphe that bore
A gyaunt babe her selfe for griefe did kill;
Or the Thessalian Tempe,[5] where of yore
Faire Daphne Phœbus hart with love did gore;

---

[1] Pleasantness.   [2] Wholesome.   [3] Than.
[4] On the frontier of Thrace.   [5] A long, deep defile.

Or Ida[1] where the gods lov'd to repaire,
Whenever they their hevenly bowres forlore;
Or sweet Parnasse,[2] the haunt of muses faire,
Or Eden selfe, if ought with Eden mote compaire.

Much wondred Guyon at the faire aspect
Of that sweet place, yet suffred no delight
To sincke into his sence nor mind affect;
But passed forth, and lookt still forward right,
Bridling his will and maistering his might:
Till that he came unto another gate;
No gate, but like one, being goodly dight
With boughes and braunches, which did broad dilate
Their clasping armes in wanton wreathings intricate.

. . . .

There the most daintie paradise on ground
Itselfe doth offer to his sober eye,
In which all pleasures plenteously abownd,
And none does others happinesse envye;
The painted flowres, the trees upshooting hye,
The dales for shade, the hilles for breathing space,
The trembling groves, the christall running by;
And that, which all faire workes doth most aggrace,[3]
The art which all that wrought appeared in no place.

One would have thought, so cunningly the rude
And scorned partes were mingled with the fine,
That nature had for wantonesse ensude[4]
Art, and that art at nature did repine;
So striving each th' other to undermine,
Each did the others worke more beautifie;
So diff'ring both in willes agreed in fine:[5]
So all agreed, through sweete diversitie,
This gardin to adorne with all varietie.

And in the midst of all a fountaine stood
Of richest substance that on earth might bee,
So pure and shiny that the silver flood
Through every channell running one might see;
Most goodly it with curious imageree

---

[1] Hill of Phrygia.   [2] Hill sacred to the Muses.   [3] Lend favor to.
[4] Followed after.   [5] End.

Was over-wrought, and shapes of naked boyes,
Of which some seemed with lively jollitee
To fly about, playing their wanton toyes,[1]
Whylest others did themselves embay[2] in liquid joyes.

And over all of purest gold was spred
A trayle of yvie in his native hew;
For the rich metall was so coloured
That wight[3] who did not well avis'd it vew,
Would surely deeme it to bee yvie trew:
Low his lascivious armes adown did creepe,
That themselves dipping in the silver dew
Their fleecy flowres they fearfully did steepe,
Which drops of christall seemed for wantones to weepe.

Infinit streames continually did well
Out of this fountaine, sweet and faire to see,
The which into an ample laver[4] fell,
And shortly grew to so great quantitie
That like a little lake it seemd to bee;
Whose depth exceeded not three cubits hight,
That through the waves one might the bottom see
All pav'd beneath with jasper shining bright,
That seemed the fountaine in that sea did sayle upright.

.   .   .   .

Eftsoones[1] they heard a most melodious sound,
Of all that mote[2] delight a daintie eare,
Such as attonce might not on living ground,
Save in this paradise, be heard elsewhere:
Right hard it was for wight, which did it heare,
To read what manner musicke that mote bee;
For all that pleasing is to living eare
Was there consorted in one harmonee;
Birdes, voices, instruments, windes, waters, all agree.

The joyous birdes, shrouded in chearefull shade,
Their notes unto the voyce attempred sweet;
Th' angelicall, soft, trembling voyces made
To th' instruments divine respondence meet;

---

[1] Sports.   [2] Bathe.   [3] Person.   [4] Basin.   [5] Forthwith.   [6] Could.

The silver sounding instruments did meet
With the base murmure of the waters fall;
The waters fall with difference discreet,[1]
Now soft, now loud, unto the wind did call;
The gentle, warbling wind low answered to all.

FURTHER READINGS—IN BOOK I.—Opening stanzas of Canto I.; some stanzas of Canto II., beginning with the seventh; opening stanzas of Canto III., and of Canto IV.; some stanzas of Canto V., beginning with the eighteenth; some stanzas of Canto X., beginning with the twelfth, and also some beginning with the fifty-first; and concluding stanzas of Canto XII., beginning at the twentieth.

LESSON 22.

THE FOUR PHASES OF THE LATER ELIZABETHAN POETRY.— "Spenser reflected in his poems the spirit of the English Renaissance. The other poetry of Elizabeth's reign reflected the whole of English Life. The best way to arrange it—omitting as yet the Drama—is in an order parallel to the growth of the national life, and the proof that it is the best way is that on the whole such an order is a true chronological order.

First, then, if we compare England after 1580, as writers have often done, to an ardent youth, we shall find, in the poetry of the first years that followed that date, all the elements of youth. It is a poetry of *love* and romance and fancy. *Secondly,* and later on, when Englishmen grew older in feeling, their unsettled enthusiasm, which had flitted here and there in action and literature over all kinds of subjects, settled down into a steady enthusiasm for England itself. The country entered on its early manhood, and parallel with this there is the great outburst of historical plays, and a set of poets whom I will call the *patriotic* poets. *Thirdly,* and later still, all enthusiasm died down into a graver and more thoughtful national life, and parallel with this are the tragedies of Shakespeare and the poets whom I will call *philosophical.* These three classes of Poets overlapped one another, and grew up

---

[1] Varied,

gradually, but on the whole their succession represents a real succession of national thought and emotion.

A *fourth* and separate phase does not represent, as these do, a new national life, a new religion, and new politics, but the despairing struggle of the old faith against the new. There were numbers of men such as Wordsworth has finely sketched in old Norton in the *Doe of Rylstone*, who vainly strove in sorrow against all the new national elements. ROBERT SOUTH- WELL, of Norfolk, a Jesuit priest, was the poet of Roman Cath- olic England. Imprisoned for three years, racked ten times, and finally executed, he wrote during his prison time his two longest poems, *St. Peter's Complaint*, and *Mary Magdalene's Funeral Tears*, and it marks not only the large Roman Cath- olic element in the country but also the strange contrasts of the time that eleven editions of poems with these titles were published between 1593 and 1600, at a time when the *Venus and Adonis* of Shakespeare led the way for a multitude of poems that sang of love and delight and England's glory. To the first three we now turn.

THE LOVE POETRY.—I have called it by this name, because in all its best work (to be found in the first book of Mr. Palgrave's 'Golden Treasury') it is almost limited to that subject—the sub- ject of youth. It is chiefly composed in the form of songs and sonnets, and was published in miscellanies in and after 1600. The most famous of these, in which men like Nicholas Breton, Henry Constable, Rd. Barnefield, and others wrote, are *Eng- land's Helicon* and *Davison's Rhapsody* and the *Passionate Pilgrim*. The latter contained some poems of Shakespeare, and he is by virtue of these, and the songs in his Dramas, the best of these lyric writers. The songs themselves are 'old and plain, and dallying with the innocence of love.' They have natural sweetness, great simplicity of speech, and directness of statement. Some, as Shakespeare's, possess a 'passionate reality;' others a quaint pastoralism like shepherd life in por- celain, such as Marlowe's well known song, 'Come live with me and be my love;' others a splendor of love and beauty as in Lodge's *Song of Rosaline*, and Spenser's on his marriage.

The sonnets were written chiefly in series, and I have already said that such writers are called amourists. Such were Shakespeare's and the *Amoretti* of Spenser, and those *to Diana* by Constable. They were sometimes mixed with Canzones and Ballatas after the Italian manner, and the best of these were a series by Sir Philip Sidney. A number of other sonnets and of longer love poems were written by the dramatists before Shakespeare, by Peele and Greene and Marlowe and Lodge, far the finest being the *Hero and Leander*, which Marlowe left as a fragment to be completed by Chapman. Mingled up with these were small religious poems, the reflection of the Puritan and the more religious Church element in English society. They were collected under such titles as the *Handful of Honeysuckles*, the *Poor Widow's Mite, Psalms and Sonnets*, and there are some good things among them written by William Hunnis.

In one Scotch poet, WILLIAM DRUMMOND OF HAWTHORNDEN, the friend of Ben Jonson, the love poet and the religious poet were united. I mention him here, though his work properly belongs to the reign of James I., because his poetry really goes back in spirit and feeling to this time. He cannot be counted among the true Scottish poets. Drummond is entirely Elizabethan and English, and he is worthy to be named among the lyrical poets below Spenser and Shakespeare. His love sonnets have as much grace as Sidney's and less quaintness, his songs have often the grave simplicity of Wyatt's, and his religious poems, especially one solemn sonnet on John the Baptist, have a distant resemblance to the grandeur of Milton.

THE PATRIOTIC POETRY.—Among all this poetry of Romance, Chivalry, Religion, and Love, rose a poetry which devoted itself to the glory of England. It was chiefly historical, and as it may be said to have had its germ in the *Mirror of Magistrates*, so it had its perfect flower in the historical drama of Shakespeare.   Men had now begun to have a great pride in England.   She had stepped into the foremost rank, had outwitted France, subdued internal foes, beaten and humbled Spain on every sea.   Hence the history of the land became precious, and the very rivers and hills and plains honorable, and to be sung and praised in verse.   This poetic impulse is best represented in the works of three men—WILLIAM WAR-NER, SAMUEL DANIEL, and MICHAEL DRAYTON.   Born within a few years of each other, about 1560, they all lived beyond the century, and the national poetry they set on foot lasted when the romantic poetry died.

WILLIAM WARNER's great book was *Albion's England*, 1586, a history of England in verse from the Deluge to Queen Elizabeth.   It is clever, humorous, crowded with stories, and runs to 10,000 lines.   Its popularity was great, and the English in which it was written deserved it.   Such stories as *Argentile and Curan* and the *Patient Countess* prove him to have had a true and pathetic vein of poetry.   His English is not, however, better than that of 'well-languaged DANIEL,' who, among tragedies and pastoral comedies and poems of pure fancy, wrote in verse a prosaic *History of the Civil Wars*, 1595, as we have already found him writing history in prose.   Spenser saw in him a new 'shepherd' of poetry who did far surpass the others, and Coleridge says that the style of his *Hymen's Triumph* may be declared 'imperishable English.'

Of the three the greatest poet was DRAYTON.   Two historical poems are his work—the *Civil Wars of Edward II. and the Barons*, and *England's Heroical Epistles*, 1598.   Not content with these, he set himself to glorify the whole of his land in the *Polyolbion*, thirty books, and more than 30,000 lines.   It is a description in Alexandrines of the ' tracts, mountains, forests, and other parts of this renowned isle of Britain, with intermixture of the most remarkable stories, antiquities, wonders, pleasures, and commodities of the same, digested into a poem.' It was not a success, though it deserved success. Its great length was against it, but the real reason was, that this kind of poetry had had its day. It appeared in 1613, in James I.'s reign.

PHILOSOPHICAL POETRY.—Before that time a change had come. As the patriotic poets came after the romantic, so the romantic were followed by the philosophical poets. The youth and early manhood of the Elizabethan poetry passed, about 1600, into its thoughtful manhood. The land was settled; enterprise ceased to be the first thing; men sat down to think, and in poetry questions of religious and political philosophy were treated with 'sententious reasoning, grave, subtile, and condensed.' Shakespeare, in his passage from comedy to tragedy, in 1601, represents this change.

The two poets who represent it are SIR JNO. DAVIES and FULKE GREVILLE, Lord Brooke. In Davies we find an admirable instance of it. His earlier poem of the *Orchestra*, 1596, in which the whole world is explained as a dance, is as gay and bright as Spenser. His later poem, 1599, is compact and vigorous reasoning, for the most part without fancy. Its very title, *Nosce te ipsum*—Know Thyself—and its divisions, 1. ' On humane learning,' 2. ' The immortality of the soul '—mark the alteration. Two little poems, one of Bacon's, on the *Life of Man*, as a bubble, and one of SIR HENRY WOTTON'S, on the *Character of a Happy Life*, are instances of the same change. It is still more marked in Greville's long, obscure poems on *Human Learning*, on *Wars*, and on *Monarchy and Religion*. They are political and historical treatises, not poems, and all in them, says Lamb, ' is made frozen and rigid by intellect.' Apart from poetry, ' they are worth notice as an indication of that thinking spirit on political science which was to produce the riper speculations of Hobbes, Harrington, and Locke.'

TRANSLATIONS.—There are three translators that take literary rank among the crowd that carried on the work of the earlier time.   Two mark the influence of Italy, one the more powerful influence of the Greek spirit.   SIR JOHN HARINGTON in 1591 translated Ariosto's *Orlando Furioso,* FAIRFAX in 1600 translated Tasso's *Jerusalem,* and his book is 'one of the glories of Elizabeth's reign.'   But the noblest *translation* is that *of Homer's* whole work by GEORGE CHAPMAN, the dramatist, the first part of which appeared in 1598.   The vivid life and energy of the time, its creative power, and its force are expressed in this poem, which is more an Elizabethan tale written about Achilles and Ulysses than a translation.   The rushing gallop of the long fourteen syllable stanza in which it is written has the fire and swiftness of Homer, but it has not his directness or dignity.   Its 'inconquerable quaintness' and diffuseness are as unlike the pure form and light and measure of Greek work as possible.   But it is a distinct poem of such power that it will excite and delight all lovers of poetry, as it excited and delighted Keats."

LESSON 23.

EARLY DRAMATIC REPRESENTATION IN ENGLAND.—"The drama, as in Greece, so in England, began in religion.   In early times none but the clergy could read the stories of their religion, and it was not the custom to deliver sermons to the people.   It was necessary to instruct uneducated men in the history of the Bible, in the Christian faith, in the lives of the Saints and Martyrs.   Hence the Church set on foot miracle-plays and mysteries.   We find the first of these about 1110, when Geoffrey, afterwards Abbot of St. Albans, prepared his miracle play of *St. Catherine* for acting.   Such plays became more frequent from the time of Henry II., and they were so common in Chaucer's time that they were the resort of idle gossips in Lent.   The wife of Bath went to 'plays of miracles and marriages.'   They were acted not only by the clergy but by the laity. About the year 1268, the town guilds began to take them into their own hands, and acted complete sets of plays, setting forth the whole of Scripture history from the Creation to the Day of Judgment. Each guild took one play in the set. They lasted sometimes three days, sometimes eight, and were represented on a great movable stage on wheels in the open spaces of the towns: Of these sets we have three remaining, the Towneley, Coventry, and Chester plays, 1300 —1600. The first set has 32, the second 42, and the third 25 plays.

The Miracle-Play was a representation of some portion of Scripture history, or of the life of some Saint of the Church. The **Mystery** was a representation of any portion of the New Testament history concerned with a mysterious subject, such as the Incarnation, the Atonement, or the Resurrection. It has been attempted to distinguish these more particularly, but they are mingled together in England into one. From the towns they went to the Court and to the houses of nobles. The Kings kept players of them, and we know that exhibiting Scripture plays at great festivals was part of the domestic regulations of the great houses, and that it was the Chaplain's business to write them. Their 'Dumb Show' and their 'Chorus' leave their trace in the regular drama. We cannot say that the modern drama arose after them, for it came in before they died out in England. They were still acted in Chester in 1577, and in Coventry in 1580."

"There were neither theatres nor professional actors in England, indeed in Europe, at the period when miracle-plays first came in vogue. The first performers in these plays were clergymen; the first stages, or scaffolds, on which they were presented were set up in churches. Evidence that this was the case has been discovered in such profusion that it is needless to specify it more particularly in this place than to remark that councils and prelates finally found it necessary to forbid such performances either in churches or by the clergy. But it is worthy of remark that evidence of the ecclesiastical character of the first actors of our drama is preserved in dramatic literature to this day in the Latin words of direction, *Exit* and *Exeunt*. After the exclusion of the clergy from the religious stage, lay-brothers, parish clerks, and the hangers-on of the priesthood naturally took the place of their spiritual fathers, under whose superintendence, or to speak precisely, management, the miracle-plays were brought out. Excluded from the church itself, the miracle-play found fitting refuge in the church-yard. But it was finally forbidden within all hallowed precincts, and was then presented upon a movable scaffold, or pageant, which was dragged through the town, and stopped for the performance at certain places designated by an announcement made a day or two before.

At last the presentation of these plays fell entirely into the hands of laymen, and handicraftsmen became their actors; the members of the various guilds undertaking respectively certain plays which they made for the time their specialty. Thus the Shearmen and Taylors would represent one; the Coppers another; and so with the Smiths, the Skinners, the Fishmongers, and others. In the Chester series, Noah's flood was very appropriately assigned to the Water-dealers and Drawers of Dee. It is almost needless to remark that female characters were always played by striplings and young men. Women did not appear upon the English stage until the middle of the seventeenth century. It would seem that the priests appeared only as amateurs, and that their performances were gratuitous. But when laymen, or, at least, when handicraftsmen undertook the business, they were paid, as we know by the memorandums of accounts still existing."—*R. G. White.*

MORAL-PLAYS.—"**The Morality** was the next step to these, and in it we come to a representation which is closely connected with the drama. It was a play in which the characters were the Vices and Virtues, with the addition afterwards of allegorical personages, such as Riches, Good Deeds, Confession, Death, and any human condition or quality needed for the play. These characters were brought together in a rough story, at the end of which Virtue triumphed, or some moral principle was established. The dramatic *fool* grew up in the Moralities out of a personage called 'The Vice,' and the humorous element was introduced by the retaining of 'The Devil' from the Miracle play, and by making *the Vice* torment him. They were continually represented, but, becoming coarser, were finally supplanted by the regular drama about the end of Elizabeth's reign.

The Transition between these and the regular Drama is not hard to trace. The Virtues and Vices were dull, because they stirred no human sympathy. Historical characters were therefore then introduced, who were celebrated for a virtue or a vice; Brutus represented patriotism, Aristides represented justice; or, as in BALE's *Kynge Johan*, historical and allegorical personages were mixed together. The transition was hastened by the impulse of the Reformation. The religious struggle came so home to men's hearts that they were not satisfied with subjects drawn from the past, and the Morality was used to support the Catholic or the Protestant side. Real men and women were shown under the thin cloaks of its allegorical characters; the vices and the follies of the time were displayed. It was the origin of satiric comedy. The stage was becoming a living power when this began. The excitement of the audience was now very different from that felt in listening to Virtues and Vices, and a demand arose for a comedy and tragedy which should picture human life in all its forms.

The **Interludes** of JOHN HEYWOOD, most of which were written for Court representation in Henry VIII.'s time, 1530, 1540, represent this further transition. They differed from the Morality in that most of the characters were drawn from real life, but they retained ' the Vice ' as a personage. The Interlude—a short, humorous piece, to be acted in the midst of the Morality for the amusement of the people—had been frequently used, but Heywood isolated it from the Morality, and made of it a kind of farce. Out of it we may say grew English comedy."

BIBLIOGRAPHY. THE DRAMA.—R. G. White's Account of the *Rise and Progress* of; Whipple's *Lit. of Age of Eliz.*; W. Hazlitt's *Lectures on the Dra. Lit. of Age of Eliz.*; T. Gilliland's *Dramatic Mirror*; H. N. Hudson's *Origin and Growth* of; J. Skelton's *Early Eng. Life* in; H. Ulrici's *Sketch of Hist. of Eng. Drama*; Nat. Quar Rev., Dec., 1873.

LESSON 24.

THE REGULAR DRAMA.—"The first stage of the regular drama begins with the first English comedy, *Ralph Roister Dois-ter*, written by NICHOLAS UDALL, master of Eton, known to have been acted before 1551, but not published till 1566. It is our earliest picture of London manners; the characters are well drawn; it is divided into regular acts and scenes and is made in rhyme. The first English tragedy is *Gorboduc*, written by SACKVILLE and NORTON, and represented in 1562. The story was taken from British legend, and the characters are gravely sustained. But the piece was heavy and too solemn for the audience, and RICHARD EDWARDS by mixing tragic and comic elements together in his play, *Damon and Pythias*, acted about 1564, succeeded better.

These two gave the impulse to a number of dramas from classical and modern story, which were acted at the Universities, Inns of Court, and the Court up to 1580, when the drama, having gone through its boyhood, entered on a vigorous manhood. More than fifty-two dramas, so quick was their production, are known to have been acted up to this time. Some were translated from the Greek, as the *Jocasta* from Euripides, and others from the Italian, as the *Supposes* from Ariosto, both by the same author, GEORGE GASCOIGNE, already mentioned as a satirist. These were acted in 1566.

THE THEATRE.—There was as yet no theatre. A patent was given in 1574 to the Earl of Leicester's servants to act plays in any town in England, and they built in 1576 the Blackfriars Theatre. In the same year two others were set up in the fields about Shoreditch—'The Theatre' and 'The Curtain.' The Globe Theatre, built for Shakespeare and his fellows in 1599, may stand as a type of the rest. In the form of a hexagon outside, it was circular within, and open to the weather except above the stage. The play began at three o'clock; the nobles and ladies sat in boxes or in stools on the stage, the people stood in the pit or yard. The stage itself, strewn with rushes, was a naked room with a blanket for a curtain. Wooden imitations of animals, towers, woods, etc., were all the scenery used, and a board, stating the place of action, was hung out from the top when the scene changed. Boys acted the female parts. It was only after the Restoration that movable scenery and actresses were introduced. No 'pencil's aid' supplied the landscape of Shakespeare's plays. The forest of Arden, the castle of Duncan were 'seen only by the intellectual eye.'"

"The private theatres were entirely roofed in, while in the others the pit was uncovered, and of course the stage and the gallery were exposed to the external air. A flag was kept flying from the staff on the roof during the performance. The price of admission to the pit, or yard, varied, according to the pretensions of the theatre, from twopence, and even a penny, to sixpence; that to the boxes or rooms, from a shilling to two shillings, and even, on extraordinary occasions, half a crown. The theatre appears to have been always artificially lighted, in the body of the house by cressets, and upon the stage by large, rude chandeliers. The small band of musicians sat, not in an orchestra in front of the stage, but, it would seem, in a balcony projecting from the proscenium. People went early to the theatre, and, while waiting for the play to begin, they read, gamed, smoked, drank, and cracked nuts and jokes together; those who set up for wits and gallants, or critics liked to appear upon the stage itself, which they were allowed to do all through the performance, lying upon the rushes, or sitting upon stools, for which they paid an extra price. Each day's exhibition was closed by a prayer for the Queen, offered by all the actors kneeling."—*R. G. White.*

THE SECOND STAGE OF THE REGULAR DRAMA.—"This ranges from 1580 to 1596. It includes the work of Lyly, author of the *Euphues*, the plays of Peele, Greene, Lodge, Marlowe, Kyd, Munday, Chettle, Nash, and the earliest works of Shakespeare. During this time we know that more than 100 different plays were performed by four out of the eleven companies; so swift and plentiful was their production. They were written in prose and in rhyme, and in blank verse mixed with prose and rhyme. Prose and rhyme prevailed before

1587, when Marlowe, in his play of *Tamburlaine,* made blank verse the fashion.

JOHN LYLY illustrates the three methods, for he wrote seven plays in prose, one in rhyme, and one (after *Tamburlaine*) in blank verse. Some beautiful little songs scattered through them are the forerunners of the songs with which Shakespeare made his dramas bright, and the witty 'quips and cranks,' repartees, and similes of their fantastic prose dialogue were the school of Shakespeare's prose dialogue. PEELE, GREENE, and MARLOWE are the three important names of the period. They are the first in whose hands the play of human passion and action is expressed with any true dramatic effect. Peele and Greene make their characters act on, and draw out, one another in the several scenes, but they have no power of making a plot, or of working out their plays, scene by scene, to a natural conclusion. They are, in one word, without art, and their characters, even when they talk in good poetry, are neither natural nor simple.

CHRISTOPHER MARLOWE, on the other hand, rose by degrees and easily into mastery of his art. The difference between the unequal and violent action and thought of his *Doctor Faustus* and the quiet and orderly progression to its end of the play of *Edward II.* is all the more remarkable when we know that he died at thirty. Though less than Shakespeare, he was worthy to precede him. As he may be said to have invented and made the verse of the drama, so he created the English tragic drama. His plays are wrought with art to their end, his characters are sharply and strongly outlined. Each play illustrates one ruling passion in its growth, its power, and its extremes. *Tamburlaine* paints the desire of universal empire; the *Jew of Malta* the passions of greed and hatred; *Doctor Faustus* the struggle and failure of man to possess all knowledge and all pleasure without toil and without law; *Edward II.* the misery of weakness and the agony of a king's ruin. Marlowe's verse is 'mighty,' his poetry strong and weak alike with passionate feeling, and expressed with a turbulent magnificence of words and images, the fault of which is a very great want of temperance. It reflects his life and the lives of those with whom he lived.

Marlowe lived and died an irreligious, imaginative, tender-hearted, licentious poet. Peele and Greene lived an even more riotous life and died as miserably, and they are examples of a crowd of other dramatists who passed their lives between the theatre, the wine-shop, and the prison. Their drama, in which we see the better side of the men, had all the marks of a wild youth. (It was daring, full of strong but unequal life, romantic, sometimes savage, often tender, always exaggerated in its treatment and expression of the human passions.) If it had no moderation, it had no tame dulness. If it was coarse, it was powerful, and it was above all national. It was a time full of strange contrasts, a time of fiery action and of senti-mental contemplation; a time of fancy and chivalry, indeli-cacy and buffoonery; of great national adventure and private brawls; of literary quiet and polemic thought; of faith and infidelity—and the whole of it is painted with truth, but with too glaring colors, in the drama of these men."

From Marlowe's *Edward II.*[*]

Enter Matrevis, Gurney, and soldiers with King Edward.

K. Edw. Friends, whither must unhappy Edward go?
Will hateful Mortimer appoint no rest?
Must I be vexèd like the nightly bird,
Whose sight is loathsome to all wingèd fowls?
When will the fury of his mind assuage?
When will his heart be satisfied with blood?
If mine will serve, unbowel straight this breast,
And give my heart to Isabel and him:
It is the chiefest mark they level at.

---

[*] Ed. II., son of Ed. I. and father of Ed. III., was King of England, 1307-27. His character was weak, and his reign disastrous. He was deposed by his nobles. This extract from the play treats of his imprisonment in the dungeon of Kenil-worth, his execution, and the feelings and doings of Ed. III. concerning his father's treatment.

Gur. Not so, my liege, the queen hath given this charge—
To keep your grace in safety:
Your passions make your dolours to increase.

K. Edw. This usage makes my misery increase.
But can my air of life continue long,
When all my senses are annoyed with stench?
Within a dungeon England's king is kept,
Where I am starv'd for want of sustenance.
My daily diet is heart-breaking sobs,
That almost rend the closet of my heart:
Thus lives old Edward not reliev'd by any,
And so must die, though pitièd by many.
Oh, water, gentle friends, to cool my thirst,)
And clear my body from foul excrements!

Mat. Why strive you thus? your labor is in vain.

K. Edw. The wren may strive against the lion's strength,
But all in vain: so vainly do I strive
To seek for mercy at a tyrant's hand.
Immortal powers, that know the painful cares
That wait upon my poor, distressèd soul,
Oh, level all your looks upon these daring men
That wrong their liege and sovereign, England's king!
O Gaveston, it is for thee that I am wrong'd!
For me both thou and both the Spensers died;
And for your sakes a thousand wrongs I'll take.
The Spensers' ghosts, wherever they remain,
Wish well to mine; then, tush, for them I'll die.

Mat. 'Twixt theirs and yours shall be no enmity.
Come, come, away! Now put the torches out,
We'll enter in by darkness to Killingworth.

Enter the younger Mortimer and Lightborn.

Y. Mort. Art thou so resolute as thou wast?
Light. What else, my lord? and far more resolute.
Y. Mort. And hast thou cast how to accomplish it?
Light. Ay, ay; and none shall know which way he died.
Y. Mort. But at his looks, Lightborn, thou wilt relent.
Light. Relent! ha, ha! I use much to relent.
Y. Mort. Well, do it bravely, and be secret.
Light. You shall not need to give instructions;
'Tis not the first time I have kill'd a man:

I learn'd in Naples how to poison flowers;
To strangle with a lawn thrust thro' the throat;
To pierce the wind-pipe with a needle's point;
Or, whilst one is asleep, to take a quill
And blow a little powder in his ears;
Or open his mouth, and pour quick-silver down.
But yet I have a braver way than these.

                                              [Exit.

[Enters Killingworth prison.

   K. Edw. Who's there? what light is that? Wherefore
com'st thou?
   Light. To comfort you, and bring you joyful news.
   K. Edw. Small comfort finds poor Edward in thy looks.
Villain, I know thou com'st to murder me.
   Light. To murder you, my most gracious lord!
Far is it from my heart to do you harm.
The queen sent me to see how you were us'd,
For she relents at this your misery:
And what eyes can refrain from shedding tears,
To see a king in this most piteous state?
   K. Edw. Weep'st thou already? list awhile to me,
And then thy heart, were it as Gurney's is,
Or as Matrevis', hewn from the Caucasus,
Yet will it melt ere I have done my tale.
This dungeon where they keep me is the sink
Wherein the filth of all the castle falls.
   Light. O villains!
   K. Edw. And there, in mire and puddle, have I stood
This ten days' space; and, lest that I should sleep,
One plays continually upon a drum.
They give me bread and water, being a king;
So that, for want of sleep and sustenance,
My mind's distemper'd, and my body's numb'd,
And whether I have limbs or no I know not.
Oh, would my blood dropp'd out from every vein,
As doth this water from my tatter'd robes!
Tell Isabel, the queen, I look'd not thus,
When for her sake I ran at tilt in France,
And there unhors'd the Duke of Cleremont.
   Light. Oh, speak no more, my lord! this breaks my heart.
Lie on this bed, and rest yourself awhile.

K. Edw. These looks of thine can harbor naught but death;
I see my tragedy written in thy brows.
Yet stay awhile; forbear thy bloody hand,
And let me see the stroke before it comes,
That even then when I shall lose my life,
My mind may be more steadfast on my God.
    Light. What means your highness to mistrust me thus?
    K. Edw. What mean'st thou to dissemble with me thus?
    Light. These hands were never stain'd with innocent blood,
Nor shall they now be tainted with a king's. ·
    K. Edw. Forgive my thought for having such a thought.
One jewel have I left; receive thou this.

                             [Giving jewel.

Still fear I, and I know not what's the cause,
But every joint shakes as I give it thee.
Oh, if thou harbor'st murder in thy heart,
Let this gift change thy mind, and save thy soul! ·
Know that I am a king: Oh, at that name
I feel a hell of grief! Where is my crown?
Gone, gone! and do I still remain alive?
    Light. You're overwatch'd, my lord; lie down and rest.
    K. Edw. But that grief keeps me waking, I should sleep;
For not these ten days have these eye-lids clos'd.
Now, as I speak, they fall; and yet with fear
Open again.   Oh, wherefore sitt'st thou here?
    Light. If you mistrust me, I'll be gone, my lord.
    K. Edw. No, no; for, if thou mean'st to murder me,
Thou wilt return again; and therefore stay.

                             [Sleeps.

    Light. He sleeps.
    K. Edw. [Waking] Oh, let me not die yet! Oh, stay awhile!
    Light. How now, my lord!
    K. Edw. Something still buzzeth in mine ears,
And tells me, if I sleep, I never wake:
This fear is that which makes me tremble thus;
And therefore tell me, wherefore art thou come?
    Light. To rid thee of thy life.—Matrevis, come!

            Enter Matrevis and Gurney.

    K. Edw. I am too weak and feeble to resist.—
Assist me, sweet God, and receive my soul!
    Light. Run for the table.

K. Edw. Oh, spare me, or despatch me in a trice!

Light. So, lay the table down, and stamp on it,
But not too hard, lest that you bruise his body.

Mat. I fear me that this cry will raise the town,
And therefore let us take horse and away.

Light. Tell me, sirs, was it not bravely done?

Gur. Excellent well, take this for thy reward.

                      [Stabs Lightborn, who dies.

Enter King Edw. III., Q. Isab., lords, and attendants.

First Lord. Fear not, my lord, know that you are a king.

K. Edw. III. Villain!

Y. Mort. How now, my lord!

K. Edw. III. Think not that I am frighted with thy words!
My father's murdered through thy treachery;
And thou shalt die, and on his mournful hearse
Thy hateful and accursèd head shall lie,
To witness to the world that by thy means
His kingly body was too soon interr'd.

Q. Isab. Weep not, sweet son!

K. Edw. III. Forbid not me to weep, he was my father;
And had you lov'd him half so well as I,
You could not bear his death thus patiently:
But you, I fear, conspir'd with Mortimer.
Ay, Mortimer, thou know'st that he is slain;
And so shalt thou be too. Why stays he here?
Bring him unto a hurdle, drag him forth,
Hang him, I say, and set his quarters up;
But bring his head back presently to me.

Q. Isab. For my sake, sweet son, pity Mortimer!

Y. Mort. Madam, entreat not, I will rather die
Than sue for life unto a paltry boy.

K. Edw. III. Hence with the traitor! with the murderer!

Y. Mort. Base Fortune, now I see that in thy wheel
There is a point, to which when men aspire,
They tumble headlong down: that point I touch'd,
And, seeing there was no place to mount up higher,
Why should I grieve at my declining fall?—
Farewell, fair queen; weep not for Mortimer,
That scorns the world, and, as a traveller,
Goes to discover countries yet unknown.

LESSON 25.

WILLIAM SHAKESPEARE.—" The greatest dramatist of the world now took up the work of Marlowe, and in twenty-eight years made the drama represent the whole of human life. He was born, it is thought, April 23, 1564, the son of a comfortable burgess of Stratford-on-Avon. While he was still young, his father fell into poverty, and an interrupted education left the son an inferior scholar. He had 'small Latin and less Greek.' But by dint of genius and by living in a society in which all sorts of information were attainable, he became an accomplished man. The story told of his deer-stealing in Charlecote woods is without proof, but it is likely that his youth was wild and passionate. At nineteen, he married Ann Hathaway, seven years older than himself, and was probably unhappy with her. For this reason or from poverty or from the driving of the genius that led him to the stage, he left Stratford about 1586–7, and went to London at the age of twenty-two, and, falling in with Marlowe, Greene and the rest, became an actor and a play-wright, and may have lived their unrestrained and riotous life for some years.

HIS FIRST PERIOD.—It is probable that before leaving Stratford he had sketched a part at least of his *Venus and Adonis.* It is full of the country sights and sounds, of the ways of birds and animals, such as he saw when wandering in Charlecote woods. Its rich and overladen poetry and its warm coloring made him, when it was published, 1591–3, at once the favorite of men like Lord Southampton, and lifted him into fame. But before that date he had done work for the stage by touching up old plays and writing new ones. We seem to trace his 'prentice hand' in many dramas of the time, but the first he is usually thought to have retouched is *Titus Andronicus,* and some time after, the *First Part of Henry VI.*

Love's Labor's Lost, the first of his original plays, in which he quizzed and excelled the Euphuists in wit, was followed by the rapid farce of the *Comedy of Errors*. Out of these frolics of intellect and action he passed into pure poetry in the *Midsummer Night's Dream*, and mingled into fantastic beauty the classic legend, the mediæval fairyland, and the clownish life of the English mechanic. Italian story then laid its charm upon him, and the *Two Gentlemen of Verona* preceded the southern glow of passion in *Romeo and Juliet*, in which he first reached tragic power. They complete, with *Love's Labor's Won*, afterwards recast as *All's Well That Ends Well*, the love plays of his early period. We may, perhaps, add to them the second act of an older play, *Edward III*. We should certainly read along with them, as belonging to the same passionate time, his *Rape of Lucrece*, a poem finally printed in 1594, one year later than the *Venus and Adonis*.

The same poetic succession we have traced in the poets is now found in Shakespeare. The patriotic feeling of England, also represented in Marlowe and Peele, now seized on him, and he turned from love to begin his great series of historical plays with *Richard II.*, 1593–4. *Richard III.* followed quickly. To introduce it and to complete the subject, he recast the *Second and Third Parts of Henry VI.* (written by some unknown authors), and ended his first period with *King John ;* five plays in a little more than two years.

HIS SECOND PERIOD, 1596—1602.—In the *Merchant of Venice* Shakespeare reached entire mastery over his art. A mingled woof of tragic and comic threads is brought to its highest point of color when Portia and Shylock meet in court. Pure comedy followed in his retouch of the old *Taming of the Shrew*, and all the wit of the world, mixed with noble history, met next in the three comedies of *Falstaff*, the *First* and *Second Parts* of *Henry IV.* and the *Merry Wives of Windsor*. The historical plays were then closed with *Henry V.;* a splendid dramatic song to the glory of England.

The Globe theatre, in which he was one of the proprietors,

was built in 1599. In the comedies he wrote for it, Shakespeare turned to write of love again, not to touch its deeper
passion as before but to play with it in all its lighter phases.
The flashing dialogue of *Much Ado About Nothing* was followed
by the far-off forest world of *As You Like It*, where 'the
time fleets carelessly,' and Rosalind's character is the play.
Amid all its gracious lightness steals in a new element, and the
melancholy of Jaques is the first touch we have of the older
Shakespeare who had 'gained his experience, and whose experience had made him sad.' As yet it was but a touch;
Twelfth Night shows no trace of it, though the play that followed, *All's Well That Ends Well*, again strikes a sadder note.
We find this sadness fully grown in the later sonnets, which
are said to have been finished about 1602. They were published in 1609.

Shakespeare's life changed now, and his mind changed with
it.   He had grown wealthy during this period and famous, and
was loved by society. He was the friend of the Earls of Southampton and Essex, and of William Herbert, Lord Pembroke.
The Queen patronized him; all the best literary society was
his own.   He had rescued his father from poverty, bought the
best house in Stratford and much land, and was a man of
wealth and comfort. Suddenly all his life seems to have
grown dark.   His best friends fell into ruin, Essex perished
on the scaffold, Southampton went to the Tower, Pembroke
was banished from the Court; he may himself, as some have
thought, have been concerned in the rising of Essex.   Added
to this, we may conjecture, from the imaginative pageantry of
the sonnets, that he had unwisely loved, and been betrayed in
his love by a dear friend. Disgust of his profession as an
actor and public and private ill weighed heavily on him, and
in darkness of spirit, though still clinging to the business of
the theatre, he passed from comedy to write of the sterner side
of the world, to tell the tragedy of mankind.

His Third Period, 1602—1608, begins with the last days

of Queen Elizabeth. It contains all the great tragedies, and opens with the fate of Hamlet, who felt, like the poet himself, that 'the time was out of joint.' *Hamlet*, the dreamer, may well represent Shakespeare as he stood aside from the crash that overwhelmed his friends, and thought on the changing world. The tragi-comedy of *Measure for Measure* was next written, and is tragic in thought throughout. *Julius Cæsar*, *Othello*, *Macbeth*, *Lear*, *Troilus and Cressida* (finished from an incomplete work of his youth), *Antony and Cleopatra*, *Coriolanus*, *Timon* (only in part his own) were all written in these five years. The darker sins of men, the unpitying fate which slowly gathers round and falls on men, the avenging wrath of conscience, the cruelty and punishment of weakness, the treachery, lust, jealousy, ingratitude, madness of men, the follies of the great, and the fickleness of the mob are all, with a thousand other varying moods and passions, painted, and felt as his own while he painted them, during this stern time.

HIS FOURTH PERIOD, 1608—1613.—As Shakespeare wrote of these things, he passed out of them, and his last days are full of the gentle and loving calm of one who has known sin and sorrow and fate but has risen above them into peaceful victory. Like his great contemporary, Bacon, he left the world and his own evil time behind him, and with the same quiet dignity sought the innocence and stillness of country life. The country breathes through all the dramas of this time. The flowers Perdita gathers in *Winter's Tale* and the frolic of the sheep-shearing he may have seen in the Stratford meadows; the song of Fidele in *Cymbeline* is written by one who already feared no more the frown of the great nor slander nor censure rash, and was looking forward to the time when men should say of him—

> ' Quiet consummation have;
> And renownèd be thy grave!'

Shakespeare probably left London in 1609, and lived in the house he had bought at Stratford-on-Avon. He was recon-

ciled, it is said, to his wife, and the plays he writes speak of
domestic peace and forgiveness. The story of *Marina*, which
he left unfinished, and which two later writers expanded into
the play of *Pericles*, is the first of his closing series of dramas.
The *Two Noble Kinsmen* of Fletcher, a great part of which is
now, on doubtful grounds, I think, attributed to Shakespeare,
and in which the poet sought the inspiration of Chaucer,
would belong to this period. *Cymbeline, Winter's Tale*, and
the *Tempest* bring his history up to 1612, and in the next
year he closed his poetic life by writing, with Fletcher, *Henry
VIII*. For three years he kept silence, and then, on the 23d
of April, 1616, the day he reached the age of fifty-two as is
supposed, he died.

HIS WORK.—We can only guess with regard to Shakespeare's life; we can only guess with regard to his character.
It has been tried to find out what he was from his sonnets
and from his plays, but every attempt seems to be a failure.
We cannot lay our hand on anything and say for certain that
it was spoken by Shakespeare out of his own character.   The
most personal thing in all his writings is one that has scarcely
been noticed.   It is the Epilogue to the *Tempest;* and if it
be, as is most probable, the last thing he ever wrote, then its
cry for forgiveness, its tale of inward sorrow, only to be
relieved by prayer, give us some dim insight into how the
silence of those three years was passed; while its declaration
of his aim in writing, 'which was to please,'—the true definition of an artist's aim—should make us very cautious in our
efforts to define his character from his works. Shakespeare
made men and women whose dramatic action on each other,
and towards a catastrophe, was intended to please the public,
not to reveal himself.

No commentary on his writings, no guesses about his life
or character are worth much which do not rest on this canon
as their foundation—What he did, thought, learned, and felt,
he did, thought, learned, and felt as an artist.   And he was

never less the artist, through all the changes of the time. Fully influenced, as we see in Hamlet he was, by the graver and more philosophic cast of thought of the later time of Elizabeth; passing on into the reign of James I., when pedantry took the place of gayety, and sensual the place of imaginative love in the drama, and artificial art the place of that art which itself is nature; he preserves to the last the natural passion, the simple tenderness, the sweetness, grace, and fire of the youthful Elizabethan poetry. The *Winter's Tale* is as lovely a love story as *Romeo and Juliet*, the *Tempest* is more instinct with imagination than the *Midsummer-Night's Dream*, and as great in fancy, and yet there are fully twenty years between them. The only change is in the increase of power and in a closer and graver grasp of human nature. Around him the whole tone and manner of the drama altered for the worse as his life went on, but his work grew to the close in strength and beauty."

NOTE.—"The dates and arrangement of Shakespeare's plays given above are only tentative. They are so placed by the conjectures of the latest criticism, and the conjectures wait for proof. *Julius Cæsar, e.g.,* is now dated 1601."

BIBLIOGRAPHY. SHAKESPEARE'S WORKS.—Clarendon Press Ed.; Mieklejohn's Ed.; J. P. Collier's Ed.; Leopold Shakespeare Ed., with an Int. by F. J. Furnivall; Knight's Ed.; H. H. Furness's New Variorum Ed.; H. N. Hudson's Ed.; Rolfe's Ed.; R. G. White's Ed.; G. C. Verplanck's Ed ; Dyce's Ed.; and others.

BIOGRAPHIES AND CRITICAL STUDIES IN.—H. N. Hudson's *Lectures on Shak.* and his *Life, Art,* and *Characters* of; S. T. Coleridge's *Notes and Lectures* upon Shak.; Dowden's *Critical Study of Mind and Art of Shak.;* T. Carlyle's *Hero as Poet ;* R. W. Emerson's *Shakespeare, or the Poet,* in *Rep. Men;* Gervinus' *Shak. Commentaries ;* H. Giles' *Human Life in Shak. ;* R. G. White's *Memoirs* of, with an *Essay toward the Expression of the Genius* of ; J. Weiss' *Wit, Humor, and Shak.;* J. R. Lowell's *Among my Books ;* Whipple's *Lit. of Age of Eliz.;* C. & M. C. Clarke's *The Shak. Key;* E. A. Abbott's *Shak. Grammar ;* H. Reed's *Lectures on Eng. Hist. and Tragic Po. as illustrated by Shak.;* Minto's *Characteristics of Eng. Poets.*

READING.—It is impossible to quote from Shakespeare as much as is needed, and so we quote nothing. His plays, admirably annotated, are published separately, and can easily be procured. We suggest that a Comedy, *As You Like It,* or *Much Ado About Nothing,* for instance ; a Tragedy, *Macbeth. King Lear, Othello,* or *Hamlet ;* and a Historical play, *Hen. IV., Part II.,* or *Hen. V.,* be read. If possible, these should be read (1) till the pupils can give the plot of the play, (2) till they fairly understand the characters, and can point out the influence of each upon the others and his agency in the development of the play, (3) till they can quote the notable passages and tell who uttered them, and (4) till they have acquired some mastery of Shakespeare's language, imagery, and thought.

LESSON 26.

BEN JONSON.—" The Decay of the Drama begins while Shakespeare is alive. At first one can scarcely call it decay, it was so magnificent. For it began with ' rare BEN JONSON,' who was born in 1573. His first play, in its very title, *Every Man in his Humor*, 1596–98, enables us to say in what the first step of this decay consisted.

The drama in Shakespeare's hands had been the painting of the whole of human nature, the painting of characters as they were built up by their natural bent, and by the play of circumstance upon them. The drama in Ben Jonson's hands was the painting of that particular human nature which he saw in his own age; and his characters are not men and women as they are, but as they may become when they are mastered by a special bias of the mind, or HUMOR. ' The Manners, now called Humors, feed the Stage,' says Jonson himself. *Every Man in his Humor* was followed by *Every Man out of his Humor*, and by *Cynthia's Revels*, written to satirize the courtiers. The fierce satire of these plays brought the town down upon him, and he replied to their ' noise ' in the *Poetaster*, in which Dekker and Marston were satirized. Dekker answered with the *Satiro-Mastix*, a bitter parody on the *Poetaster*, in which he did not spare Jonson's bodily defects. The staring Leviathan, as he calls Jonson, is not a very untrue description. Silent then for two years, he reappeared with the tragedy of *Sejanus*, and shortly after produced three splendid comedies in James I.'s reign, *Volpone the Fox, The Silent Woman*, and *The Alchemist*, 1605–9–10.

The first is the finest thing he ever did, as great in power as it is in the interest and skill of its plot; the second is chiefly valuable as a picture of English life in high society; the third is full to weariness of Jonson's obscure learning, but its character of Sir Epicure Mammon redeems it. In 1611 his *Cati-*

line appeared, and eight years after he was made Poet Laureate. Soon he became poor and palsy stricken, but his genius did not decay. The most graceful and tender thing he ever wrote was written in his old age. His pastoral drama, *The Sad Shepherd*, proves that, like Shakespeare, Jonson grew kinder and gentler as he grew near to death, and death took him in 1637. He was a great man. The power of the young Elizabethan age belonged to him; and he stands far below, but still worthily by, Shakespeare, 'a robust, surly, and observing dramatist.'"

From Jonson's *Sejanus.*[*]

Enter Arruntius.

Arr. Still dost thou suffer. heaven! will no flame,
No heat of sin make thy just wrath to boil
In thy distemper'd bosom, and o'erflow
The pitchy blazes of impiety
Kindled beneath thy throne? Still canst thou sleep
Patient, while vice doth make an antic face
At thy dread power, and blow dust and smoke
Into thy nostrils? Jove! will nothing wake thee?
Must vile Sejanus pull thee by the beard
Ere thou wilt open thy black-lidded eye,
And look him dead? Well, snore on, dreaming gods,
And let this last of that proud giant-race
Heave mountain upon mountain, 'gainst your state—
Be good unto me, Fortune and you Powers,
Whom I, expostulating, have profaned.
I see what's equal with a prodigy,
A great, a noble Roman, and an honest,
Live an old man!—

---

[*] Sejanus was the prime minister of Tiberius Claudius Nero Cæsar, Emperor of Rome, 14–37 A.D. For eight years Sejanus possessed an undivided influence over his wicked master, and procured the death or banishment of almost every one opposed to his own ambition—the attainment of imperial power. The Senate were servile to him, and the people gave him honors second only to those accorded to the Emperor. Tiberius at length became aware of the plans of Sejanus, and had him arrested, condemned, and put to an ignominious death.

This extract describes his eminence and the feelings of patriotic Romans toward him just before his fall.

Enter Lepidus.

O Marcus Lepidus,
When is our turn to bleed?   Thyself and I,
Without our boast, are almost all the few
Left to be honest in these impious times.

Lep. What we are left to be we will be, Lucius,
Though tyranny did stare as wide as death
To fright us from it.

Arr. 'T hath so on Sabinus.

Lep. I saw him now drawn from the Gemonies,[1]
And, what increased the direness of the fact,
His faithful dog, upbraiding all us Romans,
Never forsook the corps',[2] but seeing it thrown
Into the stream, leap'd in, and drown'd with it.

Arr. O act to be envied him of us men!
We are the next the hook lays hold on, Marcus.
What are thy arts, good patriot, teach them me,
That have preserved thy hairs to this white dye,
And kept so reverend and so dear a head
Safe on his[3] comely shoulders?

Lep. Arts, Arruntius!
None but the plain and passive fortitude
To suffer and be silent; never stretch
These arms against the torrent; live at home
With my own thoughts, and innocence about me,
Not tempting the wolves' jaws: these are my arts.

Arr. I would begin to study 'em if I thought
They would secure me.   May I pray to Jove
In secret and be safe?   Ay, or aloud,
With open wishes, so I do not mention
Tiberius or Sejanus?   Yes, I must
If I speak out.   'Tis hard that.   May I think
And not be rack'd?   What danger is't to dream,
Talk in one's sleep, or cough?   Who knows the law?
May I shake my head without a comment? say
It rains or it holds up, and not be thrown
Upon the Gemonies?   These now are things
Whereon men's fortune, yea, their faith depends.

---

[1] Steps near the Roman prison, down which bodies were thrown.
[2] Corpse.   [3] Its.

Nothing hath privilege 'gainst the violent ear.
No place, no day, no hour, we see, is free,
Not our religious and most sacred times,
From some one kind of cruelty; all matter,
Nay, all occasion pleaseth. Madmen's rage,
The idleness of drunkards, women's nothing,
Jester's simplicity—all, all is good
That can be catcht at. Nor is now the event
Of any person, or for any crime,
To be expected; for 'tis always one.
   I dare tell you, whom I dare better trust,
That our night-eyed Tiberius doth not see
His minion's[1] drifts; or, if he do, he's not
So arrant subtile as we fools do take him;
To breed a mongrel up, in his own house,
With his own blood, and, if the good gods please,
At his own throat, flesh him, to take a leap.
I do not beg it heaven; but, if the fates
Grant it these eyes, they must not wink.
   Lep. They must not see it, Lucius.
   Arr. Who should let[2] them?
   Lep. Zeal
And duty, with the thought he is our prince.
   Arr. He is our monster: forfeited to vice
So far as no rack'd virtue can redeem him.
His loathèd person fouler than all crimes:
An emperor only in his lusts. Retired
From all regard of his own fame or Rome's
Into an obscure island,[3] where he lives
Acting his tragedies with a comic face
Amidst his rout of Chaldees;[4] spending hours,
Days, weeks, and months, in the unkind abuse
Of grave astrology, to the bane of men,
Casting the scope of men's nativities,
And having found aught worthy in their fortune,
Kill, or precipitate them in the sea,
And boast he can mock fate. Nay, muse not; these

---

[1] Sejanus.   [2] Hinder.
  [3] Sejanus had persuaded Tiberius to retire to the island of Capreæ, now Capri, near Naples.
    [4] A Semitic people from Mesopotamia, given to astronomy and astrology,

Are far from ends[1] of evil, scarce degrees.
He hath his slaughter-house at Capreæ,
Where he doth study murder as an art;
And they are dearest in his grace that can
Devise the deepest tortures. Thither, too,
He hath his boys and beauteous girls ta'en up
Out of our noblest houses, the best form'd,
Best nurtured, and most modest; what's their good
Serves to provoke his bad. Some are allured,
Some threatened; others, by their friends detained
Are ravished hence, like captives, and, in sight
Of their most grievèd parents, dealt away
Unto his spintries,[2] sellaries,[2] and slaves.
To[3] this (what most strikes us and bleeding Rome)
He is, with all his craft, become the ward
To his own vassal, a stale catamite[4],
Whom he, upon our low and suffering necks,
Hath raised from excrement[5] to side the gods,
And have his proper sacrifice in Rome:
Which Jove beholds, and yet will sooner rive
A senseless oak with thunder than his trunk!

    Lep. I'll ne'er believe but Cæsar hath some scent
Of bold Sejanus' footing. These cross points
Of varying letters and opposing consuls,
Mingling his honors and his punishments,
Feigning now ill, now well, raising Sejanus
And then depressing him, as now of late
In all reports we have it, cannot be
Empty of practise: 'tis Tiberius' art.
For having found his favorite grown too great,
And with his greatness strong; that all the soldiers
Are, with their leaders, made at his devotion;
That almost all the senate are his creatures,
Or hold on him their main dependencies,
Either for benefit or hope or fear;
And that himself hath lost much of his own,
By parting unto him; and, by th' increase
Of his rank, lusts, and rages, quite disarm'd
Himself of love or other public means

---

[1] **His extremes.**   [2] **Lewd people.**   [3] **In addition to.**
[4] **One kept for unnatural purposes.**   [5] **The dirt.**

To dare an open contestation;—
His subtilty hath chose this doubling line
To hold him even in: not so to fear him
As wholly put him out, and yet give check
Unto his farther boldness.

Scene II. *An Apartment in* Sejanus' *House.*

Sej. Swell, swell, my joys, and faint not to declare
Yourselves as ample as your causes are.
I did not live till now; this my first hour;
Wherein I see my thoughts reach'd by my power.
My roof receives me not; 'tis air I tread,
And at each step I feel my advanced head
Knock out a star in heaven! rear'd to this height,
All my desires seem modest, poor, and slight
That did before sound impudent: 'tis place
Not blood discerns[1] the noble and the base.
Is there not something more than to be Cæsar?
Must we rest there? it irks t' have come so far
To be so near a stay. Caligula,
Would thou stood'st stiff, and many in our way!
Winds lose their strength when they do empty fly
Unmet of woods or buildings; great fires die
That want their matter to withstand them; so
It is our grief, and will be our loss, to know
Our power shall want opposites;[2] unless
The gods, by mixing in the cause, would bless
Our fortune with their conquest. That were worth
Sejanus' strife, durst fates but bring it forth.

Enter Terentius, Satrius, *and* Natta.

Ter. Safety to great Sejanus!
Sej. Now, Terentius?
Ter. Hears not my lord the wonder?
Sej. Speak it, no.
Ter. I meet it violent in the people's mouths,
Who run in routs to Pompey's theatre
To view your statue, which, they say, sends forth
A smoke, as from a furnace, black and dreadful.
Sej. Some traitor hath put fire in: you, go see,

---

[1] Separates. [2] Opponents.

And let the head be taken off to look
What 'tis. Some slave hath practised an imposture
To stir the people.
    Sat. The head, my lord, already is ta'en off,
I saw it; and, at opening, there leapt out
A great and monstrous serpent.
    Sej. Monstrous! why?
Had it a beard and horns? no heart? a tongue
Forkèd as flattery? look'd it of the hue
To such as live in great men's bosoms? was
The spirit of it Macro's? [1]
    Hat. May it please
The most divine Sejanus, in my days
I have not seen a more extended, grown,
Foul, spotted, venemous, ugly—
    Sej. Oh, the fates!
What a wild muster's here of attributes
T' express a worm, a snake!
    Ter. But how that should
Come there, my lord!
    Sej. What, and you too Terentius!
I think you mean to make 't a prodigy
In your reporting.
    Ter. Can the wise Sejanus
Think heaven hath meant it less?
    Sej. Oh, superstition!
Why, then the falling of our bed, that brake
This morning, burden'd with the populous weight
Of our expecting clients, to salute us;
Or running of the cat betwixt our legs,
As we set forth unto the Capitol,
Were prodigies.
    Ter. I think them ominous,
And would they had not happened! as, to-day
The fate of some your servants, who, declining[2]
Their way, not able, for the throng, to follow,
Slipt down the Gemonies and brake their necks!
Besides, in taking your last augury,
No prosperous bird appear'd; but croaking ravens

---

[1] Rival and successor to Sejanus.   [2] Turning from.

Flagg'd up and down, and from the sacrifice
Flew to the prison, where they sat all night
Beating the air with their obstreperous[1] beaks!
I dare not counsel but I would entreat
That great Sejanus would attempt the gods
Once more with sacrifice.

    Sej. What excellent fools
Religion makes of men! Believes Terentius,
If these were dangers, as I shame to think them,
The gods could change the certain course of fate?
Or, if they could, they would, now in a moment,
For a beeve's fat, or less, be bribed to invert
Those long decrees? Then think the gods, like flies,
Are to be taken with the steam of flesh
Or blood, diffused about their altars: think
Their power as cheap as I esteem it small.—
Of all the throng that fill th' Olympian hall
And, without pity, lade poor Atlas'[2] back,
I know not that one deity, but Fortune,
To whom I would throw up in begging smoke
One grain of incense; or whose ear I'd buy
With thus much oil. Her I, indeed, adore,
And keep her grateful image in my house,
Sometime belonging to a Roman king.
To her I care not, if, for satisfying
Your scrupulous phant'sies, sins, I go offer. Bid
Our priest prepare us honey, milk, and poppy,
His masculine odors, and night-vestments: say
Our rites are instant, which performed, you'll see
How vain and worthy laughter your fears be.

                        Exeunt all but *Sej.*

    If you will, Destinies, that, after all,
I faint now ere I touch my period,[3]
You are but cruel; and I already have done
Things great enough. All Rome hath been my slave;
The senate sate an idle looker on
And witness of my power; when I have blush'd
More to command than it to suffer: all
The fathers have sate ready and prepared

---

[1] Noisy.   [2] Doomed to hold up the heavens.   [3] Highest point.

> To give me empire, temples, or their throats
> . When I would ask 'em; and, what crowns the top,
> Rome, senate, people, all the world have seen
> Jove but my equal, Cæsar but my second.
> 'Tis then your malice, Fates, who, but your own,
> Envy and fear to have my power long known.

HIS MASQUES.—"Rugged as Jonson was, he could turn to light and graceful work, and it is with his name that we connect *the Masques*. Masques were dramatic representations made for a festive occasion, with a reference to the persons present and the occasion. Their personages were allegorical. They admitted of dialogue, music, singing, and dancing, combined by the use of some ingenious fable into a whole. They were made and performed for the court and the houses of the nobles, and the scenery was as gorgeous and varied as the scenery of the playhouse proper was poor and unchanging. Arriving for the first time at any repute in Henry VIII.'s time, they reached splendor under James and Charles I. Great men took part in them. When Ben Jonson wrote them, Inigo Jones made the scenery, and Lawes the music, and Lord Bacon, Whitelock, and Selden sat in committee for the last great masque presented to Charles. Milton himself made them worthier by writing *Comus,* and their scenic decoration was soon introduced into the regular theatres.

Beaumont and Fletcher worked together, but out of more than fifty plays, all written in James I.'s reign, not more than fourteen were shared in by Beaumont, who died at the age of thirty in 1616. Fletcher survived him, and died in 1625. Both were of gentle birth. Beaumont, where we can trace his work, is weightier and more dignified than his comrade, but Fletcher was the better poet. Fletcher wrote rapidly, but his imagination worked slowly. Their *Philaster* and *Thierry and Theodoret* are fine examples of their tragic power. Fletcher's *Faithful Shepherdess* is full of lovely poetry, and both are masters of grace and pathos and style. They enfeebled the blank verse of the drama, while they rendered it sweeter by using feminine endings and adding an eleventh syllable with great frequency. This gave freedom and elasticity to their verse and was suited to the dialogue of comedy, but it lowered the dignity of their tragedy.

These two men mark a change in politics and society from Shakespeare's time. Shakespeare's loyalty is constitutional; Beaumont and Fletcher are blind supporters of James I.'s invention of the divine right of kings. Shakespeare's society was on the whole decent, and it is so in his plays. Beaumont and Fletcher are 'studiously indecent.' In contrast with them Shakespeare is as white as snow. Shakespeare's men are of the type of Sidney and Raleigh, Burleigh and Drake. The men of these two writers represent the 'young bloods' of the Stuart Court; and even the best of their older and graver men are base and foul in thought. Their women are either monsters of badness or of goodness. When they paint a good woman (two or three at most being excepted), she is beyond nature. The fact is, that the high art, which in Shakespeare sought to give a noble pleasure by being true to human nature in its natural aspects, sank now into the baser art, which wished to excite, at any cost, the passions of the audience by representing human nature in unnatural aspects.

In **Massinger and Ford** this evil is just as plainly marked. MASSINGER'S first dated play was the *Virgin Martyr*, 1620. He lived poor, and died 'a stranger' in 1639. In these twenty years he wrote thirty-seven plays, of which the *New Way to Pay Old Debts* is the best known by its character of Sir Giles Overreach. No writer is fouler in language, and there is a want of unity of impression both in his plots and in his characters. He often sacrifices art to effect, and 'unlike Shakespeare, seems often to despise his own characters.' On the other hand, his versification and language are flexible and strong, 'and seem to rise out of the passions he describes.' He speaks the tongue of real life. His men and women are far more natural than those of Beaumont and Fletcher, and, with all his coarseness, he is the most moral of the secondary dramatists. Nowhere else is his work so great as when he represents the brave man struggling through trial to victory, the pure woman suffering for the sake of truth and love; or when he describes the terrors that conscience brings on injustice and cruelty.

JOHN FORD, his contemporary, published his first play, the *Lover's Melancholy*, in 1629, and five years after, *Perkin Warbeck*, the best historical drama after Shakespeare. Between these dates appeared others, of which the best is the *Broken Heart*. He carried to an extreme the tendency of the drama to unnatural and horrible subjects, but he did so with very great power. He has no comic humor, but no man has described better the worn and tortured human heart.

WEBSTER AND OTHER DRAMATISTS.—Higher as a poet, and possessing the same power as Ford, though not the same exquisite tenderness, was JOHN WEBSTER, whose best drama, *The Duchess of Malfi*, was acted in 1616. *Vittoria Corombona* was printed in 1612, and was followed by the *Devil's Law Case*, *Appius and Virginia*, and others. Webster's peculiar power of creating ghastly horror is redeemed from sensationalism by his poetic insight. His imagination easily saw, and expressed in short and intense lines, the inmost thoughts and feelings of characters, whom he represents as wrought on by misery or crime or remorse, at their very highest point of passion. In his worst characters there is some redeeming touch, and this poetic pity brings him nearer to Shakespeare than to the rest. He is also neither so coarse nor so great a king worshipper nor so irreligious as the others. We seem to taste the Puritan in his work. Two comedies, *Westward Ho!* and *Northward Ho!* remarkable for the light they throw on the manners of the time, were written by him along with THOMAS DEKKER.

GEORGE CHAPMAN is the only one of the later Elizabethan

dramatists who kept the old fire of Marlowe, though he never had the naturalness or temperance which lifted Shakespeare far beyond Marlowe. The same power which we have seen in his translation of Homer is to be found in his plays. The mingling of intellectual power with imagination, and swollen violence of words and images with tender and natural and often splendid passages, are entirely in the earlier Elizabethan manner. He, too, like Marlowe, to quote his own line, 'hurled instinctive fire about the world.' These were the greatest names among a crowd of dramatists. We can only mention John Marston, Henry Glapthorne, Richard Brome, William Rowley, Thomas Middleton, Cyril Tourneur, and Thomas Heywood. Of the crowd, 'all of whom,' says Lamb, 'spoke nearly the same language and had a set of moral feelings and notions in common,' JAMES SHIRLEY is the last. He lived till 1666. In him the fire and passion of the old time passes away, but some of the delicate poetry remains, and in him the Elizabethan drama dies.

In 1642, the theatres were closed during the calamitous times of the Civil War. Strolling players managed to exist with difficulty, and against the law, till 1656, when SIR WILLIAM DAVENANT had his opera of the *Siege of Rhodes* acted in London. It was the beginning of a new drama, in every point but impurity different from the old, and four years after, at the Restoration, it broke loose from the prison of Puritanism to indulge in a shameless license.

In this rapid sketch of the Drama in England, we have been carried on beyond the death of Elizabeth to the date of the Restoration. It was necessary, because it keeps the whole story together. We now return to the time that followed the accession of James I."

BIBLIOGRAPHY. BEN JONSON, BEAUMONT, AND FLETCHER.—S. A. Dunham's *Lives of Lit. Men;* W. Gifford's *Memoir* of; Taine's *Hist. of Eng. Lit.;* A. W. Ward's *Hist. Eng. Dra. Lit.;* Whipple's *Lit. of the Age of Eliz.;* T. H. Ward's *Anthology;* Littell, 1860, v. 2; Br. Quar. Rev., 1857; Ecl. Mag., Feb. and Oct., 1847; Apr., 1856; May, 1858; and Oct., 1874.

Scheme for Review.

PERIOD V.

Lesson 27.

Brief Historical Sketch.—James VI. of Scotland, son of Mary, Queen of Scots, and of Darnley, comes to the English throne, 1603, as Jas. I., and is the first of the Stuart House. Gunpowder Plot, 1605. First permanent English settlement in America, at Jamestown, Virginia, 1607. Thermometer invented, 1610. King James's Bible, a revision of Wyclif's, Tyndale's, and Coverdale's translations, issued, 1611. Harvey discovers circulation of the blood, 1616. Expedition and death of Raleigh, 1617. Settlement of New England at Plymouth, 1620, the year negro slavery was introduced into the Virginia Colony. Charles, son of James, married to Henrietta, daughter of Hen. IV. of France, became King of England, 1625. Hampden refused to pay his ship-money tax, 1637. Covenant signed in Scotland, 1638,—an agreement by which the people bound themselves to resist the re-introduction of Episcopacy into Scotland. Long Parliament met, 1640. Strafford executed, 1641, and Laud, 1644. Civil war broke out, 1642. Puritans separate into Presbyterians and Independents. Battle of Naseby, 1645. Long Parliament reduced by Pride's Purge to the Rump, 1648. King executed, 1649. Conquest of Ireland by Cromwell, same year. Coffee-houses established in London, 1652. Rump Parliament abolished, 1653. Cromwell made Lord Protector, same year. Civil marriage legalized, same year. Post-Office established, 1657. Watches for the pocket first made in England, 1658. Cromwell died, 1658. Richard Cromwell made Protector, 1658.

LESSON 28.

PROSE.—'' We have traced the decline of the drama of Eliza-beth up to the date of the Restoration. All poetry suffered in the same way after the reign of James I. It became fan-tastic in style and overwrought in thought. It was diffuse, or violent, in expression. *Prose literature*, on the contrary, gradually grew into greater excellence, spread itself over larger fields of thought, and took up a greater variety of sub-jects. The grave national struggle, while it lessened poetical, increased prose, literature. *The painting of short 'Characters'* was begun by Sir T. Overbury's book in 1614, and carried on by John Earle and Joseph Hall, afterwards made bishops. They mark the interest in individual life which now began to arise, and which soon took form in *Biography*.

THOMAS FULLER'S *Holy and Profane State*, 1642, added to sketches of 'characters' illustrations of them in the lives of famous persons, and in 1662 his *Worthies of England* still fur-ther set on foot the literature of Biography. *The historical literature*, which we have noticed already in the works of Ral-eigh and Bacon, was carried on by Fuller in his *Church His-tory of Britain*, 1656. He is a quaint and delightful writer; good sense, piety, and inventive wit are woven together in his work. We may place together ROBERT BURTON'S *Anatomy of Melancholy*, 1621, and SIR THOMAS BROWNE'S *Religio Medici*, 1642, and *Pseudodoxia* as *books which treat of miscellaneous subjects* in a witty and learned fashion. This kind of writing was greatly increased by the *setting up of libraries*, where men dipped into every kind of literature. It was in James I.'s reign that Sir Thomas Bodley established the Bodleian at Oxford, and Sir Robert Cotton a library now placed in the British Museum. A number of small writers took part in the *Puritan and Church controversies*, among whom WILLIAM PRYNNE, a violent Puritan, deserves to be mentioned for his *Histrio-Mastix*, or *Scourge of Players*.

But there were others on each side who rose above the war of party into the calm air of *spiritual religion*. JEREMY TAYLOR at the close of Charles I.'s reign published his *Great Exemplar* and his *Holy Living and Holy Dying*, and shortly afterwards his *Sermons*. They had been preceded in 1647 by his *Liberty of Prophesying*, in which he claimed full freedom of Biblical interpretation as the right of all, and asked for only one standard of faith—the Apostles' Creed. His work is especially literary. Weighty with argument, his sermons and books of devotion are still read among us for their sweet and deep devotion, for their rapidly flowing and poetic eloquence.

Towards the end of the Civil Wars, RICHARD BAXTER, the great Puritan writer, wrote a good book, which, as it still remains a household book in England, takes its place in literature. There are few cottages which do not possess a copy of *The Saint's Everlasting Rest;* and there are few parsonages in England in which ROBERT LEIGHTON's book on the Epistle of St. Peter is not also to be found. Leighton died in 1684, Archbishop of Glasgow. In philosophic literature I have already spoken of Bacon, and of the political writers, such as Hobbes and Harrington, who wrote during the Commonwealth, I will speak hereafter in their proper place.

Miscellaneous writing is further represented in the *literature of travel* by GEORGE SANDYS and THOMAS CORYAT. *Coryat's Crudities*, 1611, describes his journey through France and Italy; Sandys' book, 1615, a journey to the East. We have also from abroad some interesting letters from Sir Henry Wotton, and he gave Milton introductions to famous men in Italy. Wotton's quaint and pleasant friend IZAAK WALTON closes the list of these pre-Restoration writers with the *Compleat Angler*, 1653, a book which resembles in its quaint and garrulous style the rustic scenery and prattling rivers that it celebrates, and marks the quiet interest in the country which now began to grow up in England.

The style of all these writers links them to the age of Elizabeth.   It did not follow the weighty gravity of Hooker, or the balanced calm and splendor of Bacon, but rather the witty quaintness of Lyly and of Sydney.   The prose of men like Browne and Burton and Fuller is not as poetic as that of these Elizabethan writers, but it is just as fanciful.   Even the prose of Jeremy Taylor is over poetical, and though it has all the Elizabethan ardor, it has also the Elizabethan faults of excessive wordiness and involved periods and images.   It never knows where to stop.   Milton's prose works, which shall be mentioned in their place in his life, are also Elizabethan in style.   Their style has the fire and violence, the eloquence and diffuseness, of the earlier literature, but, in spite of the praise it has received, it is in reality scarcely to be called a style.   It has all the faults a prose style can have except obscurity and vulgarity.   Its bursts of eloquence ought to be in poetry, and it never charms except when Milton becomes purposely simple in personal narrative.   There is no pure style in prose writing till Hobbes began to write in English, indeed we may say till after the Restoration, unless we except, on grounds of weight and power, the styles of Bacon and Hooker."

BIBLIOGRAPHY.   FULLER, TAYLOR, and BROWNE.—E. Lawrence's *Lives of Brit. Historians;* H. Rogers' *Life and Writings* of; Minto's *Man. Eng. Prose Lit.;* Littell, v. 19, 1857; Cornhill Mag., v. 25, 1872; J. Foster's *Crit. Essays;* Contemp. Rev., v. 9, 1868; Quart. Rev., v. 131, 1871; Ecl. Mag., Aug., 1851; Tuckerman's *Characteristics;* Bulwer's *Crit. Writings;* S. Johnson's *Life* of; Ecl. Mag., v. 25, 1852; N. A. Rev., v. 94 1862.

From Thomas Fuller.

THE GOOD SCHOOLMASTER.—*He studieth his scholars' natures as carefully as they their books,* and ranks their dispositions into several forms. And though it may seem difficult for him in a great school to descend to all particulars, yet experienced schoolmasters may quickly make a grammar of boys' natures, and reduce them all, saving some few exceptions, to these general rules:—

1. *Those that are ingenious and industrious.*—The conjunction of two such planets in a youth presages much good unto him.   To such a lad a frown may be a whipping, and a whipping a death; yea, where their master whips them once, shame whips them all the week after.   Such natures he useth with all gentleness.

2. *Those that are ingenious and idle.*—These think, with the hare in the fable, that, running with snails, (so they count the rest of their school-fellows) they shall come soon enough to the post, though sleeping a good while before their starting. Oh! a good rod would finely take them napping!

3. *Those that are dull and diligent.*—Wines—the stronger they be, the more lees they have when they are new. Many boys are muddy-headed till they be clarified with age; and such afterwards prove the best. Bristol diamonds are both bright and squared and pointed by nature and yet are soft and worthless; whereas orient ones, in India, are rough and rugged naturally. Hard, rugged, and dull natures of youth acquit themselves afterwards the jewels of the country; and, therefore, their duleness at first is to be borne with, if they be diligent. That schoolmaster deserves to be beaten himself who beats nature in a boy for a fault. And I question whether all the whipping in the world can make their parts which are naturally sluggish rise one minute before the hour nature hath appointed.

4. *Those that are invincibly dull and negligent also.*—Correction may reform the latter, not amend the former. All the whetting in the world can never set a razor's edge on that which hath no steel in it. Such boys he consigneth over to other professions. Shipwrights and boatmakers will choose those crooked pieces of timber which other carpenters refuse. Those may make excellent merchants and mechanics who will not serve for scholars.

He is able, diligent, and methodical in his teaching. Not leading them rather in a circle than forwards. He minces his precepts for children to swallow; hanging clogs on the nimbleness of his own soul that his scholars may go along with him.

He is moderate in inflicting deserved correction. Many a schoolmaster better answereth the name *paidotribe*[1] than *paidagogos*,[2] rather "tearing his scholars' flesh with whipping than giving them good education." No wonder if his scholars hate the Muses, being presented unto them in the shapes of fiends and furies. Such an Orbilius[3] mars more scholars than he makes. Their tyranny hath caused many tongues to stammer which spake plain by nature, and whose stuttering at first was nothing else but fears quavering on their speech at their master's presence, and whose mauling them about their heads hath dulled those who in quickness exceeded their master.

He spoils not a good school to make thereof a bad college, therein to teach

---

[1] Boyflogger. [2] Boyteacher. [3] A rigid disciplinarian, an instructor of the poet Horace.

his scholars logic.   For, besides that logic may have an action of tres-
pass against grammar for encroaching on her liberties, syllogisms are
solecisms taught in the school; and, oftentimes, youth are forced afterwards, in the University, to unlearn the fumbling skill they had before.

Out of his school he is no whit pedantical in carriage or discourse, con-
tenting himself to be rich in Latin, though he doth not jingle with it in
every company wherein he comes.

MEMORY.—It is the treasure-house of the mind, wherein the monuments thereof are kept and preserved.   Plato makes it the mother
of the Muses.   Aristotle sets it one degree further, making experience
the mother of arts, memory the parent of experience.   Philosophers
place it in the rear of the head; and it seems the mine of memory lies
there, because *there* naturally men dig for it, scratching it when they
are at a loss.   This, again, is twofold; one the simple retention of
things, the other a regaining them when forgotten.

Brute creatures equal, if not exceed, men in a bare retentive memory.—
Through how many labyrinths of woods, without other clew of thread
than natural instinct, doth the hunted hare return to her muce![1]   How
doth the little bee, flying into several meadows and gardens, sipping of
many cups, yet never intoxicated, through an ocean (as I may say) of
air steadily steer herself home, without help of cord or compass!   But
these cannot play an after-game, and recover what they have forgotten,
which is done by the mediation of discourse.

First soundly infix in thy mind what thou desirest to remember.—What
wonder is it if agitation of business jog that out of thy head which was
there rather tacked than fastened?   It is best knocking in the nail over-
night, and clinching it the next morning.

Overburden not thy memory to make so faithful a servant a slave.—Remember Atlas was weary.   Have as much reason as a camel—to rise
when thou hast thy full load.   Memory is like a purse,—if it be over-full
that it cannot shut, all will drop out of it.   Take heed of a gluttonous
curiosity to feed on many things, lest the greediness of the appetite of
thy memory spoil the digestion thereof.   Beza's case was peculiar and
memorable.   Being over fourscore years of age, he perfectly could say
by heart any Greek chapter in St. Paul's Epistles, or anything else
which he had learned long before, but forgot whatsoever was newly told
him; his memory, like an inn, retaining old guests, but having no room
to entertain new.

Marshal thy notions into a handsome method.—One will carry twice

---

[1] Gap in the hedge.

more weight trussed and packed up in bundles than when it lies un-
towardly flapping and hanging about his shoulders. Things orderly
fardled [1] up under heads are most portable.

LESSON 29.

From Jeremy Taylor—*The best use of speech.*

Our conversation must be "apt to comfort" the disconsolate; and
than this, men in present can feel no greater charity. For, since half
the duty of a Christian in this life consists in the exercise of passive
graces; and the infinite variety of providence and the perpetual adversity
of chances and the dissatisfaction and emptiness that is in things themselves and the weariness and anguish of our spirit call us to the trial and
exercise of patience even in the days of sunshine, and much more in the
violent storms that shake our dwellings and make our hearts tremble;
God hath sent some angels into the world whose office it is to refresh
the sorrows of the poor and to lighten the eyes of the disconsolate. He
hath made some creatures whose powers are chiefly ordained to comfort,
—wine, and oil, and society, cordials, and variety; and time itself is
checkered with black and white; stay but till to-morrow, and your present sorrow will be weary and will lie down to rest.

But this is not all. God glories in the appellative that he is "the
Father of mercies, and the God of all comfort;" and therefore to minister
in the office is to become like God and to imitate the charities of Heaven.
And God hath fitted mankind for it; man most needs it, and he feels
his brother's wants by his own experience; and God hath given us
speech, and the endearments of society, and pleasantness of conversation, and powers of seasonable discourse, arguments to allay the sorrow
by abating our apprehensions and taking out the sting or telling the
periods of comfort or exciting hope or urging a precept and reconciling
our affections and reciting promises or telling stories of the Divine
mercy or changing it into duty or making the burden less by comparing
it with greater or by proving it to be less than we deserve and that it
is so intended and may become the instrument of virtue.

And certain it is that, as nothing can better do it, so there is nothing
greater for which God made our tongues, next to reciting his praises,
than to minister comfort to a weary soul. And what greater measure
can we have than that we should bring joy to our brother, who with his
dreary eyes looks to heaven and round about, and cannot find so much

---

[1] Bundled.

rest as to lay his eyelids close together, than that thy tongue should be tuned with heavenly accents, and make the weary soul listen for light and ease: and, when he perceives that there is such a thing in the world and in the order of things as comfort and joy, to begin to break out from the prison of his sorrows at the door of sighs and tears, and by little and little melt into showers of refreshment? This is the glory of thy voice, and employment fit for the brightest angel.

But so have I seen the Sun kiss the frozen earth, which was bound up with the images of death and the colder breath of the north: and then the waters break from their enclosures and melt with joy and run in useful channels; and the flies do rise again from their little graves in walls, and dance awhile in the air, to tell that there is joy within and that the great mother of creatures will open the stock of refreshments, become useful to mankind, and sing praises to her Redeemer. So is the heart of a sorrowful man under the discourses of a wise comforter; he breaks from the despairs of the grave, and the fetters and chains of sorrow; he blesses God and he blesses thee and he feels his life returning; for to be miserable is death, and nothing is life but to be comforted; and God is pleased with no music from below so much as in the thanksgiving songs of relieved widows, of supported orphans, of rejoicing and comforted and thankful persons. This part of communication does the work of God and of our neighbors, and bears us to Heaven in streams of joy made by the overflowings of our brother's comfort.

It is a fearful thing to see a man despairing; none knows the sorrow and the intolerable anguish but themselves, and they that are damned: and so are all the loads of a wounded spirit, when the staff of a man's broken fortune bows his head to the ground, and sinks like an osier under the violence of a mighty tempest. But therefore, in proportion to this, I may tell the excellency of the employment, and the duty of that charity which bears the dying and languishing soul from the fringes of hell to the seat of the brightest stars, where God's face shines and reflects comforts for ever and ever.

And, though God hath for this especially intrusted his ministers and servants of the Church, and hath put into their hearts and notices great magazines of promises and arguments of hope and arts of the Spirit, yet God does not always send angels on these embassies, but sends a man, that every good man in his season may be to his brother in the place of God, to comfort and restore him. And, that it may appear how much it is the duty of us all to minister comfort to our brother, we may remember that the same words and the same arguments do oftentimes much more prevail upon our spirits when they are applied by the hand of another than when they dwell in us and come from our own discoursings. This is indeed the greatest and most holy charity.

From Browne's *Hydriotaphia—Urn Burial.*

Now since these dead bones[1] have already outlasted the living ones of Methuselah, and in a yard underground, and thin walls of clay, outworn all the strong and specious[2] buildings above it, and quietly rested under the drums and tramplings of three conquests,[3] what prince can promise such diuturnity[4] unto his relics? Time, which antiquates antiquities, and hath an art to make dust of all things, hath yet spared these minor monuments.

What time the persons of these ossuaries[5] entered the famous nations of the dead and slept with princes and counsellors might admit a wide solution. But who were the proprietaries of these bones or what bodies these ashes made up were a question above antiquarism, not to be resolved by man nor easily, perhaps, by spirits, except we consult the provincial guardians, or tutelary observators. Had they made as good provision for their names as they have done for their relics, they had not so grossly erred in the art of perpetuation. But to subsist in bones and be but pyramidally extant is a fallacy in duration.

There is no antidote against the opium of time, which temporally considereth all things; our fathers find their graves in our short memories, and sadly tell us how we may be buried in our survivors. Gravestones tell truth scarce forty years.[6] Generations pass while some trees stand, and old families last not three oaks. To be read by bare inscriptions, like many in Gruter,[7] to hope for eternity by enigmatical epithets or first letters of our names, to be studied by antiquaries, who we were, and have new names given us, like many of the mummies, are cold consolations unto the students of perpetuity, even by everlasting languages.

To be content that times to come should only know that there was such a man, not caring whether they knew more of him, was a frigid ambition in Cardan,[8] disparaging his horoscopal inclination and judgment of himself. Who cares to subsist like Hippocrates's[9] patients or Achilles's horses in Homer, under naked nominations,[10] without

---

[1] Supposed to be of the Romans that occupied the island. The Romans burned the dead and buried the ashes in urns. Forty or fifty of these were dug up in Norfolk in Browne's time. [2] Showy. [3] Tell what three. [4] Duration. [5] Burial places. [6] Inscriptions wear away. [7] Born at Antwerp 1560, he lived awhile at Norwich. Browne's place, graduated at Leyden, became a learned man, a professor, and author of many works, and died 1627. [8] Born at Pavia 1501, died at Rome 1576. Was a noted astrologer. This explains the remainder of the sentence. [9] The father of physic, born about 460 B.C. [10] Merely named.

deserts and noble acts, which are the balsam[1] of our memories, the *entelechia*[2] and soul of our subsistencies? To be nameless in worthy deeds exceeds an infamous history. The Canaanitish[3] woman lives more happily without a name than Herodias[3] with one. And who had not rather have been the good thief[3] than Pilate?[3]

But the iniquity[4] of oblivion blindly scattereth her poppy, and deals with the memory of men without distinction to merit of perpetuity. Who can but pity the founder of the pyramids? Herostratus lives that burnt the temple of Diana,[5] he is almost lost that built it. Time hath spared the epitaph of Adrian's[6] horse, confounded that of himself. In vain we compute our felicities by the advantage of our good names, since bad have equal durations, and Thersites is like to live as long as Agamemnon[7] without the favor of the everlasting register. Who knows whether the best of men be known, or whether there be not more remarkable persons forgot than any that stand remembered in the known account of time?

Oblivion is not to be hired. The greater part must be content to be as though they had not been, to be found in the register of God, not in the record of man. Twenty-seven names make up the first story, and the recorded names ever since contain not one living century.[8] The number of the dead long exceedeth all that shall live. The night of time far surpasseth the day, and who knows when was the equinox?[9] Every hour adds unto that current arithmetic, which scarce stands one moment. And since death must be the Lucina[10] of life and even pagans could doubt whether thus to live were to die; since our longest sun sets at right descensions, and makes but winter arches, and therefore it cannot be long before we lie down in darkness, and have our light in ashes; since the brother of death[11] daily haunts us with dying mementos, and time, that grows old in itself, bids us hope no long duration;—diuturnity is a dream and folly of expectation.

There is nothing strictly immortal but immortality. Whatever hath no beginning may be confident of no end—all others have a dependent being and within the reach of destruction—which is the peculiar[12] of that necessary essence that cannot destroy itself, and the highest strain of omnipotency, to be so powerfully constituted as not to suffer even from

---

[1] Preserver. [2] That by which our existence (subsistences) actually *is*. [3] See John iv, Matt. xiv, and Mark xxiii. [4] Inequality, partiality. [5] Daughter of Jupiter and Latona, and goddess of the chase. [6] An illustrious Rom. Emperor, the 14th, b. 76 A.D., d. 183. [7] Commander of the Greek forces before Troy, and *Thersites* was a railler in his camp. [8] Hundred. [9] When the time past equalled that to come. [10] The goddess of childbirth. [11] Sleep. [12] Peculiarity.

the power of itself. But the sufficiency of Christian immortality frustrates all earthly glory, and the quality of either state after death makes a folly of posthumous[1] memory. God who can only destroy our souls and hath assured our resurrection, either of our bodies or names hath directly promised no duration. Wherein there is so much of chance that the boldest expectants have found unhappy frustration, and to hold long subsistence seems but a scape in oblivion. But man is a noble animal, splendid in ashes, and pompous in the grave, solemnizing nativities and deaths with equal lustre, nor omitting ceremonies of bravery in the infancy of his nature.

LESSON 30.

THE DECLINE OF POETRY.—" The various elements which we have noticed in the poetry of Elizabeth's reign, without the exception, even, of the slight Catholic element, though opposed to each other, were filled with one spirit—the love of England and the Queen. Nor were they ever sharply divided; they are found mixed together and modifying one another in the same poet, as, for instance, Puritanism and Chivalry in Spenser, Catholicism and Love in Constable; and all are mixed together in Shakespeare and the dramatists. This unity of spirit in poetry became less and less after the Queen's death. The elements remained, but they were separated. Poetry was the bundle of sticks with the cord round it in Elizabeth's time; in the time of Charles I. it was the same bundle with the cord removed and the sticks set apart. The cause of this was, that the strife in politics between the Divine Right of Kings and Liberty, and in religion between the Church and the Puritans grew so defined and intense that England ceased to be at one, and the poets, though not so strongly as other classes, were separated into sections.

A certain style, which induced Johnson to call them '*metaphysical*,' belongs more or less to all these poets. They were those, Hallam says, ' who labored after conceits, or novel turns

---

[1] After death.

of thought, usually false, and resting on some equivocation of language or exceedingly remote analogy.' This form finds its true source in the fantastic style of the *Euphues* and the *Arcadia*. It grew up again towards the close of Elizabeth's reign, and it ended by greatly lessening good sense and clearness in English poetry. It was in the reaction from it, and in the determination to bring clear thought and clear expression of thought into English verse, that the school of Dryden and Pope—the critical school—began. The poetry from the later years of Elizabeth to Milton illustrates all these remarks.

The Lyric Poetry struck a new note in the songs of Ben Jonson, such as the *Hymn to Diana*. They are less natural, less able to be sung, than Shakespeare's, more classical, more artificial. But they have no special tendency. Later on, during the reign of Charles I. and during the Civil War, the lyrics of THOMAS CAREW, SIR JOHN SUCKLING, COLONEL LOVELACE, and ROBERT HERRICK, whose *Hesperides* was published in 1648, have a special royalist and court character. They are, for the most part, light, pleasant, short songs and epigrams on the passing interests of the day, on the charms of the court beauties, on a lock of hair, a dress, on all the fleeting forms of fleeting love. Here and there we find a pure or pathetic song, and there are few of them which time has selected that do not possess a gay or a gentle grace. As the Civil War deepened, the special court poetry died, and the songs became songs of battle and marching, and devoted and violent loyalty. These have been lately collected under the title of *Songs of the Cavaliers*.

Satirical Poetry, always arising when natural passion in poetry decays, is represented in the later days of Elizabeth by JOSEPH HALL, afterwards Bishop Hall, whose *Virgidemiarum*, 1597, satires partly in poetry, make him the master satirist of this time. JOHN DONNE, Dean of St. Paul's, who also partly belongs to the age of Elizabeth, was, with John Cleveland (a furious royalist and satirist of Charles I.'s time), the most obscure and fanciful of the poets absurdly called Metaphysical. Donne, however, rose far above the rest in the beauty of thought, and in the tenderness of his religious and love poems. His satires are graphic pictures of the manners of the age of James I. GEORGE WITHER hit the follies and vices of the day so hard in his *Abuses Stript and Whipt*, 1613, that he was put into the Marshalsea prison, where he continued his satires in the *Shepherd's Hunting*. As the Puritan and the Royalist became more opposed to one another, satirical poetry naturally became more bitter; but, like the poetry of the Civil War, it took the form of short songs and pieces which went about the country, as those of Bishop Corbet did, in manuscript.

THE RURAL POETRY.—The *pastoral* now began to take a more truly rural form than the conventional pastorals of France and Italy, out of which it rose. In WILLIAM BROWNE'S *Britannia's Pastorals*, 1616, the element of pleasure in country life arises, and from this time it begins to grow in our poetry. It appears slightly in WITHER'S *Shepherd's Hunting*, but plainly in his *Mistress of Philarete*, a poem interspersed with lyrics. In dwelling so much as he did on the beauty of natural scenery away from cities, he brings a new element into English verse. Henceforth we always find a country poetry set over against a town poetry, a poetry of nature set over against a poetry of man.

It is still stronger in ANDREW MARVELL, Milton's secretary, who, with the exception of Milton, did the finest work of this kind. In imaginative intensity, in the fusing together of personal feeling and thought with the delight received from nature, his verses on *The Emigrants in the Bermudas* and *The Thoughts in a Garden*, and the little poem, *The Girl describes her Fawn*, are like the work of Wordsworth on one side, and like the best Elizabethan work on the other. They are the last and the truest echo of the lyrics of the time of Elizabeth, but they reach beyond them in the love of nature.

SPENSERIANS.—Among these broken up forms of poetry,

there was one kind which was imitative of Spenser. PHINEAS
FLETCHER, GILES FLETCHER, HENRY MORE in his *Platonical
Song of the Soul*, 1642, and JOHN CHALKHILL in his *Thealma*,
owned him as their master.   The *Purple Island*, 1633, of the
first, an elaborate allegory of the body and mind of man, has
some grace and sweetness, and tells us that the scientific element, which after the Restoration took form in the setting up
of the Royal Society, was so far spread in England at his time
as to influence the poets.

RELIGIOUS POETRY.—*The Temptation and Victory of Christ*,
1610, of GILES FLETCHER, is a lovely poem and gave hints to
Milton for the *Paradise Regained*.   It is one of the many religious poems that now began to interest the people.   Of these
The Temple, 1631, of GEORGE HERBERT, rector of Bemer-
ton, has been the most popular.   The purity and profound
devotion of its poetry have made it dear to all.   Its gentle
Church feeling has pleased all classes of churchmen ; its great
quaintness, which removes it from true poetry, has added
perhaps to its charm.   With him we must rank HENRY
VAUGHAN, the Silurist, whose *Sacred Poems* are equally devotional, pure, and quaint, and FRANCIS QUARLES, whose
Divine Emblems, 1635, is still read in the cottages of England.

On the Roman Catholic side, WILLIAM HABINGTON mingled his devotion to his religion with the praises of his wife,
under the name of *Castara*, 1634 ; and RICHARD CRASHAW,
whose rich inventiveness was not made less rich by the religious
mysticism which finally led him to become a Roman Catholic,
published his *Steps to the Temple* in 1646.   On the Puritan
side, we may now place GEORGE WITHER, whose *Hallelujah*,
1641, a series of religious poems, was sent forth just before
the Civil War began, when he left the king's side to support
the Parliament.   Finally, religious poetry, after the return of
Charles II., passed on through the *Davideis* of ABRAHAM
COWLEY, and the *Divine Love* of EDMUND WALLER to find its
highest expression in the *Paradise Lost*.

We have thus traced through all its forms the decline of poetry. It is a poetry often beautiful, but as often injured by obscurity, over-fancifulness, confusion of thought and of images. From this decay we pass into a new world when we come to speak of Milton. Between the dying poetry of the past, and the uprising of a new kind in Dryden, stands alone the majestic work of a great genius who touches the Elizabethan time with one hand and our own time with the other."

BIBLIOGRAPHY. HERBERT AND DONNE.—Ward's *Anthology;* Mrs. Thompson's *Celebrated Friendships;* S. Brown's *Lectures and Essays ;* Walton's *Lives of Herbert, Donne,* etc; Ecl. Mag., v. 32, 1854.

LESSON 31.

JOHN MILTON.—" MILTON was the last of the Elizabethans, and, except Shakespeare, far the greatest of them all. Born in 1608, in Bread-street, he may have seen Shakespeare, for Milton remained in London till he was sixteen.

His literary life may be said to begin with his entrance into Cambridge, in 1625, the year of the accession of Charles I. Nicknamed the 'lady' from his beauty and delicate taste and morality, he got soon a great fame, and during the seven years of his life at the university his poetic genius opened itself in the English poems of which I give the dates. *On the Death of a Fair Infant*, 1626. *At a Vacation Exercise*, 1628. *On the Morning of Christ's Nativity*, 1629. *On the Circumcision, The Passion, Time, At a Solemn Musick, On the May Morning, On Shakespeare*, 1630. *On the University Carrier, Epitaph on Marchioness of Worcester, Sonnet 1., To the Nightingale, Sonnet 2., On Arriving at Age of Twenty-three*, 1631. The last sonnet, when explained by a letter that accompanied it, shows that Milton, influenced by the sufferings of the Puritans, had given up his intention of becoming a clergyman.

He left, therefore, the university in 1632, and went to live at Horton, near Windsor, where he spent five years, steadily

reading the Greek and Latin writers, and amusing himsel
with mathematics and music. Poetry was not neglected.
The *L'Allegro* and *Il Penseroso* were written in 1632, and
probably the *Arcades;* *Comus* in 1634, and *Lycidas* in 1637.
They all prove that, though Milton was Puritan in heart, his
Puritanism was of that earlier type which neither disdained
literature, art, or gaiety nor despised the ancient Church nor
turned away from natural beauty. He could still enjoy the
village dance, the masque, the lists, the music in the dim
Cathedral; he could still mingle the learning of the Renaissance with his delight in the fields and flowers, with his feasting and his grief. He was as much the child of the New
Learning as Spenser was, but his Puritanism was set deeper
than Spenser's.

In 1638 he went to Italy, the second home of so many of
the English poets, and visited the great towns, making friends
in Florence, where he saw Galileo, and in Rome. At Naples
he heard the sad news of civil war, which determined him to
return; 'inasmuch as I thought it base to be travelling at my
ease for intellectual culture, while my fellow-countrymen at
home were fighting for liberty.' But, hearing that the war
had not yet arisen, he remained in Italy till the end of 1639,
and at the meeting of the Long Parliament we find him in a
house in Aldersgate, where he lived till 1645. He had projected, while abroad, a great epic poem on the subject of
Arthur (again the Welsh subject returns), but in London his
mind changed, and among a number of subjects, tended at
last to *Paradise Lost,* which he meant to throw into the form
of a Greek Tragedy with lyrics and choruses.

MILTON'S PROSE. THE COMMONWEALTH. — Suddenly his
whole life changed, and for twenty years, 1640-1660, he was
carried out of art into politics, out of poetry into prose. Before 1642, when the Civil War began, he had written five
vigorous pamphlets against episcopacy. Six more pamphlets
appeared in the next two years. One of these was the *Areo-*

pagitica, or *Speech for the Liberty of Unlicensed Printing*, 1644, a bold and eloquent attack on the censorship of the press by the Presbyterians. The four pamphlets in which he advocated conditional divorce made him still more the horror of the Presbyterians. When, on the execution of the king, 1649, England became a republic, Milton defended the act in an answer to the *Eikon Basilike*, a portraiture of the sufferings of the king by Dr. Gauden, and continued to defend it in his famous Latin *Defence for the People of England*, 1651, in which he inflicted so pitiless a lashing on Salmasius, the great Leyden scholar, that his fame went over the whole of Europe. In the next year he wholly lost his sight. But he continued his work when Cromwell was made Protector, and wrote another *Defence for the English People*, and a further defence of himself against scurrilous charges. This closed the controversy in 1655.

In the last year of the Protector's life he began the *Paradise Lost*, about the date of the last of his sonnets. The two years that came before the Restoration were employed in a fruitless effort to prevent it by the publication of six more pamphlets. It was a wonder he was not put to death, and he was in hiding and in custody for a time. At last he settled in a house near Bunhill Fields. It was here that *Paradise Lost* was finished, before the end of 1665, and then published in 1667."

"One virtue these pamphlets possess—the virtue of style. They are monuments of our language so remarkable that Milton's prose works must always be resorted to by students as long as English remains a medium of ideas. Putting Bacon aside, the condensed force and poignant brevity of whose aphoristic wisdom has no parallel in English, there is no other prosaist who possesses anything like Milton's command over the resources of our language. Neither Hooker nor Jeremy Taylor impresses the reader with a sense of unlimited power such as we feel to reside in Milton. Vast as is the wealth of magnificent words which he flings with both hands carelessly upon the page, we feel that there is still much more in reserve.

Yet even on the score of style, Milton's prose is subject to serious deductions. His negligence is such as to amount to an absence of construction. He who in his verse trained the sentence with delicate sensibility to follow his guiding hand into exquisite syntax seems in his
prose writing to abandon his meaning to shift for itself. Here Milton
compares disadvantageously with Hooker. Hooker's elaborate sentence,
like the sentence of Demosthenes, is composed of facts so hinged, of
clauses so subordinated to the main thought, that we foresee the end
from the beginning, and close the period with a sense of perfect roundness and totality. Milton does not seem to have any notion of what a
period means. He begins anywhere and leaves off, not when the sense
closes, but when he is out of breath. We might have thought this pell-
mell huddle of his words was explained, if not excused, by the exigen-
cies of the party pamphlet, which cannot wait. But the same asyntactic
disorder is equally found in the *History of Britain*, which he had in
hand for forty years. Nor is it only the Miltonic sentence which is in-
coherent, the whole arrangement of his topics is equally loose, disjointed,
and desultory.

Many of Milton's pamphlets are certainly party pleadings, choleric,
one-sided, personal. But through them all runs the one redeeming char
acteristic—they are all written on the side of liberty. He defended religious liberty against the prelates, civil liberty against the crown, the
liberty of the press against the executive, liberty of conscience against
the Presbyterians, and domestic liberty against the tyranny of canon
law."—*Mark Pattison.*

PARADISE LOST.—" We may perhaps regret that Milton was
shut away from his art for twenty years, during which no verse
was written but the sonnets. But it may be that the poems
he wrote, when the great cause he fought for had closed in
seeming defeat but real victory, gained from its solemn issues
and from the moral grandeur with which he wrought for its
ends their majestic movement, their grand style, and their
grave beauty. During the struggle he had never forgotten
his art. ' I may one day hope,' he said, speaking of his youthful studies, ' to have ye again, in a still time, when there shall
be no chiding; not in these Noises,' and the saying strikes
the note of calm sublimity which is kept in *Paradise Lost.*

It opens with the awaking of the rebel angels in hell after

their fall from heaven, the consultation of their chiefs how best to carry on the war with God, and the resolve of Satan to go forth and tempt newly created man to fall. He takes his flight to the earth and finds Eden. Eden is then described, and Adam and Eve in their innocence. The next four books, from the fifth to the eighth, contain the Arch-angel Raphael's story of the war in heaven, the fall of Satan, and the creation of the world. The last four books describe the temptation and the fall of Man, the vision shown by Michael to Adam of the future and of the redemption of Man by Christ, and the expulsion from Paradise.

The beauty of the poem is rather that of ideal purity, and of sublime thought expressed in language which has the severe loveliness of the best Greek sculpture. The interest collects round the character of Satan at first, but he grows more and more mean as the poem goes on, and seems to fall a second time, to lose all his original brightness, after his temptation of Eve. Indeed this second degradation of Satan after he has not only sinned himself but made innocence sin, and beaten back in himself the last remains of good, is one of the finest motives in the poem. In every part of the poem, in every character in it, as indeed in all his poems, Milton's intense individuality appears. It is a pleasure to find it. The egotism of such a man, said Coleridge, is a revelation of spirit."

"The first of Englishmen to whom the designation *Men of Letters* is appropriate, Milton was also the noblest example of the type. He cultivated not letters but himself, and sought to enter into possession of his own mental kingdom not that he might reign there but that he might royally use its resources in building up a work which should bring honor to his country and his native tongue. The style of *Paradise Lost* is then only the natural expression of a soul thus exquisitely nourished upon the best thoughts and finest words of all ages. It is the language of one who lives in the companionship of the great and the wise of past time. It is inevitable that when such a one speaks, his tones, his accent, the melodies of his rhythm, the inner harmonies of his linked thoughts, the grace of his allusive touch should escape the common ear. To follow Milton one should at least have tasted the same training through which he put himself. The many cannot see it, and complain that the poet is too learned.

Whatever conclusion may be the true one from the public demand, we cannot be wrong in asserting that from the first, and now as then, *Paradise Lost* has been more admired than read. The poet's wish and expectation that he should find 'fit audience though few' has been fulfilled. Partly this has been due to his limitation, his unsympathetic disposition, the deficiency of the human element in his imagination, and his presentation of mythical instead of real beings. But it is also, in part, a tribute to his excellence, and it is to be ascribed to the lofty strain which requires more effort to accompany than an average reader is able to make, a majestic demeanor which no parodist has been able to degrade, and a wealth of allusion demanding more literature than is possessed by any but the few whose life is lived with the poets. An appreciation of Milton is the last reward of consummated scholarship."—*Mark Pattison.*

MILTON'S LATER POEMS.—"It was followed by *Paradise Regained* and *Samson Agonistes*, published together in 1671. *Paradise Regained* opens with the journey of Christ into the wilderness after his baptism, and its four books describe the temptation of Christ by Satan, and the answers and victory of the Redeemer. The speeches in it drown the action, and their learned argument is only relieved by a few descriptions; but these, as in that of Athens, are done with Milton's highest power. The same solemn beauty of a quiet mind and a more severe style than that of *Paradise Lost* make us feel in it that Milton has grown older.

In *Samson Agonistes*, the style is still severer, even to the verge of a harshness which the sublimity alone tends to modify. It is a choral drama, after the Greek model. Samson in his blindness is described, is called on to make sport for the Philistines, and overthrows them in the end. Samson represents the fallen Puritan cause, and his victorious death Milton's hopes for its final triumph. The poem has all the grandeur of the last words of a great man in whom there was now 'calm of mind, all passion spent.' He wrote it blind and old and fallen on evil days. But in it, as in the others, blindness did not prevent sight. No man saw more vividly and could say more vividly what he saw. Nor did age make him lose strength. The force of thought and verse in his last poem is only less than in *Paradise Lost*. Nor did evil days touch his imagination with weakness, or make less the dignity of his art. Till the end it was

> ' An undisturbéd song of pure concent,
> Aye sung before the sapphire-colored throne,
> To Him that sits thereon.'

It ended in his death, November, 1674.

HIS WORK.—To the greatness of the artist, Milton joined the majesty of a pure and lofty character. His poetic style was as lofty as his character, and proceeded from it. Living at a time when criticism began to purify the verse of England, and being himself well acquainted with the great classical models, his work is free from the false conceits and the intemperance of the Elizabethan writers, and yet is as imaginative as theirs, and as various. He has their grace, naturalness, and intensity, when he chooses, and he adds to it a sublime dignity which they did not possess. All the kinds of poetry which he touched he touched with the ease of great strength, and with so much weight that they became new in his hands. He put a new life into the masque, the sonnet, the elegy, the descriptive lyric, the song, the choral drama; and he created the epic in England. The lighter love poem he never wrote, and he kept satire for prose.

In some points he was untrue to his descent from the Elizabethans, for he had no dramatic faculty and he had no humor. He summed up in himself all the higher influences of the Renaissance, and, when they had died in England, revived and handed them to us. His taste was as severe, his verse as polished, his method and language as strict as those of the school of Dryden and Pope that grew up when he was

old.   A literary past and present thus met in him, and, like all
the greatest men, he did not fail to make a cast into the future.
He began that pure poetry of natural description which has
no higher examples to show in Wordsworth or Scott or Keats
than his *L'Allegro* and *Il Penseroso*.   Lastly, he did not
represent in any way the England that followed the tyranny,
the coarseness, the sensuality, the falseness, or the irreligion
of the Stuarts, but he did represent Puritan England, and the
whole career of Puritanism from its cradle to its grave.

THE PILGRIM'S PROGRESS.—With Milton the great Elizabethan age of imaginative poetry and the spirit of the New Learning said their last word.   We might say that Puritanism also
said its last great words with him, were it not that its spirit
lasted in English life, were it not also that four years after his
death, in 1678, JOHN BUNYAN, who had previously written
much, published the *Pilgrim's Progress*.   It is the journey
of Christian, the Pilgrim, from the City of Destruction to the
Celestial City.   The *second part* was published in 1684, and in
1682 the allegory of the *Holy War*.

I class the *Pilgrim's Progress* here, because, in its imaginative fervor and poetry and in its quality of naturalness, it
belongs to the spirit of the Elizabethan times.   It belongs also
to that time in this, that its simple and clear form grew up out
of passionate feeling and not out of self-conscious art.   It is the
people's book and not the book of a literary class, and yet it
lives in literature, because it first revealed the poetry which
fervent belief in a spiritual world can kindle in the rudest
hearts.   In doing this, and in painting the various changes
and feelings of the pilgrim's progress towards God, the book
touched the deepest human interests, and set on foot a new
and plentiful literature.   Its language is the language of the
Bible.   It is a prose allegory conceived as an epic poem.   As
such it admits the vivid dramatic dialogue, the episodes, the
descriptions, and the clear drawing of types of character which

give a different, but an equal, pleasure to a peasant boy and to an intellect like Lord Macaulay's."

" Scholars of wide and critical acquaintance with literature are often unable to acquire an acceptably good, not to say an admirable, style; and, on the other hand, men who can read only their own language, and who have received little instruction even in that, often write and speak in a style that wins or commands attention, and in itself gives pleasure. Of these men John Bunyan is, perhaps, the most marked example. Better English there could hardly be, or a style more admirable for every excellence, than appears throughout the writings of that tinker. No person who has read *The Pilgrim's Progress* can have forgotten the fight of Christian with Apollyon, which, for vividness of description and dramatic interest, puts to shame all the combats with knights and giants and men and dragons that can be found elsewhere in romance or poetry; but there are probably many who do not remember, and not a few, perhaps, who, in the very enjoyment of it, did not notice, the clearness, the spirit, the strength, and the simple beauty of the style in which that passage is written. For example, take the sentence which tells of the beginning of the fight:—

' Then Apollyon straddled quite over the whole breadth of the way, and said, I am void of fear in this matter; prepare thyself to die; for I swear by my infernal Den that thou shalt go no further: here will I spill thy soul.'

A man cannot be taught to write like that, nor can he by any study learn the mystery of such a style."—*R. G. White.*

BIBLIOGRAPHY. MILTON.—D. Masson's *Life* of; *English Men of Letters* Series; W. E. Channing's *Char. and Writings* of; De Quincey's *Essays;* S. Johnson's *Lives of Eng. Poets*; R. W. Emerson in *Characteristics of Men of Gen.;* Macaulay's *Essays;* Brydges' *Imaginative Biography;* P. Bayne's *Essays;* W. Hazlitt's *Sonnets* of; F. D. Maurice's *Friendship of Books;* J. R. Seeley's *Politics and Poetry* of, in his *Rom. Imperialism;* Addison's *Essays* in Spectator, published in pamphlet; Ward's *Anthology;* Lowell's *Among my Books,* 2d Ser.; Ecl. Mag., Nov., 1849; Apr., 1852; and Nov., 1853.

BUNYAN.—*Eng. Men of Let.* Series; J. Tulloch's *Eng. Puritanism and its Leaders;* Macaulay's *Essays:* J. Baillie's *Life Studies;* Ecl. Mag., July, 1851; and May, 1852.

LESSON 32.

From Milton's *Areopagitica*.

Truth indeed came once into the world with her divine Master, and was a perfect shape, most glorious to look on; but, when he ascended, and his apostles after him were laid asleep, then straight arose a wicked race of deceivers, who, as that story goes of the Egyptian Typhon[1] with his conspirators, how they dealt with the good Osiris, took the virgin Truth, hewed her lovely form into a thousand pieces, and scattered them to the four winds. From that time ever since, the sad friends of truth, such as durst appear, imitating the careful search that Isis[2] made for the mangled body of Osiris, went up and down gathering up limb by limb still as they could find them. We have not yet found them all, Lords and Commons,[3] nor ever shall do till her Master's second coming; he shall bring together every joint and member, and shall mould them into an immortal feature of loveliness and perfection. Suffer not these licensing prohibitions[4] to stand at every place of opportunity, forbidding and disturbing them that continue seeking, that continue to do our obsequies to the torn body of our martyred saint.

We boast our light; but, if we look not wisely on the sun itself, it smites us into darkness. Who can discern those planets that are oft combust,[5] and those stars of brightest magnitude that rise and set with the sun, until the opposite motion of their orbs brings them to such a place in the firmament where they may be seen evening or morning? The light which we have gained was given us not to be ever staring on, but by it to discover onward things more remote from our knowledge. It is not the unfrocking of a priest, the unmitring of a bishop and the removing him from off the Presbyterian shoulders that will make us a happy nation; no, if other things as great in the church and in the rule of life, both economical and political, be not looked into and reformed, we have looked so long upon the blaze that Zwinglius[6] and Calvin[6] hath beaconed up to us that we are stark blind.

There be who perpetually complain of schisms and sects, and make it such a calamity that any man dissents from their maxims. 'Tis their own pride and ignorance which causes the disturbing, who neither will

---

[1] Brother to the Egyptian god Osiris, who was venerated under the form of a bull, whom Typhon killed, and whose body he cut into twenty-six pieces. [2] Sister and spouse of Osiris. [3] The pamphlet was addressed to Parliament. [4] An official license was needed for the publication of any book. [5] Burning. [6] Reformers—the one a Swiss, the other a Frenchman.

hear with meekness nor can convince, yet all must be suppressed which is not found in their *syntagma*.[1] They are the troublers, they are the dividers of unity who neglect and permit not others to unite those dissevered pieces which are yet wanting to the body of truth. To be still searching what we know not by what we know, still closing up truth to truth as we find it—for all her body is homogeneal and proportional—this is the golden rule in theology as well as in arithmetic, and makes up the best harmony in a church; not the forced and outward union of cold and neutral and inwardly divided minds.

Behold now this vast City,[2] a city of refuge, the mansion house of liberty, encompassed and surrounded with God's protection; the shop of war hath not there more anvils and hammers waking to fashion out the plates and instruments of armed justice in defence of beleagured truth than there be pens and heads there, sitting by their studious lamps, musing, searching, revolving new notions and ideas wherewith to present, as with their homage and their fealty, the approaching reformation; others as fast reading, trying all things, assenting to the force of reason and convincement. What could a man require more from a nation so pliant and so prone to seek after knowledge? What wants there to such a towardly[3] and pregnant soil but wise and faithful laborers to make a knowing people, a nation of prophets, of sages, and of worthies? We reckon more than five months yet to harvest; there need not be five weeks; had we but eyes to lift up, the fields are white already.

Where there is much desire to learn, there of necessity will be much arguing, much writing, many opinions; for opinion in good men is but knowledge in the making. A little generous prudence, a little forbearance of one another, and some grain of charity might win all these diligences to join and unite in one general and brotherly search after truth. I doubt not, if some great and worthy stranger should come among us, wise to discern the mould and temper of a people and how to govern it, observing the high hopes and aims, the diligent alacrity of our extended thoughts and reasonings in the pursuance of truth and freedom, but that he would cry out as Pirrhus[4] did, admiring the Roman docility and courage, If such were my Epirots, I would not despair the greatest design that could be attempted to make a church or kingdom happy.

Yet these are the men cried out against for schismatics and sectaries; as if, while the temple of the Lord was building, some cutting, some

---

[1] Works. [2] London. [3] Favoring. [4] King of Epirus, invited into Italy to aid the Tarentines against Rome.

squaring the marble, others hewing the cedars, there should be a sort of irrational men who could not consider there must be many schisms and many dissections made in the quarry and in the timber ere the house of God can be built. And when every stone is laid artfully[1] together, it cannot be united into a continuity, it can but be contiguous in this world; neither can every piece of the building be of one form; nay rather the perfection consists in this, that out of many moderate varieties and brotherly dissimilitudes, that are not vastly disproportional, arises the goodly and the graceful symmetry that commends the whole pile and structure. . . . . .

Methinks I see in my mind a noble and puissant Nation rousing herself like a strong man[2] after sleep, and shaking her invincible locks. Methinks I see her as an eagle mewing her mighty youth, and kindling her undazzled eyes at the full midday beam; purging and unsealing her long-abused sight at the fountain itself of heavenly radiance, while the whole noise of timorous and flocking birds, with those also that love the twilight, flutter about amazed at what she means, and in their envious gabble would prognosticate a year of sects and schisms.

From Bunyan's *Pilgrim's Progress*.

I beheld, then, that they all went on till they came at the foot of the hill *Difficulty*, at the bottom of which was a spring. There were also in the same place two other ways besides that which came straight from the Gate; one turned to the left hand, and the other to the right, at the bottom of the hill; but the narrow way lay right up the hill; and the name of the going up the side of the hill is called *Difficulty*. Christian now went to the spring, and drank thereof to refresh himself, and then he began to go up the hill.

The other two also came to the foot of the hill; but when they saw that the hill was steep and high, and that there were two other ways to go, and supposing also that these two ways might meet again with that up which Christian went, on the other side of the hill, therefore they were resolved to go in those ways. Now, the name of one of those was *Danger*, and the name of the other *Destruction*. So the one took the way which is called Danger, which led him into a great wood; and the other took directly up the way to Destruction, which led him into a wide field, full of dark mountains, where he stumbled and fell and rose no more.

I looked then after Christian to see him go up the hill, where I perceived he fell from running to going,[3] and from going to clambering

---

[1] With art.   [2] The allusion is to Samson.   [3] Walking.

upon his hands and his knees, because of the steepness of the place. Now, about the mid-way to the top of the hill was a pleasant arbor, made by the Lord of the hill, for the refreshment of weary travellers; thither, therefore, Christian got, where also he sat down to rest him. Then he pulled his Roll out of his bosom and read therein to his comfort; he also now began afresh to take a review of the coat or garment that was given to him as he stood by the Cross. Thus pleasing himself a while, he at last fell into a slumber, and thence into a fast sleep, which detained him in that place until it was almost night; and in his sleep his Roll fell out of his hand. Now, as he was sleeping, there came one to him, and awaked him, saying, "Go to the ant, thou sluggard, consider her ways, and be wise;" and with that, Christian suddenly started up, and sped him on his way, and went apace till he came to the top of the hill.

Now, when he was got up to the top of the hill, there came two men running to meet him again; the name of the one was *Timorous*, and of the other *Mistrust ;* to whom Christian said, Sirs, what's the matter? you run the wrong way. Timorous answered that they were going to the city of Zion, and had got up that difficult place; but said he, The farther we go, the more danger we meet with; wherefore we turned, and are going back again.

Yes, said Mistrust, for just before us lie a couple of Lions in the way, whether sleeping or waking we know not; and we could not think, if we came within reach, but they would presently pull us in pieces.

Then said Christian, You make me afraid; but whither shall I flee to be safe? If I go back to my own country, that is prepared for fire and brimstone, and I shall certainly perish there; if I can get to the Celestial City, I am sure to be in safety there. I must venture: to go back is nothing but death; to go forward is fear of death, and life everlasting beyond it: I will yet go forward. So Mistrust and Timorous ran down the hill and Christian went on his way. But, thinking again of what he had heard from the men, he felt in his bosom for his Roll that he might read therein and be comforted; but he felt and found it not. Then was Christian in great distress, and knew not what to do; for he wanted that which used to relieve him, and that which should have been his pass into the Celestial City. Here, therefore, he began to be much perplexed, and knew not what to do: at last he bethought himself that he had slept in the arbor that is on the side of the hill; and, falling down upon his knees, he asked God's forgiveness for that foolish fact, and then went back to look for his Roll. But all the way back who can sufficiently set forth the sorrow of Christian's heart? Sometimes he sighed, sometimes he wept, and oftentimes he chid himself for being so foolish to fall asleep in that place which was erected only for a little refreshment for his weariness. Thus, therefore, he went back, carefully looking on this side and on that, all the way as he went, if happily he might find his Roll that had been his comfort so many times in his journey. He went thus till he came again within sight of the arbor where he sat and slept; but that sight renewed his sorrow the more by bringing again, even afresh, his evil of sleeping into his mind. Thus, therefore, he now went on, bewailing his sinful sleep, saying, O wretched man that I am! that I should sleep in the daytime! that I should sleep in the midst of difficulty! that I should so indulge the flesh as to use that rest for ease to my flesh which the Lord of the hill hath erected only for the relief of the spirits of pilgrims!

Now by this time he was come to the arbor again, where for a while he sat down and wept; but at last, looking sorrowfully down under the settle, there he espied his Roll; the which he with trembling and haste catched up and put into his bosom. But who can tell how joyful this man was when he had gotten his Roll again! for this Roll was the assurance of his life and acceptance at the desired haven. Therefore he laid it up in his bosom, gave thanks to God for directing his eye to the place where it lay, and with joy and tears betook himself again to his journey. But O how nimbly did he go up the rest of the hill! Yet, before he got up, the sun went down upon Christian; and this made him again recall the vanity of his sleeping to his remembrance. I must walk without the sun, darkness must cover the path of my feet, and I must hear the noise of the doleful creatures because of my sinful sleep! Now also he remembered the story that Mistrust and Timorous told him, of how they were frighted with the sight of the Lions. Then said Christian to himself again, These beasts range in the night for their prey, and if they should meet with me in the dark, how should I shift them? How should I escape being by them torn in pieces? Thus he went on; but while he was thus bewailing his unhappy miscarriage, he lift up his eyes, and behold there was a very stately palace before him, the name of which was *Beautiful;* and it stood just by the highway side.

So I saw in my dream that he made haste and went forward that, if possible, he might get lodging there. Now, before he had gone far, he entered into a very narrow passage which was about a furlong off of the porter's lodge; and, looking very narrowly before him as he went, he espied two lions in the way. Then he was afraid, for he thought nothing but death was before him; but the Porter at the lodge, whose name is *Watchful*, perceiving that Christian made a halt as if he would go back, cried unto him saying, Is thy strength so small? Fear not the Lions, for they are chained, and are placed there for a trial of faith where it is, and for discovery of those that have none; keep in the midst of the path, and no hurt shall come unto thee.

Then I saw that he went on, trembling for fear of the Lions; but, taking good heed to the directions of the Porter, he heard them roar, but they did him no harm. Then he clapped his hands, and went on till he came and stood before the gate where the Porter was. Then said Christian to the Porter, Sir, what house is this? and may I lodge here to-night? The Porter answered, This house was built by the Lord of the hill, and he built it for the relief and security of pilgrims. The Porter also asked whence he was and whither he was going.

Chr. I am come from the city of Destruction, and am going to Mount Zion; but, because the sun is now set, I desire, if I may, to lodge here to-night.

Por. But how doth it happen that you come so late? The sun is set.

Chr. I had been here sooner, but that, wretched man that I am, I slept in the arbor that stands on the hill-side. Nay, I had notwithstanding that been here much sooner, but that in my sleep I lost my Evidence, and came without it to the brow of the hill; and then feeling for it and not finding it, I was forced, with sorrow of heart, to go back to the place where I slept my sleep; where I found it, and now am come.

Por. Well, I will call out one of the Virgins of this place who will, if she likes your talk, bring you in to the rest of the family, according to the rules of the house. So Watchful, the Porter, rang a bell, at the sound of which came out of the door of the house a grave and beautiful damsel, named *Discretion*, and asked why she was called.

The Porter answered, This man is on a journey from the city of Destruction to Mount Zion, but, being weary and benighted, he asked me if he might lodge here to-night.

Then she asked him whence he was and whither he was going; and he told her. She asked him also how he got into the way; and he told her. Then she asked him what he had seen and met with in the way; and he told her. And at last she asked his name. So he said, It is Christian; and I have so much the more a desire to lodge here to-night, because, by what I perceive, this place was built by the Lord of the hill for the relief and security of pilgrims. So she smiled, but the water stood in her eyes; and, after a little pause, she said, I will call forth two or three more of the family. So she ran to the door and called out Prudence, Piety, and Charity, who, after a little more discourse with him, had him in to the family; and many of them meeting him at the threshold of the house, said, Come in, thou blessed of the Lord; this house was built by the Lord of the hill on purpose to entertain such pilgrims in. Then he bowed his head, and followed them into the house.

LESSON 33.

Milton's *Hymn on the Nativity*.

It was the winter wild,
While the heaven-born child
All meanly wrapt in the rude manger lies;
Nature, in awe to him,
Had doffed her gaudy trim,
With her great Master so to sympathize:
It was no season then for her
To wanton with the Sun, her lusty paramour.

Only with speeches fair
She woos the gentle air
To hide her guilty front with innocent snow;
And, on her naked shame,
Pollute with sinful blame,
The saintly veil of maiden white to throw;
Confounded, that her Maker's eyes
Should look so near upon her foul deformities.

But he, her fears to cease,
Sent down the meek-eyed Peace;
She, crowned with olive green, came softly sliding
Down through the turning sphere,
His ready harbinger,
With turtle wing the amorous clouds dividing;
And, waving wide her myrtle wand,
She strikes a universal peace through sea and land.

No war or battle's sound
Was heard the world around;
The idle spear and shield were high uphung;
The hookèd chariot stood
Unstained with hostile blood;
The trumpet spake not to the armèd throng;
And kings sat still with awful eye,
As if they surely knew their sovran[1] Lord was by.

---

[1] Sovereign.

But peaceful was the night
Wherein the Prince of Light
His reign of peace upon the earth began.
The winds, with wonder whist,
Smoothly the waters kissed,
Whispering new joys to the mild Ocean,
Who now hath quite forgot to rave,
While birds of calm sit brooding on the charmèd wave.

The stars, with deep amaze,
Stand fixed in steadfast gaze,
Bending one way their precious influence;
And will not take their flight,
For all the morning light,
Or Lucifer[1] that often warned them thence;
But in their glimmering orbs did glow,
Until their Lord himself bespake, and bid them go.

And, though the shady gloom
Had given day her room,
The Sun himself withheld his wonted speed,
And hid his head for shame,
As his inferior flame
The new-enlightened world no more should need;
He saw a greater Sun appear
Than his bright throne or burning axletree could bear.

The shepherds on the lawn,
Or ere the point of dawn,
Sat simply chatting in a rustic row:
Full little thought they than[2]
That the mighty Pan[3]
Was kindly come to live with them below;
Perhaps their loves or else their sheep
Were all that did their silly thoughts so busy keep.

When such music sweet
Their hearts and ears did greet
As never was by mortal fingers strook;

---

[1] The morning star.   [2] Then.   [3] The pastoral god of Grecian mythology.

Divinely-warbled voice
Answering the stringèd noise,
As all their souls in blissful rapture took:
The air, such pleasure loth to lose,
With thousand echoes still prolongs each heavenly close.

Nature, that heard such sound
Beneath the hollow round
Of Cynthia's[1] seat the airy region thrilling,
Now was almost won
To think her part was done,
And that her reign had here its last fulfilling:
She knew such harmony alone
Could hold all heaven and earth in happier union.

At last surrounds their sight
A globe of circular light,
That with long beams the shame-faced Night arrayed;
The helmèd cherubim
And swordèd seraphim
Are seen in glittering ranks with wings displayed,
Harping in loud and solemn quire,
With unexpressive notes, to Heaven's new-born heir,

Such music as, 'tis said,
Before was never made,
But when of old the sons of morning sung
While the Creator great
His constellations set,
And the well-balanced world on hinges hung,
And cast the dark foundations deep,
And bid the weltering waves their oozy channel keep.

Ring out, ye crystal spheres!
Once bless our human ears,
If ye have power to touch our senses so;
And let your silver chime
Move in melodious time;
And let the bass of heaven's deep organ blow;
And with your ninefold harmony
Make up full consort to the angelic symphony.

---

[1] The moon's.

For, if such holy song
Enwrap our fancy long,
Time will run back, and fetch the age of gold;
And speckled Vanity
Will sicken soon and die,
And leprous Sin will melt from earthly mould;
And Hell itself will pass away,
And leave her dolorous mansions to the peering day.

Yea, Truth and Justice then
Will down return to men,
Orbed in a rainbow; and, like glories wearing,
Mercy will sit between,
Throned in celestial sheen,
With radiant feet the tissued clouds down steering;
And Heaven, as at some festival,
Will open wide the gates of her high palace-hall.

But wisest Fate says, No,
This must not yet be so;
The Babe yet lies in smiling infancy
That on the bitter cross
Must redeem our loss,
So both himself and us to glorify:
Yet first, to those ychained in sleep,
The wakeful trump of doom must thunder through the deep,

With such a horrid clang
As on Mount Sinai rang,
While the red fire and smouldering clouds outbrake:
The agèd Earth, aghast
With terror of that blast,
Shall from the surface to the centre shake,
When, at the world's last session,
The dreadful Judge in middle air shall spread his throne.

And then at last our bliss
Full and perfect is,
But now begins; for, from this happy day,
The old dragon under ground,
In straiter limits bound,
Not half so far casts his usurpèd sway;

And, wroth to see his kingdom fail,
Swinges[1] the scaly horror of his folded tail.

The oracles are dumb;
No voice or hideous hum
Runs through the archèd roof in words deceiving.
Apollo[2] from his shrine
Can no more divine,
With hollow shriek the steep of Delphos leaving.
No nightly trance or breathèd spell
Inspires the pale-eyed priest from the prophetic cell.

The lonely mountains o'er
And the resounding shore
A voice of weeping heard and loud lament;
From haunted spring, and dale
Edgèd with poplar pale,
The parting Genius is with sighing sent;
With flower-inwoven tresses torn,
The nymphs in twilight shade of tangled thickets mourn.

In consecrated earth
And on the holy hearth,
The Lars[3] and Lemures[3] mourn with midnight plaint.
In urns and altars round,
A drear and dying sound
Affrights the flamens[4] at their service quaint;
And the chill marble seems to sweat,
While each peculiar power forgoes his wonted seat.

Peor[5] and Baälim[6]
Forsake their temples dim,
With that twice-battered god of Palestine;
And moonèd Ashtaroth,[6]
Heaven's queen and mother both,
Now sits not girt with tapers' holy shine;
The Libyc Hammon[7] shrinks his horn;
In vain the Tyrian maids their wounded Thammuz[8] mourn.

---

[1] To move as a lash.   [2] A Grecian divinity whose temple was at Delphi.   [3] Ghosts of the dead.   [4] Priests.   [5] The national god of the Moabites, it is thought.   [6] Plural nouns denoting the gods and goddesses of Syria and Palestine.   [7] Jupiter, as worshipped in Libya. His statue there had the head and horns of a ram.   [8] A Phœnician god.

And sullen Moloch,[1] fled,
Hath left in shadows dread
His burning idol all of blackest hue;
In vain with cymbals' ring
They call the grisly king,
In dismal dance about the furnace blue,
The brutish gods of Nile as fast,
Isis and Orus and the dog Anubis, haste.

Nor is Osiris seen
In Memphian grove or green,
Trampling the unshowered grass with lowings loud;
Nor can he be at rest
Within his sacred chest;
Nought but profoundest hell can be his shroud;
In vain, with timbreled anthems dark,
The sable-stolèd sorcerers bear his worshiped ark.

He feels from Juda's land
The dreaded Infant's hand;
The rays of Bethlehem blind his dusky eyn;[2]
Nor all the gods beside
Longer dare abide,
Not Typhon huge ending in snaky twine:
Our Babe, to show his Godhead true,
Can in his swaddling bands control the damnèd crew.

So, when the Sun in bed,
Curtained with cloudy red,
Pillows his chin upon an orient wave,
The flocking shadows pale
Troop to the infernal jail,
Each fettered ghost slips to his several grave;
And the yellow-skirted fays
Fly after the night-steeds, leaving their moon-loved maze.

But see! the Virgin blest
Hath laid her Babe to rest.
Time is our tedious song should here have ending:

---

[1] National god of the Ammonites.   [2] Eyes.

Heaven's youngest-teemèd star
Hath fixed her polished car,
Her sleeping Lord with handmaid lamp attending;
And all about the courtly stable
Bright-harnessed angels sit in order serviceable.

FURTHER READING.—*L'Allegro* and *Il Penseroso* (in pamphlet form, by Clark & Maynard, as also the whole of Bk. I. of *Paradise Lost*). Of *Paradise Lost* read Bk. I., ll. 1-74; 242-330. Bk. II., 50-467; 629-883. Bk. III., 1-55. Bk. IV., 411-735. Bk. V., 153-208. Bk. VI., 171-353; 507-669; 824-892. Bk. VIII., 452-559; 618-753. Bk. IX., 205-392; 494-795. Bk. X., 845-965. Bk. XI., 226-285. Bk. XII., 606-649.

SCHEME FOR REVIEW.

PERIOD VI.

From the Restoration to Swift's Death, 1660–1745.

LESSON 34.

Brief Historical Sketch.—House of Stuart restored in the person of Charles II., 1660. Twenty-eight of the Regicides arraigned, and thirteen executed. Tea introduced, 1662. Royal Society chartered, same year. First newspaper, the Public Intelligencer, 1663. Star Chamber, monopolies, and Court of High Commission not restored. Sole right of Parliament to grant supplies to the Crown not disputed. Secret treaty made with France, by which Charles II. became a pensioner of Louis XIV. Great Plague in London, 1665–6. Great Fire, 1666. Titus Oates' affair, the "Popish Plot," 1678. Habeas Corpus act passed, 1679. Rye-House Plot, 1682. Accession of Jas. II., 1685. Revocation of Edict of Nantes, 1685. Invasion of England and of Scotland by Monmouth and Argyle, same year. Jeffreys' bloody assizes follow. Quarrel of the king with the two Universities and Declaration of Indulgence, 1687. Trial of the seven bishops for petitioning to be excused from ordering the Declaration to be read in the churches, 1688. Revolution, by which Wm. of Orange and Mary came to the English throne made vacant by the flight of James, 1688. Grand Alliance of England, Austria, Spain, and the Netherlands against France formed by William, 1689. Irish subdued, 1690. White paper manufactured in England, same year. The Ministry becomes what it is now, the executive committee of the majority of the House of Commons. Bank of England established, 1694. National Debt, 1697, £5,000,000. Second Grand Alliance of England, Holland, Hanover, and Austria, joined afterward by Prussia, the German Empire, and Portugal, is formed by William, and begins, 1702, the War of the Spanish Succession. Marlborough in command of the allied forces. Anne comes to the throne, 1702. National Debt, 1703, £14,000,000. England and Scotland united, 1707. About 1709 first daily newspaper established.   Impeachment of Dr. Sacheverell, 1709–10. Marlborough and the Whig party fall, and Oxford and Bolingbroke come into power, 1710.   Crown, during the reigns of Wm. III. and Anne, becomes less personal and more official.   Veto on bills practically given up, last exercised, 1707.   War of the Spanish Succession closed by the treaty of Utrecht, 1713.   National Debt, 1714, £54,000,000 (now £800,000,000).   George I., founder of the House of Hanover, comes to the throne, 1714.   Invasion by the Pretender, son of Jas. II., 1715. Bolingbroke and Oxford impeached, 1715.   South Sea Company established 1711, fails 1720.   Sir Robt. Walpole Prime Minister, 1721–42. A great Peace Minister, removed the duties from more than 100 articles of export and from 30 of import.   George II. comes to the throne, 1727. Methodism founded, at first within the Church, 1727–9.   Separation of Methodism from the Church, 1738.   Five great hospitals established, 1719–45.

LESSON 35.

POETRY.   CHANGE OF STYLE.—"We have seen the natural style, as distinguished from the artificial, in the Elizabethan poets.   Style became not only natural but artistic when it was used by a great genius like Shakespeare or Spenser, for a first rate poet creates rules of art ; his work itself is art.   But when the art of poetry is making, its rules are not laid down, and the second rate poets, inspired only by their feelings, will write in a natural style unrestrained by rules; that is, they will put their feelings into verse without caring much for the form in which they do it.   As long as they live in the midst of a youthful national life, and feel an ardent sympathy with it, their style will be fresh and impassioned, and give pleasure because of the strong feeling that inspires it.   But it will also be extravagant and unrestrained in its use of images and words because of its want of art.   This is the history of the style of the poets of the middle period of Elizabeth's reign.

Afterwards the national life grew chill, and the feelings of the poets also chilled.   Then the want of art in the style made itself felt.   The far-fetched images, the hazarded meanings, the over-fanciful way of putting thoughts, the sensational ex-pression of feeling in which the Elizabethan poets indulged not only appeared in all their ugliness, when they were inspired by no warm feeling, but were indulged in far more than be-fore. Men tried to produce by extravagant use of words the same results that living feeling had produced, and the more they failed, the more extravagant and fantastic they became, till at last their poetry ceased to have clear meaning. This is the history of the style of the poets from the later days of Elizabeth till the Civil War.

The natural style, unregulated by art, had thus become un-natural. When it had reached that point, men began to feel how necessary it was that the style of poetry should be sub-jected to the rules of art, and two influences partly caused and partly supported this desire. One was the influence of Milton. Milton, first by his genius, which, as I said, creates of itself an artistic style, and secondly by his knowledge and imitation of the great classical models, was able to give the first example in England of a pure, grand, and finished style, and in blank-verse and the sonnet wrote for the first time with absolute correctness. Another influence was that of the movement all over Europe towards inquiry into the right way of doing things, and into the truth of things, a movement we shall soon see at work in science, politics, and religion. In poetry it produced a school of criticism which first took form in France, and the influence of Boileau, La Fontaine, and others who were striving after greater finish and neatness of expression told on England now. It is an influence which has been ex-aggerated. It is absurd to place the 'creaking lyre' of Boileau side by side with Dryden's 'long resounding march and energy divine' of verse. Our critical school of poets have no French qualities in them even when they imitate the French.

Further, our own poets had already, before the Restoration, begun the critical work, and the French influence served only to give it a greater impulse. We shall see the growth of a colder and more correct spirit of art in Cowley, Denham, and Waller. Vigorous form was given to that spirit by Dryden, and perfection of artifice added to it by Pope. The *artificial* style succeeded to, and extinguished, the *natural*."

" During the period now under review, the whole of English literary effort, but especially poetical effort, has one aim and is governed by one principle. This is the desire to attain perfection of form, a sense of the beauty of literary composition as such. It was found to be possible to please by your manner as well as by your matter, and having been shown to be possible, it became necessary. No writer who neglected the graces of style could gain acceptance by the public.

If this definition of the literary aim which dominated all writing during the hundred years which followed 1660 be just, it follows from it that the period would be more favorable to prose than to poetry. What in fact came to pass was, that a compromise was effected between poetry and prose, and the leading writers adopted, as the most telling form of utterance, prosaic verse, metre without poetry. It is by courtesy that the versifiers of this century from Dryden to Churchill are styled poets. They wanted inspiration, lofty sentiment, the heroic soul, chivalrous devotion, the inner eye of faith—above all, love and sympathy. They could not mean greatly. But such meaning as they had they labored to express in the neatest, most terse and pointed form which our language is capable of. If not poets, they were literary artists."—*Mark Pattison.*

CHANGE OF POETIC SUBJECT.—" The subject of the Elizabethan poets was Man as influenced by the *Passions,* and it was treated from the side of natural feeling. This was fully and splendidly done by Shakespeare. But after a time the subject followed, as we have seen in speaking of the drama, the same career as the style. It was treated in an extravagant and sensational manner, and the representation of the passions tended to become, and did become, unnatural or fantastic. Milton alone redeemed the subject from this vicious excess. He wrote in a grave and natural manner of the passions of the human heart, and he made strong the religious passions of love of God, sorrow for sin, and others, in English poetry. But with him the subject of man as influenced by the passions died for a time. Dryden, Pope, and their followers turned to another. They left the passions aside, and wrote of the things in which the intellect and the conscience, the social and political instincts in man were interested. In this way the satiric, didactic, philosophical, and party poetry of a new school arose.

TRANSITION POETS.—There were a few poets, writing partly before and partly after the Restoration, who represent the passage from the fantastic to the more correct style. ABRAHAM COWLEY was one of these. His love poems, *The Mistress*, 1647, are courtly, witty, and have some of the Elizabethan imagination. His later poems, owing probably to his life in France, were more exact in verse, and more cold in form. The same may be said of EDMUND WALLER, who 'first made writing in rhyme easily an art.' He also lived a long time in France, and died in 1687. SIR JNO. DENHAM's *Cooper's Hill*, 1643, was a favorite with Dryden for the 'majesty of its style.' It may rank as one of the first of our descriptive poems, and its didactic reflectiveness and the chill stream of its verse and thought link him closely to Pope. SIR W. DAVENANT'S *Gondibert*, 1651, a heroic poem, is perhaps the most striking example of this transition. Worthless as poetry, it represents the new interest in political philosophy and in science that was arising, and preludes the intellectual poetry. Its preface discourses of rhyme and the rules of art, and represents the new critical influence which came over with the exiled court from France. The critical school had, therefore, begun even before Dryden's poems were written. The change was less sudden than it seemed.

Satiric poetry, soon to become a greater thing, was made during this transition time into a powerful weapon by two men, each on a different side. ANDREW MARVELL's *Satires*, after the Restoration, represent the Puritan's wrath with the vices of the court and king, and his shame for the disgrace of England among the nations.   The *Hudibras* of Samuel Butler, in 1663, represents the fierce reaction which had set in against Puritanism.   It is justly famed for wit, learning, good sense, and ingenious drollery, and, in accordance with the new criticism, it is absolutely without obscurity.   It is often as terse as Pope's best work.   But it is too long, its wit wearies us at last, and it undoes the force of its attack on the Puritans, by its exaggeration.   Satire should have at least the semblance of truth; yet Butler calls the Puritans cowards.   We turn now to the first of these poets in whom poetry is founded on intellect rather than on feeling, and whose best verse is devoted to argument and satire."

Bibliographa.   Cowley, Waller, and Butler.—R. Bell's and S. Johnson's *Lives Eng. Poets;* Ward's *Anthology;* Minto's *Man. Eng. Prose Lit.;* J. Coleman's *Hist. Essays;* Bentley's Miscel., v. 37, 1855; N. A. Rev., v. 91, 1860; N. Br. Rev., v. 24, 1855-6, and v. 43, 1865; Fraser's Mag., v. 53, 1856.

Lesson 36.

John Dryden.—"He was the first of the new, as Milton was the last of the elder, school of poetry.   It was late in life that he gained fame.   Born in 1631, he was a Cromwellite till the Restoration, when he began the changes which mark his life.   His poem on the death of the Protector was soon followed by the *Astræa Redux,* which celebrated the return of justice to the realm in the person of Charles II.   The *Annus Mirabilis* appeared in 1667, and in this his great power was first clearly shown.   It is the power of clear reasoning expressing itself with entire ease in a rapid succession of condensed thoughts in verse.   Such a power fitted Dryden for satire, and his *Absalom and Ahitophel* is the foremost of English satires.

He had been a playwriter till its appearance in 1681, and the rhymed plays which he had written enabled him to perfect the versification which is so remarkable in it and the poems that followed.   The satire itself, written in mockery of the Popish Plot and the Exclusion Bill, attacked Shaftesbury as Ahitophel, was kind to Monmouth as Absalom, and, in its sketch of Buckingham as Zimri, the poet avenged himself for the *Rehearsal*. It was the first fine example of that party poetry which became still more bitter and personal in the hands of Pope. It was followed by the *Medal*, a new attack on Shaftesbury, and the *Mac Flecknoe*, in which Shadwell, a rival poet, who had supported Shaftesbury's party, was made a laughing-stock. After these, Dryden taught theology in verse, and the *Religio Laici*, 1682, defends, and states the argument for, the Church of England. It was perhaps poverty that drove him, on the accession of James II., to change his religion, and the *Hind and Panther*, 1687, is as fine a model of clear reasoning in behalf of the milk-white hind of the Church of Rome as the *Religio Laici* was in behalf of the Church of England, which now becomes the spotted panther.

As a narrative poet his fables and translations, produced late in life, in 1700, give him a high rank, though the fine harmony of their verse does not win us to forget their coarseness, and their lack of that skill in arranging a story which comes from imaginative feeling.

As a lyric poet his fame rests on the animated *Ode for St. Cecilia's Day*. His translation of *Vergil* has fire, but wants the dignity and tenderness of the original. From Milton's death till his own, in 1700, Dryden reigned undisputed, and round his throne in Will's Coffeehouse, where he sat as 'Glorious John,' we may place the names of the lesser poets, the Earls of Dorset, Roscommon, and Mulgrave, Sir Charles Sedley, and the Earl of Rochester. The lighter poetry of the court lived on in the last two. JOHN OLDHAM won a short fame by his *Satires on the Jesuits*, 1679; and BISHOP KEN, 1668, set on foot, in his *Morning and Evening Hymns*, a new type of religious poetry."

" Of the best English poetry it might be said that it is understanding aërated by imagination. In Dryden the solid part too often refused to mix kindly with the leaven, either remaining lumpish, or rising to a hasty puffiness. Grace and lightness were with him much more a laborious achievement than a natural gift, and it is all the more remarkable that he should so often have attained to what seems such an easy perfection in both. He was not wholly and unconsciously a poet, but a thinker who sometimes lost himself on enchanted ground, and was transfigured by its touch.

This preponderance in him of the reasoning over the intuitive faculties, the one always there, the other flashing in when you least expect it, accounts for that inequality and even incongruousness in his writing which makes one revise his judgment at every tenth page. In his prose you come upon passages that persuade you he is a poet, in spite of his verses' so often turning state's evidence against him as to convince you he is none. Now and then we come upon something that makes us hesitate again whether, after all, Dryden was not grandiose rather than great. He is best upon a level, table land it is true, and a very high level, but still somewhere between the loftier peaks of inspiration and the plain of every day life. As I read him, I cannot help thinking of an ostrich, to be classed with flying things and capable, what with leap and flap together, of leaving the earth for a longer or shorter space, but loving the open plain, where wing and foot help each other to something that is both flight and run at once.

We always feel his epoch in him, that he was the lock which let our language down from its point of highest poetry to its level of easiest and most gently flowing prose."— *J. R. Lowell.*

THE DRAMA.—" The change that now passed over literature was as great in the drama as in poetry. Two acting companies were formed on the king's return, under Thomas Killigrew and Davenant; actresses came upon the stage for the first time, and scenery began to be used. Dryden began his dramatic work with comedies, 1663, but soon after, following Corneille, though he abjured French influence, made rhyme, instead of blank-verse, the vehicle of tragedy. His tragedies, like the rest of the time, were written in a pompous heroic style. The DUKE OF BUCKINGHAM ridiculed them in the *Rehearsal*, 1671, and sometime after Dryden changed his style, and wrote in another manner, of which *All for Love* and the *Spanish Friar*, are perhaps the best examples. His plays have but little sentiment, for Dryden's treatment of the emotions is al-

ways brutal, but they have some neat intrigue, some fine passages. JOHN CROWNE'S *Sir Courtly Nice*, NAT LEE'S *Rival
Queens*, and two pathetic tragedies by THOMAS OTWAY, *The
Orphan* and *Venice Preserved*, are of the Restoration time
and kept the stage.

It was in Comedy that the dramatists of the Restoration excelled. William Wycherley, whose gross vigor is remarkable,
introduced the prose Comedy of Manners, in 1672, and Mrs.
Behn, Sir George Etherege, and others carried it on to the
Revolution. The wit of their comedies is the wit of a vulgar
and licentious society. After the Revolution, William Congreve, Sir John Vanbrugh, and George Farquar made comedy
more gentlemanly and its intrigue more subtile. Though
without truth to nature, their plays sparkle with wit in every
line. They exaggerate the vices of the time, but their immo-
rality is partly forgotten in their swift and delightful gaiety.

Jeremy Collier's famous attack on the stage, 1698, may have
had some influence in purifying it, but it was really the growth
of a higher tone of society which improved it. It grew dull
in the stupid plays of Steele, in ADDISON'S ponderous tragedy
of *Cato*, 1713, and in the melancholy tragedies of Rowe, 1700-
13, whose name is, however, to be remembered as the first
editor of Shakespeare, 1709-10. The four folio editions of
Shakespeare had been previously set forth in 1623, 1632, 1664,
and 1685. *The Beggar's Opera*, 1728, of GAY introduced a
new form of dramatic literature, and Colley Cibber carried on
the lighter comedy into the reign of George II. Fielding then
made the stage the vehicle of criticism on the follies, literature,
and politics of the time, and the actors, Foote and Garrick, did
the same in their farces."

BIBLIOGRAPHY. DRYDEN and CONGREVE.—R. Bell's and S. Johnson's *Lives of Eng.
Poets;* Macaulay's *Essays ;* Lowell's *Among my Books ;* D. Masson's *Dryden and Lit.
of the Rest.;* H. Reed's *Lectures on Brit. Poets ;* Ward's *Anthology;* Ed. Rev., v.
102; West. Rev., v. 63, 1855; Ecl. Mag., Aug., 1854 ; Coleridge's *Northern Worthies;*
Thackeray's *Eng. Humorists ;* Thomson's *Wits and Beaux of Society.*

Dryden's *Ode in honor of St. Cecilia's Day.*

'Twas at the royal feast for Persia won
   By Philip's warlike son;
    Aloft in awful state
    The godlike hero sate
    On his imperial throne:
   His valiant peers were placed around;
Their brows with roses and with myrtles bound:
   (So should desert in arms be crowned.)
The lovely Thais, by his side,
Sate, like a blooming Eastern bride,
In flower of youth and beauty's pride.
   Happy, happy, happy pair!
      None but the brave,
      None but the brave,
  None but the brave deserves the fair.

Chorus.

Happy, happy, happy pair!
   None but the brave,
   None but the brave,
None but the brave deserves the fair.

Timotheus, placed on high
  Amid the tuneful quire,
  With flying fingers touched the lyre:
The trembling notes ascend the sky,
  And heavenly joys inspire.
The song began from Jove,
Who left his blissful seats above
(Such is the power of mighty love.)
A dragon's fiery form belied the god,
Sublime on radiant spires he rode.
  .   .   .   .
The listening crowd admire the lofty sound,
A present deity! they shout around;
A present deity! the vaulted roofs rebound:
     With ravished ears
     The monarch hears,
     Assumes the god,
     Affects to nod,
And seems to shake the spheres.

Chorus.

With ravished ears
The monarch hears,
Etc. etc. etc.

The praise of Bacchus then the sweet musician sung,
Of Bacchus ever fair and ever young.
   The jolly god in triumph comes;
   Sound the trumpets; beat the drums;
     Flushed with a purple grace,
     He shows his honest face;
Now give the hautboys breath: he comes! he comes!
   Bacchus, ever fair and young,
     Drinking joys did first ordain;
   Bacchus' blessings are a treasure,
   Drinking is the soldier's pleasure:
      Rich the treasure,
      Sweet the pleasure;
   Sweet is pleasure after pain.

Chorus.

Bacchus' blessings are a treasure,
Drinking is the soldier's pleasure:
Etc. etc. etc.

Soothed with the sound, the king grew vain;
   Fought all his battles o'er again;
And thrice he routed all his foes, and thrice he slew the slain.
   The master saw the madness rise;
   His glowing cheeks, his ardent eyes;
   And, while he heaven and earth defied,
   Changed his hand, and checked his pride.
     He chose a mournful Muse
     Soft pity to infuse:
   He sung Darius great and good,
     By too severe a fate
   Fallen, fallen, fallen, fallen,
   Fallen from his high estate,
     And welt'ring in his blood;
   Deserted at his utmost need
   By those his former bounty fed,

On the bare earth exposed he lies,
With not a friend to close his eyes.
With downcast looks the joyless victor sate,
  Revolving in his altered soul
    The various turns of chance below;
  And now and then a sigh he stole;
  And tears began to flow.

Chorus.

  Revolving in his altered soul
    The various turns of chance below;
    Etc. etc. etc.

The mighty master smiled to see
That love was in the next degree:
'Twas but a kindred sound to move,
For pity melts the mind to love.
  Softly sweet, in Lydian measures,
  Soon he soothed his soul to pleasures.
War, he sung, is toil and trouble;
Honor but an empty bubble;
  Never ending, still beginning,
Fighting still, and still destroying;
  If the world be worth thy winning,
Think, O think it worth enjoying:
  Lovely Thais sits beside thee,
  Take the good the gods provide thee!
The many rend the skies with loud applause;
So Love was crowned, but Music won the cause.
  The prince, unable to conceal his pain,
    Gazed on the fair
    Who caused his care,
  And sighed and looked, sighed and looked,
  Sighed and looked, and sighed again:
At length, with love and wine at once oppressed,
The vanquished victor sunk upon her breast.

Chorus.

The prince, unable to conceal his pain,
    Gazed on the fair
    Etc. etc. etc.

Now strike the golden lyre again:
A louder yet, and yet a louder strain.
Break his bands of sleep asunder,
And rouse him, like a rattling peal of thunder.
  Hark, hark, the horrid sound
   Has raised up his head!
   As awaked from the dead,
  And amazed, he stares around.
'Revenge! revenge!' Timotheus cries,
  'See the Furies arise,
  See the snakes that they rear,
  How they hiss in their hair,
And the sparkles that flash from their eyes!
  Behold a ghastly band,
  Each a torch in his hand!
Those are Grecian ghosts, that in battle were slain,
  And unburied remain
  Inglorious on the plain:
  Give the vengeance due
  To the valiant crew!
Behold how they toss their torches on high,
  How they point to the Persian-abodes,
And glittering temples of their hostile gods!'
The princes applaud, with a furious joy,
And the king seized a flambeau with zeal to destroy;
  Thais led the way
  To light him to his prey,
And, like another Helen, fired another Troy.

    Chorus.
And the king seized a flambeau with zeal to destroy;
  Thais led the way
   Etc. etc. etc.

   Thus, long ago,
  Ere heaving bellows learned to blow,
   While organs yet were mute,
  Timotheus, to his breathing flute
   And sounding lyre,
Could swell the soul to rage, or kindle soft desire.
  At last divine Cecilia came,
  Inventress of the vocal frame;

The sweet enthusiast, from her sacred store,
　Enlarged the former narrow bounds,
　And added length to solemn sounds,
With Nature's mother-wit, and arts unknown before.
　Let old Timotheus yield the prize,
　　Or both divide the crown;
　He raised a mortal to the skies,
　　She drew an angel down.

Grand Chorus.
At last divine Cecilia came,
Inventress of the vocal frame;
The sweet enthusiast, from her sacred store,
　Enlarged the former narrow bounds,
　And added length to solemn sounds,
With Nature's mother-wit, and arts unknown before.
　Let old Timotheus yield the prize,
　　Or both divide the crown;
　He raised a mortal to the skies,
　　She drew an angel down.

LESSON 37.

THE PROSE LITERATURE.—"I have said that towards the end of Elizabeth's reign men settled down to think and inquire. Intellectual had succeeded to active life. We have seen this in the poetry of the time; and the great work of BACON, which was then begun, represents the same thing in prose. He worked at not only all subjects of inquiry but also at the right method of enquiry. The *Advancement of Learning* and *Novum Organum* did not fulfil all he aimed at, but they did stir the whole of English intelligence into activity.

In Science, the impulse he gave was only partly right, and the work of Science in England was behind that of the Continent. The religious and the political struggle absorbed the country, and it was not till after the Restoration, with two exceptions, that scientific discovery advanced so far as to claim recognition in a history of Literature. The Royal Society was embodied in 1662, and astronomy, experimental chemistry, medicine, mineralogy, zoology, botany, vegetable physiology were all founded as studies and their literature begun in the age of the Restoration. One man's work was so great in science as to merit his name's being mentioned among the literary men of England. In 1671 ISAAC NEWTON, 1642–1727, laid his *Theory of Light* before the Royal Society; in the year before the Revolution, his *Principia* established with its proof of the theory of gravitation the true system of the universe.

It was in political and religious knowledge, however, that the intellectual inquiry of the nation was most shown. When the thinking spirit succeeds the active and adventurous in a people, the first thing they will think upon is the true method and grounds of government, both divine and human. Two sides will be taken, the side of Authority and the side of Reason in Religion; the side of Authority and the side of Individual Liberty in Politics.

The Theological Literature of those who declared that reason was supreme as a test of truth, arose with some men who met at Lord Falkland's just before the civil war, and especially with JOHN HALES and WILLIAM CHILLINGWORTH. With them Jeremy Taylor pleaded, as we have seen, the cause of religious liberty and toleration, and of rightness of life as more important than a correct theology. After the Restoration and Revolution, their work was carried on by BISHOP BURNET, ROBERT BOYLE, the philosopher, ARCHBISHOP TILLOTSON, and BISHOP BUTLER, whose *Sermons* and *Analogy of Religion, Natural and Revealed, to the Constitution and Course of Nature*, 1736, endeavor to make peace between Authority and Reason. Many other divines of the English Church took one side or another, or opposed the growing Deism. ISAAC BARROW is to be mentioned for his sedate, ROBERT SOUTH for his fierce and witty, eloquence, and in them and in men like EDWARD STILLINGFLEET and WILLIAM SHERLOCK, English theological prose took form.

POLITICAL LITERATURE.—The resistance to authority in the opposition to the theory of the Divine Right of Kings did not enter into Literature till after it had been worked out practically in the Civil War. During the Commonwealth and after the Revolution, it took the form of a discussion on the abstract question of the Science of Government, and was mingled with an inquiry into the origin of society and the ground of social life.

THOMAS HOBBES, 1588-1674, during the Commonwealth, was the first who dealt with the question from the side of reason alone, and he is also the first of all our prose writers whose style may be said to be uniform and correct, and adapted carefully to the subjects on which he wrote. His treatise, the *Leviathan*, 1651, declared (1) that the origin of all power was in the people, and (2) the end of all power was for the common weal. It destroyed the theory of a Divine Right of Kings and Priests, but it created another kind of Divine Right when it said that the power lodged in rulers by the people could not be taken away by the people. SIR R. FILMER supported the side of Divine Right in his *Patriarchä*, published in 1680. HENRY NEVILE in his *Dialogue concerning Government*, and JAMES HARRINGTON in his romance, *The Commonwealth of Oceana*, published at the beginning of the Commonwealth, contended that all secure government was to be based on property, but Nevile supported a monarchy, and Harrington— with whom I may class Algernon Sidney, executed in 1683,— a democracy, on this basis.

John Locke, 1632-1704, in his treatise on *Civil Government* followed, in 1689-1690, the two doctrines of Hobbes, but with these two important additions—(1) that the people have a right to take away the power given by them to the ruler, (2) that the ruler is responsible to the people for the trust reposed in him, and (3) that legislative assemblies are supreme as the voice of the people. This was the political philosophy of the Revolution.

Locke carried the same spirit of free inquiry into the realm of religion, and in his three *Letters on Toleration*, 1689-90-92, laid down the philosophical grounds for liberty of religious thought. He finished by entering the realm of metaphysical inquiry. In 1690 appeared his *Essay concerning the Human-Understanding*, in which he investigated its limits and traced all ideas, and therefore all knowledge, to experience. In his clear statement of the way in which the understanding works, in the way in which he guarded it and language against their errors in the inquiry after truth, he did as much for the true method of thinking as Bacon had done for the science of nature.

The intellectual stir of the time produced, apart from the great movement of thought, a good deal of **Miscellaneous Literature.** Sir William Petty, in 1667, made the first effort after a science of political economy in his *Treatise on Taxes.* Characters, essays, letter-writing, memoirs, all came to the front. The painting of short ' *characters* ' was carried on after the Restoration by Saml. Butler and W. Charleton. These ' characters ' had no personality, but, as party spirit deepened, names thinly disguised were given to characters drawn of living men, and Dryden and Pope in poetry and all the prose wits of the time of Queen Anne and George I. made personal, and often violent, sketches of their opponents a special element in literature.

After the Restoration, Cowley's small volume, and Dryden, in the masterly criticism on his art which he prefixed to some of his dramas, gave richness to *the Essay.* These two writers began, with Hobbes, the second period of English prose, in which the style is easy, unaffected, moulded to the subject, and the proper words are put in their proper places. It is as different from the style that came before it as the easy manners of a gentleman are from those of a learned man unaccustomed to society. In William III's, time Sir W. Temple's

pleasant *Essays* brings us in style and tone nearer to the great
class of essayists of whom Addison was chief.

Lady Rachel Russell's Letters begin the *letter-writing literature* of England, in which Gray and Cowper, Byron and
Beckford have done the best work.

Pepys, in 1660–69, and Evelyn, whose Diary grows full after
1640, begin that class of gossiping *memoirs* which have been
of so much use in giving color to history. *History* itself at
this time is little better than memoirs, and such a name may
be fairly given to CLARENDON'S *History of the Civil Wars*,
begun in 1641, and to BISHOP BURNET'S *History of his own
Time*, and to his *History of the Reformation*, begun in 1679,
completed in 1715. Finally, *classical criticism*, in the discussion on the genuineness of the Letters of Phalaris, was
created by Richard Bentley in 1697–99.

THE LITERATURE OF QUEEN ANNE AND THE FIRST GEORGES.
—With the closing years of William III. and the accession of
Queen Anne, 1702, a literature arose which was partly new
and partly a continuation of that of the Restoration. The
conflict between those who took the oath to the new dynasty
and the Nonjurors who refused, the hot blood that it produced, the war between Dissent and Church and between the
two parties which now took the names of Whig and Tory
produced a mass of political pamphlets, of which Daniel
Defoe's and Swift's were the best; of songs and ballads, like
Lillibullero, which were sung in every street; of squibs, reviews, and satirical poems and letters. Every one joined in it,
and it rose into importance in the work of the greater men
who mingled more literary studies with their political excitement. In politics all the abstract discussions we have mentioned ceased to be abstract and became personal and practical,
and the spirit of inquiry applied itself more closely to the
questions of every-day life. The whole of this stirring literary
life was concentrated in London, where the agitation of soci-

ety was hottest; and it is round this vivid city life that the literature of Queen Anne and the two following reigns is best grouped.

It was with a few exceptions a **Party Literature.** The Whig and Tory leaders enlisted on their sides the best poets and prose writers, who fiercely satirized and unduly praised them under names thinly disguised. Personalities were sent to and fro like shots in battle. Those who could do this work well were well rewarded, but the rank and file of writers were left to starve. Literature was thus honored not for itself, but for the sake of party. The result was that the abler men lowered it by making it a political tool, and the smaller men, the fry of Grub Street, degraded it by using it in the same way, only in a baser manner. Their flattery was as abject as their abuse was shameless, and both were stupid. They received and deserved the merciless lashing which Pope was soon to give them in the *Dunciad.*

Being a party literature, it naturally came to study and to look sharply into human character and into human life as seen in the great city. It discussed all the varieties of social life, and painted town society more vividly than was done before or has been since; and it was so wholly taken up with this that country life and its interests, except in the writings of Addison, were scarcely touched by it at all. The society of the day was one in which all subjects of intellectual and scientific inquiry were eagerly debated, and the wit of this society was stimulated by its party spirit. Its literature reflected this intellectual excitement, and at no time in our history was literary work so vigorous and masculine on the various problems of thought and knowledge. Criticism being so active, the *form* in which thought was expressed was now especially dwelt on, and the result was, that the style of English prose became for the first time absolutely simple and clear, and English verse reached a neatness of expression and a closeness of thought as exquisite as it was artificial.   At the same time, and for the same reasons, Nature, Passion, and Imagination decayed in poetry."

BIBLIOGRAPHY. HOBBES.—I. Disraeli's *Quarrels of Authors;* Grote's *Minor Works;* Hazlitt's *Literary Remains;* Tulloch *Rat. Theology in Eng.;* Contem. Rev., v. 7, 1868; West. Rev., v. 87, 1867.

LOCKE.—T. Forster's *Original Letters* of with *Sketch of Writings and Opinions;* King's *Life* of; Sir J. Mackintosh's *Miscel. Works;* R. Vaughn's *Essays; Eng. Men of Let.* Series; Lewes' *Hist. of Philosophy;* Ed. Rev., v. 99.

From Locke's *Conduct of the Understanding.*

Those who have read of everything are thought to understand everything too, but it is not always so.   Reading furnishes the mind only with materials of knowledge, it is thinking [which] makes what we read ours.   We are of the ruminating kind, and it is not enough to cram ourselves with a great load of collections; unless we chew them over again, they will not give us strength and nourishment.   There are indeed in some writers visible instances of deep thoughts, close and acute reasoning, and ideas well pursued.   The light these would give would be of great use, if their readers would observe and imitate them; all the rest at best are but particulars fit to be turned into knowledge; but that can be done only by our own meditation, and examining the reach, force, and coherence of what is said; and then, as far as we apprehend and see the connection of ideas, so far it is ours; without that it is but so much loose matter floating in our brain.   The memory may be stored, but the judgment is little better, and the stock of knowledge not increased, by being able to repeat what others have said or produce the arguments we have found in them.   Such a knowledge as this is but knowledge by hearsay, and the ostentation of it is at best but talking by rote, and very often upon weak and wrong principles.

Books and reading are looked upon to be the great helps of the understanding and instruments of knowledge, as it must be allowed that they are; and yet I beg leave to question whether these do not prove a hindrance to many, and keep several bookish men from attaining to solid and true knowledge.   This I think I may be permitted to say, that there is no part wherein the understanding needs a more careful and wary conduct than in the use of books: without which they will prove rather innocent amusements than profitable employments of our time, and bring but small additions to our knowledge.

There is not seldom to be found even amongst those who aim at knowledge [those] who with an unwearied industry employ their whole time in books, who scarce allow themselves time to eat or sleep, but read and read and read on, but yet make no great advances in real knowledge, though there be no defect in their intellectual faculties to which their little progress can be imputed. The mistake here is, that it is usually supposed that, by reading, the author's knowledge is transfused into the reader's understanding; and so it is, but not by bare reading, but by reading and understanding what he writ. Whereby I mean not barely comprehending what is affirmed or denied in each proposition, though that great readers do not always think themselves concerned precisely to do, but to see and follow the train of his reasonings, observe the strength and clearness of their connection, and examine upon what they bottom. Without this a man may read the discourses of a very rational author, writ in a language and in propositions that he very well understands, and yet acquire not one jot of his knowledge; which consisting only in the perceived, certain, or probable connection of the ideas made use of in his reasonings, the reader's knowledge is no farther increased than he perceives that so much as he sees of this connection so much he knows of the truth or probability of that author's opinions.

All that he relies on without this perception he takes upon trust, upon the author's credit, without any knowledge of it at all. This makes me not at all wonder to see some men so abound in citations, and build so much upon authorities, it being the sole foundation on which they bottom most of their own tenets; so that in effect they have but a second-hand or implicit knowledge, i.e., are in the right if such an one from whom they borrowed it were in the right in that opinion which they took from him, which indeed is no knowledge at all. Writers of this or former ages may be good witnesses of matters of fact which they deliver, which we may do well to take upon their authority; but their credit can go no farther than this, it cannot at all affect the truth and falsehood of opinions, which have no other sort of trial but reason and proof, which they themselves make use of to make themselves knowing, and so must others too that will partake in their knowledge.

Indeed, it is an advantage that they have been at the pains to find out the proofs, and lay them in that order that may show the truth or probability of their conclusions: and for this we owe them great acknowledgments for saving us the pains in searching out those proofs which they have collected for us, and which possibly, after all our pains, we might not have found, nor been able to have set them in so good a light as that which they left them us in. Upon this account we are mightily beholding to judicious writers of all ages for those discoveries and discourses they have left behind them for our instruction, if we know how to make a right use of them; which is not to run them over in a hasty perusal, and perhaps lodge their opinions or some remarkable passages in our memories, but to enter into their reasonings, examine their proofs, and then judge of the truth or falsehood, probability or improbability of what they advance, not by any opinion we have entertained of the author, but by the evidence he produces, and the conviction he affords us, drawn from things themselves. Knowing is seeing, and, if it be so, it is madness to persuade ourselves that we do so by another man's eyes, let him use ever so many words to tell us that what he asserts is very visible. Till we ourselves see it with our own eyes, and perceive it by our own understandings, we are as much in the dark and as void of knowledge as before, let us believe any learned author as much as we will.

Euclid and Archimedes are allowed to be knowing, and to have demonstrated what they say; and yet, whoever shall read over their writings without perceiving the connection of their proofs, and seeing what they show, though he may understand all their words, yet he is not the more knowing: he may believe indeed, but does not know what they say, and so is not advanced one jot in mathematical knowledge by all the reading of those approved mathematicians.

LESSON 38.

ALEXANDER POPE.—" Pope absorbed and reflected all the elements spoken of under *party literature*. Born in 1688, he wrote excellent verse at twelve years of age; the *Pastorals* appeared in 1709, and two years afterwards he took full rank as critical poet in the *Essay on Criticism*, 1711. The next year saw the first cast of his *Rape of the Lock*, the 'epos of society under Queen Anne,' and the most brilliant play of wit in English. This closed what we may call his *first* period.

He now became known to Swift and to Henry St. John, Lord Bolingbroke, a statesman who was also a writer. With these and with Gay, Parnell, Prior, and Arbuthnot, Pope formed the Scriblerus Club, and soon rose into great fame by his *Translation of the Iliad and Odyssey* under George I., 1715–1725, for which he received 7,000 pounds.

He now, being at ease, lived at Twickenham, where he had completed his Homer. It was here, retired from the literary mob, that in bitter scorn of the many petty scribblers, he wrote in 1728 the *Dunciad*, altered and enlarged in 1741. It was the fiercest of his satires and it closes his *second* period, which took much of its savageness from the influence of Swift.

The *third* phase of Pope's literary life was closely linked to his friend Bolingbroke. It was in conversation with him that he originated the *Essay on Man*, 1732–4, and the *Imitations of Horace*. The *Moral Essays*, or Epistles to men and women, were written to praise those whom he loved, and to satirize the bad poets and the social follies of the day, and all who disliked him or his party. In the last few years of his life, Bishop Warburton, the writer of the *Legation of Moses* and editor of Shakespeare, helped him to fit the *Moral Essays* into the plan of which the *Essay on Man* formed part. Warburton was Pope's last great friend; but almost his only old friend. By 1740 nearly all the members of his literary circle were dead, and a new race of poets and writers had grown up. In 1744 Pope died.

He is our greatest master in didactic poetry, not so much because of the worth of the thoughts as because of the masterly form in which they are put. The *Essay on Man*, though its philosophy is poor and not his own, is crowded with lines that have passed into daily use. The *Essay on Criticism* is equally full of critical precepts put with exquisite skill. The *Satires* and *Epistles* are also didactic. They set virtue and cleverness over against vice and stupidity, and they illustrate both by types of character, in the drawing of which Pope is without a rival in our literature.

His translation of Homer is made with great literary art, but for that very reason it does not make us feel the simplicity and directness of Homer. It has neither the manner of Homer nor the spirit of the Greek life, just as Pope's descriptions of nature have neither the manner nor the spirit of nature.

The *heroic couplet,* in which he wrote his translation and nearly all his work, he used in various subjects with a correctness that has never been surpassed, but it sometimes fails from being too smooth, and its cadences too regular.

Finally, he was a true artist, hating those who degraded his art, and, at a time when men followed it for money and place and the applause of the club and of the town, he loved it faithfully to the end for its own sake."

"In two directions, in that of condensing and pointing his meaning, and in that of drawing the utmost harmony of sound out of the couplet, Pope carried versification far beyond the point at which it was when he took it up. Because, after Pope, his trick of versification became common property, we are apt to overlook the merit of the first invention. But epigrammatic force and musical flow are not the sole elements of Pope's reputation. The matter which he worked up into his verse has a permanent value, and is indeed one of the most precious heirlooms which the eighteenth century has bequeathed us.

And here we must distinguish between Pope when he attempts general themes, and Pope when he draws that which he knew—the social life of his own day. When in the *Pastorals* he writes of natural beauty, in the *Essay on Criticism* he lays down the rules of writing, in the *Essay on Man* he versifies Leibnitzian optimism, he does not rise above the herd of eighteenth century writers, except in so far as his skill of language is more accomplished than theirs. It is where he comes to describe the one thing which he knew and about which he felt sympathy and antipathy—the court and town of his time, in the *Moral Essays,* and the *Satires* and *Epistles,* that Pope found the proper material on which to lay out his elaborate workmanship. Where he moralizes or deduces general principles, he is superficial, second-hand, and one-sided as the veriest scribbler. Wherever he recedes from what was immediately close to him, the manners, passions, prejudices, sentiments of his own day, Pope has only such merit—little enough—as wit divorced from truth can have. He is at his best only where the delicacies and subtle felicities of his diction are employed to embody some transient phase of contemporary feeling. The complex web of society, with its indefinable shades, its minute personal affinities and repulsions, is the world in which Pope lived and moved, and which he has drawn in a few vivid lines, with a keenness and intensity with which there is nothing in our literature that can compare."—*Mark Pattison.*

THE MINOR POETS.—"The minor poets who surrounded Pope in the first two thirds of his life did not write in his manner nor approach his genius. THOMAS PARNELL is known by his *Hermit*, and both he and JOHN GAY, in his six pastorals, *The Shepherd's Week*, 1714, touched on country life. Swift's poetical satires were coarse but always hit home, Addison celebrated the battle of Blenheim in the *Campaign*, and his sweet grace is found in some devotional pieces; while Prior's charming ease is best shown in the light narrative poetry which I may say began with him in the reign of William III. The *Black-eyed Susan* of Gay and TICKELL's *Colin and Lucy* and CAREY's *Sally in our Alley* and afterwards GOLDSMITH's *Edwin and Angelina* mark the rise of the *modern ballad;* a class of poetry wholly apart from the genius of Pope.

The influence of the didactic and satirical poetry of the critical school is found in Johnson's two satires on the manners of his time, the *London*, 1738, and the *Vanity of Human Wishes*, 1749; in ROBERT BLAIR's dull poem of *The Grave*, 1743; in EDWARD YOUNG's *Night Thoughts*, 1743, a poem on the immortality of the soul, and in his satires on *The Universal Passion of Fame;* in the tame work of Richard Savage, Johnson's poor friend; and in the short-lived, but vigorous, satires of Charles Churchill, who died in 1764, twenty years after Savage. The *Pleasures of the Imagination*, 1744, by MARK AKENSIDE, belongs also in spirit to the time of Queen Anne, and was suggested by Addison's essays in the *Spectator* on imagination.

THE POETRY OF NATURAL DESCRIPTION.—We have found already traces in the poets of a pleasure in rural things and the emotions they awakened. This appears chiefly among the Puritans, who, because they hated the politics of the Stuarts before the civil war and the corruption of the court after it, lived apart from the town in quietude. The best natural description we have before the time of Pope is that of two Puritans, Marvell and Milton.

But the first poem devoted to natural description appeared while Pope was yet alive, in the very midst of a vigorous town poetry. It was the *Seasons*, 1726–30; and it is curious, remembering what I have said about the peculiar turn of the Scotch for natural description, that it was the work of JAMES THOMSON, a Scotchman. It described the scenery and country life of Spring, Summer, Autumn, and Winter. He wrote with his eye upon their scenery, and even when he wrote of it in his room, it was with 'a recollected love.' The descriptions were too much like catalogues, the very fault of the previous Scotch poets, and his style was always heavy and often cold, but he was the first poet who led the English people into that new world of nature in poetry, which has moved and enchanted us in the work of Wordsworth, Shelley, Keats, and Tennyson, but which was entirely impossible for Pope to understand."

BIBLIOGRAPHY. POPE.—Elwin's *Life* of; R Bell's and S Johnson's *Lives of Eng. Poets*; Ward's *Anthology*; De Quincey's *Biog*. *Essays* and *Essays on the Poets*; I. Disraeli's *Quarrels of Authors*; L. Stephen's *Hours in a Library*; *Eng. Men of Let.* Series; J. T. Fields' *Yesterdays with Authors*; W. Howitt's *Homes of Brit. Poets*; Thackeray's *Eng. Humorists*; Lowell's *My Study Windows*; Fraser's Mag., v. 48, 1853, and v. 61, 1860; Ecl. Mag., Dec.. 1847; N. Br. Rev., v. 75, 1872.

THOMSON.—Erskine's *Essays* upon; Howitt's *Homes of Brit. Poets*; S. Johnson's *Lives of Eng. Poets*; J. Wilson's *Recreations*; Ecl. Mag., v. 20, 1853; New Monthly, June, 1855, and June, 1858.

LESSON 39.

From Pope's *Epistle to Dr. Arbuthnot.*

P. Shut, shut the door, good John! fatigued, I said,
Tie up the knocker, say I'm sick, I'm dead.
The dog star rages! nay, 'tis past a doubt,
All Bedlam or Parnassus is let out:
Fire in each eye and papers in each hand,
They rave, recite, and madden round the land.
What walks can guard me, or what shades can hide?
They pierce my thickets, through my grot they glide.
By land, by water, they renew the charge,
They stop the chariot, and they board the barge.

No place is sacred, not the church is free,
Ev'n Sunday shines no Sabbath-day to me.
  Is there a parson much be-mus'd in beer,
A maudlin poetess, a rhyming peer,
A clerk foredoom'd his father's soul to cross,
Who pens a stanza when he should engross?
Is there who, lock'd from ink and paper, scrawls
With desp'rate charcoal round his darken'd walls?
All fly to Twit'nam, and in humble strain
Apply to me to keep them mad or vain.
  Friend to my life, (which did not you prolong
The world had wanted many an idle song)
What drop or nostrum can this plague remove?
Or which must end me, a fool's wrath or love?
A dire dilemma! either way I'm sped,
If foes, they write, if friends, they read me dead.
Seiz'd and tied down to judge, how wretched I!
Who can't be silent, and who will not lie:
To laugh were want of goodness and of grace,
And to be grave exceeds all pow'r of face.
I sit with sad civility, I read
With honest anguish and an aching head;
And drop at last, but in unwilling ears,
This saving counsel, "Keep your piece nine years."
"Nine years!" cries he, who high in Drury-lane
Lull'd by soft zephyrs through the broken pane,
Rhymes ere he wakes, and prints before term ends,
Oblig'd by hunger and request of friends;
"The piece, you think, is incorrect? why take it,
I'm all submission, what you'd have it make it."
Three things another's modest wishes bound,—
My friendship and a prologue and ten pound.
  Why did I write? what sin to me unknown
Dipt me in ink,—my parents' or my own?
As yet a child, nor yet a fool to fame,
I lisp'd in numbers, for the numbers came.
I left no calling for this idle trade,
No duty broke, no father disobey'd;
The muse but serv'd to ease some friend, not wife,
To help me through this long disease, my life,

To second, Arbuthnot, thy art and care
And teach the being you preserv'd to bear.
　　Soft were my numbers; who could take offence
While pure description held the place of sense?
Like gentle Fanny's was my flow'ry theme,
A painted mistress or a purling stream.
Yet then did Gildon draw his venal quill;
I wish'd the man a dinner, and sate still.
Yet then did Dennis rave in furious fret;
I never answer'd, I was not in debt.
If want provok'd, or madness made them print,
I wag'd no war with Bedlam or the Mint.
　　Did some more sober critic come abroad;
If wrong, I smiled; if right, I kiss'd the rod.
Pains, reading, study are their just pretence,
And all they want is spirit, taste, and sense.
Commas and points they set exactly right,
And 'twere a sin to rob them of their mite.
Yet ne'er one sprig of laurel grac'd these ribalds,
From slashing Bentley down to piddling Tibalds.
Each wight who reads not, and but scans and spells,
Each word-catcher that lives on syllables,
Ev'n such small critics some regard may claim,·
Preserv'd in Milton's or in Shakespeare's name.
Pretty! in amber to observe the forms
Of hairs or straws or dirt or grubs or worms!
The things, we know, are neither rich nor rare,
But wonder how the d——l they got there.
　　Were others angry, I excused them too;
Well might they rage, I gave them but their due.
A man's true merit 'tis not hard to find;
But each man's secret standard in his mind,
That casting-weight pride adds to emptiness,—
This who can gratify? for who can guess?
The bard whom pilfered pastorals renown,
Who turns a Persian tale for half a crown,
Just writes to make his barrenness appear,
And strains from hard-bound brains eight lines a year;
He who, still wanting, tho' he lives on theft,
Steals much, spends little, yet has nothing left;

And he who now to sense, now nonsense leaning,
Means not, but blunders round about a meaning;
And he whose fustian's so sublimely bad
It is not poetry but prose run mad;—
All these my modest satire bade translate
And own'd that nine such poets made a Tate.
How did they fume and stamp and roar and chafe!
And swear not Addison himself was safe.
    Peace to all such! but were there one[1] whose fires
True genius kindles, and fair fame inspires;
Blest with each talent and each art to please,
And born to write, converse, and live with ease:
Should such a man, too fond to rule alone,
Bear, like the Turk,[2] no brother near the throne,
View him with scornful, yet with jealous, eyes,
And hate for arts that caus'd himself to rise;
Damn with faint praise, assent with civil leer,
And without sneering teach the rest to sneer;
Willing to wound, and yet afraid to strike,
Just hint a fault, and hesitate dislike;
Alike reserv'd to blame or to commend,
A timorous foe and a suspicious friend;
Dreading ev'n fools, by flatterers besieg'd,
And so obliging that he ne'er obliged;
Like Cato, give his little senate laws,
And sit attentive to his own applause;
While wits and templars ev'ry sentence raise
And wonder with a foolish face of praise:—
Who but must laugh if such a man there be?
Who would not weep if Atticus were he?
    Oh! let me live my own and die so too!
(To live and die is all I have to do)
Maintain a poet's dignity and ease,
And see what friends and read what books I please;
Above a patron, tho' I condescend
Sometimes to call a minister my friend.
I was not born for courts or great affairs;
I pay my debts, believe, and say my prayers;

---

[1] This is Pope's famous satire upon Addison.   [2] What is the allusion?

Can sleep without a poem in my head,
Nor know if Dennis be alive or dead.
　A lash like mine no honest man shall dread,
But all such babbling blockheads in his stead.
Let Sporus[1] tremble.   *A.* What? that thing of silk,
Sporus, that mere white curd of ass's milk?
Satire or sense, alas! can Sporus feel?
Who breaks a butterfly upon a wheel?
P. Yet let me flap this bug with gilded wings,

.　　　.　　　.　　　.　　　.　　　.　　　.

Whose buzz the witty and the fair annoys,
Yet wit ne'er tastes, and beauty ne'er enjoys.
So well-bred spaniels civilly delight
In mumbling of the game they dare not bite.
Eternal smiles his emptiness betray,
As shallow streams run dimpling all the way,
Whether in florid impotence he speaks,
And, as the prompter breathes the puppet squeaks;
Or at the ear of Eve, familiar toad,
Half froth, half venom, spits himself abroad
In puns or politics or tales or lies
Or spite or smut or rhymes or blasphemies.
His wit all see-saw, between that and this,
Now high, now low, now master up, now miss,
And he himself one vile antithesis.
Amphibious thing! that, acting either part,
The trifling head or the corrupted heart,
Fop at the toilet, flatterer at the board,
Now trips a lady, and now struts a lord.
Eve's temper thus the rabbins have express'd
A cherub's face, a reptile all the rest,
Beauty that shocks you, parts that none will trust,
Wit that can creep, and pride that licks the dust.
　Not fortune's worshipper nor fashion's fool,
Not lucre's madman nor ambition's tool,
Not proud nor servile, be one poet's praise
That, if he pleas'd, he pleas'd by manly ways;
That flattery ev'n to kings he held a shame,
And thought a lie in verse or prose the same.

---

[1] Lord Hervey.

That not in fancy's maze he wander'd long,
But stoop'd to truth and moraliz'd his song;
That not for fame but virtue's better end
He stood the furious foe, the timid friend,
The damning critic, half-approving wit,
The coxcomb hit or fearing to be hit;
Laughed at the loss of friends he never had,
The dull, the proud, the wicked, and the mad;
The distant threats of vengeance on his head,
The blow unfelt, the tear he never shed;
The tale reviv'd, the lie so oft o'erthrown,
Th' imputed trash, and duluess not his own;
The morals blacken'd when the writings 'scape,
The libell'd person and the pictur'd shape;
Abuse, on all he lov'd or lov'd him, spread,
A friend in exile, or a father dead;
The whisper, that, to greatness still too near,
Perhaps yet vibrates on his sovereign's ear;—
Welcome for thee, fair virtue, all the past;
For thee, fair virtue, welcome ev'n the last!
    Of gentle blood (part shed in honor's cause,
While yet in Britain honor had applause,)
Each parent sprung— *A.* What fortune, pray? *P.* Their own,
And better got than Bestia's from the throne.
Born to no pride, inheriting no strife,
Nor marrying discord in a noble wife,
Stranger to civil and religious rage,
The good man walk'd innoxious through his age.
No courts he saw, no suits would ever try,
Nor dar'd an oath, nor hazarded a lie.
Unlearn'd, he knew no schoolman's subtle art,
No language but the language of the heart.
By nature honest, by experience wise,
Healthy by temperance and by exercise,
His life, tho' long, to sickness pass'd unknown
His death was instant, and without a groan.
Oh! grant me thus to live, and thus to die,
Who sprung from kings shall know less joy than I.
    O Friend, may each domestic bliss be thine!
Be no unpleasing melancholy mine.

Me, let the tender office long engage,
To rock the cradle of reposing age,
With lenient arts extend a mother's breath,
Make languor smile and smooth the bed of death,
Explore the thought, explain the asking eye,
And keep awhile one parent from the sky!
On cares like these, if length of days attend,
May heaven, to bless those days, preserve my friend!
Preserve him social, cheerful, and serene,
And just as rich as when he serv'd a Queen.
A. Whether that blessing be denied or giv'n,
Thus far was right, the rest belongs to Heav'n.

LESSON 40.

PROSE LITERATURE.—" The prose literature of Pope's time collects itself round four great names, Swift, Defoe, Addison, and Bishop Berkeley, and they all exhibit those elements of the age of which I have spoken.

JONATHAN SWIFT, born in 1667, was the keenest of political partisans. The *Battle of the Books*, or the literary fight about the Letters of Phalaris, and the *Tale of a Tub*, a satire on the Presbyterians and the Papists, made his reputation in 1704 and established him as a satirist. Swift left the Whig for the Tory party, and his political tracts brought him Court favor and literary fame. On the fall of the Tory party at the accession of George I., he retired to the Deanery of St. Patrick in Ireland an embittered man, and the *Drapier's Letters*, 1724, written against Wood's halfpence, gained him popularity in a country that he hated. In 1726 his inventive genius, his savage satire, and his cruel indignation with life were all shown in *Gulliver's Travels*. The voyage to Lilliput and Brobdingnag satirized the politics and manners of England and Europe; that to Laputa mocked the philosophers; and the last, to the country of the Houyhnhnms, lacerated and defiled the whole body of humanity. No

English is more robust than Swift's, no wit more scathing, no life in private and public more sad and proud, no death more pitiable. He died in 1745 hopelessly insane.

DANIEL DEFOE, 1661–1731, was almost as vigorous a political writer as Swift, but he will live in literature by *Robinson Crusoe*, 1719. In it he equalled *Gulliver's Travels* in truthful representation, and excelled it in invention. The story lives and charms from day to day. With his other tales it makes him our first fine writer of fiction. But none of his stories are true novels; that is, they have no plot to the working out of which the characters and the events contribute. They form the transition, however, from the slight tale and the romance of the Elizabethan time to the finished novel of Richardson and Fielding.

Metaphysical Literature was enriched by the work of BISHOP BERKELEY, 1684–1753. His *Minute Philosopher* and other works questioned the real existence of matter, and founded on the denial of it an answer to the English Deists, round whom in the first half of the eighteenth century centred the struggle between the claims of natural and of revealed religion. Shaftesbury, Bolingbroke, and Wollaston, Tindal, Toland, and Collins, on the Deists' side, were opposed by Clarke, by Bentley, whose name is best known as the founder of the true school of classical criticism, and by Bishop Warburton.

I may mention here a social satire, *The Fable of the Bees*, by MANDEVILLE, half poem, half prose dialogue, and finished in 1729. It tried to prove that the vices of society are the foundation of civilization, and is the first of a new set of books which marked the rise in England of the bold speculations on the nature and ground of society which the French Revolution afterwards increased.

The Periodical Essay is connected with the names of JOSEPH ADDISON, 1672–1719, and SIR RICHARD STEELE, 1675-1729. This gay, light, and graceful kind of literature, differing from such Essays as Bacon's as good conversation about a subject differs from a clear analysis of all its points, was begun in France by Montaigne in 1580. Charles Cotton, a wit of Charles II.'s time, re-translated Montaigne's *Essays*, and they soon found imitators in Cowley and Sir W. Temple. But the periodical Essay was created by Steele and Addison. It was published three times a week, then daily, and it was anonymous, and both these characters necessarily changed its form from that of an Essay of Montaigne.

Steele began it in the *Tatler*, 1709, and it treated of everything that was going on in the world. He paints as a social humorist the whole age of Queen Anne—the political and literary disputes, the fine gentlemen and ladies, the characters of men, the humors of society, the new book, the new play; we live in the very streets and drawing-rooms of old London. Addison soon joined him, first in the *Tatler*, afterwards in the *Spectator*, 1711. His work is more critical, literary, and didactic than his companion's. The characters he introduces, such as Roger de Coverley, are finished studies after nature, and their talk is easy and dramatic. No humor is more fine and tender; and, like Chaucer's, it is never bitter. The style adds to the charm, and it seems to grow out of the subjects treated of.

Addison's work was a great one, lightly done. The *Spectator*, the *Guardian*, and the *Freeholder*, in his hands, gave a better tone to manners, and a gentler one to political and literary criticism. The essays published every Friday were chiefly on literary subjects, the Saturday essays chiefly on religious subjects. The former popularized literature, so that culture spread among the middle classes and crept down to the country; the latter popularized religion. 'I have brought,' he says, 'philosophy out of closets and libraries, schools and colleges, to dwell in clubs and assemblies, at tea-tables and in coffee-houses."

"Addison, appearing at a time when English literature was at a very low ebb, made an impression which his writings would not now produce, and won a reputation which was then his due, but which has long survived his comparative excellence. Charmed by the gentle flow of his thought,—which, neither deep nor strong, neither subtle nor struggling with the obstacles of argument, might well flow easily,—by his lambent humor, his playful fancy (he was very slenderly endowed with imagination), and the healthy tone of his mind, the writers of his own generation and those of the succeeding half century placed him upon a pedestal, in his right to which there has since been almost unquestioning acquiescence. He certainly did much for English literature, and more for English morals and manners, which in his day were sadly in need of elevation and refinement. But, as a writer of English, he is not to be compared, except with great peril to his reputation, to at least a score of men who have flourished in the present century, and some of whom are now living."—*R. G. White.*

" That which chiefly distinguishes Addison from almost all the other great masters of ridicule is the grace, the nobleness, the moral purity which we find even in his merriment. If, as Soame Jenyns oddly imagined, a portion of the happiness of seraphim and just men made perfect be derived from an exquisite perception of the ludicrous, their mirth must surely be none other than the mirth of Addison; a mirth consistent with tender compassion for all that is frail, and with profound reverence for all that is sublime. Nothing great, nothing amiable, no moral duty, no doctrine of natural or revealed religion has ever been associated by Addison with any degrading idea. His humanity is without a parallel in literary history. It may be confidently affirmed that he has blackened no man's character, nay, that it would be difficult, if not impossible, to find in all the volumes which he has left us a single taunt which can be called ungenerous or unkind."—*Macaulay.*

BIBLIOGRAPHY. SWIFT.—J. Forster's *Life* of; *Eng. Men. of Let.* Series; Jeffrey's *Essays;* S. Johnson's *Lives of Eng. Poets;* Thackeray's *Eng. Humorists;* Minto's *Man. Eng. Prose Lit.;* Ward's *Anthology;* Br. Quar. Rev., Oct., 1854; Black. Mag., v. 74, 1853; Fraser's Mag., v. 61, 1860, and v. 76, 1867; N. A. Rev., Jan., 1868; N. Br. Rev., v. 51, 1870; Ecl. Mag., May and Oct., 1849.

DEFOE.—W. Chadwick's *Life and Times* of; J. Forster's *Hist. and Biog. Essays;* Minto's *Man. Eng. Pr. Lit.;* L. Stephen's *Hours in a Library; Eng. Men of Let.* Series; Br Quar. Rev., Oct., 1869; Quar. Rev., v. 101, 1857; Cornhill Mag., v. 17, 1868.

ADDISON.—Minto's *Man. Eng. Pr. Lit.; Eng. Men of Let.* Series; Macaulay's *Essays;* Howitt's *Homes and Haunts of Brit. Poets;* S. Johnson's *Lives of Eng. Poets;* Taine's *Hist. Eng. Lit.;* Thackeray's *Eng. Humorists,* and in *Henry Esmond;* N. A. Rev., v. 79, 1854; Ecl. Mag., Sept., 1874, and Apr., 1879.

I have now considered Milton's *Paradise Lost* under those four great heads of the fable, the characters, the sentiments, and the language; and have shown that he excels, in general, under each of these heads. I hope that I have made several discoveries which may appear new even to those who are versed in critical learning. Were I indeed to choose my readers, by whose judgment I would stand or fall, they should not be such as are acquainted only with the French and Italian critics, but also with the ancient and moderns who have written in either of the learned languages. Above all, I would have them well versed in the Greek and Latin poets, without which a man very often fancies that he understands a critic, when in reality he does not comprehend his meaning.

It is in criticism, as in all other sciences and speculations; one who brings with him any implicit notions and observations which he has made in his reading of the poets, will find his own reflections method-ized and explained, and perhaps several little hints, that had passed in his mind, perfected and improved in the works of a good critic; whereas one who has not these previous lights is very often an utter stranger to what he reads, and apt to put a wrong interpretation upon it.

Nor is it sufficient that a man who sets up for a judge in criticism should have perused the authors above-mentioned, unless he has also a clear and logical head. Without this talent he is perpetually puzzled and perplexed amidst his own blunders, mistakes the sense of those he would confute, or, if he chances to think right, does not know how to convey his thoughts to another with clearness and perspicuity. Aristotle, who was the best critic, was also one of the best logicians that ever ap-peared in the world.

Mr. Locke's Essay on The Human Understanding would be thought a very odd book for a man to make himself master of, who would get a reputation by critical writings; though at the same time it is very certain that an author who has not learned the art of distinguishing be-tween words and things, and of ranging his thoughts and setting them in proper lights, whatever notions he may have, will lose himself in confusion and obscurity. I might further observe that there is not a Greek or a Latin critic who has not shown, even in the style of his criti-cisms, that he was a master of all the elegance and delicacy of his na-tive tongue.

The truth of it is, there is nothing more absurd than for a man to set up for a critic, without a good insight into all the parts of learning; whereas many of those who have endeavored to signalize themselves by works of this nature among our English writers are not only defective in the above-mentioned particulars but plainly discover by the phrases which they make use of, and by their confused way of thinking, that they are not acquainted with the most common and ordinary systems of arts and sciences. A few general rules extracted out of the French authors, with a certain cant of words, have sometimes set up an illiterate heavy writer for a most judicious and formidable critic.

One great mark by which you may discover a critic who has neither taste nor learning is this, that he seldom ventures to praise any passage in an author which has not been before received and applauded by the public, and that his criticism turns wholly upon little faults and errors. This part of a critic is so very easy to succeed in that we find every ordinary reader, upon the publishing of a new poem, has wit and ill-nature enough to turn several passages of it into ridicule, and very often in the right place. This Mr. Dryden has very agreeably remarked in those two celebrated lines:—

> Errors, like straws, upon the surface flow;
> He who would search for pearls must dive below.

A true critic ought to dwell rather upon excellencies than imperfections, to discover the concealed beauties of a writer, and communicate to the world such things as are worth their observation. The most exquisite words and finest strokes of an author are those which very often appear the most doubtful and exceptionable to a man who wants a relish for polite learning; and they are these, which a sour, undistinguishing critic generally attacks with the greatest violence. Tully observes that it is very easy to brand or fix a mark upon what he calls *verbum ardens*, or, as it may be rendered into English, a *glowing bold expression*, and to turn it into ridicule by a cold, ill-natured criticism. A little wit is equally capable of exposing a beauty and of aggravating a fault; and, though such a treatment of an author naturally produces indignation in the mind of an understanding reader, it has, however, its effect among the generality of those whose hands it falls into, the rabble of mankind being very apt to think that everything which is laughed at with any mixture of wit is ridiculous in itself.

Such a mirth as this is always unseasonable in a critic, as it rather prejudices the reader than convinces him, and is capable of making a beauty, as well as a blemish, the subject of derision. A man who cannot write with wit on a proper subject is dull and stupid, but one who shows it in an improper place is as impertinent and absurd. Besides, a man who has the gift of ridicule is very apt to find fault with anything that gives him an opportunity of exciting his beloved talent, and very often censures a passage, not because there is any fault in it, but because he can be merry upon it. Such kinds of pleasantry are very unfair and disingenuous in works of criticism, in which the greatest masters, both ancient and modern, have always appeared with a serious and instructive air.

As I intend in my next paper to show the defects in Milton's *Paradise Lost*, I thought fit to premise these few particulars, to the end that the reader may know I enter upon it, as on a very ungrateful work, and that I shall just point at the imperfections, without endeavoring to inflame them with ridicule. I must also observe with Longinus that the productions of a great genius, with many lapses and inadvertencies, are infinitely preferable to the works of an inferior kind of author which are scrupulously exact and conformable to all the rules of correct writing.

I shall conclude my paper with a story out of Boccalini which sufficiently shows us the opinion that judicious author entertained of the sort of critics I have been here mentioning. A famous critic, says he, having gathered together all the faults of an eminent poet, made a present of them to Apollo, who received them very graciously, and resolved to make the author a suitable return for the trouble he had been at in collecting them. In order to this he set before him a sack of wheat, as it had been just threshed out of the sheaf. He then bid him pick out the chaff from among the corn, and lay it aside by itself. The critic applied himself to the task with great industry and pleasure, and, after having made the due separation, was presented by Apollo with the chaff for his pains.

FURTHER READING.—The *Sir Roger de Coverley* papers, published in pamphlet form by Clark & Maynard.

SCHEME FOR REVIEW.

PERIOD VII.

FROM SWIFT'S DEATH TO THE FRENCH REVOLUTION,

1745-1789.

LESSON 41.

Brief Historical Sketch.—Invasion by second Pretender, son of the first, 1745. Battle of Culloden, Apr. 16, 1746. England begins, 1755, the French and Indian War, closed by Treaty of Paris in 1763. Clive's Battle of Plassey in India, 1757. Eng. aids Frederic the Great in the Seven Years' War against Austria, France, and Russia, begun 1756. Era of the Elder Pitt, the Great Commoner, afterward Lord Chatham, the third quarter of this century. Under Clive the East India Co. conquers a large part of India, 1755-67. Geo. III. succeeds Geo. II., 1760. His influence over his ministry almost supreme. Wilkes' Controversy, 1762-82. Stamp Act, 1764. Repeal of it, 1765. Watt invents Steam Engine, 1765, patents it, 1781. Arkwright's Spinning Machine, 1768. Regulation Acts, 1774. First great English Journals date from about 1770. Right of the press to criticise Parliament, ministers, and even the sovereign now established. Death of Chatham, 1778. American Revolution begins, 1775. Lord George Gordon Riots, 1780. American Independence acknowledged by Treaty of Paris, 1783. The Younger Pitt made Prime Minister, 1784. Mail Conches introduced, 1784. East Indian possessions vastly increased by Warren Hastings, 1774-85. Articles of impeachment presented against him by Burke, 1786. Trial began 1788, lasting till 1795, and resulting in his acquittal. Howard's Reform of prisons and prison discipline, 1774-90. French Revolution, 1789.

Lesson 42.

Prose Literature.—"The rapid increase of 'manufactures, science, and prosperity which began with the middle of the eighteenth century is paralleled by the growth of Literature. The general causes of this growth were:—

1. **A good prose style had been perfected,** and the method of writing being made easy, production increased. Men were born, as it were, into a good school of the art of composition, and the boy of eighteen had no difficulty in making sentences which the Elizabethan writer could not have put together after fifty years of study.

2. **The long peace** after the accession of the House of Hanover had left England at rest, and given it wealth. The reclaiming of waste tracts, and the increased wealth and trade made better communication necessary; and the country was soon covered with a network of highways. The leisure gave time to men to think and write: the quicker interchange between the capital and the country spread over England the literature of the capital, and stirred men everywhere to write. The coaching services and the post carried the new book and the literary criticism to the villages, and awoke the men of genius there, who might otherwise have been silent.

3. **The Press** sent far and wide the news of the day, and grew in importance till it contained the opinions and writinsg of men like Canning. Such seed produced literary work in the country. *Newspapers* now began to play their part in literature. They rose under the Commonwealth, but became important when the censorship which reduced them to a mere broadsheet of news was removed after the Revolution of 1688. The political sleep of the age of the first two Georges hindered their progress; but, in the reign of George III., after a struggle with which the name of John Wilkes and the author of the letters of Junius are connected, the Press claimed and

obtained the right to criticise the conduct and measures of Ministers and Parliament and the King; and, after the struggle in 1771, the right to publish and comment on the debates in the two Houses.

The great English Journals, the *Morning Chronicle*, the *Post*, the *Herald*, and the *Times*, gave an enormous impulse within the next twenty years to the production of books, and created a new class of literary men—the Journalists. Later on, in 1802, the publication of the *Edinburgh Review*, and afterwards of the *Quarterly Review* and *Blackwood's Magazine*, started another kind of prose writing, and by their criticisms on new books improved and stimulated literature.

4. **Communication with the Continent** had increased during the peaceable times of Walpole, and the wars that followed made it still easier. With its increase, two new and great outbursts of literature told upon England. France sent the works of Montesquieu, of Voltaire, Rousseau, Diderot, D'Alembert, and the rest of the liberal thinkers who were called the Encyclopædists, to influence and quicken English literature on all the great subjects that belong to the social and political life of man. Afterwards, the fresh German movement, led by Lessing and others, and carried on by Goethe and Schiller, added its impulse to the poetical school that arose in England along with the French Revolution. These were the general causes of the rapid growth of literature from the time of George III."

" It seems as if a simple and natural prose were a thing which we might expect to come easy to communities of men, and to come early to them; but we know from experience that it is not so. Poetry and the poetic form of expression naturally precede prose. We see this in ancient Greece. We see prose forming itself there gradually and with labor; we see it passing through more than one stage before it attains to thorough propriety and lucidity, long after forms of consummate adequacy have already been reached and used in poetry. It is a people's growth in practical life, and its native turn for developing this life and for making progress in it which awaken the desire for a good prose—a prose, plain, direct, intelligible, serviceable.

The practical genius of our people could not but urge irresistibly to the production of a real prose style, because, for the purposes of modern life, the old English prose, the prose of Milton and Taylor, is cumbersome, unavailable, impossible. A dead language, the Latin, for a long time furnished the nations of Europe with an instrument of the kind superior to any which they had yet discovered in their own tongue. But such nations as England and France, called to a great historic life, and with powerful interests and gifts, were sure to feel the need of having a sound prose of their own, and to bring such a prose forth. They brought it forth in the seventeenth and eighteenth centuries; France first, afterwards England."—*Matthew Arnold.*

THE NOVEL.—" The novel is perhaps the most remarkable of the forms literature now took. It began in the reign of George II. No other books have ever produced so plentiful an offspring as the novels of Richardson, Fielding, and Smollett. The novel arranges and combines round the passion of love and its course between two or more persons a number of events and of characters, which, in their action on one another, develop the plot of the story and bring about a sad or a happy close. The story may be laid at any time, in any class of society, in any place. The whole world and the whole of human life lie before it as its subject. Its vast sphere accounts for its vast production—its human interest for its vast numbers of readers.

SAMUEL RICHARDSON, 1689–1761, while Pope was yet alive, wrote in the form of letters, and in two months' time, *Pamela*, 1740, and afterwards *Clarissa Harlowe*, 1748, and *Sir Charles Grandison*. The second is the best, and all are celebrated for their subtile and tender drawing of the human heart. They are novels of Sentiment; and their intense minuteness of detail gives them reality. Henry Fielding and Tobias Smollett followed him with the novel of Real life, full of events, adventures, fun, and vivid painting of various kinds of life in England.

FIELDING, 1707–1754, began with *Joseph Andrews*, 1742; SMOLLETT, 1721–1771, with *Roderick Random*, 1748. Both wrote many other stories, but in truthful representation of common life, and in the natural growth and winding up of the story, Fielding's *Tom Jones*, 1749, is our English master-piece and model. Ten years thus sufficed to create an entirely new literature. LAURENCE STERNE, 1713–1768, in his *Tristram Shandy*, 1759, introduced the novel of Character in which events are few. His peculiar vein of labyrinthine humor and falsetto sentiment has been imitated, but never attained. We mention Johnson's *Rasselas*, 1759, as the first of our Didactic tales, and the *Fool of Quality*, by HENRY BROOKE, as the first of our Theological tales.

Under George III. new forms of fiction appeared. GOLD-SMITH'S *Vicar of Wakefield*, 1766, was the first, and perhaps the most charming, of all those novels which we may call Idyllic, which describe the loves and the simple lives of country people in country scenery. MISS BURNEY'S *Evelina*, 1778, and *Cecilia* were the first novels of Society. MRS. INCHBALD'S *Simple Story*, 1791, introduced the novel of Passion, and MRS. RADCLIFFE, in her wild and picturesque tales, the Romantic novel."

BIBLIOGRAPHY. RICHARDSON.—D. Masson's *Brit. Novelists;* Mrs. Oliphant's *Hist. Sketches;* L. Stephen's *Hours in a Library;* Fort. Rev., v. 12, 1869; Fraser's Mag., v. 62, 1860, and v. 71, 1865; West. Rev., v. 91, 1869.

FIELDING.—Thackeray's *Eng. Humorists;* Whipple's *Essays and Reviews;* Forsyth's *Novels and Novelists;* Scott's *Lives of the Novelists;* Black. Mag., v. 87, 1860; Fraser's Mag., v. 57, 1858, and v. 61, 1860; N. Br. Rev., v. 24, 1855; Quar. Rev., v. 98, 1856.

STERNE.—P. Fitzgerald's *Life* of; Thack.'s *Eng. Humorists;* Scott's *Lives of the Novelists;* Tuckerman's *Essays;* Black. Mag., v. 97, 1865; Nat. Rev., v. 18, 1864; N. A. Rev., v. 81, 1865, and v. 107, 1868; Quar. Rev., v. 94, 1854.

From Fielding's *Tom Jones*.

Mr. Jones, being at last in a state of good spirits, agreed to carry an appointment, which he had before made, into execution. This was to attend Mrs. Miller and her youngest daughter into the gallery at the playhouse, and to admit Mr. Partridge as one of the company. For, as Jones had really that taste for humor which many affect, he expected to enjoy much entertainment in the criticisms of Partridge; from whom he expected the simple dictates of nature, unimproved, indeed, but likewise unadulterated, by art.

In the first row, then, of the first gallery, did Mr. Jones, Mrs. Miller, her youngest daughter, and Partridge take their places. Partridge immediately declared it was the finest place he had ever been in. When the first music was played, he said it was a wonder how so many fiddlers could play at one time without putting one another out. While the fellow was lighting the upper candles, he cried out to Mrs. Miller, "Look, look, madam; the very picture of the man in the end of the common prayer-book, before the gunpowder treason service." Nor could he help observing with a sigh, when all the candles were lighted, that here were candles enough burned in one night to keep an honest poor family for a whole twelvemonth.

As soon as the play, which was *Hamlet, Prince of Denmark*, began, Partridge was all attention, nor did he break silence till the entrance of the ghost; upon which he asked Jones what man that was in the strange dress; "something," said he, "like what I have seen in a picture. Sure it is not armor, is it?"

Jones answered, "That is the ghost."

To which Partridge replied with a smile, "Persuade me to that, sir, if you can. Though I can't say I ever actually saw a ghost in my life, yet I am certain I should know one, if I saw him, better than that comes to. No, no, sir; ghosts don't appear in such dresses as that, neither." In this mistake, which caused much laughter in the neighborhood of Partridge, he was suffered to continue till the scene between the ghost and Hamlet, when Partridge gave that credit to Mr. Garrick which he had denied to Jones, and fell into so violent a trembling that his knees knocked against each other.

Jones asked him what was the matter, and whether he was afraid of the warrior upon the stage.

"O la! sir," said he, "I perceive now it is what you told me. I am not afraid of anything, for I know it is but a play; and, if it was really a ghost, it could do one no harm at such a distance, and in so much company; and yet, if I was frightened, I am not the only person."

"Why, who," cries Jones, "dost thou take to be such a coward here besides thyself?"

"Nay, you may call me coward if you will; but, if that little man there upon the stage is not frightened, I never saw any man frightened in my life. Ay, ay; go along with you! Ay, to be sure! Who's fool, then? Will you? Lud have mercy upon such foolhardiness! Whatever happens it is good enough for you. Follow you? I'd follow the devil as soon. Nay, perhaps it is the devil—for they say he can put on what likeness he pleases. Oh! here he is again. No farther! No, you have gone far enough already; farther than I'd have gone for all the king's dominions." Jones offered to speak, but Partridge cried, "Hush, hush, dear sir, don't you hear him?" And, during the whole speech of the ghost, he sat with his eyes fixed partly on the ghost and partly on Hamlet, and with his mouth open: the same passions which succeeded each other in Hamlet succeeding likewise in him.

When the scene was over, Jones said, "Why, Partridge, you exceed my expectations. You enjoy the play more than I conceived possible."

"Nay, sir," answered Partridge, "if you are not afraid of the devil, I can't help it; but, to be sure, it is natural to be surprised at such things, though I know there is nothing in them: not that it was the ghost that surprised me, neither; for I should have known that to have been only a man in a strange dress; but, when I saw the little man so frightened himself, it was that which took hold of me."

"And dost thou imagine then, Partridge," cries Jones, "that he was really frightened?"

"Nay, sir," said Partridge, "did not you yourself observe afterwards, when he found it was his own father's spirit, and how he was murdered in the garden, how his fear forsook him by degrees, and he was struck dumb with sorrow, as it were, just as I should have been, had it been my own case. But hush! O la! what noise is that? There he is again. Well, to be certain, though I know there is nothing at all in it, I am glad I am not down yonder where those men are." Then, turning his eyes again upon Hamlet, "Ay, you may draw your sword; what signifies a sword against the power of the devil?"

During the second act, Partridge made very few remarks. He greatly admired the fineness of the dresses; nor could he help observing upon the king's countenance. "Well," said he, "how people may be deceived by faces! Who would think, by looking in the king's face, that he had ever committed a murder?" He then inquired after the ghost; but Jones, who intended he should be surprised, gave him no other satisfaction than that he might possibly see him again soon, and in a flash of fire.

Partridge sat in fearful expectation of this; and now, when the ghost made his next appearance, Partridge cried out, "There, sir, now; what say you now? is he frightened now or no? As much frightened as you think me; and, to be sure, nobody can help some fears. I would not be in so bad a condition as—what's his name?—Squire Hamlet is there, for all the world. Bless me! what's become of the spirit? As I am a living soul, I thought I saw him sink into the earth."

"Indeed you saw right," answered Jones.

"Well," cries Partridge, "I know it is only a play; and besides, if there was anything in all this, Madam Miller would not laugh so; for, as to you, sir, you would not be afraid, I believe, if the devil was here in person. There, there; ay, no wonder you are in such a passion; shake the vile, wicked wretch to pieces. If she was my own mother, I should serve her so. To be sure, all duty to a mother is forfeited by such wicked doings. Ay, go about your business; I hate the sight of you."

Our critic was now pretty silent till the play which Hamlet introduces before the king. This he did not at first understand, till Jones explained it to him; but he no sooner entered into the spirit of it than he began to bless himself that he had never committed murder. Then turning to Mrs. Miller, he asked her if she did not imagine the king looked as if he was touched; "though he is," said he, "a good actor, and doth all he can to hide it. Well, I would not have so much to answer for as that wicked man there hath, to sit upon a much higher chair than he sits upon. No wonder he ran away; for your sake I'll never trust an innocent face again."

The grave-digging scene next engaged the attention of Partridge, who expressed much surprise at the number of skulls thrown upon the stage. To which Jones answered that it was one of the most famous burial-places about town.

"No wonder, then," cries Partridge, "that the place is haunted. But I never saw in my life a worse grave-digger. I had a sexton, when I was clerk, that should have dug three graves while he is digging one. The fellow handles a spade as if it was the first time he had ever had one in his hand. Ay, ay, you may sing. You had rather sing than work, I believe." Upon Hamlet's taking up the skull, he cried out, "Well! it is strange to see how fearless some men are; I never could bring myself to touch anything belonging to a dead man, on any account. He seemed frightened enough, too, at the ghost, I thought."

Little more worth remembering occurred during the play; at the end of which Jones asked him which of the players he had liked best. To this he answered, with some appearance of indignation at the question, "The king, without doubt."

"Indeed, Mr. Partridge," says Mrs. Miller, "you are not of the same opinion with the town; for they are all agreed that Hamlet is acted by the best player who ever was on the stage."

"He the best player!" cries Partridge, with a contemptuous sneer, "why, I could act as well as he myself. I am sure, if I had seen a ghost, I should have looked in the very same manner, and done just as he did. And then, to be sure, in that scene, as you called it, between him and his mother, where you told me he acted so fine, why, Lord help me, any man, that is, any good man, that had such a mother, would have done exactly the same. I know you are only joking with me; but, indeed, madam, though I was never at a play in London, yet I have seen acting before in the country; and the king for my money; he speaks all his words distinctly, half as loud again as the other. Anybody may see he is an actor."

Thus ended the adventure at the playhouse, where Partridge had afforded great mirth not only to Jones and Mrs. Miller but to all who sat within hearing, who were more attentive to what he said than to anything that passed on the stage. He durst not go to bed all that night for fear of the ghost; and, for many nights after, sweated two or three hours, before he went to sleep, with the same apprehensions, and waked several times in great horrors, crying out, "Lord have mercy upon us! there it is."

LESSON 43.

HISTORY.—"History, to which we now turn, was raised into the rank of literature in the latter half of the eighteenth century by three men.

DAVID HUME'S *History of England,* finished 1761, is, in the importance it gives to letters, in its clear narrative and style, and in the writer's endeavor to make it a philosophic whole, our first literary history. Of DR. ROBERTSON'S *Histories of Scotland, of Charles V.,* and *of America,* the two last are literary by their descriptive and popular style, and show how our historical interests were reaching beyond our own land.

EDWARD GIBBON, 1737–1794, excelled the others in his *Decline and Fall of the Roman Empire,* completed in 1788. The execution of his work was as accurate and exhaustive as a scientific treatise. Gibbon's conception of the whole subject was as poetical as a great picture. Rome, eastern and western, was painted in the centre, dying slowly like a lion. Around it he pictured all the nations and hordes that wrought its ruin, told their stories from the beginning, and the results on themselves and on the world of their victories over Rome. The collecting and use of every detail of the art and costume and manners of the times he described, the reading and use of all the contemporary literature, the careful geographical detail, the marshalling of all this information with his facts, the great imaginative conception of the work as a whole, and the use of a full, and perhaps too heightened, style to add importance to the subject gave a new impulse and a new model to historical literature. The contemptuous tone of the book is made still more remarkable by the heavily-laden style, and the monotonous balance of every sentence. The bias Gibbon had against Christianity illustrates a common fault of historians. The historical value of Hume's history was spoiled by his personal dislike of the principles of our Revolution."

"The faults of Gibbon's style are obvious enough, and its compensatory merits are not far to seek. No one can overlook its frequent tumidity and constant want of terseness. It lacks suppleness, ease, variety. It is not often distinguished by happy selection of epithet, and seems to ignore all delicacy of *nuance*. A prevailing grandiloquence, which easily slides into pomposity, is its greatest blemish. It seems as if Gibbon had taken the stilted tone of the old French tragedy for his model, rather than the crisp and nervous prose of the best French writers. We are constantly offended by a superfine diction lavished on barbarous chiefs and rough soldiers of the Lower Empire, which almost reproduces the high-flown rhetoric in which Corneille's and Racine's characters address each other. Such phrases as the 'majesty of the throne,' 'the dignity of the purple,' the 'wisdom of the senate' recur with a rather jarring monotony, especially when the rest of the narrative was designed to show that there was no majesty nor dignity nor wisdom involved in the matter. We feel that the writer was thinking more of his sonorous sentence than of the real fact.

On the other hand, nothing but a want of candor or taste can lead any one to overlook the rare and great excellences of Gibbon's style.

First of all, it is singularly correct—a rather common merit now, but not common in his day. But its sustained vigor and loftiness will always be uncommon; above all, its rapidity and masculine length of stride are quite admirable. When he takes up his pen to describe a campaign or any great historic scene, we feel that we shall have something worthy of the occasion, that we shall be carried swiftly and grandly through it all, without the suspicion of a breakdown of any kind's being possible. An indefinable stamp of weightiness is impressed on Gibbon's writing; he has a baritone manliness which banishes everything small, trivial, or weak. On the whole, we may say that his manner, with certain manifest faults, is not unworthy of his matter, and the praise is great."—*J. C. Morrison.*

BIOGRAPHY AND TRAVELS.—"These are linked at many points to History. The first was lifted into a higher place in literature by JOHNSON's *Lives of the Poets,* 1779–81, and by BOSWELL's *Life of Johnson,* 1791. The production of books of Travel, since James Bruce left for Africa in 1762 till the present day, has increased as rapidly almost as that of the Novel, and there is scarcely any part of the world that has not been visited and described. In this way a vast amount of materials has been collected for the use of philosophers, poets, and historians. Travel has rarely produced literature, but it has been one of its assistants.

Classic Comedy may be said to be represented by *The Goodnatured Man* and *She Stoops to Conquer* of GOLDSMITH, and by *The Rivals* and the *School for Scandal* of SHERIDAN, all of which appeared between 1768 and 1778. Both men were Irishmen, but Goldsmith has more of the Celtic grace, and Sheridan of the Celtic wit. With Sheridan we may say that the history of the English drama closes."

BIBLIOGRAPHY. HUME, ROBERTSON, and GIBBON.—*Eng. Men of Let.* Series; H. Brougham's *Lives of Men of Let.*; J. Forster's *Crit. Essays*; Hume's *My Own Life*; Contem. Rev., v. 11, 1869; E. Lawrence's *Lives of Brit. Hist.*; Bagehot's *Estimates of some Englishmen and Scotchmen;* Sainte Beuve's *Eng. Portraits;* Ecl. Mag., Nov., 1852.

From Gibbon's *Decline and Fall*.

The noblest of the Greeks and the bravest of the allies were summoned to the palace to prepare them, on the evening of the 28th, for the duties and dangers of the general assault. The last speech of Palæologus was the funeral oration of the Roman Empire; he promised, he conjured, and he vainly attempted to infuse the hope which was extinguished in his own mind. In this world all was comfortless and gloomy; and neither the gospel nor the church has proposed any conspicuous recompense to the heroes who fall in the service of their country.

But the example of their prince and the confinement of a siege had armed these warriors with the courage of despair; and the pathetic scene is described by the feelings of the historian Phranza, who was himself present at this mournful assembly. They wept, they embraced; regardless of their families and fortunes, they devoted their lives; and each commander, departing to his station, maintained all night a vigilant and anxious watch on the rampart. The emperor and some faithful companions, entered the dome of St. Sophia, which in a few hours was to be converted into a mosque, and devoutly received, with tears and prayers, the sacrament of the holy communion. He reposed some moments in the palace, which resounded with cries and lamentations; solicited the pardon of all whom he might have injured; and mounted on horseback to visit the guards and explore the motions of the enemy. The distress and fall of the last Constantine are more glorious than the long prosperity of the Byzantine Cæsars.

In the confusion of darkness, an assailant may sometimes succeed; but in this great and general attack, the military judgment and astrological knowledge of Mahomet advised him to expect the morning, the memorable 29th of May, in the fourteen hundred and fifty-third year of the Christian era. The preceding night had been strenuously employed: the troops, the cannon, and the fascines were advanced to the edge of the ditch, which in many parts presented a smooth and level passage to the breach; and his fourscore galleys almost touched with the prows and their scaling-ladders the less defensible walls of the harbor. Under pain of death, silence was enjoined; but the physical laws of motion and sound are not obedient to discipline or fear; each individual might suppress his voice and measure his footsteps; but the march and labor of thousands must inevitably produce a strange confusion of dissonant clamors, which reached the ears of the watchmen of the towers.

At daybreak, without the customary signal of the morning-gun, the Turks assaulted the city by sea and land; and the similitude of a twined or twisted thread has been applied to the closeness and continuity of their line of attack. The foremost ranks consisted of the refuse of the host, a voluntary crowd, who fought without order or command; of the feebleness of age or childhood, of peasants and vagrants, and of all who had joined the camp in the blind hope of plunder and martyrdom. The common impulse drove them onwards to the wall; the most audacious to climb were instantly precipitated; and not a dart, not a bullet of the Christians was idly wasted on the accumulated throng. But their strength and ammunition were exhausted in this laborious defence; the ditch was filled with the bodies of the slain; they supported the footsteps of their companions; and of this devoted vanguard the death was more serviceable than the life.

Under their respective bashaws and sanjaks, the troops of Anatolia and Romania were successively led to the charge; their progress was various and doubtful; but, after a conflict of two hours, the Greeks still maintained and improved their advantage; and the voice of the emperor was heard, encouraging his soldiers to achieve, by a last effort, the deliverance of their country. In that fatal moment, the janizaries arose, fresh, vigorous, and invincible. The sultan himself on horseback, with an iron mace in his hand, was the spectator and judge of their valor; he was surrounded by ten thousand of his domestic troops whom he reserved for the decisive occasions; and the tide of battle was directed and impelled by his voice and eye. His numerous ministers of justice were posted behind the line to urge, to restrain, and to punish; and, if danger was in the front, shame and inevitable death were in the rear of the fugitives. The cries of fear and of pain were drowned in the martial music of drums, trumpets, and attaballs; and experience has proved that the mechanical operation of sounds, by quickening the circulation of the blood and spirits, will act on the human machine more forcibly than the eloquence of reason and honor. From the lines, the galleys, and the bridge, the Ottoman artillery thundered on all sides; and the camp and city, the Greeks and the Turks, were involved in a cloud of smoke, which could only be dispelled by the final deliverance or destruction of the Roman Empire.

The single combats of the heroes of history or fable amuse our fancy and engage our affections; the skilful evolutions of war may inform the mind, and improve a necessary, though pernicious, science; but, in the uniform and odious pictures of a general assault, all is blood and horror and confusion: nor shall I strive, at the distance of three centuries and a thousand miles, to delineate a scene of which there could be no spectators, and of which the actors themselves were incapable of forming any just or adequate idea.

The immediate loss of Constantinople may be ascribed to the bullet, or arrow, which pierced the gauntlet of John Justiniani. The sight of his blood, and the exquisite pain appalled the courage of the chief, whose arms and counsels were the firmest rampart of the city. As he withdrew from his station in quest of a surgeon, his flight was perceived and stopped by the indefatigable emperor. "Your wound," exclaimed Palæ-ologus, "is slight; the danger is pressing; your presence is necessary; and whither will you retire?" "I will retire," said the trembling Genoese, "by the same road which God has opened to the Turks;" and at these words he hastily passed through one of the breaches of the inner wall. By this pusillanimous act he stained the honors of a military life; and the few days which he survived in Galata, or the isle of Chios, were em-bittered by his own and the public reproach. His example was imitated by the greatest part of the Latin auxiliaries, and the defence began to slacken when the attack was pressed with redoubled vigor.

The number of the Ottomans was fifty, perhaps a hundred, times superior to that of the Christians; the double walls were reduced by the cannon to a heap of ruins; in a circuit of several miles, some places must be found more easy of access or more feebly guarded; and, if the besiegers could penetrate in a single point, the whole city was irrecover-ably lost. The first who deserved the sultan's reward was Hassan, the janizary, of gigantic stature and strength. With his scimitar in one hand, and his buckler in the other, he ascended the outward fortifica-tion; of the thirty janizaries who were emulous of his valor eighteen perished in the bold adventure. Hassan and his twelve companions had reached the summit; the giant was precipitated from the rampart; he rose on one knee, and was again oppressed by a shower of darts and stones. But his success had proved that the achievement was possible; the walls and towers were instantly covered with a swarm of Turks; and the Greeks, now driven from the vantage-ground, were overwhelmed by increasing multitudes. Amidst these multitudes, the emperor, who ac-complished all the duties of a general and a soldier, was long seen, and finally lost. The nobles, who fought round his person, sustained, till their last breath, the honorable names of Palæologus and Cantacuzene; his mournful exclamation was heard, "Cannot there be found a Christian to cut off my head?" and his last fear was that of falling alive into the hands of the infidels. The prudent despair of Constantine cast away the purple; amidst the tumult he fell by an unknown hand, and his body was buried under a mountain of the slain.

After his death, resistance and order were no more; the Greeks fled towards the city, and many were pressed and stifled in the narrow pass of the gate of St. Romanus. The victorious Turks rushed through the breaches of the inner wall, and, as they advanced into the streets, they were soon joined by their brethren, who had forced the gate Phenar on the side of the harbor. In the first heat of their pursuit, about two thousand Christians were put to the sword; but avarice soon prevailed over cruelty, and the victors acknowledged that they should immediately have given quarter, if the valor of the emperor and his chosen bands had not prepared them for a similar opposition in every part of the capital. It was thus, after a siege of fifty-three days, that Constantinople was irretrievably subdued by the arms of Mahomet II. Her empire only had been subverted by the Latins; her religion was trampled in the dust by the Moslem conquerors.

LESSON 44.

PHILOSOPHICAL AND POLITICAL LITERATURE.—"These were both stimulated by the great movement of thought on all subjects pertaining to the natural rights of man which was led by Voltaire and Rousseau. In *philosophy* the historian David Hume led the way, and the transparent clearness of his style gave full force to opinions which made utility the only measure of virtue, and the knowledge of our ignorance the only certain knowledge.

In **Political Literature**, EDMUND BURKE, born 1731, is our greatest, almost our only, writer of this time. From 1756 to 1797, when he died, his treatises and speeches proved their right to the title of literature by their extraordinary influence on the country. Philosophical reasoning and poetic passion were wedded together in them on the side of conservatism, and every art of eloquence was used with the mastery that imagination gives. His *Thoughts on the Cause of the Present Discontents*, 1773, was perhaps the best of his works in point of style.

All Burke's work is more literature than oratory. Many of his speeches enthralled their hearers, but many more put them to sleep. The very men, however, who slept under him in the House read over and over again the same speech, when published, with renewed delight. Goldsmith's praise of him, that he ' wound himself into his subject like a serpent,' gives the reason why he sometimes failed as an orator, why he always succeeded as a writer."

"The varieties of Burke's literary or rhetorical method are very strik·ing. It is almost incredible that the superb imaginative amplification of the description of Hyder Ali's descent upon the Carnatic should be from the same pen as the grave, simple, unadorned *Address to the King*, 1777, where each sentence falls on the ear with the accent of some gold-en-tongued oracle of the wise gods. His stride is the stride of a giant, from the sentimental beauty of the picture of Marie Antoinette at Versailles to the learning, positiveness, and cool, judicial mastery of the *Report on the Lords' Journals*, 1794. Even in the coolest and dryest of his pieces, there is the mark of greatness, of grasp, of comprehension. In all its varieties Burke's style is noble, earnest, deep-flowing, because his sentiment was lofty and fervid, and went with sincerity and ardent disciplined travail of judgment. Burke had the style of his subjects, the amplitude, the weightiness, the laboriousness, the sense, the high flight, the grandeur, proper to a man dealing with imperial themes— the freedom of nations, the justice of rulers, the fortunes of great socie-ties, the sacredness of law.

Burke will always be read with delight and edification, because, in the midst of discussions on the local and the accidental, he scatters apothegms that take us into the regions of lasting wisdom. In the midst of the torrent of his most strenuous and passionate deliverances, he sud-denly rises aloof from his immediate subject, and in all tranquility re-minds us of some permanent relation of things, some enduring truth of human life or society. We do not hear the organ tones of Milton, for faith and freedom had other notes in the seventeenth century. There is none of the complacent and wise-browed sagacity of Bacon, for Burke's were days of eager, personal strife and party fire and civil division. We are not exhilarated by the cheerfulness, the polish, the fine man-ners of Bolingbroke, for Burke had an anxious conscience, and was earnest and intent that the good should triumph. And yet Burke is among the greatest of those who have wrought marvels in the prose of our English tongue."—*John Morley*.

POLITICAL ECONOMY.—" Before Burke, a new class of politi-cal writings had arisen which concerned themselves with social and economical reform. The immense increase of the industry, wealth, and commerce of the country, from 1720 to 1770, aroused inquiry into the laws that regulate wealth, and ADAM SMITH, 1723–1790, a professor at Glasgow, who had in 1759 written his book on the *Moral Sentiments*, published in 1776 the *Wealth of Nations*. By its theory, that labor is the source of wealth, and that to give the laborer absolute freedom to pursue his own interest in his own way is the best means of increasing the wealth of the country; by its proof that all laws made to restrain or to shape or to promote commerce were stumbling-blocks in the way of the wealth of any state, he created the Science of Political Economy, and started the theory and practice of Free Trade. All the questions of labor and capital were now placed on a scientific basis, and since that time the literature of the whole of the subject has engaged great thinkers. Connected with this were all the writings on the subjects of the *poor* and *education* and *reform*.

MISCELLANEOUS LITERATURE.—During the whole of the time from the days of Addison onwards, the finer literature of prose had flourished. With SAMUEL JOHNSON, born 1709, began the literary man such as we know him in modern times, who, independent of patronage or party, lives by his pen, and finds in the public his only paymaster. The Essay was continued by him in his *Rambler*, 1750–2, and *Idler*, but, in these papers, lightness, the essence of Addison's and Steele's Essays in the *Spectator* and *Tatler*, is not found.

His celebrated letter to Lord Chesterfield gave the death-blow to patronage. The great *Dictionary of the English Language*, 1755, at which he worked unhelped, and which he published without support, was the first book that appealed solely to the public. He represents thus a new class. But he was also the last representative of the literary king who, like Dryden and Pope, held a kind of court in London. When he died, 1784, London was no longer the only literary centre, and poetry and prose were produced from all parts of the country."

"Johnson's sentences seem to be contorted, as his gigantic limbs used to twitch, by a kind of mechanical, spasmodic action. The most obvious peculiarity is the tendency, which he noticed himself, to use too big words and too many of them. It was not, however, the mere bigness of the words that distinguished his style, but a peculiar love of putting the abstract for the concrete, of using awkward inversions, and of balancing his sentences in a monotonous rhythm, which give the appearance, as they sometimes correspond to the reality, of elaborate, logical discrimination.

With all its faults the style has the merits of masculine directness. The inversions are not such as to complicate the construction. As Boswell remarks, he never uses a parenthesis; and his style, though ponderous and wearisome, is as transparent as the smarter snip-snap of Macaulay. This singular mannerism appears in his earliest writings; it is most marked at the time of the *Rambler;* whilst, in the *Lives of the Poets,* although I think that the trick of inversion has become commoner, the other peculiarities have been so far softened as to be inoffensive."—*Leslie Stephen.*

"GOLDSMITH'S *Citizen of the World,* a series of letters supposed to be written by a Chinese traveller in England, and collected in 1762, satirizes the manners and fashionable follies of the time. Several other series followed, but they are now unreadable. One man alone in our own century caught the old inspiration, and with a humor less easy, but more subtile, than Addison's. It was Charles Lamb, in the *Essays of Elia,* and the fineness of perception he showed in these was equally displayed in his criticisms on the old dramatists.

The miscellaneous literature of the latter half of the eighteenth century includes, also, the admirable *Letters* of GRAY, the poet; THOMAS WARTON'S *History of English Poetry,* which founded a new school of poetic criticism; the many collections of periodical essays, all of which ceased in 1787; Burke's *Inquiry into the Origin of our Ideas of the Sublime and Beautiful;* and the *Letters of Junius,* political invectives, written in a style which has preserved them to this day."

BIBLIOGRAPHY. BURKE.—T. Macknight's *Life and Times* of; *Eng. Men of Let.* Series; J. Timbs' *Anecdote Biog.*; Brougham's *Sketches of Statesmen;* F. D. Mau-

rice's *Friendship of Books* ; S. Rogers'*Recollections ;* Minto's *Man. of Eng. Pr. Lit.;* G. Croly's *Hist. Sketches ;* Ecl. Mag., Jan. and Feb., 1852, and Feb. and March, 1862; N. A. Rev., v. 88, 1859.
JOHNSON.—Boswell's *Life* of ; Hawthorne's *Our Old Home;* Macaulay's *Essays; Eng. Men of Let.* Series: A. Murphy's *Essay on Life and Genius* of ; N. Drake's *Essays;* T. Carlyle's *Heroes and Hero Worship;* Ed. Rev., Oct., 1859; Quar. Rev., v. 103, 1858, and v. 105, 1859; Allibone's *Crit. Dictionary.*
JUNIUS.—C. Chabot's *The Hand-Writing of Junius professionally investigated;* J. Jaques' *Hist. of Junius and His Works:* De Quincey's *Lit. Reminiscences;* J. Forster's *Crit. Essays;* West. Rev., Oct., 1871; Quar. Rev., Apr., 1871; Temple Bar, Oct., 1873.

LESSON 45.

POETRY.—THE ELEMENTS AND FORMS OF THE NEW POETRY.

—"The period we are now studying may not improperly be called a time of transition in poetry. The influence of the poetry of the past lasted; new elements were added to poetry, and new forms of it took shape. There was a change also in the style and in the subject of poetry. Under these heads I shall bring together the various poetical works of this period.

1. *The study of the Greek and Latin classics revived,* and with it a more artistic poetry. Not only correct form, for which Pope sought, but beautiful form was sought after. Men like Thomas Gray and William Collins strove to pour into their work that simplicity of beauty which the Greek poets and Italians like Petrarca had reached as the last result of genius restrained by art. Their poems, published between 1746 and 1757, remain apart as a unique type of poetry. The refined workmanship of these poets, their manner of blending together natural feeling and natural scenery, their studious care in the choice of words are worthy of special study.

2. *The study of the Elizabethan and of the earlier poets like Chaucer and of the whole course of poetry in England was taken up with great interest.* Shakespeare and Chaucer had engaged both Dryden and Pope; but the whole subject was now enlarged. Gray, like Pope, projected a history of English poetry, and his *Ode on the Progress of Poesy* illustrates this new interest. Thomas Warton wrote his *History of English*

Poetry, 1774–78, and in doing so gave fresh material to the poets. They began to take delight in the childlikeness and naturalness of Chaucer as distinguished from the artificial and critical verse of the school of Pope. Shakespeare was studied in a more accurate way. Pope's, Theobald's, Sir Thomas Hanmer's, and Warburton's editions of Shakespeare were succeeded by Johnson's in 1765; and Garrick, the actor, began the restoration of the genuine text of Shakespeare's plays for the stage.

Spenser formed the spirit and work of some poets, and T. Warton wrote an essay on the *Faerie Queen*. WILLIAM SHEN-STONE'S *Schoolmistress*, 1742, was one of these Spenserian poems, and so was the *Castle of Indolence*, 1748, by JAMES THOMSON, author of the *Seasons*. JAMES BEATTIE, in the *Minstrel*, 1774, a didactic poem, followed the stanza and manner of Spenser.

3. A new element, *interest in the romantic past*, was added by the publication of Dr. Percy's *Reliques of Ancient English Poetry*, 1765. The narrative ballad and the narrative romance, afterwards taken up and perfected by Sir Walter Scott, now struck their roots afresh in English poetry. Men began to seek among the ruder times of history for wild, natural stories of human life; and the pleasure in these increased and accompanied the growing love of lonely, even of savage, scenery. The *Ossian*, 1762, of JAMES MACPHERSON, which gave itself out as a translation of Gaelic epic poems, is an example of this new element.

Still more remarkable in this way were the poems of THOM-AS CHATTERTON, the 'marvellous boy,' who died by his own hand in 1770, at the age of seventeen. They were imitations of old poetry. He pretended to have discovered, in a muniment room at Bristol, the *Death of Sir Charles Bawdin* and other poems by an imaginary monk named Thomas Rowley. Written with quaint spelling, and with a great deal of lyrical invention, they raised around them a great controversy. J may mention as an instance of the same tendency, even before the *Reliques*, Gray's translations from the Norse and British poetry, and his poem of the *Bard*, in which the bards of Wales are celebrated.

CHANGE OF STYLE.—We have seen how the natural style of the Elizabethan poets had ended by producing an unnatural style. In reaction from this, the critical poets set aside natural feeling, as having nothing to do with the expression of thought in verse, and wrote according to rules of art which they had painfully worked out. Their style in doing this lost life and fire; and, losing these, lost art, which has its roots in emotion, and gained artifice, which has its roots in intellectual analysis. Being unwarmed by any natural feeling, it became as unnatural, considered as a poetic style, as that of the later Elizabethan poets. We may sum up, then, the whole history of the style of poetry from Elizabeth to George I.—the style of the first-rate poets being excepted—in these words: *Nature without Art, and Art without Nature, had reached similar but not identical results in style.*

But in the process two things had been learned. *First,* that artistic rules were necessary, and, *secondly*, that natural feeling was necessary in order that poetry should have a style fitted to express nobly the emotions and thoughts of man. The way was therefore now made ready for a style in which the Art should itself be Nature, and it sprang at once into being in the work of the poets of this time. The style of Gray and Collins is polished to the finest point, and yet is instinct with natural feeling. Goldsmith is natural even to simplicity, and yet his verse is even more accurate than Pope's. Cowper's style, in such poems as the *Lines to his Mother's Picture,* and in lyrics like the *Loss of the Royal George,* arises out of the simplest pathos, and yet is as pure in expression as Greek poetry. The work was then done; but as yet the element of fervent passion did not enter into poetry. We shall see how that came in after 1789.

CHANGE OF SUBJECT—NATURE.—Up to the age of Pope
the subject of man was treated, and we have seen how many
phases it went through. There remained the subject of Nature and of man's relation to it; that is, of the visible landscape,
sea, and sky, and all that men feel in contact with them.
Natural scenery had been hitherto used only as a background
to the picture of human life. It now began to take a much
larger place in poetry, and after a time grew to occupy a distinct place of its own apart from Man.

The impulse given by Thomson to poetry of this kind was
soon followed. Men left the town to visit the country and
record their feelings. WILLIAM SOMERVILLE'S *Chase*, 1735,
and JOHN DYER'S *Grongar Hill*, 1726, a description of a
journey in South Wales, and his *Fleece*, 1757, are full of
country sights and scenes: even Akenside mingled his spuri-
ous philosophy with pictures of solitary natural scenery.

Foreign travel now enlarged the love of nature. The *Letters* of GRAY, 1716-1771, some of the best in the English language, describe natural scenery with a minuteness quite new
in English Literature. In his poetry he used the description
of nature as 'its most graceful ornament,' but never made it
the subject. In the *Elegy in a Country Churchyard*, and in
the *Ode on a Distant Prospect of Eton College*, natural scenery is interwoven with reflections on human life, and used to
point its moral. COLLINS observes the same method in his
Ode on the Passions and the *Ode to Evening*. There is, then,
as yet no love of nature for its own sake.

A further step was made by OLIVER GOLDSMITH, 1728-74,
in his *Traveller*, 1764, a sketch of national manners and governments, and in his *Deserted Village*, 1770. He describes
natural scenery with less emotion than Collins, and does not
moralize it like Gray. The scenes he paints are pure pictures,
and he has no personal interest in them.

The next step was made by men like the two Wartons and
by John Logan, 1782. Their poems do not speak of nature

and human life, but of nature and themselves. They see the reflection of their own joys and sorrows in the woods and streams, and for the first time the pleasure of being alone with nature apart from men became a distinct element in modern poetry. In the later poets it becomes one of their main subjects. These were the steps towards that love of nature for its own sake which we shall find in the poets who followed Cowper. One poem of the time almost anticipates it. It is the *Minstrels,* 1771, of JAMES BEATTIE. This poem represents a young poet educated almost altogether by lonely communion with and love of nature, and both in the spirit and in the treatment of the first part of the story resembles very closely Wordsworth's description of his own education by nature, in the beginning of the *Prelude,* and the history of the peddler in the first book of the *Excursion.*"

" Goldsmith was peculiarly happy in writing bright and airy verses; the grace and lightness of his touch have rarely been approached. The *Deserted Village* is one of the most graceful and touching poems in the English language. It is clear bird-singing; but there is a pathetic note in it. No one better knew than himself the value of those finished and musical lines he was gradually adding to the beautiful poem, the grace and sweetness and tender pathetic charm of which make it one of the literary treasures of the English people."— *William Black.*

BIBLIOGRAPHY. GRAY.—Mitford's *Life* of; S. Johnson's *Lives of Eng. Poets;* Howitt's *Homes of Brit. Poets;* Ward's *Anthology;* Black. Mag., v. 75, 1854; N. A. Rev., v. 96, 1863; Quar. Rev., v. 94, 1854.

COLLINS.—Brydges' *Imagin. Biog.;* J. Coleman's *Hist. Essays;* N. Drake's *Literary Hours;* Ward's *Anthology.*

GOLDSMITH.—Irving's *Life* of; Forster's *Life and Times* of; De Quincey's *Essays on the Poets;* H. Giles' *Lectures and Essays ;* Thack.'s *Eng. Humorists;* J. Timbs' *Wits and Humorists; Eng. Men of Let.* Series; Macaulay's *Essays;* Ecl. Mag., May, 1850, and Jan., 1855.

READINGS.—Gray's *Elegy* and Goldsmith's *Deserted Village* and *Traveller,* published in pamphlet form by Clark & Maynard.

LESSON 46.

FURTHER CHANGE OF SUBJECT—MAN.—"During this time the interest in Mankind, that is, in Man independent of nation, class, and caste, which we have seen in prose, and which was stimulated by the works of Voltaire and Rousseau, began to influence poetry. It broke out into a fierce extreme in the French Revolution, but long before that event it entered into poetry in various ways as it had entered into society and politics. One form of it appeared in the interest the poets began to take in men of other nations than England; another form of it—and this was increased by the Methodist revival—was the interest in the lives of the poor. Thomson speaks with sympathy of the Siberian exile and the Mecca pilgrim, and the *Traveller* of Goldsmith enters into foreign interests. His *Deserted Village*, Shenstone's *Schoolmistress*, Gray's *Elegy* celebrate the annals of the poor. Michael Bruce in his *Lochleven* praises the 'secret primrose path of rural life,' and Dr. John Langhorne in his *Country Justice* pleads the cause of the poor and paints their sorrows. Connected with this new element is the simple ballad of simple love, such as Shenstone's *Jemmy Dawson*, Mickle's *Mariner's Wife*, Goldsmith's *Edwin and Angelina*, poems which started a new type of human poetry, afterwards worked out more completely in the *Lyrical Ballads* of Wordsworth.

In a class apart I call attention to the *Song of David*, a long poem written by CHRISTOPHER SMART, a friend of Johnson's. It will be found in Chambers' ' Cyclopædia of English Literature.' Composed for the most part in a madhouse, the song has a touch here and there of the overforcefulness and the lapsing thoughts of a half insane brain. But its power of metre and of imaginative presentation of thoughts and things, and its mingling of sweet and grand religious poetry ought to make it better known. It is unique in style and in character-

SCOTTISH POETRY illustrates and anticipates the poetry of the poor and the ballad. We have not mentioned it since Sir David Lyndsay, for, with the exception of stray songs, its voice was silent for a century and a half. It revived in ALLAN RAMSAY, a friend of Pope and Gay. His light pieces of rustic humor were followed by the *Tea Table Miscellany* and the *Ever-Green*, collections of existing Scottish songs mixed up with some of his own. They carried on the song of rural life and love and humor which Burns perfected. Ramsey's pastoral drama of the *Gentle Shepherd*, 1725, is a pure, tender, and genuine picture of Scottish life and love among the poor and in the country.

ROBERT FERGUSON deserves to be named, because he kindled the muse of Burns, and his occasional pieces, 1773, are chiefly concerned with the rude and humorous life of Edinburgh. The Ballad, always continuous in Scotland, took a more modern but very pathetic form in such productions as *Auld Robin Gray* and the *Flowers of the Forest*, a mourning for those who fell at Flodden Field. The peculiarities I have dwelt on already continue in this revival. There is the same nationality, the same rough wit, the same love of nature, but the love of color has lessened.

The new elements and the changes on which I have dwelt are expressed by three poets—Cowper, Crabbe, and Burns. But before these we must mention the poems of WILLIAM BLAKE, the artist, and for three reasons.

1. They represent the new elements. *The Poetical Sketches*, written in 1777, illustrate the new study of the Elizabethan poets. Blake imitated Spenser, and, in his short fragment of *Edward III.*, we hear again and again the note of Marlowe's violent imagination. A short poem *To the Muses* is a cry for the restoration to English poetry of the old poetic passion it had lost. In some ballad poems we trace the influence represented by Ossian and given by the publication of Percy's *Reliques*.

2. We find also in his work certain elements which belonged to the second period of which I shall now speak. The love of animals is one. A great love of children and the poetry of home is another. He also anticipated, in 1789 and 1794, when his *Songs of Innocence* and *Experience* were written, the simple natural poetry of ordinary life which Wordsworth perfected in the Lyrical Ballads, 1798. Further still, we find in these poems traces of the democratic element, of the hatred of priestcraft, and of the war with social wrongs which came much later into English poetry. We even find traces of the mysticism and the search after the problem of life that fill so much of our poetry after 1832.

3. But that which is most special in Blake is his extraordinary reproduction of the spirit, tone, and ring of the Elizabethan songs, of the inimitable innocence and fearlessness which belong to the childhood of a new literature. The little poems too in the *Songs of Innocence*, on infancy and first motherhood, and on subjects like the *Lamb*, are without rival in our language for ideal simplicity and a perfection of singing joy. The *Songs of Experience* give the reverse side of the *Songs of Innocence*, and they see the evil of the world as a child with a man's heart would see it—with exaggerated and ghastly horror. Blake stands alone in our poetry, and his work coming where it did, between 1777 and 1794, makes it the more remarkable. We turn now to William Cowper, who represents fully and more widely than either Crabbe or Burns the new elements on which I have dwelt.

WILLIAM COWPER.—The first poems of WILLIAM COWPER, 1731–1800, were the *Olney Hymns*, 1779, written along with John Newton, and in these the religious poetry of Charles Wesley was continued. The profound personal religion, gloomy even to insanity as it often became, which fills the whole of Cowper's poetry, introduced a theological element into English poetry which continually increased till within the last ten years, when it has gradually ceased.

His didactic and satirical poems, 1782, link him backwards to the last age. His translation of Homer, 1791, and of shorter pieces from the Latin and Greek, connects him with the classical influence, his interest in Milton with the revived study of the English Poets. The playful and gentle vein of humor which he showed in *John Gilpin* and other poems reminds us of Addison, and opened a new kind of verse to poets. With this kind of humor is connected a simple pathos of which Cowper is our greatest master. The *Lines to Mary Unwin* and to his *Mother's Picture* prove, with the work of Blake, that pure natural feeling, wholly free from artifice, had returned to English song. A wholly new element was also introduced by him and Blake—the love of animals, and the poetry of their relation to man, a vein plentifully worked by after poets.

His greatest work was the *Task*, 1785. It is mainly a description of himself and his life in the country, his home, his friends, his thoughts as he walked, the quiet landscape of Olney, the life of the poor people about him, mixed up with disquisitions on political and social subjects, and, at the end, a prophecy of the victory of the Kingdom of God. *The change in it in relation to the subject of Nature is very great.* Cowper is the first poet who loves Nature entirely for her own sake. He paints only what he sees, but he paints it with the affection of a child for a flower and with the minute observation of a man.

The change in relation to the subject of Man is equally great. The idea of *Mankind as a whole*, which we have seen growing up, is fully formed in Cowper's mind. The range of his interests is as wide as the world, and all men form one brotherhood. All the social questions of Education, Prisons, Hospitals, city and country life, the state of the poor and their sorrows, the question of universal freedom and of slavery, of human wrong and oppression, of just and free government, of international intercourse and union, and, above all, the entirely new question of the future destiny of the race, as a whole, are introduced by Cowper into English poetry. And though splendor and passion were added, by the poets who succeeded him, to the new poetry, yet they worked on the thoughts he had laid down, and he is their leader."

" Cowper is one of the first symptoms, if not the originator, of a revolution in style which is soon to become a revolution in ideas. The 'clear, crisp English' of his verse is not the work of a man who belongs to a school, or follows some conventional pattern. It is for his amusement, he repeats again and again in his letters, that he is a poet; just as it has been for his amusement that he has worked in the garden and made rabbit-hutches. He writes because it pleases him, without a thought of his fame or of contriving what the world will admire.

The Task, his most characteristic poem, is indeed a work of great labor; but the labor is not directed, as Pope's labor was directed, towards methodizing or arranging the material, towards working up the argument, towards forcing the ideas into the most striking situations. The labor is in the cadences and the language; as for the thoughts, they are allowed to show themselves just as they come, in their natural order, so that the poem reads like the speech of a man talking to himself. To turn from a poem of Cowper's to a poem of Pope's, or even of Goldsmith's, is to turn from one sphere of art to quite another, from unconscious to conscious art. 'Formal gardens in comparison with woodland scenery,' as Southey said. And how much that means! It means that the day of critical, and so-called classical, poetry is over; that the day of spontaneous, natural, romantic poetry has begun. Burns and Wordsworth are not yet, but they are close at hand. We read Cowper not for his passion or for his ideas, but for his love of nature and his faithful rendering of her beauty, for his truth of portraiture, for his humor, for his pathos; for the refined honesty of his style, for the melancholy interest of his life, and for the simplicity and the loveliness of his character."—*Thomas H. Ward.*

BIBLIOGRAPHY. COWPER.—Cowper's *Letters;* Southey's *Life* of; Bagehot's *Estimates of some Eng. and Scotchmen;* F. Jeffrey's *Essays;* Thomson's *Celebrated Friendships; Eng. Men of Let.* Series; Ward's *Anthology;* Black. Mag., v. 109, 1871; Fort. Rev., v. 3, 1865; Fraser's Mag., v. 64, 1861;. Nat. Quar. Rev., v. 7, 1863; N. Br. Rev., v. 22, 1854; Quar. Rev., v. 107, 1860.

LESSON 47.

Cowper's *On the Receipt of my Mother's Picture.*

Oh that those lips had language! Life has passed
With me but roughly since I heard thee last.
Those lips are thine—thy own sweet smiles I see,
The same that oft in childhood solaced me;
Voice only fails, else how distinct they say,
"Grieve not, my child, chase all thy fears away!"
The meek intelligence of those dear eyes—
Blest be the art that can immortalize,
The art that baffles time's tyrannic claim
To quench it—here shines on me still the same.
　　Faithful remembrancer of one so dear,
O welcome guest, though unexpected here,
Who bidst me honor with an artless song,
Affectionate, a mother lost so long,
I will obey, not willingly alone
But gladly, as the precept were her own.
And, while that face renews my filial grief,
Fancy shall weave a charm for my relief,
Shall steep me in Elysian reverie,
A momentary dream that thou art she.
　　My mother! when I learned that thou wast dead,
Say, wast thou conscious of the tears I shed?
Hovered thy spirit o'er thy sorrowing son,
Wretch even then life's journey just begun?
Perhaps thou gavest me, though unfelt, a kiss;
Perhaps a tear, if souls can weep in bliss—
Ah, that maternal smile! it answers—Yes.
I heard the bell tolled on thy burial-day,
I saw the hearse that bore thee slow away,
And, turning from my nursery window, drew
A long, long sigh, and wept a last adieu.
But was it such? It was. Where thou art gone,
Adieus and farewells are a sound unknown.
May I but meet thee on that peaceful shore,
The parting sound shall pass my lips no more.
Thy maidens, grieved themselves at my concern,
Oft gave me promise of thy quick return,

What ardently I wished I long believed,
And, disappointed still, was still deceived;
By disappointment every day beguiled,
Dupe of *to-morrow* even from a child.
Thus many a sad-to-morrow came and went,
Till, all my stock of infant sorrow spent,
I learned at last submission to my lot,
But, though I less deplored thee, ne'er forgot.
   Where once we dwelt our name is heard no more,
Children not thine have trod my nursery floor;
And where the gardener Robin day by day
Drew me to school along the public way,
Delighted with my bauble coach, and wrapt
In scarlet mantle warm, and velvet-capped,
'Tis now become a history little known,
That once we called the pastoral house our own.
Short-lived possession! but the record fair
That memory keeps of all thy kindness there
Still outlives many a storm that has effaced
A thousand other themes less deeply traced.
Thy nightly visits to my chamber made
That thou mightst know me safe and warmly laid;
Thy morning bounties ere I left my home,
The biscuit or confectionery plum;
The fragrant waters on my cheeks bestowed
By thy own hand, till fresh they shone and glowed;
All this, and more endearing still than all,
Thy constant flow of love, that knew no fall,
Ne'er roughened by those cataracts and breaks
That humor interposed too often makes;—
All this, still legible in memory's page,
And still to be so to my latest age,
Adds joy to duty, makes me glad to pay
Such honors to thee as my numbers may;
Perhaps a frail memorial, but sincere,
Not scorned in heaven, though little noticed here.
   Could Time, his flight reversed, restore the hours,
When, playing with thy vesture's tissued flowers,
The violet, the pink, and jessamine,
I pricked them into paper with a pin—

And thou wast happier than myself the while,
Wouldst softly speak and stroke my head and smile—
Could those few pleasant hours again appear,
Might one wish bring them, would I wish them here?
I would not trust my heart—the dear delight
Seems so to be desired, perhaps I might.
But no—what here we call our life is such,
So little to be loved, and thou so much,
That I should ill requite thee to constrain
Thy unbound spirit into bonds again.

   Thou, as a gallant bark from Albion's coast
(The storms all weathered and the ocean crossed)
Shoots into port at some well-havened isle,
Where spices breathe, and brighter seasons smile,
There sits quiescent on the floods that show
Her beauteous form reflected clear below,
While airs, impregnated with incense, play
Around her, fanning light her streamers gay;
So thou, with sails how swift! hast reached the shore
"Where tempests never beat nor billows roar."
And thy loved consort on the dangerous tide
Of life long since has anchored by thy side.
But me, scarce hoping to attain that rest,
Always from port withheld, always distressed,—
Me howling blasts drive devious, tempest-tost,
Sails ripped, seams opening wide, and compass lost,
And day by day some current's thwarting force
Sets me more distant from a prosperous course.
Yet, oh, the thought that thou art safe, and he!
That thought is joy, arrive what may to me.
My boast is not that I deduce my birth
From loins enthroned and rulers of the earth;
But higher far my proud pretensions rise—
The son of parents passed into the skies!
And now, farewell—Time, unrevoked, has run
His wonted course, yet what I wished is done.
By contemplation's help, not sought in vain,
I seem to have lived my childhood o'er again;
To have renewed the joys that once were mine,
Without the sin of violating thine,

And, while the wings of Fancy still are free,
And I can view this mimic show of thee,
Time has but half succeeded in his theft—
Thyself removed, thy power to soothe me left.

From *The Task—The Winter Evening.*

Hark! 'tis the twanging horn! O'er yonder bridge,
That with its wearisome but needful length
Bestrides the wintry flood, in which the moon
Sees her unwrinkled face reflected bright,
He comes, the herald of a noisy world,
With spattered boots, strapped waist, and frozen locks,
News from all nations lumbering at his back.
True to his charge, the close-packed load behind,
Yet careless what he brings, his one concern
Is to conduct it to the destined inn,
And, having dropped the expected bag, pass on.
He whistles as he goes, light-hearted wretch,
Cold and yet cheerful: messenger of grief
Perhaps to thousands, and of joy to some,
To him indifferent whether grief or joy.
Houses in ashes, and the fall of stocks,
Births, deaths, and marriages, epistles wet
With tears that trickled down the writer's cheeks
Fast as the periods from his fluent quill,
Or charged with amorous sighs of absent swains,
Or nymphs responsive, equally affect
His horse and him, unconscious of them all.
But oh the important budget! ushered in
With such heart-shaking music—who can say
What are its tidings? Have our troops awaked?
Or do they still, as if with opium drugged,
Snore to the murmurs of the Atlantic wave?
Is India free? and does she wear her plumed
And jewelled turban with a smile of peace,
Or do we grind her still? The grand debate,
The popular harangue, the tart reply,
The logic, and the wisdom, and the wit,
And the loud laugh—I long to know them all;
I burn to set the imprisoned wranglers free,
And give them voice and utterance once again.

Now stir the fire, and close the shutters fast,
Let fall the curtains, wheel the sofa round,
And while the bubbling and loud hissing urn
Throws up a steamy column, and the cups
That cheer but not inebriate wait on each,
So let us welcome peaceful evening in.

　.　　.　　.　　.　　.　　　.

O Winter! ruler of the inverted year,
Thy scattered air with sleet like ashes filled,
Thy breath congealed upon thy lips, thy cheeks
Fringed with a beard made white with other snows
Than those of age, thy forehead wrapt in clouds,
A leafless branch thy sceptre, and thy throne
A sliding car, indebted to no wheels,
But urged by storms along its slippery way,—
I love thee, all unlovely as thou seemest,
And dreaded as thou art.　Thou hold'st the sun
A prisoner in the yet undawning east,
Shortening his journey between morn and noon,
And hurrying him, impatient of his stay,
Down to the rosy west; but kindly still
Compensating his loss with added hours
Of social converse and instructive ease,
And gathering, at short notice, in one group
The family dispersed, and fixing thought,
Not less dispersed by daylight and its cares,
I crown thee king of intimate delights,
Fireside enjoyments, homeborn happiness,
And all the comforts that the lowly roof
Of undisturbed retirement and the hours
Of long, uninterrupted evening know.
No rattling wheels stop short before these gates;
No powdered pert, proficient in the art
Of sounding an alarm, assaults these doors
Till the street rings; no stationary steeds
Cough their own knell, while, heedless of the sound,
The silent circle fan themselves and quake:
But here the needle plies its busy task,
The pattern grows, the well-depicted flower,
Wrought patiently into the snowy lawn,
Unfolds its bosom; buds and leaves and sprigs

And curling tendrils, gracefully disposed,
Follow the nimble finger of the fair;
A wreath that cannot fade, of flowers that blow
With most success when all besides decay.
The poet's or historian's page, by one
Made vocal for the amusement of the rest,
The sprightly lyre, whose treasure of sweet sounds
The touch from many a trembling chord strikes out,
And the clear voice symphonious, yet distinct,
And in the charming strife triumphant still,
Beguile the night, and set a keener edge
On female industry: the threaded steel
Flies swiftly, and, unfelt, the task proceeds.

LESSON 48.

BURNS.—" One element, the passionate treatment of love, had been on the whole absent from our poetry since the Restoration. It was restored by ROBERT BURNS, 1759–1796. In his love songs we hear again, only with greater truth of natural feeling, the same music which in the age of Elizabeth enchanted the world. It was as a love-poet that he began to write, and the first edition of his poems appeared in 1786.

He was not only the poet of love, but also of the new excitement about Man. Himself poor, he sang the poor. Neither poverty nor low birth made a man the worse—the man was 'a man for a' that.' He did the same work in Scotland in 1786 which Crabbe began in England in 1783 and Cowper in 1785, and it is worth remarking how the dates run together. As in Cowper so also in Burns, the further widening of human sympathies is shown in the new tenderness for animals. The birds, sheep, cattle, and wild creatures of the wood and field fill as large a space in the poetry of Burns as in that of Wordsworth and Coleridge.

He carried on also the Celtic elements of Scotch poetry, but he mingled them with others specially English. The rattling fun of the *Jolly Beggars* and of *Tam o'Shanter* is united to a life-like painting of human character which is peculiarly

English. A certain large gentleness of feeling often made his wit into that true humor which is more English than Celtic, and the passionate pathos of such poems as *Mary in Heaven* is connected with this vein of humor, and is also more English than Scotch. The special nationality of Scotch poetry is as strong in Burns as in any of his predecessors, but it is also mingled with a larger view of man than the merely national one. Nor did he fail to carry on the Scotch love of nature, though he shows the English influence in using natural description, not for the love of nature alone, but as a background for human love. It was the strength of his passions and the weakness of his moral will which made his poetry and spoilt his life.

With Robert Burns poetry written in the Scotch dialect may be said to say its last word of genius, though it lingered on in JAMES HOGG's pretty poem of *Kilmeny* in *The Queen's Wake*, 1813, and continues a song-making existence to the present day."

"Burns' poetry shares with all poetry of the first order of excellence the life and movement not of one age but of all ages, that which belongs to what Wordsworth calls 'the essential passions' of human nature. It is the voice of nature which we hear in his poetry, and it is of that nature one touch of which makes the whole world kin. It is doubtful whether any other poet, ancient or modern, has evoked as much personal attachment of a fervid and perfervid quality as Burns has been able to draw to himself. It is an attachment the amount and quality of which are not to be explained by anything in the history of the man, anything apart from the exercise of his genius as a poet. What renders it at all intelligible is, that human nature, in its most ordinary shapes, is more poetical than it looks, and that, exactly at those moments of its consciousness in which it is most truly, because most vividly and powerfully and poetically, itself, Burns has a voice to give to it.

He is not the poet's poet, which Shelley no doubt meant to be, or the philosopher's poet, which Wordsworth, in spite of himself, is. He is the poet of homely human nature, not half so homely or prosaic as it seems. The passions which live in his poetry and by which it lives are the essential passions of human nature. His imagination, humor, pathos, the qualities in respect to which his genius is most powerful and opulent, are without reserve placed at their disposal and submitted to their dictation. His claim to be considered the first of song-writers is hardly disputed. His lyrical passion drew its strength from various and opposite sources, from the clashing experiences, habits, and emotions of a nature which needed nothing so much as regulation and harmony. But it is itself harmony as perfect as the song of the linnet and the thrush piping to a summer evening of peace on earth and glory in the western sky. Whatever the poet's eye had seen of beauty, or his heart had felt of mirth or sadness or madness, melts into and becomes a tone, a chord of music of which, but for one singer, the world should hardly have known the power to thrill the universal heart." —*John Service.*

BIBLIOGRAPHY. BURNS.—Chambers' *Life and Works* of; T. Carlyle's *Essays;* Eng. *Men of Let.* Series; H. Giles' *Illus. of Genius;* Howitt's *Homes and Haunts of Brit. Poets;* John Wilson's *Essays;* Ward's *Anthology;* H. Miller's *Essays;* At. Monthly, v. 6, 1860; Nat. Quar. Rev., v, 6, 1863, and v. 18, 1869; N. Br. Rev., v. 16, 1851-2.

Burns' *Afton Water.*

Flow gently, sweet Afton, among thy green braes,[1]
Flow gently, I'll sing thee a song in thy praise;
My Mary's asleep by thy murmuring stream,
Flow gently, sweet Afton, disturb not her dream.

Thou stock-dove, whose echo resounds thro' the glen,
Ye wild, whistling black birds in yon thorny den,
Thou green-crested lapwing, thy screaming forbear,
I charge you, disturb not my slumbering fair.

How lofty, sweet Afton, thy neighboring hills,
Far marked with the courses of clear, winding rills;
There daily I wander as noon rises high,
My flocks and my Mary's sweet cot in my eye.

How pleasant thy banks and green valleys below,
Where wild in the woodlands the primroses blow;
There oft as mild ev'ning weeps over the lea,[2]
The sweet scented birk[3] shades my Mary and me.

Thy crystal stream, Afton, how lovely it glides,
And winds by the cot where my Mary resides;
How wanton thy waters her snowy feet lave,
As, gathering sweet flowrets, she stems thy clear wave.

---

[1] Declivities.   [2] Field.   [3] Birch-tree.

Flow gently, sweet Afton, among thy green braes,
Flow gently, sweet river, the theme of my lays;
My Mary's asleep by thy murmuring stream,
Flow gently, sweet Afton, disturb not her dream.

For A' That and A' That.

Is there, for honest poverty,
    That hangs his head, and a' that?
The coward-slave, we pass him by—
    We dare be poor for a' that!
For a' that, and a' that,
    Our toils obscure, and a' that,
The rank is but the guinea's stamp—
    The man's the gowd [1] for a' that.

What tho' on hamely fare we dine,
    Wear hoddin-grey, [2] and a' that?
Gie [3] fools their silks, and knaves their wine—
    A man's a man for a' that.
For a' that, and a' that,
    Their tinsel show, and a' that;
The honest man, tho' e'er sae poor,
    Is king o' men for a' that.

Ye see yon birkie, [4] ca'd a lord,
    Wha struts and stares and a' that;
Tho' hundreds worship at his word,
    He's but a coof [5] for a' that:
For a' that, and a' that,
    His ribband, star, and a' that;
The man of independent mind,
    He looks and laughs at a' that.

A prince can mak' a belted knight,
    A marquis, duke, and a' that;
But an honest man's aboon [6] his might,
    Gude faith, he mauna fa' that! [7]
For a' that, and a' that,
    Their dignities and a' that;

---

[1] Gold.   [2] Coarse woollen cloth.   [3] Give.   [4] Conceited fellow.
[5] Ninny.   [6] Above.   [7] Must not try that.

The pith o' sense and pride o' worth
  Are higher rank than a' that.

Then let us pray that come it may,
  As come it will for a' that,
That sense and worth, o'er a' the earth,
  May bear the gree [1] and a' that:
For a' that, and a' that,
  It's comin' yet for a' that,
That man to man, the world [2] o'er,
  Shall brothers be for a' that!

To a Mountain Daisy.

Wee, modest, crimson-tipped flow'r,
Thou's met me in an evil hour;
For I maun crush amang the stoure[3]
    Thy slender stem:
To spare thee now is past my pow'r,
    Thou bonie gem.

Alas! it's no thy neebor sweet,
The bonie Lark, companion meet!
Bending thee 'mang the dewy weet![4]
    Wi' [5] speckl'd breast,
When upward springing, blythe, to greet
    The purpling East.

Cauld blew the bitter-biting North
Upon thy early, humble birth;
Yet cheerfully thou glinted forth
    Amid the storm,
Scarce rear'd above the parent-earth
    Thy tender form.

The flaunting flow'rs our gardens yield,
High-shelt'ring woods and wa's[6] maun shield;
But thou, beneath the random bield [7]
    O' clod or stane,
Adorns the histic stibble[8]-field,
    Unseen, alane.

---

[1] Be victor.	[2] A dissyllable.	[3] Dust.	[4] Moisture.	[5] With.
[6] Walls.	[7] Shelter.		[8] Dry stubble.	

There, in thy scanty mantle clad,
Thy snawie bosom sun-ward spread,
Thou lifts thy unassuming head
    In humble guise;
But now the share[1] uptears thy bed,
    And low thou lies!

Such is the fate of artless maid,
Sweet flow'ret of the rural shade!
By love's simplicity betray'd,
    And guileless trust,
Till she, like thee, all soiled, is laid
    Low i' the dust.

Such is the fate of simple bard,
On life's rough ocean luckless starr'd!
Unskilful he to note the card
    Of prudent lore,
Till billows rage, and gales blow hard,
    And whelm him o'er!

Such fate to suffering worth is giv'n,
Who long with wants and woes has striv'n,
By human pride or cunning driv'n
    To mis'ry's brink,
Till wrench'd of ev'ry stay but heav'n,
    He, ruin'd, sink!

Ev'n thou who mourn'st the daisy's fate,
That fate is thine—no distant date;
Stern ruin's plough-share drives, elate,
    Full on thy bloom,
Till crush'd beneath the furrow's weight
    Shall be thy doom!

My Wife's a Winsome Wee Thing.

She is a winsome[2] wee thing,
She is a handsome wee thing,
She is a bonie wee thing,
    This sweet wee wife o' mine.

- Plough-share.   [2] Light-hearted.

I never saw a fairer,
I never lo'ed a dearer,
And neist[1] my heart I'll wear her,
    For fear my jewel tine.[2]

She is a winsome wee thing,
She is a handsome wee thing,
She is a bonie wee thing,
    This sweet wee wife o' mine.
The warld's wrack[3] we share o't,
The warstle[4] and the care o't;
Wi' her I'll blythely bear it,
    And think my lot divine.

Epistle to a Young Friend.

I lang hae thought, my youthfu' friend,
    A something to have sent you,
Tho' it should serve nae other end
    Than just a kind memento;
But how the subject-theme may gang,[5]
    Let time and chance determine;
Perhaps it may turn out a sang,
    Perhaps, turn out a sermon.

Ye'll try the world soon, my lad,
    And, Andrew dear, believe me,
Ye'll find mankind an unco squad[6]
    And muckle they may grieve ye:
For care and trouble set your thought,
    Ev'n when your end's attained;
And a' your views may come to nought,
    When ev'ry nerve is strained.

I'll no say men are villains a';
    The real, hardened wicked
Wha hae nae check but human law
    Are to a few restricked.
But, och! mankind are unco weak,
    An' little to be trusted;
If self the wavering balance shake,
    It's rarely right adjusted!

---

[1] Next.   [2] To lose.   [3] Trouble.   [4] Struggle.   [5] Co.   [6] Strange crew.

Yet they wha fa'[1] in fortune's strife,
　Their fate we shouldna censure,
For still the important end of life
　They equally may answer:
A man may hae an honest heart,
　Tho' poortith[2] hourly stare him;
A man may tak a neebor's part
　Yet hae nae cash to spare him.

Aye free, aff-han',[3] your story tell,
　When wi' a bosom crony;
But still keep something to yoursc
　Ye scarcely tell to ony.[4]
Conceal yoursel as weel's ye can
　Frae critical dissection;
But keek[5] thro' ev'ry other man
　Wi' sharpen'd, sly inspection.

The sacred lowe[6] o' weel-plac'd lcv
　Luxuriantly indulge it;
But never tempt th' illicit rove,
　Tho' naething should divulge it;
I wave the quantum[7] o' the sin,
　The hazard o' concealing;
But, och! it hardens a' within,
　And petrifies the feeling!

To catch Dame Fortune's golden smile
　Assiduous wait upon her;
And gather gear[8] by ev'ry wile
　That's justified by honor:
Not for to hide it in a hedge,
　Nor for a train attendant,
But for the glorious privilege
　Of being independent.

The fear o' hell's a hangman's whip
　To haud[9] the wretch in order;
But where ye feel your honor grip[10]
　Let that aye be your border:

---

[1] Who fall.	[3] Poverty.	[3] Off-hand.	[4] Any.	[5] Peep.
[6] Flame.	[7] Amount.	[8] Riches.	[9] Hold.	[10] Touched.

Its slightest touches, instant pause—
  Debar a' side pretences;
And resolutely keep its laws,
  Uncaring consequences.

The great Creator to revere
  Must sure become the creature:
But still the preaching cant forbear,
  And ev'n the rigid feature;
Yet ne'er with wits profane to range
  Be complaisance[1] extended;
An atheist laugh's a poor exchange
  For Deity offended!

When ranting round in pleasure's ring,
  Religion may be blinded;
Or, if she gie[2] a random sting,
  It may be little minded;
But when on life we're tempest-driv'n,—
  A conscience but[3] a canker,
A correspondence fix'd wi' Heav'n
  Is sure a noble anchor!

Adieu, dear, amiable youth!
  Your heart can ne'er be wanting!
May prudence, fortitude, and truth
  Erect your brow undaunting!
In ploughman phrase, " God send you speed,"[4]
  Still daily to grow wiser;
And may ye better reck the rede[5]
  Then ever did th' Adviser!

Highland Mary.

Ye banks and braes and streams around
  The castle o' Montgomery!
Green be your woods, and fair your flowers,
  Your waters never drumlie:[6]
There simmer[7] first unfauld her robes,
  And there the langest tarry;
For there I took the last fareweel
  O' my sweet Highland Mary.

---

[1] Courtesy. [2] Give. [3] Without. [4] Success. [5] Heed the advice. [6] Muddy. [7] Summer.

How sweetly bloomed the gay, green birk,
How rich the hawthorn's blossom,
As underneath their fragrant shade
I clasped her to my bosom!
The golden hours on angel wings
Flew o'er me and my dearie;
For dear to me, as light and life,
Was my sweet Highland Mary.

Wi' mony a vow and locked embrace
Our parting was fu' tender;
And, pledging aft to meet again,
We tore oursels asunder:
But, oh! fell death's untimely frost,
That nipt my flower sae early!
Now green's the sod, and cauld's the clay
That wraps my Highland Mary.

O pale, pale now, those rosy lips
I aft hae kissed sae fondly!
And closed for aye the sparkling glance
That dwelt on me sae kindly!
And mould'ring now in silent dust
That heart that lo'ed me dearly!
But still within my bosom's core
Shall live my Highland Mary.

Scheme for Review.

PERIOD VIII.

FROM THE FRENCH REVOLUTION ONWARDS,

1789 ——.

LESSON 49.

Brief Historical Sketch.—In 1793 war began with France; it ended June 18, 1815. Vaccination introduced, 1796. Rebellion in Ireland put down, 1800. Union of Ireland with England, 1800. Undulatory theory of light established, 1802. Battle of Trafalgar and death of Nelson, 1805. Death of Pitt, 1806. Slave Trade abolished, 1807. Against Napoleon's Berlin decree, 1806, which made it lawful for French vessels to seize neutral vessels sailing from English ports with English merchandise, the celebrated retaliatory Orders in Council are issued, 1807, declaring France and all subject states in a state of blockade and that vessels attempting to trade with their ports may be seized. In 1807 the American Congress retaliates with the Embargo, and in 1809 prohibits intercourse with England and France till the restrictions on neutral commerce are relaxed. War declared against the U. S. in 1812, ended, 1814. Streets of London first lighted with gas, 1814. Holy Alliance formed, 1815. First steamer, the Savannah, crosses the Atlantic, 1819. George IV. comes to the throne, 1820. Roman Catholics admitted to Parliament, 1829. First Railway, from Liverpool to Manchester, 1830. Wm. IV. succeeds Geo. IV., 1830. Reform Bill, 1832. Slavery abolished in British colonies, 1833. East India trade thrown open, 1833. Great "Tractarian Movement" by Newman, Pusey, and Keble begun, 1833. System of National Education begun, 1834. Victoria succeeds William IV., 1837. The Opium War with China, 1839. Penny Postage, 1840. Transportation for Crime abandoned, 1840. Ashburton Treaty respecting our N. E. boundary, 1842. Potato famine in Ireland, 1845. Treaty determining the boundary of Oregon, 1846. Corn Laws repealed, 1846. French Revolution and flight of Louis Philippe to England, 1848. Suppression of the Chartists and of Irish rebels, 1848. Peel's death, 1850. Crystal Palace Exhibition, 1851. Crimean War, 1854–5. Sepoy Mutiny in India, 1857–8. East India Co. abolished, and sovereignty of

India transferred to the Crown, 1858. Jews admitted to Parliament, 1858. Death of Prince Albert, 1861. Civil War in the U. S., 1861–5. First Cable between Europe and America, 1866. Irish Church dis-established, 1869. Abolition of religious tests in the Universities and of purchase in the army, 1871. Alabama Claims Treaty negotiated at Washington, 1871. Tribunal of Arbitration meets at Geneva, same year, and awards for loss of ships and cargoes and for interest, $15,500,000. Victoria becomes Empress of India, 1876. Irish Land Bill, 1881.

LESSON 50.

PROSE—NOVELS.—"The interest kindled in political questions by the French Revolution showed itself in a new class of novels, and the Political stories of HOLCROFT and WILLIAM GODWIN opened a new realm to the novelist, while the latter excluded love altogether from his story of *Caleb Williams.* MRS. OPIE made Domestic life the sphere of her graceful and pathetic stories, 1806. MISS EDGEWORTH, in her Irish stories, gave the first impulse to the novel of National character, and, in her other tales, to the novel with a Moral purpose, 1801–1811. MISS AUSTEN, 1775–1817, with 'an exquisite touch which renders commonplace things and characters interesting from truth of description and sentiment,' produced the best stories we have of everyday English society. *Sense and Sensibility, Pride and Prejudice, Emma, Mansfield Park,* and *Persuasion* were all written between 1811 and 1817.

SIR WALTER SCOTT, 1771–1832, the great Enchanter, now began the long series of his novels. Men are still alive who well remember the wonder and delight of the land when *Waverley,* 1814, was published. In the rapidity of his work, Scott recalls the Elizabethan time. *Guy Mannering,* his next tale, was written in six weeks. The *Bride of Lammermoor,* as great in fateful pathos as *Romeo and Juliet,* was done in a fortnight.

His national tales, such as *The Heart of Midlothian* and *The Antiquary,* are written as if he saw directly all the char-.

acters and scenes, and, when he saw them, enjoyed them so much that he could not help writing them down. And the art with which this was done was so inspired that, since Shakespeare, there is nothing we can compare to it. 'All is great in the Waverley Novels,' says Goethe, 'material, effects, characters, execution.' In the vivid portraiture and dramatic telling of such tales as *Kenilworth* and *Quentin Durward*, he created the Historical Novel. His last tale of power was the *Fair Maid of Perth* in 1828; his last effort in 1831 was made the year before he died. He raised the whole of the literature of the novel into one of the greatest influences that bear on the human mind. The words his uncle once said to him may be applied to the work he did,—'God bless thee, Walter, my man! Thou hast risen to be great, but thou wast always good.' "

"I do not think one of his successors can compare with him for a moment in the ease and truth with which he painted not merely the life of his own time and country—seldom, indeed, that of precisely his own time—but that of days long past, and often, too, of scenes far distant. Scott needed a certain largeness of type, a strongly marked class-life, and, where it was possible, a free, out-of-doors life, for his delineations. No one could paint beggars and gipsies and wandering fiddlers and mercenary soldiers and peasants and farmers and lawyers and magistrates and preachers and courtiers and statesmen and, best of all, perhaps, queens and kings with anything like his ability. But, when it came to describing the small differences of manner, differences not due to external habits so much as to internal sentiment or education or mere domestic circumstance, he was beyond his proper field. And it was well for the world that it was so. The domestic novel, when really of the highest kind, is no doubt a perfect work of art, and an unfailing source of amusement; but it has nothing of the tonic influence, the large instructiveness, the stimulating air of Scott's historic tales.

His conception of women of his own or of a higher class was always too romantic. He hardly ventured, as it were, in his tenderness for them, to look deeply into their little weaknesses and intricacies of character. With women of an inferior class he had not this feeling. But once make a woman beautiful or in any way an object of homage to him, and Scott bowed so low before the image of her that he could not go deep into her heart. He could no more have analyzed such a woman, as Thackeray analyzed Lady Castlewood or Amelia or Becky, or as George Eliot analyzed Rosamond Vincy, than he could have vivisected Camp or Maida[1]. To some extent, therefore, Scott's pictures of women remain something in the style of the miniatures of the last age—bright and beautiful beings without any special character in them. But then how living are his men, whether coarse or noble!"—*Richard H. Hutton.*

BIBLIOGRAPHY. SCOTT.—Lockhart *Life* of; D. Masson's *Brit. Novelists;* W. H. Prescott's *Miscellanies;* Bulwer's *Crit. Writings;* Carlyle's *Essays; Eng. Men of Let.* Series; L. Stephen's *Hours in a Library;* H. Martineau's *Miscellanies;* Harper's Month., vs. 26, 36, 43, and 44; N. A. Rev., v. 87, 1858; Quar. Rev., v. 124, 1868; Allibone's *Crit. Dictionary.*

From Scott's *Guy Mannering.*

This was Abel Sampson, commonly called, from his occupation as a pedagogue, Dominie Sampson. He was of low birth, but having evinced, even from his cradle, an uncommon seriousness of disposition, the poor parents were encouraged to hope that their *bairn,*[2] as they expressed it, "might wag his pow[3] in a pulpit yet." With an ambitious view to such a consummation, they pinched and pared, rose early and lay down late, ate dry bread and drank cold water, to secure to Abel the means of learning. Meantime, his tall, ungainly figure, his taciturn and grave manners, and some grotesque habits of swinging his limbs and screwing his visage while reciting his task made poor Sampson the ridicule of all his school-companions. The same qualities secured him at Glasgow College a plentiful share of the same sort of notice. Half the youthful mob of "the yards" used to assemble regularly to see Dominie Sampson (for he had already attained that honorable title) descend the stairs from the Greek class, with his lexicon under his arm, his long misshapen legs sprawling abroad, and keeping awkward time to the play of his immense shoulder blades, as they raised and depressed the loose and threadbare black coat which was his constant and only wear. When he spoke, the efforts of the professor (professor of divinity, though he was) were totally inadequate to restrain the inextinguishable laughter of the students, and sometimes even to repress his own. The long, sallow visage, the goggle eyes, the huge under jaw, which appeared not to open and shut by an act of volition, but to be dropped and hoisted up again by some complicated machinery within the inner man, the harsh and dissonant voice, and the screech-owl notes to which

---

[1] His favorite dogs.   [2] Child.   [3] Head.

it was exalted when he was exhorted to pronounce more distinctly,—all added fresh subject for mirth to the torn cloak and shattered shoe, which have afforded legitimate subjects of raillery against the poor scholar, from Juvenal's[1] time downward. It was never known that Sampson either exhibited irritability at this ill usage, or made the least attempt to retort upon his tormentors. He slunk from college by the most secret paths he could discover, and plunged himself into his miserable lodging, where, for eighteen-pence a week, he was allowed the benefit of a straw mattress, and, if his landlady was in good humor, permission to study his task by her fire. Under all these disadvantages, he obtained a competent knowledge of Greek and Latin, and some acquaintance with the sciences.

In progress of time, Abel Sampson, probationer of divinity, was admitted to the privileges of a preacher. But, alas! partly from his own bashfulness, partly owing to a strong and obvious disposition to risibility, which pervaded the congregation upon his first attempt, he became totally incapable of proceeding in his intended discourse—gasped, grinned hideously, rolled his eyes till the congregation thought them flying out of his head—shut the Bible—stumbled down the pulpit-stairs, trampling upon the old women who generally take their station there,—and was ever after designated as a "stickit[2] minister." And thus he wandered back to his own country, with blighted hopes and prospects, to share the poverty of his parents. As he had neither friend nor confidant, hardly even an acquaintance, no one had the means of observing closely how Dominie Sampson bore a disappointment which supplied the whole town with a week's sport. To all appearance, the equanimity of Sampson was unshaken. He sought to assist his parents by teaching a school, and soon had plenty of scholars, but very few fees. In fact, he taught the sons of farmers for what they chose to give him, and the poor for nothing; and, to the shame of the former be it spoken, the pedagogue's gains never equalled those of a skilful ploughman. He wrote, however, a good hand, and added something to his pittance by copying accounts and writing letters for Ellangowan.

Now it must be confessed that our friend Sampson, although a profound scholar and mathematician, had not travelled so far in philosophy as to doubt the reality of witchcraft or apparitions. Born, indeed, at a time when a doubt in the existence of witches was interpreted as equivalent to a justification of their infernal practices, a belief of such legends

---

[1] A noted Roman Satirist.   [2] Incompetent.

had been impressed upon the Dominie as an article indivisible from his religious faith; and perhaps it would have been equally difficult to have induced him to doubt the one as the other. With these feelings, and in a thick, misty day, which was already drawing to its close, Dominie Sampson did not pass the Kairn of Derncleugh without some feelings of tacit horror.

What, then, was his astonishment, when, on passing the door—that door which was supposed to have been placed there by one of the later Lairds of Ellangowan to prevent presumptuous strangers from incurring the dangers of the haunted vault—that door supposed to be always locked, and the key of which was popularly said to be deposited with the presbytery—that door, that very door opened suddenly, and the figure of Meg Merrilies, well known, though not seen for many a revolving year, was placed at once before the eyes of the startled Dominie! She stood immediately before him in the foot-path, confronting him so absolutely that he could not avoid her except by fairly turning back, which his manhood prevented him from thinking of.

"I kenn'd[1] ye wad[2] be here," she said with her harsh and hollow voice; "I ken wha[3] ye seek, but ye maun[4] do my bidding."

"Get thee behind me!" said the alarmed Dominie—"Avoid ye!— *Conjuro te scelestissima—iniquissima—atque miserrima—Conjuro te!!!*[5]

Meg stood her ground against this tremendous volley of superlatives, which Sampson hawked up from the pit of his stomach, and hurled at her in thunder. "Is the carl daft,"[6] she said, "wi' his glamour?"[7]

"*Conjuro,*" continued the Dominie, "*abjuro,*[8] *contestor*[8] —"

"What, in the name of Sathan, are ye feared for, wi' your French gibberish[9] that would make a dog sick? Listen, ye stickit stibbler,[10] to what I tell ye, or ye sall rue[11] it while there's a limb o' ye hings to anither! Tell Colonel Mannering that I ken he's seeking me. He kens, and I ken, that the blood will be wiped out, and the lost will be found,

> And Bertram's right and Bertram's might
> Shall meet on Ellangowan height.

Hae, there's a letter to him; I was gaun[12] to send it in another way.—I canna write mysell; but I hae[13] them that will baith write and read, and ride and rin for me. Tell him the time's coming now and the weird's dreed[14]

---

[1] Knew. [2] Would. [3] Who. [4] Must. [5] I adjure thee thou most accursed, spiteful, and wretched one, I adjure thee. [6] Man foolish. [7] Spell. [8] I swear and attest. [9] Inarticulate babble. [10] Good-for-nothing minister. [11] Shall repent. [12] Going. [13] Have. [14] Fate is accomplished.

and the wheel's turning. Bid him look at the stars, as he has looked at them before.—Will ye mind a' this?"

"Assuredly," said the Dominie, "I am dubious—for, woman, I am perturbed at thy words, and my flesh quakes to hear thee."

"They'll do you nae[1] ill though, and may be muckle gude."[2]

"Avoid ye! I desire no good that comes by unlawful means."

"Fule-body that thou art!" said Meg, stepping up to him with a frown of indignation that made her dark eyes flash like lamps from under her bent brows—"Fule-body! If I meant ye wrang, couldna I clod[3] ye over that craig, and wad man ken how ye cam by your end mair than Frank Kennedy? Hear ye that, ye worricow?"[4]

"In the name of all that is good," said the Dominie, recoiling, and pointing his long pewter-headed walking-cane like a javelin at the supposed sorceress,—"in the name of all that is good, bide[5] off hands! I will not be handled—woman, stand off, upon thine own proper peril!—desist, I say—I am strong—lo, I will resist!" Here his speech was cut short; for Meg, armed with supernatural strength, (as the Dominie asserted) broke in upon his guard, put by a thrust which he made at her with his cane, and lifted him into the vault, "as easily," said he, "as I could sway a Kitchen's Atlas."

"Sit down there," she said, pushing the half-throttled preacher with some violence against a broken chair—"sit down there, and gather your wind and your senses, ye black barrow-tram[6] of the Kirk[7] that ye are! Are ye fou[8] or fasting?"

"Fasting—from all but sin," answered the Dominie, who, recovering his voice, and finding his exorcisms only served to exasperate the intractable sorceress, thought it best to affect complaisance and submission, inwardly conning over, however, the wholesome conjurations which he durst no longer utter aloud. But as the Dominie's brain was by no means equal to carry on two trains of ideas at the same time, a word or two of his mental exercise sometimes escaped, and mingled with his uttered speech in a manner ludicrous enough, especially as the poor man shrunk himself together after every escape of the kind, from terror of the effect it might produce upon the irritable feelings of the witch.

Meg, in the meanwhile, went to a great black cauldron that was boiling on a fire on the floor, and, lifting the lid, an odor was diffused through the vault, which, if the vapors of a witch's cauldron could in aught be trusted, promised better things than the hell-broth which such vessels are usually supposed to contain. It was, in fact, the savor of a

---

[1] No. [2] Much good. [3] Throw. [4] Scarecrow. [5] Keep. [6] A term derisive of his ministerial office. [7] Church. [8] Drunk.

goodly stew, composed of fowls, hares, partridges, and moorgame, boiled in a large mess with potatoes, onions, and leeks, and, from the size of the cauldron, appeared to be prepared for half a dozen people at least.

"So ye hae eat naething a' day?" said Meg, heaving a large portion of this mess into a brown dish, and strewing it savorily with salt and pepper.

"Nothing," answered the Dominie—"*scelestissima*—that is, gude wife."

"Hae, then," said she, placing the dish before him, "there's what will warm your heart."

"I do not hunger—*malefica*[1]—that is to say—Mrs. Merrilies!" for he said unto himself, "The savor is sweet, but it hath been cooked by a Canidia[2] or an Erichthoe."[3]

"If ye dinna eat instantly, and put some saul in ye, by the bread and the salt, I'll put it down your throat wi' the cutty[4] spoon, scaulding as it is, and whether ye will or no. Gape,[5] sinner, and swallow."

Sampson, afraid of eye of newt,[6] and toe of frog, tigers' chaudrons,[7] and so forth, had determined not to venture; but the smell of the stew was fast melting his obstinacy, which flowed from his chops as it were in streams of water, and the witch's threats decided him to feed. Hunger and fear are excellent casuists.

"Saul," said Hunger, "feasted with the witch of Endor." "And," quoth Fear, "the salt which she sprinkled upon the food showeth plainly it is not a necromantic banquet, in which that seasoning never occurs." "And besides," says Hunger, after the first spoonful, "it is savory and refreshing viands."

"So ye like the meat?" said the hostess.

"Yea," answered the Dominie, "and I give thee thanks—*sceleratissima!*[8]—which means—Mrs. Margaret."

"Aweel, eat your fill, but, an[9] ye kenn'd how it was gotten, ye may be wadna like it sae weel." Sampson's spoon dropped, in the act of carrying its load to his mouth. "There's been mony a moonlight watch to bring a' that trade thegither," [10] continued Meg,—"the folk that are to eat that dinner thought little o' your game-laws."

"Is that all?" thought Sampson, resuming his spoon, and shovelling away manfully; "I will not lack my food upon that argument."

"Now, ye maun tak a dram."

"I will," quoth Sampson—"*Conjuro te*—that is, I thank you heartily,"

---

[1] Evil-doer. [2] A reputed sorceress at Rome. [3] A Thessalian witch. [4] A large dish spoon. [5] Open the mouth. [6] Lizard. [7] Entrails—an allusion to the witch scene in *Macbeth*. [8] Most wicked one. [9] If. [10] Stuff together.

for he thought to himself, in for a penny in for a pound; and he fairly drank the witch's health in a cupful of brandy. When he had put this cope-stone[1] upon Meg's good cheer, he felt, as he said, mightily elevated and afraid of no evil which could befall unto him.

" Will ye remember my errand now?" said Meg Merrilies; "I ken by the cast o' your ee[2] that ye're anither man than when ye cam in."

" I will, Mrs. Margaret," repeated Sampson stoutly; "I will deliver unto him the sealed yepistle, and I will add what you please to send by word of mouth."

"Then I'll make it short," says Meg. "Tell him to look at the stars without fail this night, and to do what I desire him in that letter, as he would wish

> That Bertram's right and Bertram's might
> Should meet on Ellangowan height.

I have seen him twice when he saw na me; I ken when he was in the country first, and I ken what's brought him back again. Up, an' to the gate! ye're ower lang here—follow me."

Sampson followed the sibyl accordingly, who guided him about a quarter of a mile through the woods, by a shorter cut than he could have found for himself; they then entered upon the common, Meg still marching before him at a great pace, until she gained the top of a small hillock which overhung the road.

"Here," she said, "stand still here. Look how the setting sun breaks through yon cloud that's been darkening the lift[3] a' day. See where the first stream o' light fa's[4]—it's upon Donagild's round tower—the auldest tower in the Castle of Ellangowan—that's no for naething! See as it's glooming[5] to seaward abune[6] yon sloop in the bay—that's no for naething, neither. Here I stood on this very spot," said she, drawing herself up so as not to lose one hair-breadth of her uncommon height, and stretching out her long, sinewy arm and clenched hand—" here I stood when I tauld the last Laird o' Ellangowan what was coming on his house; and did that fa' to the ground? Na—it hit even ower sair![7] And here, where I broke the wand of peace ower him—here I stand again—to bid God bless and prosper the just heir of Ellangowan, that will sure be brought to his ain;[8] and the best laird he shall be that Ellangowan has seen for three hundred years. I'll no live to see it, maybe; but there will be mony a blythe ee see it, though mine be closed. And now, Abel Sampson, as ever ye lo'ed the house of Ellangowan,

---

[1] Top-stone. [2] Eye. [3] Sky. [4] Falls. [5] Darkening. [6] Above. [7] Too sorely. [8] Own.

away wi' my message to the English Colonel, as if life and death were upon your haste."

So saying, she turned suddenly from the amazed Dominie, and regained with swift and long strides the shelter of the wood from which she had issued, at the point where it most encroached upon the common. Sampson gazed after her for a moment in utter astonishment, and then obeyed her directions, hurrying to Woodbourne at a pace very unusual for him, exclaiming three times, "Prodigious! prodigious! pro-di-gi-ous!"

LESSON 51.

NOVELS.—"JOHN GALT and MISS FERRIER followed Scott in describing Scottish life and society. With the peace of 1815 arose new forms of fiction and travel, which became very popular when the close of the war with Napoleon opened the world again to Englishmen, and gave birth to the tale of Foreign scenery and manners. THOMAS HOPE's *Anastasius*, 1819, was the first. LOCKHART began the Classical novel in *Valerius*. Fashionable society was now painted by THEODORE HOOK, MRS. TROLLOPE, and MRS. GORE; and Rural life by MISS MITFORD in *Our Village*.

EDWARD BULWER LYTTON, 1805–1873, began with the Fashionable novel in *Pelham*, 1827, and followed it with a long succession of tales on historical, classical, and romantic subjects. Towards the close of his life, he changed his manner altogether, and *The Caxtons* and those that followed are novels of Modern Society. The tone of them all from the beginning to the end is too high-pitched for real life, but each of them, being kept in the same key throughout, has a reality of its own.

CHARLOTTE BRONTË, 1816–1855, revived in *Jane Eyre* the novel of Passion, and Miss Yonge set on foot the Religious novel in support of a special school of theology. We need only mention Captain Marryatt, whose delightful sea stories carry on the seamen of Smollett to our own times. Miss Martineau and Mr. Disraeli continued the novel of Political opinion and economy, and Charles Kingsley applied the novel to the social and theological problems of our own day.   Three other great names are too close to us to admit of comment— CHARLES DICKENS, 1812–1870, WILLIAM M. THACKERAY, 1811–1863, and the novelist who is known as GEORGE ELIOT. It will be seen then that the Novel claims almost every sphere of human interest as its own, and it has this special character, that it is the only kind of literature in which women have done excellently.

HISTORY.—W. MITFORD's *History of Greece*, completed in 1810, is made untrue by his hatred of a democracy; and DR. LINGARD's excellent *History of England*, 1819, is influenced by his dislike of the Reformation.   HENRY HALLAM, 1778– 1859, was the first who wrote history in England with so careful a love of truth and with so accurate a judgment of the relative value of facts and things that prejudice was ex- cluded.   His *Europe during the Middle Ages*, 1818, and his *Literature of Europe*, 1837–8, are distinguished for their ex- haustive and judicial summing up of facts; and his *Constitu- tional History of England*, 1827, set on foot a new kind of history in the best way.

Our own history now engaged a number of writers.   The great work of LORD MACAULAY, 1800–1859, told the story of the Revolution of 1688 in a style sometimes too emphatic, often monotonous from its mannerism, but always clear.   Its vivid word-painting of characters and great events, and the splendid use, in such descriptions, of his vast knowledge of details, gave as great an impulse to the literature of history as Gibbon had done in his day, and his *Historical Essays* on the times and statesmen between the Restoration and Pitt are masterpieces of their kind.

SIR FRANCIS PALGRAVE gave interest to the study of the early English period, and in our own day a critical English history school has arisen, of which MR. FREEMAN and PRO- FESSOR STUBBS are the leaders.

As the interest in the history of our own land increased, our interest in the history of the world increased. DEAN MILMAN's *History of Latin Christianity* well deserves, by its brilliant and romantic style, the title of fine literature. Greece old and new found her best historians in Bishop Thirlwall, George Grote, and Mr. Finlay; Rome in Dr. Arnold. The history of events near at hand on the Continent was also taken up with care. Among the books of this class, I mention, for their special literary character and style, SIR WILLIAM NAPIER's *History of the Peninsular War*, and THOMAS CARLYLE's *History of the French Revolution*. Both are written in too poetic prose, and the latter is a kind of epic, and is full of his realistic, fantastic, and unequal power of representing persons and things.

BIOGRAPHY.—Since Boswell a multitude of biographies have poured from the press, and have formed useful materials for history. Few of . them have reached literary excellence. SOUTHEY's *Life of Nelson*, LOCKHART's *Life of Scott*, MOORE's *Life of Lord Byron;* or in our own days, FORSTER's *Life of Goldsmith*, and DEAN STANLEY's *Life of Arnold* rise out of a crowd of inferior books.

Theological Literature received a new impulse in 1738–91 from the evangelizing work of John Wesley and Whitfield; and their spiritual followers, Thos. Scott, Newton, and Cecil made by their writings the Evangelical school. WILLIAM PALEY, in his *Evidences*, and Sidney Smith, well known as a wit and an essayist, defended Christianity from the common-sense point of view; while the sermons of Robert Hall and of Dr. Chalmers are, in different ways, fine examples of devotional and philosophical eloquence.

The decay of the Evangelical school was hastened by the writings of COLERIDGE, 1772–1834, whose religious philosophy, in the *Aids to Reflection* and other books, created the school which has been called the Broad Church. Dr. Arnold's sermons supplied it with an element of masculine good sense.

Frederick Maurice in his numerous works added to it mystical piety and one-sided learning, Charles Kingsley a rough and ready power, and Frederick Robertson gave it passion, sentiment, subtilty, and a fine form. At the same time that Maurice began to write, 1830–32, the common-sense school of theology was continued by Archbishop Whately's works; and, in strong reaction against the Evangelicals, the High Church party rose into prominence in Oxford, and was chiefly supported by the tracts and sermons of JOHN HENRY NEWMAN, born in 1801, whose work, with KEBLE's *Christian Year*, a collection of exquisitely wrought hymns, belongs to literature.

The Methodist movement gave the first impulse to popular education, and stirred men to take interest in the cause of the poor. This new philanthropy, stirred still more by the theories of the French Revolution concerning the right of men to freedom and equality, took up the subjects of slavery, of prison reform, of the emancipation of the Catholics, and of a wider representation of the people, and their literature fills a large space till 1832, when Reform brought forward new subjects, and the old subjects under new forms."

BIBLIOGRAPHY. BRONTE.—Mrs. Gaskell's *Life* of; P. Bayne's *Essays;* Black. Mag., v. 82, 1857; Fraser's Mag., v. 55, 1857; N. A. Rev., v. 85, 1857; West. Rev., v. 59, 1853; Ecl. Mag., July, 1855, and Feb., 1878.

DICKENS.—Forster's *Life* of; Whipple's *Lectures on Lit. and Life* and *Success and its Conditions;* Timbs' *Lives of the Later Wits;* Field's *Yesterdays with Authors;* R. H. Horne's *New Spirit of the Age;* Black. Mag., v. 77,1855; 81, 1857; and 109, 1871; Contem. Rev., v. 10, 1869; Fort. Rev., v. 17, 1872; Nat. Quar. Rev., v. 1, 1860; West. Rev., v. 82, 1864.

THACKERAY —*Eng. Men of Let.* Series; P. Bayne's *Essays;* J. Hannay's *Studies on Thack.;* G. Brimley's *Essays;* J. Brown's *Spare Hours*, 2d Ser.; Taine's *Hist. Eng. Lit.;* At. Month.,v. 13,1864; Black. Mag.,v. 77, 1855, and 111, 1872; Ed. Rev.,Jan., 1873; Fraser's Mag., v. 46, 1852; 47, 1853; and 69, 1864; Harper's Mo., vs. 28, 41, and 49; Macmillan, Feb., 1864; Nat. Rev., v. 18, 1864; N. A. Rev., v. 77, 1853; N. Br. Rev., v. 24, 1855; v. 40, 1864; Quar. Rev., v. 97, 1855; West. Rev., v. 59, 1853; 74, 1860; and 82, 1864.

GEORGE ELIOT (Mrs. Lewes).—Black. Mag., vs. 85, 87, 100, 103, and 112; Ed. Rev., vs. 110, 124, and 128; West. Rev., vs. 74, 86, and 90; Contem. Rev., vs. 3, 8, and 20; N. Br. Rev., v. 45; Macmillan, May, 1870; Aug. 1866; and June, 1877; Fraser's Mag., v. 78; At. Mo., vs. 18 and 38; N. A. Rev., v.107; Br. Quar. Rev., Apr., 1873, and Oct., 1876; Scrib. Mo., v. 8; Fort. Rev., Nov., 1876; Ecl. Mag., March and April, 1881.

MACAULAY.—Trevelyan's *Life and Letters* of; Bagehot's *Estimates,* etc.; P.

Bayne's *Essays*; Minto's *Man. Eng. Pr. Lit.*; J. H. Sterling's *Crit. Essays*; Whipple's *Essays*; Maddyn's *Chiefs of Parties*; Black. Mag., v. 80, 1856; Littell. vs. 1, 2, and 4, 1860, and 4, 1870; Fraser's Mag., v. 56, 1857; Macmillan, Feb., 1860; N. Br. Rev., v. 27, 1857, and 33, 1860; Ecl. Mag., Feb., 1862.

LESSON 52.

Thackeray.—"In *painting*, however mechanical, the painter's mind finds always some expression. In *photography* it is difficult for the most accomplished artist to put into his mirror any trace of individual genius. Perfect and admirable as a photograph seems, it is a cold and lifeless image of what, in the reality, was animated with the breath of God.

We find this photographic quality in Thackeray's early writings. There seems to be no sympathy between the writer and his characters. They are, as it were, on the further side of the glass he holds to them. He scrutinizes them with an anatomical microscope; he submits them calmly to vivisection. This attitude of mind gives a peculiar tone to his productions. Even in his later works we think Mr. Thackeray has been over-influenced by this negative element. In *Pendennis* it is the lesson embodied in the hero. The Colonel of the *Newcomes*, of all Thackeray's creations the noblest and most gracious, is sacrificed to his daughter-in-law by a certain odious and improbable identification in the displays of her folly and pettiness.

Thus it is natural that a peculiar ironical sadness, a negative element, should rarely be unfelt in the pages of this great writer. The sense of the irony of things suggests a true picture of the world so nearly like the false picture which might be drawn by the satirist that we must not be surprised if Mr. Thackeray has more than occasionally fallen into satire or mockery. A tone of over-severity, more than a hint of irony infect *Esmond* and the *Virginians*, are painfully prominent in *Vanity Fair* and and in *Pendennis*. It is true that Thackeray's admirable humor, a quality of his so well-known and appreciated that an allusion to it will be enough, springs from the contrasts of life which this irony affords him, and is his justification for recurrence to it. It is equally true that a hundred examples may be produced, displaying the sweet and noble nature, the scorn of baseness, and the 'love of love' which in reality underlie the sneer and the smartness, yet these naturally tell on readers with the greater vividness.

We cannot sum up this criticism better than by suggesting a contrast to the reader. Compare the tone of mind impressed on us by the writings of that great-hearted man to whose honors as laureate of living novelists Mr. Thackeray has unquestionably succeeded. Scott's *Bride of Lammermoor* certainly contains not less than *Pendennis* of the mean

ness of man and the coldness of woman.   Each has the same defect—
want of depth in passionate delineation.   Each is deficient in what it is
fashionable to call 'a high view of life.'   Each, again, presents a drama
of human existence with magnificent power.   Yet, in final impression,
the difference we feel is wider than the difference between the atmosphere of a theatre and the atmosphere of fresh-water; of a ball supper-
room and of the 'incorruptible sea.'   We close the *Bride of Lammermoor* with a sense of healthy pain and healthy pleasure; *Pendennis* with
a *vanitas vanitatum*."—*George Eliot*.

From Thackeray's *Newcomes*.

A crow, who had flown away with a cheese from a dairy window, sat
perched on a tree, looking down at a great, big frog in a pool underneath him.   The frog's hideous, large eyes were goggling out of his
head in a manner which appeared quite ridiculous to the old black-a-
moor, who watched the splay-footed, slimy wretch with that peculiar
grim humor belonging to crows.   Not far from the frog a fat ox was
browsing; while a few lambs frisked about the meadow, or nibbled the
grass and buttercups there.

Who should come into the farther end of the field but a wolf?   He
was so cunningly dressed up in sheep's clothing that the very lambs did
not know master wolf; nay, one of them, whose dam the wolf had just
eaten, after which he had thrown her skin over his shoulders, ran up in-
nocently toward the devouring monster, mistaking him for mamma.

"He-he!" says a fox, sneaking round the hedge-paling, over which
the tree grew whereupon the crow was perched, looking down on the
frog who was staring with his goggle eyes fit to burst with envy, and
croaking abuse at the ox.   "How absurd those lambs are!   Yonder silly,
little, knock-kneed, baah-ling does not know the old wolf dressed in the
sheep's fleece.   He is the same old rogue who gobbled up little Red
Riding Hood's grandmother for lunch, and swallowed little Red Riding
Hood for supper.   He-he!"

An owl, that was hidden in the hollow of the tree, woke up.   "O ho,
master fox," says she, "I cannot see you, but I smell you!   If some
folks like lambs, other folks like geese," says the owl.

"And your ladyship is fond of mice," says the fox.

"The Chinese eat them," says the owl, "and I have read that they
are very fond of dogs," continued the old lady.

"I wish they would exterminate every cur of them off the face of the
earth," said the fox.

"And I have also read in works of travel that the French eat frogs,"
continued the owl.   "Aha, my friend Crapaud! are you there?   That
was a very pretty concert we sang together last night!"

"If the French devour my brethren, the English eat beef," croaked out the frog—"great, big, brutal, bellowing oxen!"

"Ho, whoo!" says the owl, "I have heard that the English are toad-eaters, too!"

"But who ever heard of them eating an owl or a fox, madam?" says Reynard, "or their sitting down and taking a crow to pick," adds the polite rogue, with a bow to the old crow, who was perched above them with the cheese in his mouth. "We are privileged animals, all of us; at least, we never furnish dishes for the odious orgies of man."

"I am the bird of wisdom," says the owl; "I was the companion of Pallas Minerva; I am frequently represented in the Egyptian monuments."

"I have seen you over the British barn-doors," said the fox, with a grin. "You have a deal of scholarship, Mrs. Owl. I know a thing or two myself; but am, I confess it, no scholar—a mere man of the world—a fellow that lives by his wits—a mere country gentleman."

"You sneer at scholarship," continues the owl, with a sneer on her venerable face. "I read a good deal of a night."

"When I am engaged deciphering the cocks and hens at roost," says the fox.

"It's a pity for all that you can't read; that board nailed over my head would give you some information."

"What does it say?" says the fox.

"I can't spell in the daylight," answered the owl; and, giving a yawn, went back to sleep till evening in the hollow of her tree.

"A fig for her hieroglyphics!" said the fox, looking up at the crow in the tree. "What airs our slow neighbor gives herself! She pretends to all the wisdom; whereas, your reverences, the crows, are endowed with gifts far superior to those benighted old big-wigs of owls, who blink in the darkness and call their hooting singing. How noble it is to hear a chorus of crows! There are twenty-four brethren of the Order of St. Corvinus who have builded themselves a convent near a wood which I frequent; what a droning and a chanting they keep up! I protest their reverences' singing is nothing to yours! You sing so deliciously in parts, do for the love of harmony favor me with a solo!"

While this conversation was going on, the ox was champing the grass; the frog was eying him in such a rage at his superior proportions that he would have spurted venom at him if he could, and that he would have burst, only that is impossible, from sheer envy: the little lambkin was lying unsuspiciously at the side of the wolf in fleecy hosiery, who did not as yet molest her, being replenished with the mutton, her mamma. But now the wolf's eyes began to glare and his sharp, white teeth to show, and he rose up with a growl, and began to think he should like lamb for supper.

"What large eyes you have got!" bleated out the lamb, with rather a timid look.

"The better to see you with, my dear."

"What large teeth you have got!"

"The better to —"

At this moment such a terrific yell filled the field that all its inhabitants started with terror. It was from a donkey, who had somehow got a lion's skin, and now came in at the hedge, pursued by some men and boys with sticks and guns.

When the wolf in sheep's clothing heard the bellow of the ass in the lion's skin, fancying that the monarch of the forest was near, he ran away as fast as his disguise would let him. When the ox heard the noise, he dashed round the meadow-ditch, and with one trample of his hoof squashed the frog who had been abusing him. When the crow saw the people with guns coming, he instantly dropped the cheese out of his mouth, and took to wing. When the fox saw the cheese drop, he immediately made a jump at it (for he knew the donkey's voice, and that his asinine bray was not a bit like his royal master's roar), and, making for the cheese, fell into a steel-trap, which snapped off his tail; without which he was obliged to go into the world, pretending, forsooth, that it was the fashion not to wear tails any more, and that the fox-party were better without 'em.

Meanwhile, a boy with a stick came up, and belabored master donkey until he roared louder than ever. The wolf, with the sheep's clothing draggling about his legs, could not run fast, and was detected and shot by one of the men. The blind old owl, whirring out of the hollow tree, quite amazed at the disturbance, flounced into the face of a plowboy, who knocked her down with a pitchfork. The butcher came and quietly led off the ox and the lamb; and the farmer, finding the fox's brush in the trap, hung it over his mantel-piece and always bragged that he had been in at his death.

"What a farrago of old fables is this! What a dressing up in old clothes!" says the critic. (I think I see such a one—a Solomon that sits in judgment over us authors, and chops up our children.) "As sure as I am just and wise, modest, learned, and religious, so surely I have read something very like this stuff and nonsense about jackasses and foxes before. That wolf in sheep's clothing!—do I not know him? That fox discoursing with the crow!—have I not previously heard of him? Yes, in Lafontaine's fables. Let us get the Dictionary and the Fable and the Biographic Universelle, article Lafontaine, and confound the impostor."

"Then in what a contemptuous way," may Solomon go on to remark, "does this author speak of human nature! There is scarce one of these characters he represents but is a villain. The fox is a flatterer; the frog is an emblem of impotence and envy; the wolf in sheep's clothing a bloodthirsty hypocrite, wearing the garb of innocence; the ass in the lion's skin a quack trying to terrify by assuming the appearance of a forest monarch; the ox a stupid common-place; the only innocent being in the writer's (stolen) apologue is a fool—the idiotic lamb, who does not know his own mother." And then the critic, if in a virtuous mood, may indulge in some fine writing regarding the holy beauteousness of maternal affection.

Why not? If authors sneer, it is the critic's business to sneer at them for sneering. He must pretend to be their superior, or who would care about his opinion? And his livelihood is to find fault. Besides, he is right sometimes; and the stories he reads, and the characters drawn in them are old, sure enough. What stories are new? All types of all characters march through all fables: tremblers and boasters; victims and bullies; dupes and knaves; long-eared Neddies, giving themselves leonine airs; Tartuffes, wearing virtuous clothing; lovers and their trials, their blindness, their folly and constancy. With the very first page of the human story do not love and lies, too, begin? So the tales were told ages before Æsop: and asses under lions' manes roared in Hebrew; and sly foxes flattered in Etruscan; and wolves in sheep's clothing gnashed their teeth in Sanscrit, no doubt. The sun shines to-day as he did when he first began shining; and the birds in the tree overhead, while I am writing, sing very much the same note they have sung ever since they were finches. Nay, since last he besought good-natured friends to listen once a month to his talking, a friend of the writer has seen the New World, and found the (featherless) birds there exceedingly like their brethren of Europe. There may be nothing new under and including the sun; but it looks fresh every morning, and we rise with it to toil, hope, scheme, laugh, struggle, love, suffer, until the night comes and quiet. And then will wake Morrow, and the eyes that look on it.

This, then, is to be a story, may it please you, in which jackdaws will wear peacock's feathers, and awaken the just ridicule of the peacocks; in which, while every justice is done to the peacocks themselves, the splendor of their plumage, the gorgeousness of their dazzling necks, and the magnificence of their tails, exception will yet be taken to the absurdity of their rickety strut, and the foolish discord of their pert squeaking;

in which lions in love will have their claws pared by sly virgins; in which rogues will sometimes triumph, and honest folks, let us hope, come by their own; in which there will be black crape and white favors; in which there will be tears under orange-flower wreaths and jokes in mourning-coaches; in which there will be dinners of herbs with contentment and without; and banquets of stalled oxen where there is care and hatred—ay, and kindness and friendship, too, along with the feast. It does not follow that all men are honest because they are poor; and I have known some who were friendly and generous, although they had plenty of money. There are some great landlords who do not grind down their tenants; there are actually bishops who are not hypocrites; there are liberal men even among the Whigs, and the Radicals themselves are not all Aristocrats at heart.

But who ever heard of giving the moral before the Fable? Children are only led to accept the one after their delectation over the other: let us take care lest our readers skip both; and so let us bring them on quickly —our wolves and lambs, our foxes and lions, our roaring donkeys, our billing ring-doves, our motherly partlets, and crowing chanticleers.

Macaulay.—"There is little to notice in Macaulay's vocabulary except its copiousness. He has no eccentricities like De Quincey or Carlyle; he employs neither slang nor scholastic technicalities, and he never coins a new word. He cannot be said to use an excess of Latin words, and he is not a purist in the matter of Saxon. His command of expression was proportioned to the extraordinary compass of his memory. The copiousness appears not so much in the Shakespearian form of accumulating synonyms one upon another as in a profuse way of repeating a thought in several different sentences. This is especially noticeable in the opening passages of some of his essays.

Macaulay's is a style that may truly be called 'artificial' from his excessive use of striking artifices of style—balanced sentences, abrupt transitions, and pointed figures of speech. The peculiarities of the mechanism of his style are expressed in such general terms as 'abrupt,' 'pointed,' 'oratorical.' His sentences have the compact finish produced by the frequent occurrence of the periodic arrangement. He is not uniformly periodic; he often prefers a loose structure, and he very rarely has recourse to the forced inversions that we find occasionally in De Quincey. Yet there is a sufficient interspersion of periodic arrangements to produce an impression of firmness.

We may notice incidentally his lavish use of antithesis. The contrasts are really more numerous than might be thought at first glance; the bare framework is so overlaid and disguised by the extraordinary fulness of expression that many of them escape notice. When we look narrowly, we see that there is a constant play of antithesis. Not only is word set over against word, clause against clause, and sentence against sentence; there are contrasts on a more extensive scale. One group of sentences answers to another, and paragraphs are balanced against paragraphs. His pages are illuminated not only by little sparks of antithesis but by broad flashes.

A rhetorician of so decided a turn as Macaulay could not fail to use the rhetorician's greatest art—the climax. In every paragraph that rises above the ordinary level of feeling, we are conscious of being led on to a crowning demonstration.

Macaulay's composition is as far from being abstruse as printed matter can well be. One can trace in his writing a constant effort to make himself intelligible to the meanest capacity. He loves to dazzle and to argue, but above everything else he is anxious to be understood. His ideal evidently is to turn a subject over on every side, to place it in all lights, and to address himself to every variety of prejudice and preoccupation in his audience."— *William Minto.*

From Macaulay's *Essay on Warren Hastings.*

Burke's knowledge of India was such as few, even of those Europeans who have passed many years in that country, have attained, and such as certainly was never attained by any other public man who had not quitted Europe. He had studied the history, the laws, and the usages of the East with an industry such as is seldom found united to so much genius and so much sensibility. Others have, perhaps, been equally laborious, and have collected an equal mass of materials. But the manner in which Burke brought his higher powers of intellect to work on statements of facts, and on tables of figures, was peculiar to himself. In every part of those huge bales of Indian information, which repelled almost all other readers, his mind, at once philosophical and poetical, found something to instruct or to delight. His reason analyzed and digested those vast and shapeless masses; his imagination animated and colored them.

Out of darkness and dulness and confusion, he formed a multitude of ingenious theories and vivid pictures. He had, in the highest degree, that noble faculty whereby man is able to live in the past and in the future, in the distant and in the unreal. India and its inhabitants were not to him, as to most Englishmen, mere names and abstractions, but a real country and a real people. The burning sun, the strange vegetation of the palm and the cocoa tree, the rice-field, the tank, the huge trees, older than the Mogul Empire, under which the village crowds assemble, the thatched roof of the peasant's hut, the rich tracery of the mosque where the imaum prays with his face to Mecca, the drums and banners and gaudy idols, the devotee swinging in the air, the graceful maiden, with the pitcher on her head, descending the steps to the river side, the black faces, the long beards, the yellow streaks of sect, the turbans and the flowing robes, the spears and the silver maces, the elephants with their canopies of state, the gorgeous palanquin of the prince, and the close litter of the noble lady,—all these things were to him as the objects amidst which his own life had been passed, as the objects which lay on the road between Beaconsfield and St. James Street.

All India was present to the eye of his mind, from the halls where suitors laid gold and perfumes at the feet of sovereigns to the wild moor where the gipsy camp was pitched, from the bazar, humming like a bee-hive with the crowd of buyers and sellers, to the jungle where the lonely courier shakes his bunch of iron rings to scare away the hyænas. He had just as lively an idea of the insurrection at Benares as of Lord George Gordon's riots, and of the execution of Nuncomar as of the execution of Dr. Dodd.

From Macaulay's *History*.

The Pontificate, exposed to new dangers more formidable than had ever before threatened it, was saved by a new religious order, which was animated by intense enthusiasm and organised with exquisite skill. When the Jesuits came to the rescue, they found the Papacy in extreme peril; but from that moment the tide of battle turned. Protestantism, which had, during a whole generation, carried all before it, was stopped in its progress, and rapidly beaten back from the foot of the Alps to the shores of the Baltic. Before the Order had existed a hundred years, it had filled the whole world with memorials of great things done and suffered for the faith. No other religious community could produce a list of men so variously distinguished; none had extended its operations over so vast a space; yet in none had there ever been such perfect unity of feeling and action. There was no region of the globe, no walk of specula-tive or of active life in which Jesuits were not to be found. They guided the counsels of kings. They deciphered Latin inscriptions. They observed the motions of Jupiter's satellites. They published whole libraries, controversy, casuistry, history, treatises on optics, Alcaic odes, editions of the fathers, madrigals, catechisms, and lampoons. The liberal education of youth passed almost entirely into their hands, and was conducted by them with conspicuous ability. They appeared to have discovered the precise point to which intellectual culture can be carried without risk of intellectual emancipation. Enmity itself was compelled to own that, in the art of managing and forming the tender mind, they had no equals

Meanwhile they assiduously and successfully cultivated the eloquence of the pulpit. With still greater assiduity and still greater success they applied themselves to the ministry of the confessional. Throughout Roman Catholic Europe the secrets of every government and of almost every family of note were in their keeping. They glided from one Protestant country to another under innumerable disguises, as gay cavaliers, as simple rustics, as Puritan preachers. They wandered to countries which neither mercantile avidity nor liberal curiosity had ever impelled any stranger to explore. They were to be found in the garb of Mandarins, superintending the observatory at Pekin. They were to be found spade in hand, teaching the rudiments of agriculture to the savages of Paraguay.

Yet, whatever might be their residence, whatever might be their employment, their spirit was the same, entire devotion to the common cause, unreasoning obedience to the central authority. None of them had chosen his dwelling-place or his vocation for himself. Whether the Jesuit should live under the arctic circle or under the equator, whether he should pass his life in arranging gems and collating manuscripts at the Vatican or in persuading naked barbarians under the Southern Cross not to eat each other, were matters which he left with profound submission to the decision of others. If he was wanted at Lima, he was on the Atlantic in the next fleet. If he was wanted at Bagdad, he was toiling through the desert with the next caravan. If his ministry were needed in some country where his life was more insecure than that of a wolf, where it was a crime to harbor him, where the heads and quarters of his brethren, fixed in the public places, showed him what he had to expect, he went without remonstrance or hesitation to his doom.

Nor is this heroic spirit yet extinct. When, in our own time, a new and terrible pestilence passed round the globe, when, in some great cities, fear had dissolved all the ties which hold society together, when the secular clergy had forsaken their flocks, when medical succor was not to be purchased by gold, when the strongest natural affections had yielded to the love of life, even then the Jesuit was found by the pallet which bishop and curate, physician and nurse, father and mother, had deserted, bending over infected lips to catch the faint accents of confession, and holding up to the last, before the expiring penitent, the image of the expiring Redeemer.

From Newman's *Grammar of Assent.*

Science gives us the grounds, or premises, from which religious truths are to be enforced; but it does not set about inferring them, much less does it reach the inference—that is not its province. It brings before us phenomena, and it leaves us, if we will, to call them works of design, wisdom, or benevolence; and, further still, if we will, to proceed to confess an intelligent Creator. We have to take its facts, and to give them a meaning and to draw our own conclusions from them. First comes knowledge, then a view, then reasoning, and then belief. This is why science has so little of a religious tendency—deductions have no power of persuasion. The heart is commonly reached, not through the reason, but through the imagination, by means of direct impressions, by the testimony of facts and events, by history, by description. Persons influence us, voices melt us, looks subdue us, deeds inflame us.

Many a man will live and die upon a dogma; no man will be a martyr for a conclusion. A conclusion is but an opinion; it is not a thing which *is*, but which we are *quite sure about;* and it has often been observed that we never say we are sure and certain without implying that we doubt. To say that a thing *must* be is to admit that it *may not* be. No one, I say, will die for his own calculations; he dies for realities. This is why a literary religion is so little to be depended upon. It looks well in fair weather; but its doctrines are opinions, and, when called to suffer for them, it slips them between its folios, or burns them at its hearth. And this again is the secret of the distrust and raillery with which moralists have been so commonly visited. They say, and do not. Why? Because they are contemplating the fitness of things, and they live by the square when they should be realizing their high maxims in the concrete.

I have no confidence, then, in philosophers who cannot help being religious, and are Christians by implication. They sit at home, and reach forward to distances which astonish us; but they hit without grasping, and are sometimes as confident about shadows as about realities. They have worked out by a calculation the lay of a country which they never saw, and mapped it by means of a gazetteer; and, like blind men, though they can put a stranger on his way, they cannot walk straight themselves, and do not feel it quite their business to walk at all.

Logic makes but a sorry rhetoric with the multitude; first shoot round corners, and you may not despair of converting by a syllogism. Tell men to gain notions of a Creator from his works, and, if they were to set about it, (which nobody does) they would be jaded and wearied by the labyrinth they were tracing. Their minds would be gorged and sur-feited by the logical operation. Logicians are more set upon conclud-ing rightly than on right conclusions. They cannot see the end for the process. Few men have that power of mind which may hold fast and firmly a variety of thoughts. We ridicule men of one idea; but a great many of us are born to be such, and we should be happier if we knew it. To most men argument makes the point in hand only more doubtful, and considerably less impressive.

After all, man is *not* a reasoning animal; he is a seeing, feeling, con-templating, acting animal. He is influenced by what is direct and precise. It is very well to freshen our impressions and convictions from physics, but to create them we must go elsewhere. Sir Robert Peel "never can think it possible that a mind can be so constituted that, after being familiarized with the wonderful discoveries which have been made in every part of experimental science, it can retire from such con-templation without more enlarged conceptions of God's providence, and a higher reverence for his name." If he speaks of religious minds, he perpetrates a truism; if of irreligious, he insinuates a paradox.

Life is not long enough for a religion of inferences; we shall never have done beginning, if we determine to begin with proof. We shall ever be laying our foundations, we shall turn theology into evidences and divines into textuaries. We shall never get at our first principles. Resolve to believe nothing, and you must prove your proof and analyze your elements, sinking farther and farther, and finding in the lowest depth a lower deep, till you come to the broad bosom of skepticism. I would rather be bound to defend the reasonableness of assuming that Christianity is true than to demonstrate a moral governance from the physical world. Life is for action. If we insist on proofs for every-thing, we shall never come to action; to act you must assume, and that assumption is faith.

LESSON 53.

George Eliot.—" We feel that, however much we may admire the other great English novelists, there is none who would make the study of George Eliot superfluous. The sphere which she made her own is that quiet English country life which she knew in early youth. It has been described with more or less vivacity and sympathy by many observers. Nobody has approached George Eliot in the power of seizing its essen-tial characteristics and exhibiting its real charm. She has done for it what Scott did for the Scotch peasantry, or Fielding for the eighteenth century Englishman, or Thackeray for the higher social stratum of his time. Its last traces are vanishing so rapidly amidst the changes of modern revolution, that its picture could hardly be drawn again, even if there were an artist of equal skill and penetration. And thus, when the name of George Eliot is mentioned, it calls up, to me at least, and, I suspect, to most readers, not so much her later and more ambitious works, as the exquisite series of scenes so lovingly and vividly presented in the earlier stage.

She has been approached, if she has not been surpassed, by other writers in her idyllic effects. But there is something less easily paralleled in the peculiar vein of humor which is the essential complement of the more tender passages. Mrs. Poyser is necessary to balance the solemnity of Dinah Morris; Silas Marner would lose half his impressiveness if he were not in contrast with the inimitable party in the ' Rainbow ' parlor.

It is enough to take note of the fact that George Eliot possessed a vein of humor. of which it is little to say that it is incomparably superior in depth, if not in delicacy, to that of any feminine writer. It is the humor of a calm, contemplative mind, familiar with wide fields of knowledge, and capable of observing the little dramas of rustic life from a higher standing-point. It is not—in these earlier books at any rate—that she obtrudes her acquirements upon us; for, if here and there we find some of those scientific illusions which afterward became a kind of mannerism, they are introduced without any appearance of forcing. It is simply that she is awake to those quaint aspects of the little world before her, which only show their quaintness to the cultivated intellect.

There is the breadth of touch, the large-minded equable spirit of loving, contemplative thought, which is fully conscious of the narrow limitations of the actor's thoughts and habits, but does not cease on that account to sympathize with his joys and sorrows. We are on a petty stage, but not in a stifling atmosphere, and we are not called upon to accept the prejudices of the actors, or to be angry with them, but simply to understand and be tolerant."—*Leslie Stephen.*

From George Eliot's *Adam Bede.*

Hetty was coming down stairs, and Mrs. Poyser, in her plain bonnet and shawl, was standing below. If ever a girl looked as if she had been made of roses, that girl was Hetty in her Sunday hat and frock. For her hat was trimmed with pink, and her frock had pink spots sprinkled on a white ground. There was nothing but pink and white about her, except in her dark hair and eyes and her little buckled shoes. Mrs. Poyser was provoked at herself, for she could hardly keep from smiling, as any mortal is inclined to do at the sight of pretty, round things. So she turned without speaking and joined the group outside the house door, followed by Hetty, whose heart was fluttering so at the thought of some one she expected to see at church that she hardly felt the ground she trod on.

And now the little procession set off. Mr. Poyser was in his Sunday suit of drab, with a red and green waistcoat, and a green watch-ribbon, having a large cornelian seal attached, pendent like a plumb-line from that promontory where his watch-pocket was situated; a silk handkerchief of a yellow tone round his neck, and excellent gray-ribbed stockings, knitted by Mrs. Poyser's own hands, setting off the proportions of his leg. Mr. Poyser had no reason to be ashamed of his leg, and suspected that the growing abuse of top-boots and other fashions tending to disguise the nether limbs, had their origin in a pitiable degeneracy of the human calf. Still less had he reason to be ashamed of his round, jolly face, which was good-humor itself, as he said, "Come, Hetty,— come, little uns!" and, giving his arm to his wife, led the way through the causeway gate into the yard.

The "little uns" addressed were Marty and Tommy, boys of nine and seven, in little fustian tailed coats and knee-breeches, relieved by rosy cheeks and black eyes; looking as much like their father as a very small elephant is like a very large one. Hetty walked between them, and behind came patient Molly, whose task it was to carry Totty through the yard and over all the wet places on the road; for Totty, having speedily recovered from her threatened fever, had insisted on going to church to-day, and especially on wearing her red-and-black necklace outside her tippet. And there were many wet places for her to be carried over this afternoon, for there had been heavy showers in the morning, though now the clouds had rolled off and lay in towering silvery masses on the horizon.

You might have known it was Sunday if you had only waked up in the farm-yard. The cocks and the hens seemed to know it, and made only crooning subdued noises; the very bull-dog looked less savage, as if he would have been satisfied with a smaller bite than usual. The sunshine seemed to call all things to rest and not to labor; it was asleep itself on the moss-grown cow-shed; on the group of white ducks nestling together with their bills tucked under their wings; on the old black sow stretched languidly on the straw, while her largest young one found an excellent spring-bed on his mother's fat ribs; on Alick, the shepherd, in his new smock-frock, taking an uneasy siesta, half-sitting, half-standing on the granary steps. Alick was of opinion that church, like other luxuries, was not to be indulged in often by a foreman who had the weather and the ewes on his mind. "Church! nay—I'n gotten summat else to think on," was an answer which he often uttered in a tone of bitter significance that silenced farther question. I feel sure Alick meant no irreverence; indeed, I know that his mind was not of a speculative, negative cast, and he would on no account have missed going to church on Christmas-day, Easter Sunday, and "Whissuntide. But he had a general impression that public worship and religious cere- monies, like other non-productive employments, were intended for peo- ple who had leisure.

"There's father a-standing at the yard gate," said Martin Poyser. "I reckon he wants to watch us down the field. It's wonderful what sight he has, and him turned seventy-five."

"Ah! I often think it's wi' th' old folks as it is wi' the babbies," said Mrs. Poyser; "they're satisfied wi' looking, no matter what they're looking at. It's God Almighty's way o' quietening 'em, I reckon, afore they go to sleep."

Old Martin opened the gate as he saw the family procession approach- ing, and held it wide open, leaning on his stick—pleased to do this bit of work; for, like all old men whose life has been spent in labor, he liked to feel that he was still useful—that there was a better crop of onions in the garden because he was by at the sowing, and that the cows would be milked the better if he staid at home on a Sunday afternoon to look on. He always went to church on Sacrament Sundays, but not very regularly at other times; on wet Sundays, or whenever he had a touch of rheumatism, he used to read the three first chapters of Genesis instead.

"They'll ha putten Thias Bede i' the ground afore ye get to the church- yard," he said, as his son came up. "It 'ud ha' been better luck if they'd ha' buried him i' the forenoon when the rain was fallin'; there's no likelihoods of a drop now, an' the moon lies like a boat there, dost see? That's a sure sign of fair weather; there's a many as is false, but that's sure."

"Ay, ay," said the son, "I'm in hopes it'll hold up now."

"Mind what the parson says—mind what the parson says, my lads," said grandfather to the black-eyed youngsters in knee-breeches, con- scious of a marble or two in their pockets, which they looked forward to handling a little, secretly, during the sermon.

And when they were all gone, the old man leaned on the gate again, watching them across the lane, along the Home Close, and through the far gate, till they disappeared behind a bend in the hedge. For the hedgerows in those days shut out one's view, even on the better-managed farms; and this afternoon the dog-roses were tossing out their pink wreaths, the night-shade was in its yellow and purple glory, the pale honeysuckle grew out of reach, peeping high up out of a holly bush, and, over all, an ash or a sycamore every now and then threw its shadow across the path.

There were acquaintances at other gates who had to move aside and let them pass; at the gate of the Home Close there was half the dairy of cows standing one behind the other, extremely slow to understand that their large bodies might be in the way; at the far gate there was the mare holding her head over the bars, and beside her the liver-colored foal with its head toward its mother's flank, apparently still much embarrassed by its own straddling existence. The way lay entirely through Mr. Poyser's own fields till they reached the main road leading to the village, and he turned a keen eye on the stock and the crops as they went along, while Mrs. Poyser was ready to supply a running commentary on them all. The woman who manages a dairy has a large share in making the rent, so she may well be allowed to have her opinion on stock and their "keep"—an exercise which strengthens her understanding so much that she finds herself able to give her husband advice on most other subjects.

"There's that short-horned Sally," she said, as they entered the Home Close, and she caught sight of the meek beast that lay chewing the cud, and looking at her with a sleepy eye. "I begin to hate the sight o' the cow; and I say now what I said three weeks ago, the sooner we get rid of her th' better, for there's that little yellow cow as doesn't give half the milk and yet I've twice as much butter from her."

"Why, thee't not like the women in general," said Mr. Poyser; "they like the short-horns, as give such a lot of milk. There's Chowne's wife wants him to buy no other sort."

"What's it sinnify what Chowne's wife likes? a poor soft thing, wi' no more head-piece nor a sparrow. She'd take a big cullender to strain her lard wi', and then wander as the scratchin's run through. I've seen enough of her to know as I'll niver take a servant from her house again—all huggermugger—and you'd niver know, when you went in, whether it was Monday or Friday, the wash draggin' on to th' end o' the week; and as for her cheese, I know well enough it rose like a loaf in a tin last year. An' then she talks o' the weather bein' i' fault, as there's folks 'ud stand on their heads and then say the fault was i' their boots."

"Well, Chowne's been wanting to buy Sally, so we can get rid of her, if thee lik'st," said Mr. Poyser, secretly proud of his wife's superior power of putting two and two together; indeed, on recent market days, he had more than once boasted of her discernment in this very matter of short-horns.

"Ay, them as choose a soft for a wife may's well buy up the short-horns, for, if you get your head stuck in a bog, your legs may's well go after it. Eh! talk o' legs, there's legs for you," Mrs. Poyser continued, as Totty, who had been set down now the road was dry, toddled on in front of her father and mother. "There's shapes! An' she's got such a long foot, she'll be her father's own child."

"Ay, she'll be welly such a one as Hetty i' ten years time, ony she's got thy colored eyes. I niver remember a blue eye i' my family; my mother had eyes as black as sloes, just like Hetty's."

"The child 'ull be none the worse for having summat as isn't like Hetty. An' I'm none for having her so over pretty. Though, for the matter o' that, there's people wi' light hair an' blue eyes as pretty as them wi' black. If Dinah had got a bit o' color in her cheeks, an' didn't stick that Methodist cap on her head, enough to frighten the crows, folks 'ud think her as pretty as Hetty."

"Nay, nay," said Mr. Poyser, with rather a contemptuous emphasis, "thee dostna know the pints of a woman. The men 'ud niver run after Dinah as they would after Hetty."

"What care I what the men 'ud run after? It's well seen what choice the most of 'em know how to make, by the poor draggle-tails o' wives you see, like bits o' gauze ribbin, good for nothing when the color's gone."

"Well, well, thee canstna say but what I know'd how to make a choice when I married thee," said Mr. Poyser, who usually settled little conjugal disputes by a compliment of this sort, "and thee was twice as buxom as Dinah ten years ago."

"I niver said as a woman had need to be ugly to make a good missis of a house. There's Chowne's wife ugly enough to turn the milk an' save the rennet, but she'll niver save nothing any other way. But as for Dinah, poor child, she's niver likely to be buxom as long as she'll make her dinner o' cake and water, for the sake o' giving to them as want. She provoked me past bearing sometimes; and, as I told her, she went clean again' the Scriptur, for that says, 'Love your neighbor as yourself;' but I said, 'if you loved your neighbor no better nor you do yourself, Dinah, it's little enough you'd do for him. You'd be thinking he might do well enough on a half-empty stomach.' Eh, I wonder where she is this blessed Sunday! sitting by that sick woman, I daresay, as she'd set her heart on going to all of a sudden."

" Ah! it was a pity she should take such megrims int' her head, when she might ha' stayed wi' us all summer, and eaten twice as much as she wanted, and it 'ud niver ha' been missed. She made no odds in th' house at all, for she sat as still at her sewing as a bird on the nest, and was uncommon nimble at running to fetch anything. If Hetty gets married, thee'dst like to ha' Dinah wi' thee constant."

" It's no use thinkin' o' that," said Mrs. Poyser. " You might as well beckon to the flyin' swallow, as ask Dinah to come an' live here comfortable like other folks. If any thing could turn her I should ha' turned her, for I've talked to her for an hour on end, and scolded her too; for she's my own sister's child, and it behoves me to do what I can for her. But eh, poor thing, as soon as she'd said us 'good-bye,' an' got into the cart, an' looked back at me with her pale face, as is welly like her aunt Judith come back from heaven, I begun to be frightened to think o' the set downs I'd given her; for it comes over you sometimes as if she'd a way o' knowing the rights o' things more nor other folks have. But I'll niver give in as that's 'cause she's a Methodist, no more nor a white calf's white 'cause it eats out o' the same bucket wi' a black un."

" Nay," said Mr. Poyser, with as near an approach to a snarl as his good-nature would allow; " I've no opinion o' the Methodists. It's ony trades-folks as turn Methodists, you niver knew a farmer bitten wi' them maggots. There's maybe a workman now and then, as isn't over cliver at's work, takes to preachin' an' that, like Seth Bede. But you see Adam, as has got one of the best head-pieces hereabout, knows better; he's a good Churchman, else I'd niver encourage him for a sweetheart for Hetty."

. . . .

Adam was hungering for a sight of Dinah; and when that sort of hunger reaches a certain stage, a lover is likely to still it though he may have to put his future in pawn.

But what harm could he do by going to Snowfield? Dinah could not be displeased with him for it; she had not forbidden him to go; she must surely expect that he would go before long. By the second Sunday in October, this view of the case had become so clear to Adam, that he was already on his way to Snowfield, on horseback this time, for his hours were precious now, and he had borrowed Jonathan Burge's good nag for the journey.

What keen memories went along the road with him! He had often been to Oakbourne and back since that first journey to Snowfield, but beyond Oakbourne, the gray stone walls, the broken country, the meagre trees, seemed to be telling him afresh the story of that painful past which he knew so well by heart.˙ But no story is the same to us after a lapse of time; or rather, we who read it are no longer the same interpreters; and Adam this morning brought with him new thoughts through that gray country—thoughts which gave an altered significance to its story of the past.

That is a base and selfish, even a blasphemous, spirit which rejoices and is thankful over the past evil that has blighted or crushed another, because it has been made the source •of unforeseen good to ourselves; Adam could never cease to mourn over that mystery of human sorrow which had been brought so close to him; he could never thank God for another's misery. And if I were capable of that narrow-sighted joy in Adam's behalf, I should still know he was not the man to feel it for him. self; he would have shaken his head at such a sentiment, and said, "Evil's evil, and sorrow's sorrow, and you can't alter its nature by wrapping it up in other words. Other folks were not created for my sake, that I should think all square when things turn out well for me."

But it is not ignoble to feel that the fuller life which a sad experience has brought us is worth our own personal share of pain; surely it is not possible to feel otherwise, any more than it would be possible for a man with cataract to regret the painful process by which his dim, blurred sight of men as trees walking had been exchanged for clear outline and effulgent day. The growth of higher feeling within us is like the growth of faculty, bringing with it the sense of added strength; we can no more wish to return to a narrower sympathy than a painter or a musician can wish to return to his cruder manner, or a philosopher to his less complete formula.

Something like this sense of enlarged being was in Adam's mind this Sunday morning, as he rode along in vivid recollection of the past. His feeling toward Dinah, the hope of passing his life with her had been the distant unseen point toward which that hard journey from Snowfield eighteen months ago had been leading him. "It's like as if it was a new strength to me," he said to himself, "love her, and know as she loves me. I shall look t' her to help me to see things right. For she's better than I am—there's less o' self in her, and pride. And it's a feeling as gives you a sort o' liberty, as if you could walk more fearless, when you've more trust in another than y' have in yourself. I've always been thinking I knew better than them as belonged to me, and that's a poor sort o' life, when you can't look to them nearest to you t' help you with a bit better thought than what you've got inside you a'ready."

It was more than two o'clock in the afternoon when Adam came in sight of the gray town on the hill-side, and looked searchingly toward the green valley below for the first glimpse of the old thatched roof near the ugly red mill. The scene looked less harsh in the soft October sunshine than it had done in the eager time of early spring; and the one grand charm it possessed, in common with all wide-stretching woodless regions—that it filled you with a new consciousness of the over-arching sky—had a milder, more soothing influence than usual on this almost cloudless day. Adam's doubts and fears melted under this influence as the delicate web-like clouds had gradually melted away into the clear blue above him. He seemed to see Dinah's gentle face assuring him, with its looks alone, of all he longed to know.

He did not expect Dinah to be at home at this hour, but he got down from his horse and tied it at the little gate that he might ask where she was gone to-day. He had set his mind on following her and bringing her home. She was gone to Sloman's End, a hamlet about three miles off, over the hill, the old woman told him; had set off directly after morning chapel, to preach in a cottage there, as her habit was. Any body at the town would tell him the way to Sloman's End. So Adam got on his horse again and rode to the town, putting up at the old inn, and taking a hasty dinner there in the company of the too chatty landlord, from whose friendly questions and reminiscences he was glad to escape as soon as possible, and set out toward Sloman's End. With all his haste, it was nearly four o'clock before he could set off, and he thought that as Dinah had gone so early, she would, perhaps, already be near returning. The little, gray, desolate-looking hamlet, unscreened by sheltering trees, lay in sight long before he reached it; and, as he came near, he could hear the sound of voices singing a hymn. "Perhaps that's the last hymn before they come away," Adam thought; "I'll walk back a bit, and turn again to meet her, farther off the village." He walked back till he got nearly to the top of the hill again, and seated himself on a loose stone against the low wall, to watch till he should see the little black figure leaving the hamlet and winding up the hill. He chose this spot, almost at the top of the hill, because it was away from all eyes—no house, no cattle, not even a nibbling sheep near,—no presence but the still lights and shadows, and the great embracing sky.

She was much longer coming than he expected; he waited an hour at least, watching for her and thinking of her, while the afternoon shadows lengthened, and the light grew softer. At last he saw the little black figure coming from between the gray houses, and gradually approaching the foot of the hill. Slowly, Adam thought; but Dinah was really walking at her usual pace, with a light, quiet step. Now she was beginning to wind along the path up the hill, but Adam would not move yet; he would not meet her too soon; he had set his heart on meeting her in this assured loneliness. And now he began to fear lest he should startle her too much; "Yet," he thought, "she's not one to be overstartled; she's always so calm and quiet, as if she was prepared for anything."

What was she thinking of as she wound up the hill? Perhaps she had found complete repose without him, and had ceased to feel any need of his love. On the verge of a decision we all tremble; hope pauses with fluttering wings.

But now at last she was very near, and Adam rose from the stone wall. It happened that, just as he walked forward, Dinah had paused and turned around to look back at the village: who does not pause and look back in mounting a hill? Adam was glad, for, with the fine instinct of a lover, he felt that it would be best for her to hear his voice before she saw him. He came within three paces of her, and then said, "Dinah!" She started without looking round, as if she connected the sound with no place. "Dinah!" Adam said again. He knew quite well what was in her mind. She was so accustomed to think of impressions as purely spiritual monitions, that she looked for no material visible accompaniment of the voice.

But this second time she looked around. What a look of yearning love it was that the mild gray eyes turned on the strong dark-eyed man! She did not start again at the sight of him; she said nothing, but moved toward him so that his arm could clasp her round.

And they walked on so in silence, while the warm tears fell. Adam was content, and said nothing. It was Dinah who spoke first.

"Adam," she said, "it is the Divine Will. My soul is so knit to yours that it is but a divided life I live without you. And this moment, now you are with me, and I feel that our hearts are filled with the same love, I have a fullness of strength to bear and do our heavenly Father's will, that I had lost before."

Adam paused and looked into her sincere, loving eyes.

"Then we'll never part any more, Dinah, till death parts us."

And they kissed each other with a deep joy.

What greater thing is there for two human souls, than to feel that they are joined for life—to strengthen each other in all labor, to rest on each other in all sorrow, to minister to each other in all pain, to be one with each other in silent, unspeakable memories at the moment of the last parting.

From Dickens's *Pickwick Papers.*

"Nathaniel Winkle!" said Mr. Skimpin.

"Here!" replied a feeble voice. Mr. Winkle entered the witness-box, and, having been duly sworn, bowed to the judge with considerable deference.

"Don't look at me, sir," said the judge, sharply, in acknowledgment of the salute; "look at the jury."

Mr. Winkle obeyed the mandate, and looked at the place where he thought it most probable the jury might be; for seeing anything in his then state of intellectual complication was wholly out of the question.

Mr. Winkle was then examined by Mr. Skimpin, who, being a promising young man of two or three and forty, was of course anxious to confuse a witness who was notoriously predisposed in favor of the other side, as much as he could.

"Now, sir," said Mr. Skimpin, "have the goodness to let his lordship and the jury know. what your name is, will you?" And Mr. Skimpin inclined his head on one side to listen with great sharpness to the answer, and glanced at the jury meanwhile, as if to imply that he rather expected Mr. Winkle's natural taste for perjury would induce him to give some name which did not belong to him.

"Winkle," replied the witness.

"What is your Christian name, sir?" angrily inquired the little judge.

"Nathaniel, sir."

"Daniel,—any other name?"

"Nathaniel, sir,—my lord, I mean."

"Nathaniel Daniel, or Daniel Nathaniel?"

"No, my lord, only Nathaniel,—not Daniel at all."

"What did you tell me it was Daniel for then, sir?" inquired the judge.

"I didn't, my lord," replied Mr. Winkle.

"You did, sir," replied the judge, with a severe frown. "How could I have got Daniel on my notes unless you told me so, sir?"

This argument was of course unanswerable.

"Mr. Winkle has rather a short memory, my lord," interposed Mr. Skimpin, with another glance at the jury. "We shall find means to refresh it before we have quite done with him, I dare say."

"You had better be careful, sir," said the little judge, with a sinister look at the witness.

Poor Mr. Winkle bowed, and endeavored to feign an easiness of manner, which, in his then state of confusion, gave him rather the air of a disconcerted pickpocket.

"Now, Mr. Winkle," said Mr. Skimpin, "attend to me, if you please, sir; and let me recommend you, for your own sake, to bear in mind his lordship's injunctions to be careful. I believe you are a particular friend of Pickwick, the defendant, are you not?"

"I have known Mr. Pickwick now, as well as I recollect at this moment, nearly—"

"Pray, Mr. Winkle, do not evade the question. Are you, or are you not, a particular friend of the defendant's?"

"I was just about to say, that—"

"Will you, or will you not, answer my question, sir?"

"If you don't answer the question, you'll be committed, sir," interposed the little judge, looking over his note-book.

"Come, sir," said Mr. Skimpin; "yes or no, if you please."

"Yes, I am," replied Mr. Winkle.

"Yes, you are. And why couldn't you say that at once, sir? Perhaps you know the plaintiff too,—eh, Mr. Winkle?"

"I don't know her; I've seen her."

"O, you don't know her, but you've seen her? Now, have the goodness to tell the gentlemen of the jury what you mean by *that*, Mr. Winkle?"

"I mean that I am not intimate with her, but that I have seen her when I went to call on Mr. Pickwick, in Goswell Street."

"How often have you seen her, sir?"

"How often?"

"Yes, Mr. Winkle, how often? I'll repeat the question for you a dozen times, if you require it, sir." And the learned gentleman, with a firm and steady frown, placed his hands on his hips and smiled suspiciously at the jury.

On this question there arose the edifying brow-beating customary on such points. First of all, Mr. Winkle said it was quite impossible for him to say how many times he had seen Mrs. Bardell. Then he was asked if he had seen her twenty times, to which he replied, "Certainly,—more than that." Then he was asked whether he hadn't seen her a hundred times,—whether he couldn't swear that he had seen her more than fifty times,—whether he didn't know that he had seen her at least seventy-five times,—and so forth; the satisfactory conclusion which was arrived at at last being, that he had better take care of himself, and mind what he was about. The witness having been by these means reduced to the requisite ebb of nervous perplexity, the examination was continued as follows:—

"Pray, Mr. Winkle, do you remember calling on the defendant Pick-wick, and these apartments in the plaintiff's house in Goswell Street, on one particular morning in the month of July last?"

"Yes, I do."

"Were you accompanied on that occasion by a friend of the name of Tupman, and another of the name of Snodgrass?"

"Yes, I was."

"Are they here?"

"Yes, they are," replied Mr. Winkle, looking very earnestly towards the spot where his friends were stationed.

"Pray attend to me, Mr. Winkle, and never mind your friends," said Mr. Skimpin with another expressive look at the jury. "They must tell their stories without any previous consultation with you, if none has yet taken place (another look at the jury). Now, sir, tell the gentlemen of the jury what you saw on entering the defendant's room on this partic-ular morning. Come; out with it, sir; we must have it sooner or later."

"The defendant, Mr. Pickwick, was holding the plaintiff in his arms, with his hands clasping her waist," replied Mr. Winkle, with natural hesitation, "and the plaintiff appeared to have fainted away."

"Did you hear the defendant say anything?"

"I heard him call Mrs. Bardell a good creature, and I heard him ask her to compose herself, for what a situation it was if anybody should come, or words to that effect."

"Now, Mr. Winkle, I have only one more question to ask you, and I beg you to bear in mind his lordship's caution. Will you undertake to swear that Pickwick, the defendant, did not say on the occasion in question, 'My dear Mrs. Bardell, you're a good creature; compose your-self to this situation, for to this situation you must come,' or words to *that* effect?"

"I—I didn't understand him so, certainly," said Mr. Winkle, as-tounded at this ingenious dove-tailing of the few words he had heard. "I was on the staircase and couldn't hear distinctly; the impression on my mind is—"

"The gentlemen of the jury want none of the impressions on your mind, Mr. Winkle, which I fear would be of little service to honest, straight-forward men," interposed Mr. Skimpin. "You were on the staircase, and didn't distinctly hear; but you will not swear that Pickwick did not make use of the expressions I have quoted? Do I understand that?"

"No, I will not," replied Mr. Winkle; and down sat Mr. Skimpin with a triumphant countenance.

Susannah Sanders was then called, and examined by Serjeant Buzfuz, and cross-examined by Serjeant Snubbin. Had always said and believed that Pickwick would marry Mrs. Bardell; knew that Mrs. Bardell's being engaged to Pickwick was the current topic of conversation in the neighborhood after the fainting in July; had been told it herself by Mrs. Mudberry, which kept a mangle, and Mrs. Bunkin, which clear-starched, but did not see either Mrs. Mudberry or Mrs. Bunkin in court. Had heard Pickwick ask the little boy how he should like to have another father. Did not know that Mrs. Bardell was at that time keeping company with the baker, but did know that the baker was then a single man, and is now married. Couldn't swear that Mrs. Bardell was not very fond of the baker, but should think that the baker was not very fond of Mrs. Bardell, or he wouldn't have married somebody else. Thought Mrs. Bardell fainted away on the morning in July, because Pickwick asked her to name the day. Knew that she (witness) fainted away stone-dead when Mr. Sanders asked *her* to name the day, and believed that everybody as called herself a lady would do the same under similar circumstances. Heard Pickwick ask the boy the question about the marbles, but upon her oath did not know the difference between an alley tor and a commoney.

Serjeant Buzfuz now rose with more importance than he had ever exhibited, if that were possible, and vociferated, "Call Samuel Weller."

It was quite unnecessary to call Samuel Weller; for Samuel Weller stepped briskly into the box the instant his name was pronounced; and, placing his hat on the floor and his arms on the rail, took a bird's-eye view of the bar, and a comprehensive survey of the bench, with a remarkably cheerful and lively aspect.

"What's your name, sir?" inquired the judge.

"Sam Weller, my lord," replied that gentleman.

"Do you spell it with a 'V' or a 'W?'" inquired the judge.

"That depends upon the taste and fancy of the speller, my lord," replied Sam. "I never had occasion to spell it more than once or twice in my life; but I spells it with a 'V.'"

Here a voice in the gallery exclaimed aloud, "Quite right too, Samevil,—quite right. Put it down a we, my lord, put it down a we."

"Who is that, who dares to address the court?" said the little judge, looking up. "Usher."

"Yes, my lord."

"Bring that person here instantly."

"Yes, my lord."

But as the usher didn't find the person, he didn't bring him; and, after a great commotion, all the people who had got up to look for the culprit sat down again. The little judge turned to the witness as soon as his indignation would allow him to speak, and said, "Do you know who that was, sir?"

"I rayther suspect it was my father, my lord," replied Sam.

"Do you see him here now?" said the judge.

"No, I don't, my lord," replied Sam, staring right up into the lantern in the roof of the court.

"If you could have pointed him out, I would have committed him instantly," said the judge.

Sam bowed his acknowledgments, and turned with unimpaired cheerfulness of countenance towards Serjeant Buzfuz.

"Now, Mr. Weller," said Serjeant Buzfuz.

"Now, sir," replied Sam.

"I believe you are in the service of Mr. Pickwick, the defendant in this case. Speak up, if you please, Mr. Weller."

"I mean to speak up, sir," replied Sam. "I am in the service o' that 'ere gen'l'm'n, and a wery good service it is."

"Little to do, and plenty to get, I suppose?" said Serjeant Buzfuz, with jocularity.

"O, quite enough to get, sir, as the soldier said ven they ordered him three hundred and fifty lashes," replied Sam.

"You must not tell us what the soldier, or any other man said, sir," interposed the judge; "it's not evidence."

"Wery good, my lord," replied Sam.

"Do you recollect anything particular happening on the morning when you were first engaged by the defendant; eh, Mr. Weller?" said Serjeant Buzfuz.

"Yes, I do, sir," replied Sam.

"Have the goodness to tell the jury what it was."

"I had a reg'lar new fit-out o' clothes that mornin', gen'l'm'n of the jury," said Sam; "and that was a wery partickler and uncommon circumstance with me in those days."

Hereupon there was a general laugh; and the little judge, looking with an angry countenance over his desk, said, "You had better be careful, sir."

"So Mr. Pickwick said at the time, my lord," replied Sam; "and I was wery careful o' that 'ere suit o' clothes,—wery careful indeed, my lord."

The judge looked sternly at Sam for full two minutes; but Sam's features were so perfectly calm and serene that the judge said nothing, and motioned Serjeant Buzfuz to proceed.

"Do you mean to tell me, Mr. Weller," said Serjeant Buzfuz, folding his arms emphatically, and turning half round to the jury, as if in mute assurance that he would bother the witness yet,—"do you mean to tell me, Mr. Weller, that you saw nothing of this fainting on the part of the plaintiff in the arms of the defendant, which you have heard described by the witnesses?"

"Certainly not," replied Sam. "I was in the passage till they called me up, and then the old lady was not there."

"Now, attend, Mr. Weller," said Serjeant Buzfuz, dipping a large pen into the inkstand before him, for the purpose of frightening Sam with a show of taking down his answer. "You were in the passage, and yet saw nothing of what was going forward. Have you a pair of eyes, Mr. Weller?"

"Yes, I have a pair of eyes," replied Sam; "and that's just it. If they was a pair o' patent double-million magnifyin' gas microscopes of hextra power, p'r'aps I might be able to see through a flight o' stairs and a deal door; but bein' only eyes, you see my wision's limited."

At this answer, which was delivered without the slightest appearance of irritation, and with the most complete simplicity and equanimity of manner, the spectators tittered, the little judge smiled, and Serjeant Buzfuz looked particularly foolish. After a short consultation with Dodson and Fogg, the learned Serjeant again turned toward Sam, and said, with a painful effort to conceal his vexation, "Now, Mr. Weller, I'll ask you a question on another point, if you please."

"If you please, sir," said Sam, with the utmost good-humor.

"Do you remember going up to Mrs. Bardell's house one night in November last?"

"O, yes, wery well."

"O, you *do* remember that, Mr. Weller," said Serjeant Buzfuz, recovering his spirits; "I thought we should get at something at last."

"I rayther thought that, too, sir," replied Sam; and at this the spectators tittered again.

"Well, I suppose you went up to have a little talk about this trial,—eh, Mr. Weller?" said Serjeant Buzfuz, looking knowingly at the jury.

"I went up to pay the rent; but we *did* get a talkin' about the trial," replied Sam.

"O, you did get a talking about the trial," said Serjeant Buzfuz, brightening up with the anticipation of some important discovery. "Now what passed about the trial? Will you have the goodness to tell us, Mr. Weller?"

"Vith all the pleasure in life, sir," replied Sam. "Arter a few unimportant observations from the two wirtuous females as has been examined here to-day, the ladies gets into a wery great state o' admiration at the honorable conduct of Mr. Dodson and Fogg,—them two gen'l'm'n as is settin' near you now." This of course drew general attention to Dodson and Fogg, who looked as virtuous as possible.

"The attorneys for the plaintiff," said Mr. Serjeant Buzfuz. "Well, they spoke in high praise of the honorable conduct of Messrs. Dodson and Fogg, the attorneys for the plaintiff, did they?"

"Yes," said Sam, "they said what a wery gen'rous thing it was o' them to have taken up the case on spec. and to charge nothin' at all for costs, unless they got 'em out of Mr. Pickwick."

At this very unexpected reply the spectators tittered again, and Dodson and Fogg, turning very·red, leant over to Serjeant Buzfuz, and in a hurried manner whispered something in his ear.

"You are quite right," said Serjeant Buzfuz aloud, with affected composure. "It's perfectly useless, my lord, attempting to get at any evidence through the impenetrable stupidity of this witness. I will not trouble the court by asking him any more questions. Stand down, sir."

"Would any other gen'l'm'n like to ask me anythin'?" inquired Sam, taking up his hat, and looking around most deliberately.

"Not I, Mr. Weller, thank you," said Serjeant Snubbin, laughing.

"You may go down, sir," said Serjeant Buzfuz, waving his hand impatiently. Sam went down accordingly, after doing Messrs. Dodson and Fogg's case as much harm as he conveniently could, and saying just as little respecting Mr. Pickwick as might be, which was precisely the object he had had in view all along.

LESSON 54.

PHILOSOPHICAL AND POLITICAL LITERATURE.—"An eloquent school of Scotch metaphysicians came after Hume, and, for the most part, opposed the ideal system on which he had founded his famous argument on causation. Dr. Reid, Dr. Stewart, and Dr. Brown carried this school on to 1820. The Utilitarian view of morals was put forth with great power by Jeremy Bentham, and in our own day by JOHN STUART MILL, 1806–1873, whose name, with that of SIR W. HAMILTON, 1788–1856, and Professor Whewell's, belongs to the literature of philosophy. The philosophy of Jurisprudence may be said to have been founded by JEREMY BENTHAM, 1748–1832, and law

was for the first time made a little clear to common minds by
BLACKSTONE'S *Commentaries.*

BURKE'S *Reflections on the French Revolution*, 1790, and
the *Letters on a Regicide Peace*, 1796–7, were most powerful.
The first of these two spread all over England a terror of the
principles of the Revolution; the second increased the eagerness of England to carry on the war with France.

MISCELLANEOUS LITERATURE. — The miscellaneous literature
of the early part of the nineteenth century took mainly the
form of long ess ys, most of which were originally published in
the Reviews and Magazines.   It was in *Blackwood's Magazine*
that Christopher North (Professor Wilson) published the
Noctes Ambrosianæ—lively conversations that treated of all
the topics of the day.   It was in the *Edinburgh Review* that
Macaulay and Sydney Smith and Jeffrey wrote essays on literature, politics, and philosophy.   It was in *Fraser's Magazine*
that THOMAS CARLYLE, 1795–1881, first came before the public with *Sartor Resartus* and the *Lectures on Heroes*, books
which gave an entirely new impulse to the generation in which
we live.   Of all these miscellaneous writers, Carlyle was the
most original, and Thomas De Quincey the greatest writer of
English prose.   The style of DE QUINCEY, 1785–1859, has so
peculiar a quality that it stands alone.   The sentences are built
up like passages in a fugue, and there is nothing in English
Literature which can be compared in involved melody with the
prose of the *Confessions of an English Opium Eater.*

One man alone in our own day is as great a master of English prose, JOHN RUSKIN, born in 1819.   He has created a new
literature, that of art, and all the subjects related to it; and
the work he has done has more genius and is more original than
any other prose work of our time.   Some of De Quincey's best
work was done on the lives of the poets of his day; and, indeed,
a great part of the miscellaneous literature consisted of *Criticism on Poetry*, past and present.   Coleridge, Charles Lamb,
and Campbell carried on that study of the Elizabethan and

Prose—Philosophical and Miscellaneous. 309

earlier poetry which Warton had begun in the eighteenth century. Wordsworth wrote admirable prose on poetry, and the prose of his Essays, just now published, especially of that on the *Convention of Cintra*, is quite stately. W. Hazlitt, W. S. Landor, Jeffrey, and a host of others added to the literature of criticism, and the ceaseless discussion of the works of the poets made them the foremost literary figures of the day."

BIBLIOGRAPHY. HAMILTON.—J. Veitch's *Memoir* of; T. S. Baynes' *Edinburgh Essays;* De Quincey's *Essays on Ph. Writers;* H. Calderwood's *Philos. of the Infinite;* J. Martineau's *Essays;* Mill's *Exam. of Sir Wm. Ham.'s Philos.;* J. H. Stirling's *Ham.'s Philos. of Perception;* Black. Mag., v. 86, 1859; N. A. Rev., vs. 70, 92, and 99; N. Br. Rev., v. 18, 1852.

CARLYLE.—J. Morley's *Crit. Miscellanies;* J. Martineau's *Essays;* Minto's *Man. Eng. Pr. Lit.;* Lowell's *My Study Windows;* P. Bayne's *Lessons from my Masters;* W. R. Greg's *Lit. Judgments;* J. Sterling's *Essays;* H. Giles' *Lectures and Essays;* Fras. Mag., v. 72, 1865; Quar. Rev., v. 132, 1872; Ecl. Mag , v. 18, 1849; 22, 1851; 26 and 7, 1852, and April and June, 1881; Froude's *Life* of.

DE QUINCEY.—P. Bayne's *Essays;* L. Stephen's *Hours in a Library;* H. Giles' *Illus. of Genius;* Minto's *Man. Eng. Pr. Lit.;* Fras. Mag., vs. 62 and 63; Nat. Quar. Rev., v. 23, 1871; N. A. Rev., v. 14, 1852, and 88, 1859; Quar. Rev., v. 110, 1861; Ecl. Mag., July, 1850; July, 1854; Dec., 1863; and Oct., 1868.

LAMB.—*Eng. Men of Let.* Series ; Talfourd's *Life and Memorials* of; Bulwer's *Prose Works;* De Quincey's *Biog.*, *Essays* and *Lit. Reminis.;* At. Mo., v. 3, 1859; Ed. Rev., v. 124, 1866; Fras. Mag., v. 75, 1867; Harper's Mo., vs. 20 and 39; Macmillan, Apr., 1867; N. A. Rev., v. 104, 1867; Quar. Rev., v. 122, 1867; Temple Bar, Apr., 1862; West. Rev., Oct., 1874.

"Carlyle's subject,—almost his only subject,—whether he wrote history or biography, or the sort of musings which contained his conceptions of life, was always the dim struggle of man's nature with the passions, doubts, and confusions by which it is surrounded, with special regard to the grip of the infinite spiritual cravings, whether good or evil, upon it. He was always trying to paint the light shining in darkness and the darkness comprehending it not, and therefore it was that he strove so hard to invent a new sort of style which should express not simply the amount of human knowledge but also, so far as possible, the much vaster amount of human ignorance against which that knowledge sparkled in mere radiant points breaking the gloom.

Some critics have attempted to account for the difference in style between his early reviews in the *Edinburgh* and his later productions, by the corrections of Jeffrey. But Jeffrey did not correct Carlyle's *Life of Schiller*, and, if any one who possesses the volume containing both the life of Schiller and the life of Sterling will compare the one with the other, he will see at once that, between the two, Carlyle had deliberately developed a new organon for his own characteristic genius, and that, so far from losing, his genius gained enormously by the process. And I say this not without fully recognizing that simplicity is, after all, the highest of all qualities of style, and that no one can pretend to find simplicity in Carlyle's mature style.

The purpose of style is to express thought, and if the central and pervading thought of all which you wish to express and must express if you are to attain the real object of your life, is inconsistent with simplicity, let simplicity go to the wall, and let us have the real drift. And this seems to me to be exactly Carlyle's case. It would have been impossible to express adequately in such English as was the English of his *Life of Schiller*, the class of convictions which had most deeply engraved themselves on his own mind. That class of convictions was, to state it shortly, the result of his belief—a one-sided belief no doubt, but full of significance—that human language, and especially our glib, cultivated use of it, had done as much or more to conceal from men how little they do know, and how ill they grasp even that which they partly know, as to define and preserve for them the little that they have actually puzzled out of the riddle of life.

To expose the pretensions of human speech, to show us that it seems much clearer than it is, to warn us habitually that ' it swims as a mere superficial film ' on a wide, unplumbed sea of undiscovered reality, is a function hardly to be discharged at all by plain and limited speech. Genuine Carlylese—which, of course, in its turn is in great danger of becoming a deceptive mask, and often does become so in Carlyle's own writings, so that you begin to think that all careful observation, sound reasoning, and precise thinking are useless, and that a true man would keep his intellect foaming and gasping, as it were, in an eternal epileptic fit of wonder—is intended to keep constantly before us the relative proportions between the immensity on every subject which we fail to apprehend, and the few well-defined focal spots of light that we can clearly discern and take in. Nothing is so well adapted as Carlyle's style to teach one that the truest language on the deepest subjects is thrown out, as it were, with more or less happy effect, at great realities far above our analysis or grasp, and not a triumphant formula which contains the whole secret of our existence."—*Richard H. Hutton.*

From Carlyle's *Death of Goethe.*

To measure and estimate all this, as we said, the time is not come; a century hence will be the fitter time. He who investigates it best will find its meaning greatest, and be the readiest to acknowledge that it transcends him. Let the reader have *seen*, before he attempts to *oversee*. A poor reader, in the mean while were he, who discerned not here the authentic rudiments of that same new era, whereof we have so often had false warning. Wondrously, the wrecks and pulverized rubbish of ancient things, institutions, religions, forgotten noblenesses, made alive again by the breath of genius, lie here in new coherence and incipient union, the spirit of art working creative through the mass: that *chaos*, into which the eighteenth century with its wild war of hypocrites and sceptics had reduced the past, begins here to be once more a *world*. This, the highest that can be said of written books, is to be said of these: there is in them a new time, the prophecy and beginning of a new time. The corner-stone of a new social edifice for mankind is laid there; firmly, as before, on the natural rock, far extending traces of a ground-plan we can also see, which future centuries may go on to enlarge, amend, and work into reality. These sayings seem strange to some; nevertheless they are not empty exaggerations, but expressions, in their way, of a belief, which is not now of yesterday; perhaps when Goethe has been read and meditated· for another generation, they will not seem so strange.

Precious is the new light of knowledge which our teacher conquers for us; yet small to the new light of love which also we derive from him; the most important element of any man's performance is the life he has accomplished. Under the intellectual union of man and man, which works by precept, lies a holier union of affection, working by example; the influences of which latter, mystic, deep-reaching, all-embracing, can still less be computed. For love is ever the beginning of knowledge, as fire is of light; works also more in the manner of *fire*. That Goethe was a great teacher of men means already that he was a good man; that he himself learned; in the school of experience had striven and proved victorious. To how many hearers languishing, nigh dead, in the airless dungeon of unbelief (a true vacuum and nonentity) has the assurance that there was such a man, that such a man was still possible, come like tidings of great joy! He who would learn to reconcile reverence with clearness, to deny and defy what is false, yet believe and worship what is true; amid raging factions, bent on what is either altogether empty or has substance in it only for a day, which stormfully convulse and tear hither and thither a distracted, expiring system of society, to adjust himself aright; and, working for the world, and in the world, keep himself unspotted from the world—let him look here.

This man, we may say, became morally great, by being in his own age what in some other ages many might have been—a genuine man.

His grand excellency was this, that he was genuine. As his primary faculty, the foundation of all others, was intellect, depth and force of vision, so his primary virtue was justice, was the courage to be just. A giant's strength we admired in him; yet, strength ennobled into softest mildness; even like that "silent rock-bound strength of a world," on whose bosom, that rests on the adamant, grow flowers. The greatest of hearts was also the bravest; fearless, unwearied, peacefully invincible. A completed man; the trembling sensibility, the wild enthusiasm of a Mignon can assort with the scornful world-mockery of a Mephistophiles; and each side of many-sided life receives its due from him.

Goethe reckoned Schiller happy that he died young, in the full vigor of his days; that he could "figure him as a youth forever." To himself a different, higher destiny was appointed. Through all the changes of man's life, onward to its extreme verge, he was to go; and through them all nobly. In youth, flatterings of fortune, uninterrupted outward prosperity cannot corrupt him; a wise observer must remark, "only a Goethe, at the sum of earthly happiness, can keep his Phœnix wings unsinged." Through manhood, in the most complex relation, as poet, courtier, politician, man of business, man of speculation; in the middle of revolutions and counter-revolutions, outward and spiritual; with the world loudly for him, with the world loudly or silently against him; in all seasons and situations, he holds equally on his way. Old age itself, which is called dark and feeble, he was to render lovely; who that looked upon him there, venerable in himself, and in the world's reverence, ever the clearer, the purer, but could have prayed that he too were such an old man? And did not the kind Heavens continue kind, and grant to a career so glorious the worthiest end?

Such was Goethe's life; such has his departure been—he sleeps now beside his Schiller and his Carl August; so had the Prince willed it, that between these two should be his own final rest. In life they were united, in death they are not divided. The unwearied workman now rests from his labors; the fruit of these is left growing and to grow. His earthly years have been numbered and ended; but of his activity (for it stood rooted in the eternal) there is no end. All that we mean by the higher literature of Germany, which is the higher literature of Europe, already gathers round this man as its creator; of which grand object, dawning mysterious on a world that hoped not for it, who is there that can assume the significance and far-reaching influences? The literature of Europe will pass away: Europe itself, the earth itself will pass away; this little life-boat of an earth, with its noisy crew of mankind, and all their troubled history, will one day have vanished, faded like a cloud-speck from the azure of the All! What then is man? What then is man? He endures but for an hour, and is crushed before the moth. Yet in the being and in the working of a faithful man is there already (as all faith, from the beginning, gives assurance) a something that pertains not to this wild death-element of TIME; that triumphs over time, and *is*, and will be, when time shall be no more.

And now we turn back into the world, withdrawing from this new-made grave. The man whom we love lies there: but glorious, worthy; and his spirit yet lives in us with an authentic life. Could each here vow to do his little task, even as the departed did his great one; in the manner of a true man, not for a day, but for eternity! To live, as he counselled and commanded, not commodiously in the reputable, the plausible, the half, but resolutely in the whole, the good, the true.

From Carlyle's *Life of Stirling*.

Nothing could be more copious than Coleridge's talk; and, furthermore, it was always, virtually or literally, of the nature of a monologue; suffering no interruption, however reverent; hastily putting aside all foreign additions, annotations, or most ingenuous desires for elucidation, as well-meant superfluities which would never do. Besides, it was talk not flowing any whither like a river; but spreading every whither in inextricable currents and regurgitations, like a lake or sea; terribly deficient in definite goal or aim—nay, often in logical intelligibility; *what* you were to believe or do, on any earthly or heavenly thing, obstinately refusing to appear from it. So that, most times, you felt logically lost; swamped near to drowning in this tide of ingenious vocables, spreading out boundless as if to submerge the world.

To sit as a passive bucket and be pumped into, whether you consent or not, can in the long run be exhilarating to no creature, how eloquent soever the flood of utterance that is descending. But if it be withal a confused, unintelligible flood of utterance, threatening to submerge all known landmarks of thought, and drown the world and you! I have heard Coleridge talk with eager, musical energy, two stricken hours, his face radiant and moist, and communicate no meaning whatsoever to any individual of his hearers,—certain of whom, I for one, still kept eagerly listening in hope; the most had long before given up, and formed (if the room were large enough) secondary humming groups of their own. He began anywhere; you put some question to him, made some suggestive observation. Instead of answering this, or decidedly setting out towards answer of it, he would accumulate formidable apparatus, logical swim-bladders, transcendental life-preserv ers, and other precautionary and vehiculatory gear, for setting out; perhaps did at last get under way, but was swiftly solicited, turned aside by the glance of some radiant new game on this hand or that, into new courses, and ever into new, and before long into all the Universe, where it was uncertain what game you would catch, or whether any.

His talk, also, was distinguished, like himself, by irresolution; it disliked to be troubled with conditions, abstinences, definite fulfilments; loved to wander at its own sweet will, and make its auditor and his claims and humble wishes a mere passive bucket for itself! He had knowledge about many things and topics, much curious reading; but generally all topics led him, after a pass or two, into the high-seas of theosophic philosophy, the hazy infinitude of Kantian transcendental-ism, with its "sum-m-mjects" and "om-m-mjects." Sad enough; for with such indolent impatience of the claims and ignorances of others, he had not the least talent for explaining this or anything unknown to them, and you swam and fluttered in the mistiest, wide, unintelligible deluge of things, for most part in a rather profitless, uncomfortable manner. Glorious islets, too, I have seen rise out of the haze; but they were few, and soon swallowed in the general element again. Balmy, sunny islets, islets of the blessed and the intelligible;—on which occasions those secondary humming groups would all cease humming, and hang breathless upon the eloquent words; till once your islet got wrapt in the mist again, and they would recommence humming. Eloquent, artistically expressive words you always had; piercing radiances of a most subtle insight came at intervals; tones of noble, pious sympathy, recognizable as pious, though strangely colored, were never wanting long; but, in general, you could not call this aimless, cloud-capt, cloud-based, lawlessly meandering human discourse of reason by the name of excellent talk, but only of "surprising;" and were reminded bitterly of Hazlitt's account of it, "Excellent talker, very—if you let him start from no premises and come to no conclusion."

Coleridge was not without what talkers call wit, and there were touches of prickly sarcasm in him, contemptuous enough of the world and its idols and popular dignitaries; he had traits even of poetic humor; but, in general, he seemed deficient in laughter, or indeed in sympathy for concrete human things either on the sunny or on the stormy side. One right peal of concrete laughter at some convicted flesh-and-blood absurdity, one burst of noble indignation at some injus-tice or depravity, rubbing elbows with us on this solid Earth—how strange would it have been in that Kantian haze world, and how in-finitely cheering amid its vacant air-castles and dim-melting ghosts and shadows! None such ever came. His life had been an abstract thinking and dreaming, idealistic, passed amid the ghosts of defunct bodies and of unborn ones. The moaning sing-song of that theosophic and metaphysical monotony left on you at last a very dreary feeling.

The constant gist of his discourse was lamentation over the sunk condition of the world, which he recognized to be given up to atheism and materialism, full of mere sordid misbeliefs, mispursuits, and misresults. All science had become mechanical; the science not of men, but of a kind of human beavers. Churches themselves had died away into a godless, mechanical condition, and stood there as mere cases of articles, mere forms of churches; like the dried carcasses of once swift camels, which you find left withering in the thirst of the universal desert,— ghastly portents for the present, beneficent ships of the desert no more. Men's souls were blinded, hebetated, sunk under the influence of atheism and materialism, and Hume and Voltaire: the world for the present was as an extinct world, deserted of God, and incapable of well-doing till it changed its heart and spirit. This, expressed, I think, with less of indignation and with more of long-drawn querulousness, was always recognizable as the ground-tone.

De Quincey.—"De Quincey ranges with great freedom over the accumulated wealth of the language, his capacious memory giving him a prodigious command of words. His range is perhaps wider than Macaulay's or Carlyle's, as he is more versatile in the pitch of his style, and does not disdain to use the slang of all classes, from Cockney to Oxonian.

In his diction, taken as a whole, there is a great preponderance of words derived from the Latin. Lord Brougham's opinion, that 'the Saxon part of our English idiom is to be favored at the expense of that part which has so happily coalesced from the Latin and Greek,' he puts aside as 'resembling that restraint which some metrical writers have imposed upon themselves—of writing a long copy of verses from which some particular letter, or from each line of which some different letter, should be carefully excluded.' From various causes he himself makes an excessive use of Latinized phraseology. First, his ear was deeply enamoured of a dignified rhythm; none but long words of Latin origin were equal to the lofty march of his periods. Secondly, by the use of Latinized and *quasi* technical terms, he gained greater precision than by the use of homely words of looser signification. And, thirdly, it was part of his peculiar humor to write concerning common objects in unfamiliar language.

Although De Quincey complained of the 'weariness and repulsion' of the periodic style, he carried it to excess in his own composition. His sentences are stately, elaborate, and crowded with qualifying clauses and parenthetical allusions to a degree unparalleled among modern writers. He maintained, and justly, that 'stateliness the most elaborate, in an *absolute* sense, is no fault at all, though it may be so in relation to a given subject, or to any subject under given circumstances.' Whether in his own practice he always conforms to circumstances is a question that must be left to individual taste. There is a certain stateliness in his sentences under almost all circumstances—a stateliness arising from his habitual use of periodic suspensions.

Explicitness of connection is the chief merit of De Quincey's paragraphs. He cannot be said to observe any other principle. He is carried into violations of all the other rules by his inveterate habit of digression. Often, upon a mere casual suggestion, he branches off into a digression of several pages, sometimes even digressing from the subject of his first digression. The enormity of these offences is a good deal palliated by his being conscious that he is digressing, and his taking care to let us know when he strikes off from the main subject and when he returns.

The melody of De Quincey's prose is pre-eminently rich and stately. He takes rank with Milton as one of our greatest masters of stately cadence as well as of sublime composition. If one may trust one's ear for a general impression, Milton's melody is sweeter and more varied; but, for magnificent effects, at least in prose, the palm must probably be assigned to De Quincey. In some of his grandest passages the language can be compared only to the swell and crash of an orchestra."— *William Minto.*

From De Quincey's *Essay on Style.*

There were two groups, or clusters, of Grecian wits—two depositions, or stratifications, of the national genius; and these were about a century apart. What makes them specially rememberable is the fact that each of these brilliant clusters had gathered separately about that man as central pivot who, even apart from this relation to the literature, was otherwise the leading spirit of his age. It is important for our purpose to notice the distinguishing character, or marks, by which the two clusters are separately recognized—the marks both personal and chronological. As to the personal distinctions, we have said that in each case severally the two men who offered the nucleus to the gathering happened to be otherwise the most eminent and splendid men of the period. Who were they? The one was PERICLES, the other was ALEXANDER OF MACEDON.

Except Themistocles, who may be ranked as senior to Pericles by just one generation, in the whole deduction of Grecian annals no other public man, statesman, captain-general, administrator of the national resources can be mentioned as approaching to these two men in splendor of reputation or even in real merit.

Thus far our purpose prospers. No man can pretend to forget two such centres as Pericles for the elder group, or Alexander of Macedon, "the strong he-goat" of Jewish prophecy, for the junior. Round these two *foci*, in two different but adjacent centuries gathered the total starry heavens, the galaxy, the Pantheon, of Grecian intellect. All that Greece produced of awful solemnity in her tragic stage, of riotous mirth and fancy in her comic stage, of power in her eloquence, of wisdom in her philosophy; all that has since tingled in the ears of twenty-four centuries, of her prosperity in the arts, her sculpture, her architecture, her painting, her music—everything, in short, excepting only her higher mathematics, which waited for a further development, which required the incubation of the musing intellect for yet another century, revolved, like two neighboring planetary systems, about these two solar orbs. Two mighty vortices, Pericles and Alexander the Great, drew into strong eddies about themselves all the glory and the pomp of Greek literature, Greek eloquence, Greek wisdom, Greek art.

Next, that we may still more severely search the relations in all points between the two systems, let us assign the chronological *locus* of each, because that will furnish another element towards the exact distribution of the chart representing the motion and the oscillations of human genius. Pericles had a very long administration. He was Prime Minister of Athens for upwards of one entire generation. He died in the year 429 B.C., and in a very early stage of that great Peloponnesian war, which was the one sole intestine war for Greece, affecting every nook and angle in the land. Now, in this long public life of Pericles, we are at liberty to fix on any year as his chronological *locus*. On good reasons, not called for in this place, we fix on the year 444. This is too remarkable to be forgotten. *Four, four, four*, what at some games of cards is called a *prial*, forms an era which no man can forget. It was the fifteenth year before the death of Pericles, and not far from the bisecting year of his political life. Now, passing to the other system, the *locus* of Alexander is quite as remarkable, as little liable to be forgotten when once indicated, and more easily determined, because selected from a narrower range of choice. The exact chronological *locus* of Alexander the Great is 333 B.C. Everybody knows how brief was the career of this great man, it terminated in the year 320. But the *annus mirabilis* of his pub-

lic life, the most effective and productive year throughout his oriental
anabasis, was the year 333 before Christ. Here we have another *prial*,
a prial of threes, for the *locus* of Alexander. Thus far the elements are
settled, the chronological longitude and latitude of the two great planetary systems into which the Greek literature breaks up and distributes
itself: 444 and 333 are the two central years for the two systems, allowing, therefore, an interspace of 111 years between their *foci*.

And next, we request the reader thoughtfully to consider who they are
of whom the elder system is composed. In the centre, as we have already explained, is Pericles, the great practical statesman, and that orator of whom (amongst so many that vibrated thunderbolts) it was said
peculiarly that he thundered and lightened as if he held this Jovian at-
tribute by some individual title. Passing onwards from Pericles, you
find that all the rest in *his* system were men in the highest sense creative; absolutely setting the very first examples, each in his peculiar walk
of composition; themselves without previous models, and yet destined,
every man of them, to become models for all after-generations; themselves without fathers or mothers, and yet having all posterity for their
children. First come the three men, *divini spiritus*, under a heavenly
afflatus, Æschylus, Sophocles, Euripides, the creators of tragedy out of
a village mummery. Next comes Aristophanes, who breathed the
breath of life into comedy. Then comes the great philosopher, Anax-
agoras, who first theorized successfully upon man and the world. Next
come, whether great or not, the still more famous philosophers, Socrates,
Plato, Xenophon. Then comes, leaning upon Pericles, as sometimes
Pericles leaned upon him, the divine artist, Phidias; and behind this
immortal man walk Herodotus and Thucydides. What a procession to
Eleusis would these men have formed! What a frieze, if some great
artist could arrange it as dramatically as Chaucer has arranged the *Pilgrimage to Canterbury!*

Now, let us step on a hundred years forward. We are now within
hail of Alexander; and a brilliant consistory of Grecian men that is by
which he is surrounded. There are now exquisite masters of the more
refined comedy; there are, again, great philosophers, for all the great
schools are represented by able successors; and, above all others, there
is the one philosopher who played with men's minds, according to
Lord Bacon's comparison, as freely as ever his princely pupil with
their persons—there is Aristotle. There are great orators, and, above
all others, there is that orator whom succeeding generations, wisely or
not, have adopted as the representative name for what is conceivable in
oratorical perfection—there is Demosthenes. Aristotle and Demosthe-

nes are in themselves bulwarks of power, many hosts lie in these two names. For artists, again, to range against Phidias, there is Lysippus, the sculptor, and there is Apelles, the painter. For great captains and masters of strategic art, there is Alexander himself, with a glittering *cortège* of general officers, well qualified to wear the crowns which they will win, and to head the dynasties which they will found. Historians there are now as in that former age. And, upon the whole, it cannot be denied that the "turn-out" is showy and imposing.

Here, reader, we would wish to put a question. Saving your presence, did you ever see what is called a dumb-bell? We have, and know it by more painful evidence than that of sight. You, therefore, O reader, if personally cognizant of dumb-bells, we shall remind, if not, we shall inform, that it is a cylindrical bar of iron, issuing at each end in a globe of the same metal, and usually it is sheathed in green baize; but perfidiously so, if that covering is meant to deny or to conceal the fact of those heart-rending thumps which it inflicts upon one's too confiding fingers every third *ictus*. Now, reader, it is under this image of the dumb bell we couch an allegory. Those globes at each end are the two systems, or separate clusters, of Greek literature; and that cylinder which connects them is the long man that ran into each system, binding the two together. Who was that? It was Isocrates. *Great* we cannot call him in conscience; and, therefore, by way of compromise, we call him *long*, which, in one sense, he certainly was, for he lived through four and twenty Olympiads, each containing four solar years. He narrowly escaped being a hundred years old; and, though that did not carry him from centre to centre, yet, as each system might be supposed to portend a radius each way of twenty years, he had, in fact, a full personal cognizance of the two systems, remote as they were, which composed the total world of Grecian genius. It is for this quality of length that Milton honors him with a touching memorial; for Isocrates was "that old man eloquent" of Milton's sonnet, whom the battle of Chæronea, "fatal to liberty, killed with report."

LESSON 55.

AMERICAN LITERATURE.—THE LAW OF COLONIES.—Transplanting a tree is often at the risk of its life. Some of the larger roots are destroyed in the removal, and innumerable rootlets are injured. With many of the parts which nourished it wanting, and with what remains impaired, the tree cannot instantly adapt itself to its strange surroundings. Before it can derive life from its new environment, the stock which it has accumulated is largely drawn upon, perhaps exhausted, and the experiment proves fatal to the tree.

The first movement of a *people*, taken up, however carefully, from its old home and set down in a new, must be a step backward. The sunderings of its old relations is a wrench that leaves the colony weak. The difficulties that confront it and the dangers that menace it are multiplied; while to it in its enfeebled condition each mole-hill seems and is a mountain. These difficulties and dangers are strange to it—its previous experience has not taught it how to meet and master them. Its energies, hitherto employed in continuing a life transmitted to it, must now be spent in beginning one. It must get a footing for itself in the new region, wresting or purchasing land, and subduing the same by cultivation. It must build houses, construct implements, accumulate necessities, and create and set going the manifold machinery of life, domestic, social, religious, and political. Is it any wonder that with so much more to do than it had before, and with less strength to work with, we should everywhere detect retrogression in the life of the transplanted people? Need we wonder, indeed, if their civilization does not stop short of barbarism in its decline, and they of extinction?

THE PLANTING OF THE AMERICAN COLONIES.—In addition to the disabilities which colonies ordinarily suffer and the difficulties they encounter, the American colonists experienced some that were extraordinary. They did not swarm out from the old hive because the home quarters were crowded. They left, because they had reached convictions and were striving after ideals with which the mother had no sympathy, and to which she gave no hospitality; for the world had not yet learned to tolerate what it did not approve. She subjected them to a discipline unloving and unnatural. They were made to feel that they were no longer welcome about the old hearth, and at last were driven forth into the wilderness without the loaf of bread and the bottle of water which even the bond-woman and the child Ishmael received. Not the mother's care but her oppressions planted them in America, it was afterwards confessed, and we can easily believe it.

The climate in which many of them found themselves here was inhospitable, unlike that they had left. The land was covered with dense forests, which had to be cleared before bread could be obtained; and, when subdued, the sterile soil was niggard in its returns. Human foes pressed in upon the settlements all along the coast. The Indians were a constant terror, appearing when least expected, ravaging and killing, and disappearing as silently and as mysteriously as they came.

If ever the mother's heart softened, and a wish entered it to atone for her harshness, the child never knew it. But if her love did not cross the three thousand miles of water that rolled between parent and son, her authority did. She must rule the boy even in the strange land to which she had driven him. And so, while the exiles were groping here after a freedom denied them at home, a freedom like that for which the Puritans were contending before and during the Commonwealth, but broader than any one there, except perhaps Milton, understood, the mother's repressive purpose was seen and her iron hand was felt. Upon those who grew restive under the Stamp Act and the Tea Tax and the Boston Port Bill and the Restraining Acts and the Military Act she imposed, in her Regulation, or Reconstruction, Acts, a regimen subversive of English traditions—a regimen unknown at home, or, if not unknown, one "from which British nobles and commons had long before fought out their exemption. These acts, radical and revolutionary, went to the foundations of our public system, and sought to reconstruct it from the base on a theory of parliamentary omnipotence and kingly sovereignty." It was not our fathers who were the revolutionists, it was the king and the parliament. The child was striving to uphold existing institutions, the mother was seeking to overthrow them. Such treatment it was that drove the boy, before he had come of age and his gristle had hardened into bone, into antagonism and then into open collision, by which he reached his majority, and his independence of maternal guidance was achieved.

And then came those other extraordinary difficulties encountered in organizing and carrying on a new government—a government for constructing which the England they had left furnished few precedents, as did, indeed, every other nation of modern times or of ancient.

Those who reproach us for our scanty literature, and for our stunted growth in everything but industrial energy and material prosperity do not always take these extraordinary obstacles into account. They overlook the fact that by these much of the progress we might have made has been prevented; that not all even of the few years of our life here should be counted. We could not start out from the point which the English people, and our fathers with them, had reached, and run on side by side with them. By the ordinary obstructions of colonial life, but still more by the extraordinary impediments peculiar to ourselves, we were set back near the goal of starting, and were handicapped for the race.

THE RELATION OF LITERATURE TO THE NATION.—The people modify, though they do not make, the literature. If not the thinkers, they are the soil out of which the thinkers spring;

if they do not immediately produce the literature, they nourish those who do. This relation, natural and always existing, is especially noticeable now. Less than ever before are writers a class, living apart and aloof from the rest of the nation. No healthful literature, prose or poetry, can come from those who are indifferent to others, cut off from the general movement of their generation; and none is now attempted. There is such a community of interests between those who write and those who do not, each party giving and taking, acting and acted upon, that no lines of cleavage between them can be traced. The writer is a teacher; the lessons he teaches must be such, in subject and in treatment, as his pupils will study. The topics he selects must be such as the needs of the people force upon him, and the handling must interest them. His very words must be those which have "sucked up the feeding juices secreted for them in the rich mother-earth of common folk." His highest inspiration must come from close contact with the people; he must have been drawn, in some measure, into the current of his times, must be in it and of it in order to direct it.

"In order that an organism—plant or animal—should exist at all, there must be a certain correspondence between the organism and its environment," says Professor Dowden. We do not look in vain into a nation's literature to see what the national spirit is, what the surroundings, attainments, and limitations of the people are. How, for example, the insular position of England and the self-centred and intense home life of her people color her literature! How a great war, civil or national, gives a martial cast to the thought and the style of the period! How a great popular movement in taste, in politics, in religion, voiced, if not initiated, by the literary men but speedily escaping their control it may be, gives a trend to the literature of the times, and regulates the width and depth of the current! Study carefully a great author, then, and you will read more than he is conscious of saying;

he speaks only for himself, he supposes; but, in reality, his generation of countrymen speak through him, and all the more truly because he is not cognizant of it.

AMERICAN LITERATURE OF THE SEVENTEENTH CENTURY.— 1. Our **first writers** were the early **colonists** themselves, men born and bred in England, and coming here and settling Virginia and Massachusetts.

2. Their **education** and their **training in literature** were such as Englishmen at that time were receiving. These first colonies were planted during the reign of the first Stuart—of him who "stood out in grotesque contrast" with his predecessors, and so violently "jarred against the conception of an English ruler which had grown up under the Tudors." Subsequent colonizations took place under his Stuart successors. More despicable sovereigns than the Stuarts never sat on the English throne. Theirs was the age when, says the historian Green, "two theories, which contained within them the seeds of a death-struggle between the people and the crown, the divine right of kings and the divine right of bishops," were insisted on—an age of prerogative and of persecution. Education was mainly in clerical hands, and literature was controlled by clerical licensers, mere creatures of the crown. Whether even *Paradise Lost* should see the light depended upon the gracious permission of a youthful prig, wearing the gown, and appointed to this post of licenser by the primate of England. Under such men, bound to a minute and definite system of doctrine, to join whose ranks, says Milton, was to write one's self *slave*, all intellectual culture was fettered, as was civil liberty by the royal prerogative. The early colonists were men cramped and stunted by this tyranny, civil and ecclesiastical; and those at least who came to New England were men chafing under these restrictions. The literature produced by them must bear, branded upon it, marks of such discipline.

3. * The **surroundings** of these men here did much to shape what they wrote. Those **peopling Virginia** were largely of the cavalier element. The ideal of life which they strove to realize was that of the country squire of England. They dwelt apart from each other on large estates. The religion was that of the Church of England. The governors did not favor general education, and the separation of colonist from colonist caused its neglect. Sir Wm. Berkeley thanked God that there were no free schools in Virginia; for learning, he thought, had brought disobedience and heresy and sects into the world, and printing had developed them. No record exists of a printing-press in Virginia before 1681. The government was not tolerant of Quakers, Baptists, Moravians, or Methodists.

The early **New England colonists** were Puritan dissenters. They believed in the right to think for themselves in matters religious and political, and came here that they might do it without restraint. They believed in universal education, and by 1649 public instruction was compulsory in nearly every colony. Among these people there was a liberal sprinkling of university men, from Cambridge especially. The men who in culture rose above all others were the clergy; it was in the service of religion that the intellect of the people was enlisted. Politics was but a department of theology, and in some places citizenship depended upon certain church relations. The clergy, who led in everything, were men who by their wisdom and by the purity of their lives deserved to lead. But they could not completely emancipate themselves from traditions and the influence of early training, or fail to take damage from the exalted positions into which they were here suddenly thrust. They became intolerant of all who did not agree with

---

* For many of the facts in this account of our early literature, we are greatly indebted to the able and admirable work of Prof. Moses Coit Tyler on American Literature.

them in what the world now calls the narrowness of their moral and religious creeds.

It cannot be said that the environment of the Virginians or of the New England colonists, during the seventeenth century, was favorable to literature; and, had it been, the stream could not have risen here higher than its source in the mother country.   And in England, we must remember, this was the age of reaction and decline from the Elizabethan era —the age of "crabbed learning and quaint conceits," of fancy supplanting imagination, of extravagant expression in place of real feeling.   In the hard struggle for existence here, little leisure could be had, and little incitement could be found, for the cultivation of literature as an art.   Nevertheless, some works were produced.   In Virginia books were written descriptive of the strange land, and of the strange life the colonists were living in it—books to gratify English curiosity, to correct misapprehensions, and to develop a better spirit and a higher life among the colonists themselves.   The first book written in America, *A True Relation of Virginia*, was by that remarkable man—traveller, soldier, and adventurer—CAPTAIN JOHN SMITH.   The following extract illustrates its style, both in matter and in treatment:—

Of the Natural Inhabitants of Virginia.—The land is not populous, for the men be few; their far greater number is of women and children. Within 60 miles of *James Towne*, there are about some 5000 people, but of able men fit for their wars scarce 1500.   To nourish so many together they have yet no means, because they make so small a benefit of their land, be it never so fertile.   Six or seven hundred have been the most hath been seen together, when they gathered themselves to have surprised me at Pamavnkee, having but fifteen to withstand the worst of their fury.   As small as the proportion of ground that hath yet been discovered is in comparison of that yet unknown.   The people differ very much in stature, especially in language, as before is expressed.   Some being very great as the *Sasquesahanocks;* others very little, as the *Wighcocomocoes:* but generally tall and straight, of a comely proportion, and of a color brown when they are of any age, but they are born white. Their hair is generally black, but few have any beards.   The men wear half their beards shaven, the other half long; for barbers they use their women, who with two shells will grate away the hair of any fashion they please. The women are cut in many fashions, agreeable to their years, but ever some part remaineth long. They are very strong, of an able body and full of agility, able to endure to lie under a tree by the fire, in the worst of winter, or in the weeds and grass, in ambuscado in the summer. They are inconstant in everything, but what fear constraineth them to keep. Crafty, timorous, quick of apprehension, and very ingenious. Some are of disposition fearful, some bold, most cautelous, all savage. Generally covetous of copper, beads, and such like trash. They are soon moved to anger, and so malicious that they seldom forget an injury; they seldom steal one from another, lest their conjurers should reveal it, and so they be pursued and punished. That they are thus feared is certain, but that any can reveal their offences by conjuration I am doubtful. Their women are careful not to be suspected of dishonesty without the leave of their husbands. Each household knoweth their own lands and gardens, and most live of their own labors.

For their apparel, they are sometimes covered with the skins of wild beasts, which in winter are dressed with the hair but in summer without. The better sort use large mantles of deer skins, not much differing in fashion from the Irish mantles. Some imbroidered with white beads, some with copper, other painted after their manner. But the common sort have scarce to cover their nakedness, but with grass, the leaves of trees, or such like. We have seen some use mantles made of turkey feathers, so prettily wrought and woven with threads that nothing could be discovered but the feathers. That was exceeding warm and very handsome. But the women are always covered about their waists with a skin, and very shamefast to be seen bare. They adorn themselves most with copper, beads, and paintings. Their women, some have their legs, hands, breasts, and face cunningly imbroidered with divers works, as beasts, serpents, artificially wrought into their flesh with black spots. In each ear commonly they have 3 great holes, whereat they hang chains, bracelets, or copper. Some of their men wear in these holes a small green and yellow colored snake, near half a yard in length, which crawling and lapping herself about his neck oftentimes familiarly would kiss his lips. Others wear a dead rat, tied by the tail. Some on their heads wear the wing of a bird, or some large feather with a rattle. Those rattles are somewhat like the shape of a rapier, but less, which they take from the tail of a snake. Many have the whole skin of a hawk, or some strange fowl, stuffed with the wings

abroad. Others a broad piece of copper, and some the hand of their
enemy dried. Their heads and shoulders are painted red with the root
pocone brayed to powder, mixed with oil; this they hold in summer to
preserve them from the heat, and in winter from the cold. Many other
forms of paintings they use, but he is the most gallant that is the most
monstrous to behold.

Their buildings and habitations are for the most part by the rivers or
not far distant from some fresh spring. Their houses are built like our
arbors, of small young sprigs bowed and tied, and so close covered with
mats, or the barks of trees very handsomely, that notwithstanding either
wind, rain, or weather, they are as warm as stoves, but smoky, yet at
the top of the house there is a hole made for the smoke to go into right
over the fire. Their fire they kindle presently by chafing a dry pointed
stick in a hole of a little square piece of wood, that firing itself, will so
fire the moss, leaves, or any such like dry thing, that will quickly burn.

The literature of the New England colonies during this
century is largely theological. This was the age of the learned
JOHN COTTON, who was called the Patriarch of New England;
of THOMAS HOOKER, who moved from his parish in Newton,
Mass., and with 100 others settled Hartford, Conn., and
became "priest and king" of his people; and of the renowned
MATHERS, father, son, and grandson,—RICHARD, INCREASE,
and COTTON,—men of vast and varied attainments, and of wonderful power and influence. INCREASE MATHER lived on till
1723, and COTTON till 1728, so that they belong partly to the
18th century. INCREASE was the author, it is said, of ninety-
two works, of which the most noteworthy is *An Essay for the
Recording of Illustrious Providences*, appearing in 1684; and
COTTON of nearly 400, great and small, the best known of
which is his celebrated *Magnalia Christi Americana*, written
before the close of the century, but not published till 1702.

Some attempts in verse were made during this century.
MRS. ANNE BRADSTREET, daughter of Gov. Dudley and wife
of Gov. Bradstreet, coming over in 1630, was the first who
aspired to poetry as a vocation. Quotations, illustrating her
muse, would hardly be edifying or pleasing now, though she
was much admired in her day.

LESSON 56.

AMERICAN LITERATURE OF THE EIGHTEENTH CENTURY.—
Before the opening of the eighteenth century, English colonies
dotted the Atlantic coast from Maine to Georgia. These have
been grouped into (1) the Northern, or New England, cluster;
(2) the Middle, including New York, New Jersey, and Pennsylvania; and (3) the Southern, composed of Maryland, Virginia, North and South Carolina, and Georgia. The literature of the seventeenth century was almost entirely produced
by those born in England; that of these groups, during the
eighteenth century, by their sons, born here. There is lacking in this eighteenth century literature what we should
expect to miss—the filial and submissive tone of the seventeenth. It was obvious, even before the century opened, and
it became more and more patent as it progressed, that the
colonies were outgrowing their pupilage and becoming self-
reliant. We catch this note early and distinctly. This spirit
is revealed and developed by the French and Indian war of
1755–63. This war was the school, too, in which many of the
best soldiers of the Revolutionary struggle graduated; and
it may be questioned whether, without the training received
in it, this great struggle, opening with the last third of the
century, would have been successful, even if attempted.

THE NEW ENGLAND GROUP.—If, as may be questioned, the
ascendancy of the clergy here was not as complete during the
eighteenth century as during the seventeenth, it was not from
any decline in ministerial scholarship and ability. The people
had grown. Pines do not tower when standing among spruce
and hemlocks as when among lowlier cedars. In SAMUEL
HOPKINS, the hero of Mrs. Stowe's *Minister's Wooing*, in
NATHANIEL EMMONS (living well into the next century), and
in JONATHAN EDWARDS, we find men of even broader culture
and keener discrimination. If not the peers of their prede-

cessors, or of some of their contemporaries, in pulpit eloquence, it cannot be denied that they discussed more profoundly than these the great problems of divine government and human responsibility. EDWARDS was a clergyman at Northampton, Mass., from 1727 to 1750, afterwards for some years a missionary among the Housatonic Indians, and died in 1758 while President of Princeton College. His *Inquiry into the Freedom of the Will* is a work without superior for subtility of reasoning.

Many other clergymen eminent in the pulpit deserve mention. Some of these became known as historians. WM. HUBBARD wrote his *General History of New England*, down to 1680, and his more celebrated *Narrative of the Troubles with the Indians in New England*, down to 1677. THOMAS PRINCE'S *Chronological History of New England* appeared in 1736.

The laity pressed toward the front during this century, and shared with the clergy in literary labor and honors.

THE MIDDLE GROUP.—WM. LIVINGSTON of New York, afterwards celebrated as a statesman, published, in 1747, a poem called *Philosophic Solitude*. WM. SMITH of New York, in 1757, published his *History of New York from the First Discovery to the Year* 1732. JONATHAN DICKINSON, of Elizabethtown, New Jersey, was a noted clergyman, a physician, and a voluminous author. Philadelphia, during this period, was second only to Boston in literature. Before the Revolution, 425 original books and pamphlets were printed there. Of the host of writers there the greatest was BENJAMIN FRANKLIN, editor, scientist, diplomat, and statesman, as well as author. He was born in Boston in 1706, and died in Philadelphia, whither he early moved, in 1790. The most celebrated of his writings is his *Autobiography*, begun in 1771, and continued in 1784 and 1788. It is charming for the simplicity and purity of its style, and is one of the most popular books ever issued.

THE SOUTHERN GROUP.—The pioneer of literary activity in Virginia, during this period, was JAMES BLAIR, the founder of the College of William and Mary, and president of it for fifty years. ROBERT BEVERLY published, in 1705, a history of Virginia, and in 1724 HUGH JONES appeared with another history of this colony. Jones was a professor in William and Mary College, and wrote text-books also.

Professor Tyler says, "In general, the characteristic note of American literature in the colonial time is, for New England, scholarly, logical, speculative, unworldly, rugged, sombre; and, as one passes southward along the coast, this literary note changes rapidly toward lightness and brightness, until it reaches the sensuous mirth, the frank and jovial worldliness, the satire, the persiflage, the gentlemanly grace, the amenity, the jocular coarseness of literature in Maryland, Virginia, and farther south."

A growing tendency is observable, as the century progresses, towards a union of the colonies in closer fellowship. This tendency is strikingly apparent as we near the last third of the century, and takes distinct form as the oppressions of the mother country arouse first the spirit of resentment and then that of resistance. From this time on, political questions swallow up all others. The mere literary man, if he can be said to exist in this country during this century, gives place to the political orator and the statesman. And mighty is the race of these that now appear all along the line, called into existence by the terrible crisis; since of them, at the *beginning* of the struggle, assembled in the Continental Congress at Philadelphia in 1774, even Chatham could say, "I must declare and avow that, in the master states of the world, I know not the people nor the senate who, under such a complication of difficult circumstances, can stand in preference to the delegates of America assembled in General Congress at Philadelphia. For genuine sagacity, for singular moderation, for solid wisdom, manly spirit, sublime sentiments, and sim-

plicity of language—for everything respectable and honorable—they stand unrivalled." Of these men during the
Revolutionary struggle we cannot here speak further, nor of
them during the years immediately succeeding, when the
Herculean labors of recuperation and reorganization were upon
them. A new Constitution was framed. The masterly papers
of ALEXANDER HAMILTON, JAMES MADISON, and JOHN JAY,
essays now gathered together and composing *The Federalist*,.
were written to urge the adoption of this Constitution; the
colonies were transformed into States, and the Union was
created.

With an added word or two we pass to quote briefly from
some of the works of this century. The first newspaper in
America was printed in Boston in 1690, and called *Public
Occurrences;* the first that lived was *The Boston News-Letter*,
started in 1704. Before the close of 1765, forty-three newspapers had been established in the American colonies—twenty
in New England, thirteen in the Middle group, and ten in
the Southern. Before the close of this year, seven colleges
also were established—Harvard in 1636; William and Mary in
1693; Yale in 1700; New Jersey (Princeton) in 1746; King's
(Columbia) in 1754; Philadelphia (University of Pennsylvania)
in 1755; Rhode Island (Brown University) in 1764. Their
work in cementing together the colonies was great, and their
influence upon our literature can scarcely be over-estimated.

From Edwards's *Inquiry into the Freedom of the Will.*

With respect to the degree of the idea of the future pleasure. With
regard to things which are the subject of our thoughts, either past, present, or future, we have much more of an idea or apprehension of some
things than others; that is, our idea is much more clear, lively, and
strong. Thus, the ideas we have of sensible things by immediate sensation are usually much more lively than those we have by mere imagination, or by contemplation of them when absent. My idea of the sun,
when I look upon it, is more vivid than when I only think of it. Our
idea of the sweet relish of a delicious fruit is usually stronger when we
taste it than when we only imagine it. And sometimes the ideas we have

of things by contemplation are much stronger and clearer than at other times. Thus, a man at one time has a much stronger idea of the pleasure which is to be enjoyed in eating some sort of food that he loves than at another. Now the degree, or strength, of the idea, or sense, that men have of future good or evil is one thing that has great influence on their minds to excite choice, or volition. When, of two kinds of future pleasure which the mind considers of and are presented for choice, both are supposed exactly equal by the judgment, and both equally certain, and all other things are equal, but only one of them is what the mind has a far more lively sense of than of the other, this has the greatest advantage by far to affect and attract the mind, and move the will. It is now more agreeable to the mind to take the pleasure it has a strong and lively sense of than that which it has only a faint idea of. The view of the former is attended with the strongest appetite, and the greatest uneasiness attends the want of it; and it is agreeable to the mind to have uneasiness removed, and its appetite gratified. And, if several future enjoyments are presented together as competitors for the choice of the mind, some of them judged to be greater and others less, the mind also having a greater sense and more lively idea of the good of some of them and of others a less, and some are viewed as of greater certainty or probability than others, and those enjoyments that appear most agreeable in one of these respects, appear least so in others, —in this case, all other things being equal, the agreeableness of a proposed object of choice will be in a degree some way compounded of the degree of good supposed by the judgment, the degree of apparent probability, or certainty, of that good, and the degree of the view, or sense, or liveliness of the idea the mind has of that good; because all together concur to constitute the degree in which the object appears at present agreeable; and accordingly volition will be determined.

I might further observe, the state of mind that views a proposed object of choice is another thing that contributes to the agreeableness or disagreeableness of that object; the particular temper which the mind has by nature, or that has been introduced and established by education, example, custom, or some other means; or the frame, or state, that the mind is in on a particular occasion. That object which appears agreeable to one does not so to another. And the same object does not always appear alike agreeable to the same person at different times. It is most agreeable to some men to follow their reason; and to others, to follow their appetite; to some men it is more agreeable to deny a vicious inclination than to gratify it; others it suits best to gratify the vilest appetites. It is more disagreeable to some men than to others to counteract a former resolution. In these respects, and many others which might be mentioned, different things will be most agreeable to different persons; and not only so, but to the same persons at different times.

But possibly it is needless and improper to mention the frame and state of the mind as a distinct ground of the agreeableness of objects from the other two mentioned before; viz., the apparent nature and circumstances of the objects viewed, and the manner of the view; perhaps, if we strictly consider the matter, the different temper and state of the mind makes no alteration as to the agreeableness of objects any other way than as it makes the objects themselves appear differently beautiful or deformed, having apparent pleasure or pain attending them; and, as it occasions the manner of the view to be different, causes the idea of beauty or deformity, pleasure or uneasiness, to be more or less lively.

However, I think so much is certain, that volition, in no one instance that can be mentioned, is otherwise than the greatest apparent good is, in the manner which has been explained. The choice of the mind never departs from that which at that time, and with respect to the direct and immediate objects of that decision of the mind, appears most agreeable and pleasing, all things considered. If the immediate objects of the will are a man's own actions, then those actions which appear most agreeable to him he wills. If it be now most agreeable to him, all things considered, to walk, then he wills to walk. If it be now, upon the whole of what at present appears to him, most agreeable to speak, then he chooses to speak; if it suits him best to keep silence, then he chooses to keep silence. There is scarcely a plainer and more universal dictate of the sense and experience of mankind than that, when men act voluntarily, and do what they please, then they do what suits them best, or what is most agreeable to them. To say that they do what they please, or what pleases them, but yet do not do what is agreeable to them, is the same thing as to say they do what they please, but do not act their pleasure; and that is to say that they do what they please, and yet do not do what they please.

It appears from these things that, in some sense, the will always follows the last dictate of the understanding. But then the understanding must be taken in a large sense, as including the whole faculty of perception, or apprehension, and not merely what is called reason, or judgment. If by the dictate of understanding is meant what reason declares to be best or most for the person's happiness, taking in the whole of his duration, it is not true that the will always follows the last dictate of the understanding. Such a dictate of reason is quite a different matter from things appearing now most agreeable; all things being put together which pertain to the mind's present perception, apprehensions, or ideas, in any respect. Although that dictate of reason, when it takes place, is one thing that is put into the scales, and is to be considered as a thing that has concern in the compound influence which moves and induces the will, and is one thing that is to be considered in estimating the degree of that appearance of good which the will always follows; either as having its influence added to other things, or subducted from them. When it concurs with other things, then its weight is added to them, as put into the same scale; but when it is against them, it is as a weight in the opposite scale, where it resists the influence of other things: yet its resistance is often overcome by their greater weight, and so the act of the will is determined in opposition to it.

The things which I have said may, I hope, serve in some measure to illustrate and confirm the position I laid down in the beginning of this section; viz., that the will is always determined by the strongest motive, or by that view of the mind which has the greatest degree of previous tendency to excite volition. But, whether I have been so happy as rightly to explain the thing wherein consists the strength of motives, or not, yet my failing in this will not overthrow the position itself; which carries much of its own evidence with it, and is the thing of chief importance to the purpose of the ensuing discourse; and the truth of it, I hope, will appear with great clearness, before I have finished what I have to say on the subject of human liberty.

From Franklin's *Autobiography.*

And now I set on foot my first project of a public nature, that for a subscription library. I drew up the proposals, got them put into form by our great scrivener, Brockden, and, by the help of my friends in the Junto, procured fifty subscribers of forty shillings each to begin with, and ten shillings a year for fifty years, the term our company was to continue. We afterwards obtained a charter, the company being increased to one hundred; this was the mother of all the North American subscription libraries, now so numerous. It is become a great thing itself, and continually goes on increasing. These libraries have improved the general conversation of the Americans, made the common tradesmen and farmers as intelligent as most gentlemen from other countries, and perhaps have contributed in some degree to the stand so generally made throughout the colonies in defence of their privileges.

At the time I established myself in Pennsylvania, there was not a good bookseller's shop in any of the colonies to the southward of Boston,

In New York and Philadelphia, the printers were indeed stationers, but they sold only paper, almanacs, ballads, and a few common-school books. Those who loved reading were obliged to send for their books from England; the members of the Junto had each a few. We had left the ale-house, where we first met, and hired a room to hold our club in. I proposed that we should all of us bring our books to that room, where they would not only be ready to consult in our conferences, but become a common benefit, each of us being at liberty to borrow such as he wished to read at home. This was accordingly done, and for some time contented us.

Finding the advantage of this little collection, I proposed to render the benefit from the books more common, by commencing a public subscription library. I drew a sketch of the plan and rules that would be necessary, and got a skilful conveyancer, Mr. Charles Brockden, to put the whole in form of articles of agreement to be subscribed; by which each subscriber engaged to pay a certain sum down for the first purchase of the books, and an annual contribution for increasing them. So few were the readers at that time in Philadelphia, and the majority of us so poor, that I was not able with great industry to find more than fifty persons, mostly young tradesmen, willing to pay down for this purpose forty shillings each, and ten shillings per annum. With this little fund we began. The books were imported; the library was opened one day in the week for lending them to the subscribers, on their promissory notes to pay double the value if not duly returned. The institution soon manifested its utility, was imitated by other towns, and in other provinces. The libraries were augmented by donations; reading became fashionable; and our people, having no public amusements to divert their attention from study, became better acquainted with books, and in a few years were observed by strangers to be better instructed and more intelligent than people of the same rank generally are in other countries.

When we were about to sign the abovementioned articles, which were to be binding on us, our heirs, etc., for fifty years, Mr. Brockden, the scrivener, said to us, "You are young men, but it is scarcely probable that any of you will live to see the expiration of the term fixed in the instrument." A number of us, however, are yet living; but the instrument was after a few years rendered null by a charter that incorporated and gave perpetuity to the company.

The objections and reluctances I met with, in soliciting the subscriptions, made me soon feel the impropriety of presenting one's self as the proposer of any useful project that might be supposed to raise one's reputation in the smallest degree above that of one's neighbors, when one has need of their assistance to accomplish that project. I therefore put myself as much as I could out of sight, and stated it as a scheme of a *number of friends*, who had requested me to go about and propose it to such as they thought lovers of reading. In this way my affair went on more smoothly, and I ever after practised it on such occasions; and, from my frequent successes, can heartily recommend it. The present little sacrifice of your vanity will afterwards be amply repaid. If it remains a while uncertain to whom the merit belongs, some one more vain than yourself may be encouraged to claim it, and then even envy will be disposed to do you justice, by plucking those assumed feathers, and restoring them to their right owner.

This library afforded me the means of improvement by constant study, for which I set apart an hour or two each day, and thus repaired in some degree the loss of the learned education my father once intended for me. Reading was the only amusement I allowed myself. I spent no time in taverns, games, or frolics of any kind; and my industry in my business continued as indefatigable as it was necessary. I was indebted for my printing-house; I had a young family coming on to be educated, and I had two competitors to contend with for business, who were established in the place before me. My circumstances, however, grew daily easier. My original habits of frugality continuing, and my father having, among his instructions to me when a boy, frequently repeated a proverb of Solomon, "Seest thou a man diligent in his calling, he shall stand before kings, he shall not stand before mean men," I thence considered industry as a means of obtaining wealth and distinction, which encouraged me, though I did not think that I should ever literally *stand before kings*, which, however, has since happened; for I have stood before *fire*, and even had the honor of sitting down with one, the King of Denmark, to dinner.

We have an English proverb that says, "He that would thrive must ask his wife." It was lucky for me that I had one as much disposed to industry and frugality as myself. She assisted me cheerfully in my business, folding and stitching pamphlets, tending shop, purchasing old linen rags for the paper-makers, etc. We kept no idle servants, our table was plain and simple, our furniture of the cheapest. For instance, my breakfast was for a long time bread and milk (no tea), and I ate it out of a two-penny earthen porringer, with a pewter spoon. But mark how luxury will enter families, and make a progress, in spite of principle: being called one morning to breakfast, I found it in a china bowl, with a spoon of silver! They had been bought for me without my knowledge by my wife, and had cost her the enormous sum of three and twenty shillings; for which she had no other excuse or apology to make, but that she thought *her* husband deserved a silver spoon and china bowl as well as any of his neighbors. This was the first appearance of plate and china in our house; which afterwards, in the course of years, as our wealth increased, augmented gradually to several hundred pounds in value.

In 1732, I first published my Almanac, under the name of *Richard Saunders ;* it was continued by me about twenty-five years, and commonly called "Poor Richard's Almanac." I endeavored to make it both entertaining and useful, and it accordingly came to be in such demand that I reaped considerable profit from it, vending annually near ten thousand. And, observing that it was generally read, scarce any neighborhood in the province being without it, I considered it as a proper vehicle for conveying instruction among the common people, who bought scarcely any other books. I therefore filled all the little spaces, that occurred between the remarkable days in the calendar, with proverbial sentences, chiefly such as inculcated industry and frugality as the means of procuring wealth, and thereby securing virtue; it being more difficult for a man in want to act always honestly, as, to use here one of those proverbs, *It is hard for an empty sack to stand upright.*   -

These proverbs, which contained the wisdom of many ages and nations, I assembled and formed into a connected discourse prefixed to the Almanac of 1757, as the harangue of a wise old man to the people attending an auction. The bringing all these scattered counsels thus into a focus enabled them to make greater impression. The piece, being universally approved, was copied in all the newspapers of the American Continent, reprinted in Britain on a large sheet of paper, to be stuck up in houses; two translations were made of it in France, and great numbers bought by the clergy and gentry to distribute gratis among their poor parishioners and tenants. In Pennsylvania, as it discouraged useless expense in foreign superfluities, some thought it had its share of influence in producing that growing plenty of money, which was observable for several years after its publication.

From John Adams's *Letters to his Wife.*

Yesterday, the greatest question was decided which ever was debated in America, and a greater, perhaps, never was nor will be decided among men. A Resolution was passed without one dissenting Colony "That these United Colonies are, and of right ought to be, free and independent States, and as such they have, and of right ought to have, full power to make war, conclude peace, establish commerce, and to do all other acts and things which other States may rightfully do." You will see, in a few days, a Declaration setting forth the causes which have impelled us to this mighty revolution, and the reasons which will justify it in the sight of God and man. A plan of confederation will be taken up in a few days.

When I look back to the year 1761, and recollect the argument concerning writs of assistance in the superior court, which I have hitherto considered as the commencement of this controversy between Great Britain and America, and run through the whole period from that time to this, and recollect the series of political events, the chain of causes and effects, I am surprised at the suddenness as well as greatness of this revolution. Britain has been filled with folly, and America with wisdom; at least, this is my judgment. Time must determine. It is the will of Heaven that the two countries should be sundered forever. It may be the will of Heaven that America shall suffer calamities still more wasting, and distresses yet more dreadful. If this is to be the case, it will have this good effect at least. It will inspire us with many virtues which we have not, and correct many errors, follies, and vices which threaten to disturb, dishonor, and destroy us. The furnace of affliction produces refinement in States as well as individuals. And the new governments we are assuming in every part will require a purification from our vices, and an augmentation of our virtues, or they will be no blessings. The people will have unbounded power, and the people are extremely addicted to corruption and venality, as well as the great. But I must submit all my hopes and fears to an overruling Providence, in which, unfashionable as the faith may be, I firmly believe.

Had a Declaration of Independency been made seven months ago, it would have been attended with many great and glorious effects.

But on the other hand, the delay of this Declaration to this time has many great advantages attending it. The hopes of reconciliation which were fondly entertained by multitudes of honest and well-meaning, though weak and mistaken people, have been gradually, and at last totally extinguished. Time has been given for the whole people maturely to consider the great question of independence, and to ripen their judgment, dissipate their fears, and allure their hopes by discussing it in newspapers and pamphlets, by debating it in assemblies, conventions, committees of safety and inspection, in town and county meetings, as well as in private conversations, so that the whole people, in every colony of the thirteen, have now adopted it as their own act. This will cement the union, and avoid those heats, and perhaps convulsions, which might have been occasioned by such a Declaration six months ago.

But the day is past. The second* day of July, 1776, will be the most memorable epocha in the history of America. I am apt to believe that it will be celebrated by succeeding generations as the great anniversary festival. It ought to be commemorated as the day of deliverance, by solemn acts of devotion to God Almighty. It ought to be solemnized with pomp and parade, with shows, games, sports, guns, bells, bonfires, and illuminations, from one end of this continent to the other, from this time forward forevermore.

You will think me transported with enthusiasm, but I am not. I am well aware of the toil and blood and treasure that it will cost us to maintain this Declaration and support and defend these States. Yet through all the gloom I can see the rays of ravishing light and glory. I can see that the end is more than worth all the means. And that posterity will triumph in that day's transaction, even although we should rue it, which I trust in God we shall not.

LESSON 57.

AMERICAN LITERATURE OF THE NINETEENTH CENTURY.— We shall touch upon a few points in which, as it seems to us, our literature differs to-day from the English, and leave the American authors from whom we shall hereafter quote to illustrate, if they may, the little here said, and the much left unsaid. In comparison with the English of the present, we think American literature, in the *main*,

(1) **LACKS SOBRIETY AND SEDATENESS.**—Our authors are somewhat wanting in justness of perception—they do not see things precisely as they are. They do not show that ripe and unerring judgment that comes from the habit of patient looking upon things from all sides. They are imposed upon by

---

* The practice has been to celebrate the 4th of July, the day upon which the form of the Declaration of Independence was agreed to, rather than the 2d, the day upon which the resolution making that declaration was determined upon by the Congress.

the specious. They have the magnifying eyes of children, cannot see without feeling and allowing the feeling to color the opinion and inflame the account. They are impatient of exact statement, easily run into extravagance, and this whether speaking without imagery or with it. What modern English author of note would say in cool narrative, as a noted American has done, that the *warmth* of a certain man's kindly aspect was so *excessive* that "an extra pass of the water-carts was found essential in order to lay the dust occasioned by so much extra sunshine;" or compare Indian cakes, in the bright yellow of their color, with "the bread which was changed to glistening gold when Midas tried to eat it"?. Delicacy of touch, so common in the old country, is rare here. Lack of it and of sobriety is especially seen in our broad and audacious humor. We betray that incredulity, so characteristic of the uncultivated, that the reader can take up a suggestion, and infer what is only implied. The restlessness of American life infects our literature—it lacks repose. In the comparison, we must add that American literature

(2) **LACKS SIMPLICITY**—that highest outcome of culture, as it has been called. There is in it a surplusage of expression. Adjectives abound, and these in the superlative degree. How hard for Americans to use the simple *yea, yea; nay, nay,* forgetting that in communication " Whatsoever is more than these cometh of evil." Are not our heads still a little turned and our style affected by the extent of our territory and our marvellous material success ? With a certain character in Longfellow's *Kavanagh,* do we not dream of a literature commensurate in style with our prairies, our Niagaras, and our Great Lakes; and in American letters do we not occasionally meet an author who has studied at school with Elijah Pogram? How hard for us to be colloquial, call things by their simple and homely names, keep clear of tumid expression, avoid " fine writing," and undertake only what we can thoroughly accomplish! We seem to think, as our orators assure us, that

the eyes of the world are still upon us; and we find it difficult not to pose and attitudinize as if upon the stage. American literature, we think,

(3) **LACKS RESPECT FOR AUTHORITY.**—We are a young nation, cut off from the old world, and trying the experiment of a new form of government. European experience should certainly count for more than it does in our politics and statesmanship. We seem to think that difference of climate, of race, of pursuit, and of government changes principles, and suppose, with Pascal, that "a meridian is decisive of truth and a few years of possession, that fundamental laws change, and that right has its epochs." This indocility has in some measure infected our writers. Were we not, for our highest good in literature as in other interests, forced too early from the state of pupilage? we are sometimes tempted to ask. Grievous as that condition was, would it not have been better for us in the end, could we have borne it, to have remained longer in it, and to have emerged from it in a natural way, and not suddenly and violently. It would have kept down the flaunting weeds of self-conceit, and cultivated in us a spirit of docility, and respect and reverence for authority—qualities not obtrusive in our national character or in our writings. We add, lastly, that, in the comparison, American literature

(4) **LACKS SCHOLARSHIP AND PROFUNDITY.**—We are not willing to serve needed apprenticeships; are ambitious to stand at the top of the ladder, but dislike to climb to it round after round. For instance, the thorough education in the preparatory and higher schools, and the five years in the medical college, required in France as preliminary to practice, we abbreviate. In business and in every profession, including that of literature, we would walk before we have learned to creep, and run before we can walk; and, unfortunately, the market for "green fruit" of all kinds, especially literary, is "brisk" here. Our readers are many, if not profound. They

create a demand that must be supplied; it is, and at paying rates. The field for writers here is broad, and largely untilled; the tempting rewards held out are not for master workmanship; and competition in the higher departments is not severe, because the laborers there are few. American literature, then, like American agriculture, we are compelled to say, ploughs shallowly and spreads itself over vast areas; does not, with German thoroughness, or even with the English, cultivate its fields.

THE REVERSE SIDE OF THE PICTURE.—But, after all, it is the likeness, rather than the unlikeness, of American literature to the English that strikes the candid and thoughtful reader. We almost wonder that so long and so distant a separation of the two peoples from each other has not wrought more, and more essential, differences between them and between their literatures. Those which exist are mostly on the surface. They arise in part from antagonism to the mother, into which once and again the child was driven; and in part are vanishing as this hostility is dying out. They come somewhat from our new environment—from our being compelled in so many things to be a law to ourselves. But they come chiefly from our youth; and, in so far as they are faults, we hope and expect that they will disappear with that.

The spirit of our literature is good. It does not come from men who deny kinship with the race, or from men moved by hatred of those socially above them. It is eminently humane. It is sensitive to the influence of nature, and alive with regard for her teachings. Our writers are open to new truth and receptive of it.

Our language is English, and theirs is American. Some words, and the forms, pronunciations, and meanings of some words, discarded in England, are retained here; but these are found rather in common speech, are seldom employed by the better educated and by those who write. New words and old words in new senses are seen here; but the lexical differences, as the syntactic, between English here and English in England are fewer and less important than those between the English of Edinburgh and that of London; fewer and less important than those which adjacent shires in England exhibit.

English literature is everywhere read here, and ours there, and the number of those here who read deeply, smaller though it be than that in England, is rapidly increasing. We acknowledge, with Everett, "the incalculable advantages derived to this land out of the deep fountains of civil, moral, and intellectual truth from which we have drawn in England."

The ties of every other kind which are holding the two peoples together and drawing into closer unity the two literatures are multiplying in number and increasing in strength. We need not apprehend a divergence of these literatures and the consequent deterioration of our own.

AMERICAN PROSE.—WASHINGTON IRVING was born in New York City in 1783, and admitted to the bar in 1807. Commenced with his brother William and James K. Paulding the serial *Salmagundi* in 1807; published *Knickerbocker's History of New York* in 1808; *Sketch-Book* in 1818; *Bracebridge Hall* in 1822; *Tales of a Traveller* in 1824; *Life and Voyages of Columbus* in 1828; *Conquest of Granada* in 1829; *Companions of Columbus* in 1831; *The Alhambra* in 1832; *Astoria* in 1836; *The Adventures of Captain Bonneville* in 1837; *Oliver Goldsmith* in 1849; *Mahomet and his Successors* in 1850; the 1st volume of *Life of Washington* in 1855 and the 5th and last in 1859. He was American Minister to Spain, 1842–6. Died at Sunnyside (Tarrytown) Nov. 28, 1859.

"Irving was by nature a retrospective man. His face was set towards the past, not towards the future. He never caught the restlessness of this century, nor the prophetic light that shone in the faces of Coleridge, Shelley, and Keats; if he apprehended the stir of the new spirit, he still, by mental affiliation, belonged rather to the age of Addison than to that of Macaulay. His writings induce to reflection, to quiet musing, to tenderness for tradition; they amuse, they entertain, they call a check to the feverishness of modern life; but they are rarely stimulating or suggestive. They are better adapted, it must be owned, to please the many than the critical few, who demand more incisive treatment and a deeper consideration of the problems of life.

I do not know how to account, on principles of culture which we recognize, for our author's style. His education was exceedingly defective, nor was his want of discipline supplied by subsequent desultory application. He seems to have been born with a rare sense of literary proportion and form; into this, as into a mould, were run his apparently lazy and really acute observations of life. That he thoroughly mastered such literature as he fancied there is abundant evidence; that his style was influenced by the purest English models is also apparent. But there remains a large margin for wonder how, with his want of training, he could have elaborated a style which is distinctly his own, and is as copious, felicitous in the choice of words, flowing, spontaneous, flexible, engaging, clear, and as little wearisome when read continuously in quantity as any in the English tongue."—*C. D. Warner.*

From Irving's *History of New York.*

It is a maxim practically observed in all honest, plain-thinking, regular cities that an alderman should be fat, and the wisdom of this can be proved to a certainty. That the body is in some measure an image of the mind, or rather that the mind is moulded to the body, like melted lead to the clay in which it is cast, has been insisted on by many philosophers who have made human nature their peculiar study; for, as a learned gentleman of our own city observes, "There is a constant relation between the moral character of all intelligent creatures and their physical constitution, between their habits and the structure of their bodies."

Thus we see that a lean, spare, diminutive body is generally accompanied by a petulant, restless, meddling mind: either the mind wears down the body by its continual motion or else the body, not affording the mind sufficient house-room, keeps it continually in a state of fretfulness, tossing and worrying about from the uneasiness of its situation. Whereas your round, sleek, fat, unwieldy periphery is ever attended by a mind like itself, tranquil, torpid, and at ease; and we may always observe that your well-fed, robustious burghers are in general very tenacious of their ease and comfort, being great enemies to noise, discord, and disturbance,—and surely none are more likely to study the public tranquility than those who are so careful of their own. Who ever heard of fat men heading a riot or herding together in turbulent mobs? No, no,—it is your lean, hungry men who are continually worrying society, and setting the whole community by the ears.

The divine Plato, whose doctrines are not sufficiently attended to by philosophers of the present age, allows to every man three souls: one, immortal and rational, seated in the brain that it may overlook and regulate the body; a second, consisting of the surly and irascible passions which, like belligerent powers, lie encamped around the heart; a third, mortal and sensual, destitute of reason, gross and brutal in its propensities, and enchained below that it may not disturb the divine soul by its ravenous howlings. Now, according to this excellent theory, what can be more clear than that your fat alderman is most likely to have the most regular and well-conditioned mind? His head is like a huge, spherical chamber, containing a prodigious mass of soft brains, whereon the rational soul lies softly and snugly couched, as on a feather bed; and the eyes, which are the windows of the bed-chamber, are usually half closed that its slumberings may not be disturbed by external objects.

A mind thus comfortably lodged, and protected from disturbance, is manifestly most likely to perform its functions with regularity and ease. By dint of good feeding, moreover, the mortal and malignant soul, confined below, and which by its raging and roaring puts the irritable soul in the neighborhood of the heart in an intolerable passion, and thus renders men crusty and quarrelsome when hungry, is completely pacified, silenced, and put to rest,—whereupon a host of honest, good-fellow qualities and kind-hearted affections, which had lain perdue, slyly peeping out of the loop-holes of the heart, finding this Cerberus asleep, do pluck up their spirits, turn out one and all in their holiday suits, and gambol up and down the diaphragm, disposing their possessor to laughter, good-humor, and a thousand friendly offices towards his fellow-mortals.

As a board of magistrates, formed on this principle, think but very little, they are the less likely to differ and wrangle about favorite opinions; and, as they generally transact business upon a hearty dinner, they are naturally disposed to be lenient and indulgent in the administration of their duties. Charlemagne was conscious of this, and therefore ordered in his cartularies that no judge should hold a court of justice except in the morning, on an empty stomach. A pitiful rule, which I can never forgive, and which I warrant bore hard upon all the poor culprits in the kingdom. The more enlightened and humane generation of the present day have taken an opposite course, and have so managed that the aldermen are the best-fed men in the community; feasting lustily on the fat things of the land, and gorging so heartily on oysters and turtles that in process of time they acquire the activity of the one, and the form, the waddle, and the green fat of the other. The consequence is, as I have just said, these luxurious feastings do produce such a dulcet equanimity and repose of the soul, rational and irrational, that their transactions are proverbial for unvarying monotony; and the profound laws which they enact in their dozing moments, amid the labors of digestion, are quietly suffered to remain as dead letters, and never enforced when awake. In a word, your fair, round-bellied burgomaster, like a full-fed mastiff, dozes quietly at the house-door, always at home, and always at hand to watch over its safety; but as to electing a lean, meddling candidate to the office, as has now and then been done, I would as lief put a grey-hound to watch the house, or a race-horse to draw an ox-wagon.

The burgomasters, then, as I have already mentioned, were wisely chosen by weight, and the schepens, or assistant aldermen, were appointed to attend upon them and help them eat; but the latter, in the course of time, when they had been fed and fattened into sufficient bulk of body and drowsiness of brain, became very eligible candidates for the burgomasters' chairs, having fairly eaten themselves into office, as a mouse eats his way into a comfortable lodgment in a goodly, blue-nosed, skimmed-milk, New England cheese.

From the *Conquest of Granada.*

The night which had passed so gloomily in the sumptuous halls of the Alhambra had been one of joyful anticipation in the Christian camp. In the evening, proclamation had been made that Granada was to be surrendered on the following day, and the troops were all ordered to assemble at an early hour under their several banners. The cavaliers, pages, and esquires were all charged to array themselves in their richest and most splendid style, for the occasion; and even the royal family determined to lay by the mourning they had recently assumed for the sudden death of the prince of Portugal, the husband of the princess Isabella. In a clause of the capitulation, it had been stipulated that the troops destined to take possession should not traverse the city, but should ascend to the Alhambra by a road opened for the purpose outside of the walls. This was to spare the feelings of the afflicted inhabitants, and to prevent any angry collision between them and their conquerors. So rigorous was Ferdinand in enforcing this precaution that the soldiers were prohibited under pain of death from leaving the ranks to enter into the city.

The rising sun had scarce shed his rosy beams upon the snowy summits of the Sierra Nevada, when three signal guns boomed heavily from the lofty fortress of the Alhambra. It was the concerted sign that all was ready for the surrender. The Christian army forthwith poured out of the city, or rather camp, of Sante Fé, and advanced across the vega. The king and queen with the prince and princess, the dignitaries and ladies of the court took the lead, accompanied by the different orders of monks and friars, and surrounded by the royal guards splendidly arrayed. The procession moved slowly forward, and paused at the village of Armilla, at the distance of half a league from the city.

In the mean time, the grand cardinal of Spain, escorted by three thousand foot and a troop of cavalry, and accompanied by the commander and a number of prelates and hidalgos, crossed the Xenil and proceeded in the advance to ascend to the Alhambra, and take possession of that royal palace and fortress. The road which had been opened for the purpose led by the Gate of Mills up a defile to the esplanade on the summit of the Hill of Martyrs. At the approach of this detachment, the Moorish king sallied forth from a postern gate of the Alhambra, having left his vizier to deliver up the palace. The gate by which he sallied passed through a lofty tower of the outer wall, called the Tower of the Seven Floors. He was accompanied by fifty cavaliers, and approached the grand cardinal on foot. The latter immediately alighted, and advanced to meet him with the utmost respect. They stepped aside a few paces, and held a brief conversation in an undertone, when Bobadil, raising his voice, exclaimed, "Go, Señor, and take possession of those fortresses in the name of the powerful sovereigns to whom God has been pleased to deliver them in reward of their great merits, and in punishment of the sins of the Moors." The grand cardinal sought to console him in his reverses, and offered him the use of his own tent during any time he might sojourn in the camp. Bobadil thanked him for the courteous offer, adding some words of melancholy import, and then, taking leave of him gracefully, passed mournfully on to meet the Catholic sovereigns, descending to the vega by the same road by which the cardinal had come. The latter, with the prelates and cavaliers who attended him, entered the Alhambra, the gates of which were thrown wide open by the alcalde, Aben Comixa. At the same time the Moorish guards yielded up their arms, and the towers and battlements were taken possession of by the Christian troops.

While these transactions were passing in the Alhambra and its vicinity, the sovereigns remained with their retinue and guards near the village of Armilla, their eyes fixed on the towers of the royal fortress, watching for the appointed signal of possession. The time that had elapsed since the departure of the detachment seemed to them more than necessary for the purpose, and the anxious mind of Ferdinand began to entertain doubts of some commotion in the city. At length they saw the silver cross, the great standard of this crusade, elevated on the Torre de la Vela, or the Great Watch-Tower, and sparkling in the sun-beams. This was done by Hernando de Talavera, bishop of Avila. Beside it was planted the pennon of the glorious apostle St. James, and a great shout of "Santiago! Santiago!" rose throughout the army. Lastly was reared the royal standard by the king of arms, with the shout of "Castile! Castile! For King Ferdinand and Queen Isabella!" These words were echoed by the whole army with acclamations that resounded across the vega. At sight of these signals of possession, the sovereigns sank upon their knees, giving thanks to God for this great triumph; the whole assembled host followed their example, and the choristers of the royal chapel broke forth into the solemn anthem of "*Te Deum laudamus.*"

The king now advanced with a splendid escort of cavalry and the sound of trumpets, until he came to a small mosque near the banks of the Xenil, and not far from the foot of the Hill of Martyrs, which edifice remains to the present day consecrated as the hermitage of St. Sebastian. Here he beheld the unfortunate King of Granada approaching on horseback, at the head of his slender retinue. Bobadil, as he drew near, made a movement to dismount, but, as had previously been concerted, Ferdinand prevented him. He then offered to kiss the king's hand, which, according to arrangement, was likewise declined, whereupon he leaned forward and kissed the king's right arm; at the same time he delivered the keys of the city with an air of mingled melancholy and resignation. "These keys," said he, "are the last relics of the Arabian empire in Spain: thine, O King, are our trophies, our kingdom, and our person. Such is the will of God! Receive them with the clemency thou hast promised, and which we look for at thy hands."

King Ferdinand restrained his exultation into an air of serene magnanimity. "Doubt not our promises," replied he, "nor that thou shalt regain from our friendship the prosperity of which the fortune of war has deprived thee."

Being informed that Don Inigo Lopez de Mendoza, the good count of Tendilla, was to be governor of the city, Bobadil drew from his finger a gold ring, set with a precious stone, and presented it to the count. "With this ring," said he, "Granada has been governed; take it, and govern with it, and God make you more fortunate than I."

He then proceeded to the village of Armilla, where the queen Isabella remained with her escort and attendants. The queen, like her husband, declined all acts of homage, and received him with her accustomed grace and benignity. She at the same time delivered to him his son, who had been held as a hostage for the fulfilment of the capitulation. Bobadil pressed his child to his bosom with tender emotion, and they seemed mutually endeared to each other by their misfortunes.

Having rejoined his family, the unfortunate Bobadil continued on towards the Alpuxarras that he might not behold the entrance of the Christians into his capital. His devoted band of cavaliers followed him in gloomy silence; but heavy sighs burst from their bosoms, as shouts of joy and strains of triumphant music were borne on the breeze from the victorious army.

Having rejoined his family, Bobadil set forward with a heavy heart for his allotted residence in the Valley of Purchena. At two leagues' distance the cavalcade, winding into the skirts of the Alpuxarras, ascended an eminence commanding the last view of Granada. As they arrived at this spot, the Moors paused involuntarily to take a last farewell gaze at their beloved city, which a few steps more would shut from their sight forever. Never had it appeared so lovely in their eyes. The sunshine, so bright in that transparent climate, lit up each tower and minaret, and rested gloriously upon the crowning battlements of the Alhambra; while the vega spread its enameled bosom of verdure below, glistening with the silver windings of the Xenil. The Moorish cavaliers gazed with a silent agony of tenderness and grief upon that delicious abode, the scene of their loves and pleasures. While they yet looked, a light cloud of smoke burst from the citadel, and presently a peal of artillery, faintly heard, told that the city was taken possession of, and that the throne of the Moslem kings was lost forever. The heart of Bobadil, softened by misfortune and overcharged with grief, could no longer contain itself. "Allah Achbar! God is great!" said he; but the words of resignation died upon his lips, and he burst into tears.

LESSON 56.

AMERICAN PROSE.—WILLIAM HICKLING PRESCOTT was born at Salem, Mass., 1796, and was graduated at Harvard, 1814. Devoted several years to the study of ancient and modern history and literature; published the *History of the Reign of Ferdinand and Isabella*, 1837; *History of the Conquest of Mexico*, 1843; a volume of *Biographical and Critical Miscellanies*,

1845; *Conquest of Peru,* 1847; two volumes of a *History of the Reign of Philip the Second,* 1855, and a third, 1858; and edited Robertson's *Charles the Fifth,* 1857. Was at work on his *Philip the Second,* to comprise six volumes, when he died at Boston, January 28, 1859. By common consent Prescott is ranked with Irving at the head of the American authors of the first half of the nineteenth century.

JOHN LOTHROP MOTLEY was born at Dorchester, Mass., in 1814, and was graduated at Harvard in 1831. Was admitted to the bar in 1836; was secretary of legation at St. Petersburg in 1841; U. S. Minister to Austria, 1866–67; and to England, 1869–70. Published *The Rise of the Dutch Republic,* 1856; *The History of the United Netherlands,* between 1861 and 1868; and *Life of John Van Barneveld,* 1874. He died in 1877.

OLIVER WENDELL HOLMES was born at Cambridge, Mass., 1809, and was graduated at Harvard, 1829. Received the degree of M.D., 1836. Became professor of anatomy and physiology at Dartmouth College, 1838, and was called to the same chair in the Harvard Medical School, Boston, 1847. An edition of his poems appeared 1836, and other poems, 1843, 1846, and 1850. His *Autocrat of the Breakfast Table,* abounding in witty and brilliant thoughts in prose, with occasional poems, came out in the *Atlantic Mo.,* 1857–58. It was followed by two similar works, in the same magazine—the *Professor at the Breakfast Table* and the *Poet at the Breakfast Table.* Published *Elsie Venner,* 1861; and the *Guardian Angel,* 1868.

From the *Autocrat of the Breakfast Table.—My last walk with the Schoolmistress.*

I can't say just how many walks she and I had taken together before this one. I found the effect of going out every morning was decidedly favorable on her health. Two pleasing dimples, the places for which were just marked when she came, played, shadowy, in her freshening cheeks when she smiled and nodded good-morning to me from the school-house steps.

I am afraid I did the greater part of the talking. At any rate, if I should try to report all that I said during the first half-dozen walks we took together, I fear that I might receive a gentle hint from my friends, the publishers, that a separate volume, at my own risk and expense, would be the proper method of bringing them before the public.

I would have a woman as true as Death. At the first real lie which works from the heart outward, she should be tenderly chloroformed into a better world, where she can have an angel for a governess, and feed on strange fruits which will make her all over again, even to her bones and marrow. Whether gifted with the accident of beauty or not, she should have been moulded in the rose-red clay of Love, before the breath of life made a moving mortal of her. Love-capacity is a congenital endowment; and I think, after a while, one gets to know the warm-hued natures it belongs to from the pretty pipe-clay counterfeits of it. Proud she may be, in the sense of respecting herself; but pride, in the sense of contemning others less gifted than herself, deserves the two lowest circles of a vulgar woman's Inferno, where the punishments are Small-pox and Bankruptcy.

She who nips off the end of a brittle courtesy, as one breaks the tip of an icicle, to bestow upon those whom she ought cordially and kindly to recognize, proclaims the fact that she comes not merely of low blood but of bad blood. Consciousness of unquestioned position makes people gracious in proper measure to all; but, if a woman puts on airs with her real equals, she has something about herself or her family she is ashamed of, or ought to be. Middle and more than middle-aged people, who know family histories, generally see through it. An official of standing was rude to me once. Oh, that is the maternal grandfather,— said a wise old friend to me,—he was a boor. Better too few words from the woman we love than too many: while she is silent, Nature is working for her; while she talks, she is working for herself. Love is sparingly soluble in the words of men; therefore they speak much of it; but one syllable of woman's speech can dissolve more of it than a man's heart can hold.

Whether I said any or all of these things to the schoolmistress, or not, whether I stole them out of Lord Bacon, whether I cribbed them from Balzac, whether I dipped them from the ocean of Tupperian wisdom, or whether I have just found them in my head, laid there by that solemn fowl, Experience, (who, according to my observation, cackles oftener than she drops real live eggs,) I cannot say. Wise men have said more foolish things, and foolish men, I don't doubt, have said as wise things. Anyhow, the schoolmistress and I had pleasant walks and long talks, all of which I do not feel bound to report.

——You are a stranger to me, Ma'am, I don't doubt you would like to know all I said to the schoolmistress. I sha'n't do it; I had rather get the publishers to return the money you have invested in this. Besides, I have forgotten a good deal of it. I shall tell only what I like of what I remember.

——My idea was, in the first place, to search out the picturesque spots which the city affords a sight of, to those who have eyes. I know a good many, and it was a pleasure to look at them in company with my young friend. There were the shrubs and flowers in the Franklin Place front-yards or borders; Commerce is just putting his granite foot upon them. Then there are certain small seraglio-gardens, into which one can get a peep through the crevices of high fences,—one in Myrtle Street, or backing on it,—here and there one at the North and South Ends. Then the great elms in Essex Street. Then the stately horse-chestnuts in that vacant lot in Chambers Street, which hold their out-spread hands over your head, (as I said in my poem the other day) and look as if they were whispering, "May grace, mercy, and peace be with you!"—and the rest of that benediction. Nay, there are certain patches of ground, which, having lain neglected for a time, Nature, who always has her pockets full of seeds, and holes in all her pockets, has covered with hungry plebeian growths, which fight for life with each other, until some of them get broad-leaved and succulent, and you have a coarse vegetable tapestry which Raphael would not have disdained to spread over the foreground of his masterpiece. The Professor pretends that he found such a one in Charles Street, which, in its dare-devil impudence of rough-and-tumble vegetation, beat the pretty-behaved flower-beds of the Public Garden as ignominiously as a group of young tatter-demalions playing pitch-and-toss beats a row of Sunday-school boys with their teacher at their head.

But then the Professor has one of his burrows in that region, and puts everything in high colors relating to it. That is his way about everything. I hold any man cheap, he said, of whom nothing stronger can be uttered than that all his geese are swans. How is that, Professor?—said I; I should have set you down for one of that sort. Sir, said he, I am proud to say that Nature has so far enriched me that I cannot own so much as a *duck* without seeing in it as pretty a swan as ever swam the basin in the garden of the Luxembourg. And the Professor showed the whites of his eyes devoutly, like one returning thanks after a dinner of many courses.

I don't know anything sweeter than this leaking in of Nature through all the cracks in the walls and floors of cities. You heap up a million tons of hewn rocks on a square mile or two of earth which was green once. The trees look down from the hill-sides and ask each other, as they stand on tiptoe, "What are these people about?" And the small herbs at their feet look up and whisper back, "We will go and see." So the small herbs pack themselves up in the least possible bundles, and wait until the wind steals to them at night and whispers, "Come with me." Then they go softly with it into the great city,—one to a cleft in the pavement, one to a spout on the roof, one to a seam in the marbles over a rich gentleman's bones, and one to the grave without a stone where nothing but a man is buried,—and there they grow, looking down on the generations of men from mouldy roofs, looking up from between the less-trodden pavements, looking out through iron cemetery-railings. Listen to them, when there is only a light breath stirring, and you will hear them saying to each other, "Wait awhile!" The words run along the telegraph of those narrow green lines that border the roads leading from the city, until they reach the slope of the hills, and the trees repeat in low murmurs to each other, "Wait awhile!" By-and-by the flow of life in the streets ebbs, and the old leafy inhabitants—the smaller tribes always in front—saunter in, one by one, very careless seemingly, but very tenacious, until they swarm so that the great stones gape from each other with the crowding of their roots, and the feldspar begins to be picked out of the granite to find them food. At last the trees take up their solemn line of march, and never rest until they have encamped in the market-place. Wait long enough and you will find an old doting oak hugging a huge worn block in its yellow underground arms; that was the corner-stone of the State-House. Oh, so patient she is, this imperturbable Nature!

——Let us cry!——

But all this has nothing to do with my walks and talks with the schoolmistress. I did not say that I would not tell you something about them. Let me alone, and I shall talk to you more than I ought to, probably. We never tell our secrets to people that pump for them.

Books we talked about, and education. It was her duty to know something of these, and of course she did. Perhaps I was somewhat more learned than she, but I found that the difference between her reading and mine was like that of a man's and a woman's dusting a library. The man flaps about with a bunch of feathers; the woman goes to work softly with a cloth. She does not raise half the dust, nor fill her own eyes and mouth with it,—but she goes into all the corners, and attends to the leaves as much as the covers.

Books are the *negative* pictures of thought, and the more sensitive the mind that receives their images, the more nicely the finest lines are reproduced. A woman (of the right kind) reading after a man, follows him as Ruth followed the reapers of Boaz, and her gleanings are often the finest of the wheat.

But it was in talking of Life that we came most nearly together. I thought I knew something about that,—that I could speak or write about it somewhat to the purpose.

To take up this fluid earthly being of ours as a sponge sucks up water; to be steeped and soaked in its realities as a hide fills its pores lying seven years in a tan-pit; to have winnowed every wave of it as a mill-wheel works up the stream that runs through the flume upon its float-boards; to have curled up in the keenest spasms and flattened out in the laxest languors of this breathing-sickness, which keeps certain parcels of matter uneasy for three or four score years; to have fought all the devils and clasped all the angels of its delirium;—and then, just at the point when the white-hot passions have cooled down to cherry red, plunge our experience into the ice-cold stream of some human language or other, one might think would end in a rhapsody with something of spring and temper in it. All this I thought my power and province.

The schoolmistress had tried life, too. Once in a while one meets with a single soul greater than all the living pageant that passes before it. As the pale astronomer sits in his study with sunken eyes and thin fingers, and weighs Uranus or Neptune as in a balance, so there are meek, slight women who have weighed all that this planetary life can offer, and hold it like a bauble in the palm of their slender hands. This was one of them. Fortune had left her, sorrow had baptized her; the routine of labor and the loneliness of almost friendless city-life were before her. Yet, as I looked upon her tranquil face, gradually regaining a cheerfulness that was often sprightly, as she became interested in the various matters we talked about and places we visited, I saw that eye and lip and every shifting lineament were made for love,—unconscious of their sweet office as yet, and meeting the cold aspect of Duty with the natural graces which were meant for the reward of nothing less than the Great Passion.

I never spoke one word of love to the schoolmistress in the course of these pleasant walks. It seemed to me that we talked of everything but love on that particular morning. There was, perhaps, a little more timidity and hesitancy on my part than I have commonly shown among our people at the boarding-house. In fact, I considered myself the master at the breakfast-table; but, somehow, I could not command myself just then so well as usual. The truth is, I had secured a passage to Liverpool in the steamer which was to leave at noon,—with the condition, however, of being released in case circumstances occurred to detain me. The schoolmistress knew nothing about all this, of course, as yet.

It was on the Common that we were walking. The *mall*, or boulevard of our Common, you know, has various branches leading from it in different directions. One of these runs downward from opposite Joy Street southward across the whole length of the Common to Boylston Street. We called it the long path, and were fond of it.

I felt very weak indeed (though of a tolerably robust habit) as we came opposite the head of this path on that morning. I think I tried to speak twice without making myself distinctly audible. At last I got out the question, "Will you take the long path with me?" "Certainly," said the schoolmistress, "with much pleasure." "Think," I said, "before you answer; if you take the long path with me now, I shall interpret it that we are to part no more!" The schoolmistress stepped back with a sudden movement, as if an arrow had struck her.

One of the long granite blocks used as seats was hard by,—the one you may still see close by the Gingko-tree. "Pray, sit down," I said. "No, no," she answered softly, "I will walk the *long path* with you!"

The old gentleman who sits opposite met us walking, arm in arm, about the middle of the long path, and said, very charmingly, "Good morning, my dears!"

LESSON 57.

AMERICAN PROSE.—RALPH WALDO EMERSON, was born in Boston in 1803, and graduated at Harvard in 1821. Began his long and splendid service as a lecturer in 1833; made Concord, Mass., his home in 1835; published a volume, called *Nature*, in 1836; two other volumes of *Essays* in 1841 and 1844; his *Poems* in 1846; his miscellaneous addresses in 1849; *Representative Men* in 1850; *English Traits* in 1856; *The Conduct of Life* in 1860, *May Day and other Poems* and *Society and Solitude* in 1869. He died in 1882.

"Before those for whom alone he writes, those who think, Emerson holds up perpetually the great end and aim of attaining absolute truth; it was so in his earliest, it is so in his latest, works; but there is in the later the recognition that the thinker's business is for the present rather with the corner-stone than the coping-stone of his tower of vision. It is an age of preparations rather than attainments. The scholar is to gain his freedom, to get rid of his gilded gyves rather than to try his wings; he is to demonstrate his liberty rather than press it. Here, in *The Conduct of Life* and in *Society and Solitude*, are rules of life that go to the very generation of the thinker, and estimate the virginal elements of which he is born; his diet, health, habits, physical as well as mental, are anxiously discussed; for with him is the hope of the world."—*M. D. Conway.*

"The bother with Mr. Emerson is, that, though he writes in prose, he is essentially a poet. If you undertake to paraphrase what he says and to reduce it to words of one syllable for infant minds, you will make as sad work of it as the good monk did with his analysis of Homer in the *Epistolæ Obscurorum Virorum.* We look upon him as one of the few men of genius whom our age has produced, and there needs no better proof of it than his masculine faculty of fecundating other minds. Search for his eloquence in his books, and you will perchance miss it, but meanwhile you will find that it has kindled all your thoughts.

For choice and pith of language he belongs to a better age than ours, and might rub shoulders with Fuller and Browne,—though he does use that abominable word *reliable.* His eye for a fine, telling phrase that will carry true is like that of a backwoodsman for a rifle: and he will dredge you up a choice word from the mud of Cotton Mather himself. A diction at once so rich and so homely as his I know not where to match in these days of writing by the page; it is like homespun cloth-of-gold. The many cannot miss his meaning, and only the few can find it. It is the open secret of all true genius. It is wholesome to angle in those profound pools, though one be rewarded with nothing more than the leap of a fish that flashes his freckled side in the sun and as suddenly absconds in the dark and dreamy waters again. There is keen excitement, though there be no ponderable acquisition. If we carry nothing home in our baskets, there is ample gain in dilated lungs and stimulated blood."—*J. R. Lowell.*

From *Culture* in *Conduct of Life.*

Culture is the suggestion from certain best thoughts, that a man has a range of affinities through which he can modulate the violence of any master-tones that have a droning preponderance in his scale, and succor him against himself. Culture redresses his balance, puts him among his equals and superiors, revives the delicious sense of sympathy, and warns him of the dangers of solitude and repulsion.

'Tis not a compliment but a disparagement to consult a man only on horses or on steam or on theatres or on eating or on books, and, whenever he appears, considerately to turn the conversation to the bantling he is known to fondle. In the Norse heaven of our forefathers, Thor's house had five hundred and forty floors, and man's house has five hundred and forty floors. His excellence is facility of adaptation and of transition through many related points, to wide contrasts and extremes. Culture kills his exaggeration, his conceit of his village or his city. We must leave our pets at home when we go into the street, and meet men on broad grounds of good meaning and good sense.

'Tis incident to scholars that each of them fancies he is pointedly odious in his community. Draw him out of this limbo of irritability. Cleanse with healthy blood his parchment skin. If you are the victim of your doing, who cares what you do? We can spare your opera, your gazetteer, your chemic analysis, your history, your syllogisms. Your man of genius pays dear for his distinction. His head runs up into a spire, and, instead of a healthy man, merry and wise, he is some mad dominie. Nature is reckless of the individual. When she has points to carry, she carries them. To wade in marshes and sea-margins is the destiny of certain birds, and they are so accurately made for this that they are imprisoned in those places. Each animal out of its *habitat* would starve. To the physician each man, each woman, is an amplification of one organ. A soldier, a locksmith, a bank-clerk, and a dancer could not exchange functions. And thus we are victims of adaptation.

The antidotes against this organic egotism are the range and variety of attractions, as gained by acquaintance with the world, with men of merit, with classes of society, with travel, with eminent persons, and with the high resources of philosophy, art, and religion, books, travel, society, solitude.

The hardiest skeptic who has seen a horse broken, a pointer trained, or who has visited a menagerie or the exhibition of the Industrious Fleas will not deny the validity of education. "A boy," says Plato, "is the most vicious of all wild beasts;" and, in the same spirit, the old English poet Gascoigne says, "A boy is better unborn than untaught." The city breeds one kind of speech and manners; the back-country a different style; the sea another; the army a fourth. We know that an army which can be confided in may be formed by discipline; that by systematic discipline all men may be made heroes. Marshal Lannes said to a French officer, "Know, Colonel, that none but a poltroon will boast that he never was afraid." A great part of courage is the courage of having done the thing before. And in all human action those faculties will be strong which are used. Robert Owen said, "Give me a tiger and I will educate him." 'Tis inhuman to want faith in the power of education, since to meliorate is the law of nature; and men are valued precisely as they exert onward or meliorating force. On the other hand, poltroonery is the acknowledging an inferiority to be incurable.

Let us make our education brave and preventive. Politics is an afterwork, a poor patching. We are always a little late. The evil is done, the law is passed, and we begin the up-hill agitation for repeal of that of which we ought to have prevented the enacting. We shall one day learn to supersede politics by education. What we call our root-and-branch reforms of slavery, war, gambling, intemperance, is only medicating the symptoms. We must begin higher up, namely, in Education.

Our arts and tools give to him who can handle them much the same advantage over the novice, as if you extended his life ten, fifty, or a hundred years. And I think it the part of good sense to provide every fine soul with such culture, that it shall not, at thirty or forty years, have to say, "This which I might do is made hopeless through my want of weapons."

But it is conceded that much of our training fails of effect; that all success is hazardous and rare; that a large part of our cost and pains is thrown away. Nature takes the matter into her own hands, and, though we must not omit any jot of our system, we can seldom be sure that it has availed much, or that as much good would not have accrued from a different system.

Books, as containing the finest records of human wit, must always enter into our notion of culture. The best heads that ever existed, Pericles, Plato, Julius Cæsar, Shakespeare, Goethe, Milton, were well-read, universally educated men, and quite too wise to undervalue letters. Their opinion has weight, because they had means of knowing the opposite opinion. We look that a great man should be a good reader, or, in proportion to the spontaneous power should be the assimilating power. Good criticism is very rare, and always precious. I am always happy to meet persons who perceive the transcendent superiority of Shakespeare over all other writers. I like people who like Plato, because this love does not consist with self-conceit.

But books are good only as far as a boy is ready for them. He sometimes gets ready very slowly. You send your child to the schoolmaster, but 'tis the school-boys who educate him. You send him to the Latin class, but much of his tuition comes, on his way to school, from the shop-windows. You like the strict rules and the long terms; and he finds his best leading in a by-way of his own, and refuses any companions but of his choosing. He hates the grammar and *Gradus*, and loves guns, fishing-rods, horses, and boats. Well, the boy is right; and you are not fit to direct his bringing-up, if your theory leaves out his gymnastic training. Archery, cricket, gun and fishing-rod, horse and boat, are all educators, liberalizers; and so are dancing, dress, and the street talk; and,—provided only the boy has resources, and is of a noble and ingenuous strain,—these will not serve him less than the books.

There is also a negative value in these arts. Their chief use to the youth is not amusement, but to be known for what they are, and not to remain to him occasions of heart-burn. We are full of superstitions. Each class fixes its eye on the advantages it has not; the refined on rude strength; the democrat on birth and breeding. One of the benefits of college education is to show the boy its little avail. I knew a leading man in a leading city who, having set his heart on an education at the university, and missed it, could never quite feel himself the equal of his own brothers who had gone thither.

His easy superiority to multitudes of professional men could never quite countervail to him this imaginary defect. Balls, riding, wine-parties, and billiards pass to a poor boy for something fine and romantic, which they are not; and a free admission to them on an equal footing, if it were possible, only once or twice, would be worth ten times its cost by undeceiving him.

I am not much an advocate for travelling, and I observe that men run away to other countries, because they are not good in their own, and run back to their own, because they pass for nothing in the new places. For the most part, only the light characters travel. Who are you that have no task to keep you at home? I have been quoted as saying captious things about travel; but I mean to do justice. I think there is a restlessness in our people which argues want of character. All educated Americans, first or last, go to Europe; perhaps, because it is their mental home, as the invalid habits of this country might suggest. An eminent teacher of girls said, "The idea of a girl's education is whatever qualifies them for going to Europe." Can we never extract this tapeworm of Europe from the brain of our countrymen? One sees very well what their fate must be. He that does not fill a place at home cannot abroad. He only goes there to hide his insignificance in a larger crowd. You do not think you will find anything there which you have not seen at home? The stuff of all countries is just the same.

Do you suppose there is any country where they do not scald milk-pans and swaddle the infants and burn the brushwood and broil the fish? What is true anywhere is true everywhere. And let him go where he will, he can only find so much beauty or worth as he carries.

Cities give us collision. 'Tis said London and New York take the nonsense out of a man. A great part of our education is sympathetic and social. Boys and girls who have been brought up with well-informed and superior people show in their manners an inestimable grace. Fuller says, "William, Earl of Nassau, won a subject from the King of Spain every time he put off his hat." You cannot have one well-bred man without a whole society of such. They keep each other up to any high point. Especially women; it requires a good many cultivated women,—saloons of bright, elegant, reading women, accustomed to ease and refinement, to spectacles, pictures, sculpture, poetry, and to elegant society, in order that you should have one Madame de Staël. The head of a commercial house, or a leading lawyer or politician, is brought into daily contact with troops of men from all parts of the country, and those too the driving-wheels, the business men of each section; and one can hardly suggest for an apprehensive man a more searching culture. Besides, we must remember the high social possibilities of a million of men. The best bribe which London offers to-day to the imagination is, that, in such a vast variety of people and conditions, one can believe there is room for persons of romantic character to exist, and that the poet, the mystic, and the hero may hope to confront their counterparts.

The fossil strata show us that Nature began with rudimental forms, and rose to the more complex as fast as the earth was fit for their dwelling-place; and that the lower perish as the higher appear. Very few of our race can be said to be yet finished men. We still carry, sticking to us, some remains of the preceding inferior quadruped organization. We call these millions men; but they are not yet men. Half-engaged in the soil, pawing to get free, man needs all the music that can be brought to disengage him. If Love, red Love, with tears and joy, if Want with his scourge, if War with his cannonade, if Christianity with its charity, if Trade with its money, if Art with its portfolios, if Science with her telegraphs through the deeps of space and time, can set his dull nerves throbbing, and, by loud taps on the tough chrysalis, can break its walls and let the new creature emerge erect and free—make way, and sing pæan! The age of the quadruped is to go out, the age of the brain and of the heart is to come in. The time will come when the evil forms we have known can no more be organized.

AMERICAN PROSE.—NATHANIEL HAWTHORNE was born July 4, 1804, at Salem, Mass., and graduated at Bowdoin College in 1825. Went to Boston in 1836 and edited the *American Magazine.* First series of *Twice-told Tales* appeared in 1837, and the second series in 1842. *Mosses from an Old Manse* in 1846. Was surveyor of the port of Salem 1846–50. Wrote there *The Scarlet Letter.* *The House of the Seven Gables* appeared in 1851, and *The Blithedale Romance* in 1852. U. S. consul at Liverpool 1853–7. *The Snow Image* appeared in 1852, and *The Marble Faun* in 1860. Published other works. Died at Plymouth, N. H., 1864.

" *The House of the Seven Gables* is the longest of his three American novels; it is the most elaborate, and, in the judgment of some persons, it is the finest. It is a rich, delightful, imaginative work, larger and more various than its companions, and full of all sorts of deep intentions, of interwoven threads of suggestion. If it be true of the others, that the pure natural quality of the imaginative strain is their great merit, this is at least as true of *The House of the Seven Gables,* the charm of which is, in a peculiar degree, of the kind that we fail to reduce to its grounds—like that of the sweetness of a piece of music, or the softness of fine September weather. It is vague, indefinable, ineffable; but it is the sort of thing we must always point to in justification of the high claims that we make for Hawthorne. . . .

Hawthorne was a beautiful, natural, original genius, and his life had been singularly exempt from worldly preoccupations and vulgar efforts. It had been as pure, as simple, as unsophisticated, as his work. He had lived primarily in his domestic affections, which were of the tenderest kind; and then—without eagerness, without pretension, but with a great deal of quiet devotion—in his charming art. His work will remain; it is too original and exquisite to pass away; among the men of imagination he will always have his niche. No other one has had just that vision of life, and no one has had a literary form that more successfully expressed his vision. He was not a moralist, and he was not simply a poet. The moralists are weightier, denser, richer, in sense; the poets are more purely inconclusive and irresponsible. He combined, in a singular degree, the spontaneity of the imagination with a haunting care for moral problems. Man's conscience was his theme, but he saw it in the light of a creative fancy, which added, out of its own substance, an interest, and, I may almost say, an importance."—*Henry James, Jr.*

From Hawthorne's *The House of the Seven Gables.*

The Pyncheon Hens.—One of the available means of amusement, of which Phœbe made the most, in Clifford's behalf, was that feathered society, the hens, a breed of whom, as we have already said, was an immemorial heirloom in the Pyncheon family. In compliance with a whim of Clifford's, as it troubled him to see them in confinement, they had been set at liberty, and now roamed at will about the garden; doing some little mischief, but hindered from escape by buildings on three sides, and the difficult peaks of a wooden fence on the other. They spent much of their abundant leisure on the margin of Maule's well, which was haunted by a kind of snail, evidently a tidbit to their palates; and the brackish water itself, however nauseous to the rest of the world, was so greatly esteemed by these fowls that they might be seen tasting, turning up their heads, and smacking their bills, with precisely the air of wine-bibbers round a probationary cask. Their generally quiet, yet often brisk and constantly diversified, talk, one to another, or sometimes in soliloquy,—as they scratched worms out of the rich black soil, or pecked at such plants as suited their taste,—had such a domestic tone that it was almost a wonder why you could not establish a regular interchange of ideas about household matters, human and gallinaceous. All hens are well worth studying for the piquancy and rich variety of their manners; but by no possibility can there have been other fowls of such odd appearance and deportment as these ancestral ones. They probably embodied the traditionary peculiarities of their whole line of progenitors, derived through an unbroken succession of eggs; or else this individual Chanticleer and his two wives had grown to be humorists, and a little crack-brained withal, on account of their solitary way of life, and out of sympathy for Hepzibah, their lady-patroness.

Queerly, indeed, they looked. Chanticleer himself, though stalking on two stilt-like legs, with the dignity of interminable descent in all his gestures, was hardly bigger than an ordinary partridge; his two wives were about the size of quails; and, as for the one chicken, it looked small enough to be still in the egg, and, at the same time, sufficiently old, withered, wizened, and experienced to have been the founder of the antiquated race. Instead of being the youngest of the family, it rather seemed to have aggregated into itself the ages not only of these living specimens of the breed but of all its forefathers and foremothers, whose united excellences and oddities were squeezed into its little body. Its mother evidently regarded it as the one chicken of the world, and as necessary, in fact, to the world's continuance, or, at any rate, to the equilibrium of the present system of affairs, whether in church or state. No lesser sense of the infant fowl's importance could have justified, even in a mother's eyes, the perseverance with which she watched over its safety, ruffling her small person to twice its proper size, and flying in everybody's face that so much as looked towards her hopeful progeny. No lower estimate could have vindicated the indefatigable zeal with which she scratched, and her unscrupulousness in digging up the choicest flower or vegetable, for the sake of the fat earth-worm at its root. Her nervous cluck, when the chicken happened to be hidden in the long grass or under the squash-leaves; her gentle croak of satisfaction, while sure of it beneath her wing; her note of ill-concealed fear and obstreperous defiance, when she saw her arch-enemy, a neighbor's cat, on the top of the high fence;—one or other of these sounds was to be heard at almost every moment of the day. By degrees the observer came to feel nearly as much interest in this chicken of illustrious race as the mother-hen did.

Phœbe, after getting well acquainted with the old hen, was sometimes permitted to take the chicken in her hand, which was quite capable of grasping its cubic inch or two of body. While she curiously examined its hereditary marks,—the peculiar speckle of its plumage, the funny tuft on its head, and a knob on each of its legs,—the little biped, as she insisted, kept giving her a sagacious wink. The daguerreotypist once whispered her that these marks betokened the oddities of the Pyncheon family, and that the chicken itself was a symbol of the life of the old house, embodying its interpretation likewise, although an unintelligible one, as such clews generally are. It was a feathered riddle; a mystery hatched out of an egg, and just as mysterious as if the egg had been addle!

The second of Chanticleer's two wives, ever since Phœbe's arrival, had been in a state of heavy despondency, caused, as it afterwards appeared, by her inability to lay an egg. One day, however, by her self-important gait, the side-way turn of her head, and the cock of her eye, as she pried into one and another nook of the garden,—croaking to herself all the while with inexpressible complacency,—it was made evident that this identical hen, much as mankind undervalued her, carried something about her person, the worth of which was not to be estimated either in gold or precious stones. Shortly after, there was a prodigious cackling and gratulation of Chanticleer and all his family, including the wizened chicken, who appeared to understand the matter quite as well as did his sire, his mother, or his aunt. That afternoon Phœbe found a diminutive egg—not in the regular nest, it was far too precious to be trusted there—but cunningly hidden under the currant-bushes, on some dry

stalks of last year's grass. Hepzibah, on learning the fact, took possession of the egg and appropriated it to Clifford's breakfast, on account of
a certain delicacy of flavor, for which, as she affirmed, these eggs had
always been famous. Thus unscrupulously did the old gentlewoman
sacrifice the continuance, perhaps, of an ancient feathered race, with no
better end than to supply her brother with a dainty that hardly filled the
bowl of a teaspoon! It must have been in reference to this outrage that
Chanticleer, the next day, accompanied by the bereaved mother of the
egg, took his post in front of Phœbe and Clifford, and delivered himself
of a harangue that might have proved as long as his own pedigree, but
for a fit of merriment on Phœbe's part. Hereupon the offended fowl
stalked away on his long stilts, and utterly withdrew his notice from
Phœbe and the rest of human nature, until she made her peace with an
offering of spice-cake, which, next to snails, was the delicacy most in
favor with his aristocratic taste.

We linger too long, no doubt, beside this paltry rivulet of life that
flowed through the garden of the Pyncheon-house. But we deem it
pardonable to record these mean incidents and poor delights, because
they proved so greatly to Clifford's benefit. They had the earth-smell
in them, and contributed to give him health and substance. Some of
his occupations wrought less desirably upon him. He had a singular
propensity, for example, to hang over Maule's well, and look at the
constantly shifting phantasmagoria of figures produced by the agitation
of the water over the mosaic-work of colored pebbles at the bottom.
He said that faces looked upward to him there—beautiful faces, arrayed
in bewitching smiles,—each momentary face so fair and rosy and every
smile so sunny that he felt wronged at its departure, until the same
flitting witchcraft made a new one. But sometimes he would suddenly cry out, "The dark face gazes at me!" and be miserable the whole
day afterwards. Phœbe, when she hung over the fountain by Clifford's
side, could see nothing of all this—neither the beauty nor the ugliness—
but only the colored pebbles, looking as if the gush of the water shook
and disarranged them. And the dark face, that so troubled Clifford,
was no more than the shadow thrown from a branch of one of the dam-
son-trees, and breaking the inner light of Maule's well. The truth was,
however, that his fancy—reviving faster than his will and judgment,
and always stronger than they—created shapes of loveliness that were
symbolic of his native character, and now and then a stern and dreadful
shape, that typified his fate.

LESSON 58.

POETRY.—THE FRENCH REVOLUTION AND THE POETS.—
" Certain ideas relating to Mankind, considered as a whole, had
been growing up in Europe for more than a century, and we
have seen their influence on the work of Cowper and Burns.
These ideas spoke of natural rights that belonged to every
man and which united all men to one another.   All men were
by right equal and free and brothers.   There was, therefore,
only one class, the class of Man; only one nation, the nation
of Man, of which all were equal citizens.   All the old divisions
therefore which wealth and rank and class and caste and national boundaries had made were put aside as wrong and useless.

Such ideas had been for a long time expressed by France in
her literature.   They were now waiting to be expressed in action, and, in the overthrow of the Bastille in 1789, and in the
proclamation of the new Constitution in the following year,
France threw them abruptly into popular and political form.

Immediately they became living powers in the world, and
it is round the excitement they kindled in England that the
work of the poets from 1790 to 1830 can best be grouped.
Wordsworth, Coleridge, and Southey accepted them with joy,
but receded from them when they ended in the violence of
the Reign of Terror and in the imperialism of Napoleon.
Scott hated them, and, in disgust at the present, turned to
write of the romantic past.   Byron did not express them themselves, but he expressed the whole of the revolutionary spirit
in its action against old social opinions.   Shelley took them up
after the reaction against them had begun to die away, and
re-expressed them.   Two men, Rogers and Keats, were wholly
untouched by them.   One special thing they did for poetry.
By the powerful feelings they kindled in men, they brought
back passion into its style, into all its work about Man, and
through that, into its work about nature.

George Crabbe took up the side of the poetry of Man which had to do with the lives of the poor, in the *Village*, 1783, and in the *Parish Register*, 1807. In the short tales related in these books we are brought face to face with the sternest pictures of humble life, its sacrifices, temptations, righteousness, love, and crimes. The prison, the workhouse, the hospital, and the miserable cottage are all sketched with a truthfulness perhaps too unrelenting, and the effect of this poetry in widening human sympathies was very great. The *Borough* and *Tales in Verse* followed, and finally the *Tales of the Hall* in 1819. His work wanted the humor of Cowper, and, though often pathetic and always forcible, was too forcible for pure pathos. His work on Nature is as minute and accurate, but as limited in range of excellence, as his work on Man.

I may mention here in connection with the poetry of the poor, the work of ROBERT BLOOMFIELD, himself a poor shoemaker. The *Farmer's Boy*, 1798, and the *Rural Tales* are poems as cheerful as Crabbe's were stern, and his descriptions of rural life are brighter and not less faithful. The kind of poetry thus started long continued in our verse. Wordsworth took it up and added to it new features, and THOMAS HOOD in short pieces, like the *Song of the Shirt*, gave it a direct bearing on social evils.

ROBERT SOUTHEY, 1774–1843, began his poetical life with the revolutionary poem of *Wat Tyler*, 1794; and between 1802 and 1814 wrote *Thalaba, Madoc, The Curse of Kehama*, and *Roderick the Last of the Goths*. His *Vision of Judgment*, written on the death of George III., and ridiculed by Byron in another *Vision*, proves him to have become a Tory of Tories.

SAMUEL T. COLERIDGE, 1772–1834, could not turn round so completely, but the wild enthusiasm of his early poems was lessened when in 1796 he wrote the *Ode to the Departing Year* and the *Ode to France*, poems which nearly reach sublimity. When France, however, ceasing to be the champion of freedom,

attacked Switzerland, Coleridge as well as Wordsworth ceased
to believe in her, and fell back on the old English ideas of
patriotism and of tranquil freedom. Still the disappointment
was bitter, and the *Ode to Dejection* is instinct not only with
his own wasted life but with the sorrow of one who has had
golden ideals, and has found them turn in his hands to clay.
His best work is but little, but of its kind it is perfect and
unique. For exquisite music of metrical movement and for
an imaginative phantasy, such as might belong to a world
where men always dreamt, there is nothing in our language to
be compared with *Christabel* and *Kubla Khan* and to the
Ancient Mariner, published as one of the *Lyrical Ballads* in
1798. The little poem called *Love* is not so good, but it
touches with great grace that with which all sympathize. All
that he did excellently might be bound up in twenty pages, but
it should be bound in pure gold."

" The main phenomenon of Coleridge's poetic life is not, as with most
poets, the gradual development of a poetic gift, determined, enriched,
retarded by the circumstances of the poet's life, but the sudden blossom-
ing, through one short season, of such a gift already perfect in its kind,
which thereafter deteriorates as suddenly, with something like premature
old age.   *Christabel* and the *Ancient Mariner* belong to the great year of
Coleridge's poetic production, his twenty-fifth year, 1797-8.   In poetic
quality, above all in that most poetic of all qualities, a keen sense of and
delight in beauty, the infection of which lays hold upon the reader, they
are quite out of proportion to all his other composition.

It is in a highly sensitive apprehension of the aspects of external nature
that Coleridge identifies himself most closely with one of the main tendencies of the 'Lake School;' a tendency instinctive, and no mere matter of theory, in him as in Wordsworth.   There is yet one other sort of
sentiment, connected with the love of outward nature, in which he is at
one with that school, yet all himself—his sympathy with the animal
world.

Coleridge's verse, with the exception of his avowedly political poems,
is singularly unaffected by any moral or professional or personal effort
and ambition, written, as he says, after the more violent emotions of sorrow, to give him pleasure when perhaps nothing else could, but coming
thus, indeed, very close to his own most intimately personal character-

ıstics, and having a certain languidly soothing grace or cadence for its most fixed quality from first to last."— *Walter H. Pater.*

BIBLIOGRAPHY. SOUTHEY.—Southey's *Life and Corresp.* of; De Quincey's *Essays;* Howitt's *Homes of Brit. Poets;* W. S. and R. J. Austin's *Poets-Laureate;* Ward's *Anthology;* Quar. Rev. v. 98, 1856; Ecl. Mag., May and July, 1850, and Dec., 1873.

COLERIDGE.—P. Bayne's *Essays;* De Quincey's *Essays;* Hazlitt's *Lit. Remains;* J. S. Mill's *Dissertations* and *Discussions;* J. C. Shairp's *Studies in Poetry and Philos.;* J. A. Hart's *Camb. Essays;* Ward's *Anthology;* Black. Mag., v. 110, 1871; Harper's Mo., vs. 14 and 39; N. Br. Rev., v. 43, 1865; Quar. Rev., July, 1868; West. Rev., vs. 85, 93, and 94.

READING.—*The Village* and *The Ancient Mariner,* in pamphlet, by Clark and Maynard.

LESSON 59.

WORDSWORTH.—" Of all the poets, misnamed Lake Poets, WILLIAM WORDSWORTH was the greatest. Born in 1770, educated on the banks of Esthwaite, he loved the scenery of the Lakes as a boy, lived among it in his manhood, and died in 1850 at Rydal Mount, close to Rydal lake. He took his degree in 1791 at Cambridge. The year before, he had made a short tour on the Continent, and stepped on the French shore at the very time when the whole land was ' mad with joy.' The end of 1791 saw him again in France and living at Orleans. He threw himself eagerly into the Revolution, joined the ' patriot side,' and came to Paris just after the September massacre of 1792. Narrowly escaping the fate of his friends, the Brissotins, he got home to England before the execution of Louis XVI. in 1793, and published his *Descriptive Sketches.* His sympathy with the French continued, and he took their side against his own country, hating the war that England now set on foot against France.

He was poor, but his friend Raisley Calvert left him £900, and enabled him to live the simple life he had now chosen, the life of a retired poet. At first we find him at Racedown, where in 1797 he made friendship with Coleridge, and then at Alfoxden, in Somerset, where he and Coleridge planned and published in 1798 the *Lyrical Ballads.* After a winter in

Germany with Coleridge, where the *Prelude* was begun, he
took a small cottage at Grasmere, and there in 1805–6 finished
the *Prelude*, not published till 1850.   Another set of the
Lyrical Ballads appeared in 1802, and in 1814 his philosophical poem, the *Excursion.*   From that time till his death he
produced from his home at Rydal Mount a great succession of
poems.

   WORDSWORTH AND NATURE.—The *Prelude* is the history
of Wordsworth's poetical growth from a child till 1806.   It
reveals him as the poet of Nature and of Man.   His view of
Nature was entirely different from that which up to his time
the poets had held.   They had believed that the visible universe was dead matter set in motion like a machine and regu-
lated by fixed laws.   Wordsworth, on the contrary, said that
it was alive.   There is a soul, he said, in all the worlds; 'an
active principle subsists' in Nature.

   This soul of Nature was entirely distinct from the mind
of man, and acted upon it.   It had powers of its own, desires, feelings, and thought of its own, and by these it
gave education, impulses, comfort, and joy to the man
who opened his heart to receive them.   The human mind
receiving these impressions, reflected on them and added to
them its own thoughts and feelings, and that union of the
mind of man to the mind in Nature then took place which
Wordsworth thought the true end of the pre-arranged harmony he conceived between Nature and Humanity.   This is
the idea which runs through all his poetry, and one thing
especially followed from it, that he was the first who loved
Nature with a personal love.   He could do that because he
did not mix up Nature with his own mind, nor make her the
reflection of himself, nor look upon her as dead matter.   She
was a person to him, distinct from himself, and therefore
capable of being loved as a man loves a woman.   He could
brood on her character, her ways, her words, her life, as he
did on those of his wife or sister.   Hence arose his minute

and loving observation of her and his passionate description
of all her forms.   There was nothing, from the daisy's 'star-
shaped shadow on the naked stone' to the vast landscape seen
at sunrise from the mountain top, that he did not describe,
that he has not made us love.

WORDSWORTH AND MAN.—We have seen the vivid interest
that Wordsworth took in the new ideas about man as they
were shown in the French Revolution.   But even before that
he relates in the *Prelude* how he had been led through his
love of Nature to honor Man.   The shepherds of the Lake
hills, the dalesmen, had been seen by him as part of the wild
scenery in which he lived, and he mixed up their life with the
grandeur of Nature and came to honor them as part of her
being.   The love of Nature led him to the love of Man.   It
was exactly the reverse order to that of the previous poets.
At Cambridge and afterwards in the crowd of London and in
his first tour on the Continent, he received new impressions of
the vast world of Man, but Nature still remained the first.
It was only during his life in France and in the excitement of
the new theories and their activity that he was swept away
from Nature, and found himself thinking of Man as distinct
from her, and first in importance.

But the hopes he had formed from the Revolution broke
down.   All his dreams about a new life of man were made
vile when France gave up liberty for Napoleon; and he was
left without love of Nature or care for Man.   It was then that
his sister Dorothy, herself worthy of mention in a history of
literature, led him back to his early love of Nature and restored
his mind.   Living quietly at Grasmere, he sought in the simple lives of the dalesmen round him for the foundations of a
truer view of mankind than the theories of the Revolution
afforded.   And in thinking and writing of the common duties
and faith, kindnesses and truth of lowly men, he found in
Man once more

'an object of delight,
Of pure imagination and of love.'

With that he recovered also his interest in the larger movements of mankind. His love of liberty and hatred of oppression
revived. He saw in Napoleon the enemy of man. A whole
series of sonnets followed the events on the Continent. One
recorded his horror at the attack on the Swiss, another mourned
the fate of Venice, another the fate of Toussaint the negro
chief, others celebrated the struggle of Hofer and the Tyrolese,
others the struggle of Spain. Two thanksgiving odes rejoiced
in the overthrow of the oppressor at Waterloo.

He became conservative in his old age, but his interest in
social and national movements did not decay. He wrote on
Education, the Poor Laws, and other subjects. When almost
seventy he took the side of the Carbonari, and sympathized
with the Italian struggle. He was truly a poet of Mankind.
But his chief work was done in his own country and among
his own folk; and he was the first who threw around the lives
of homely men and women the glory and sweetness of song,
and taught us to know the brotherhood of all men in a more
beautiful way than the wild way of the Revolution. He lies
asleep now among the people he loved, in the green church-
yard of Grasmere, by the side of the stream of Rothay, in a
place as quiet as his life. Few spots on earth are more sacred
than his grave.

Criticism must needs confess that much of his work is prosaic in thought, but the form of it is always poetic; that is,
the thoughts are expressed in a way prose never would express
them. His theory about poetic diction, that it should be the
ordinary language men use in strong emotion, may seem to
contradict this; but, as Coleridge has shown, Wordsworth did
not practice his theory, and where he did the result was not
poetry. His style in blank-verse is the likest to Milton's that
we possess, but it is more feminine than Milton's. He is like
Milton also in this, that he excelled in the Sonnet, which we
may say he restored to modern poetry. Along with the rest
of all the poets of the time he revived old measures and in-

vented new. His philosophy of Nature we have explained; his human philosophy, of which the *Excursion* is the best example, was no deeper than a lofty and grave morality created, in union with an imaginative Christianity. He believed in himself when all the world disbelieved in him, and he has been proved right and the world wrong."

"What was special in Wordsworth was the penetrating power of his perceptions of poetical elements, and his fearless reliance on the simple forces of expression in contrast to the more ornate ones. He had an eye to see these elements where I will not say no one had seen or felt them, but where no one appears to have recognized that he had seen or felt them. He saw that the familiar scene of human life—nature as affecting human life and feeling, and man as the fellow-creature of nature but also separate and beyond it in faculties and destiny—had not yet rendered up even to the mightiest of former poets all that they had in them to touch the human heart. And he accepted it as his mission to open the eyes and widen the thoughts of his countrymen, and to teach them to discern in the humblest and most unexpected forms the presence of what was kindred to what they had long recognized as the highest and greatest. Of all poets who ever wrote, Wordsworth made himself most avowedly the subject of his own thinking. In one way this gives special interest and value to his work. But this habit of perpetual self-study, though it may conduce to wisdom, does not always conduce to life or freedom of movement. It spreads a tone of individuality and apparent egotism, which, though very subtle and undefinable, is yet felt even in some of his most beautiful compositions. We miss the spirit of aloofness and self-forgetfulness, which, whether spontaneous or the result of the highest art, marks the highest types of poetry." —*R. W. Church.*

"It is important to hold fast to this: poetry is at bottom a criticism of life: the greatness of a poet lies in his powerful and beautiful application of ideas to life,—to the question, How to live. Wordsworth deals with life, because he deals with that in which life really consists. Wordsworth deals with it, and his greatness lies in his dealing with it so powerfully. His superiority to other poets is here—he deals with more of life than they do, deals with life, as a whole, more powerfully.

Wordsworth's poetry is great, because of the extraordinary power with which he feels the joy offered to us in nature, the joy offered to us in the simple primary affections and duties; and because of the extraordinary power with which, in case after case, he shows us this joy, and renders it so as to make us share it. The source of joy from which he thus draws is the truest and most unfailing source of joy accessible to man. It is also accessible universally.

Wordsworth has no style. Every one who has any sense for these things feels the subtle turn, the heightening, which is given to a poet's verse by his genius for style. We can feel it in the 'After life's fitful fever, he sleeps well,' of Shakespeare. Wordsworth was too conversant with Milton not to catch at times his master's manner, and he has fine Miltonic lines; but he has no assured poetic style of his own. Nature herself seems to take the pen out of his hand, and to write for him with her own bare, sheer, penetrating power. This arises from the profound sincereness with which Wordsworth feels his subject, and also from the profoundly sincere and natural character of his subject itself. He can and will treat such a subject with nothing but the most plain, first hand, almost austere naturalness. His expression may often be bald, but it is bald as the bare mountain-tops are bald, with a baldness which is full of grandeur."—*Matthew Arnold.*

BIBLIOGRAPHY. WORDSWORTH.—C. Wordsworth's *Memoirs of;* W. S. and R. J. Austin's *Poets-Laureate;* De Quincey's *Essays;* Field's *Yesterdays with Authors;* H. Giles' *Illus. of Genius;* Howitt's *Homes of Brit. Poets;* Lowell's *Among my Books,* 2d Ser.; Whipple's *Characteristics of Men of Genius,* his *Essays and Reviews,* and his *Lit. and Life;* F. W. Robertson's *Lectures and Addresses;* J. C. Shairp's *Studies in Poetry;* Ward's *Anthology;* M. Arnold's *Preface* to his Ed. of W.'s Poems; J. Wilson's *Essays;* Black. Mag., v. 110, 1871; Fort. Rev., Apr., 1874; Macmillan, Nov., 1860, and Aug., 1873; N. A. Rev., v. 100, 1865; Quar. Rev., v. 92, 1853; Temple Bar, Feb., 1872; Ecl. Mag., Apr., 1853; March and Apr., 1865; Oct., 1876; and Jan. and Oct. 1880.

LESSON 60.

Wordsworth's *The Solitary Reaper.*

Behold her, single in the field,
 Yon solitary Highland Lass!
Reaping and singing by herself;
 Stop here, or gently pass!
Alone she cuts and binds the grain,
And sings a melancholy strain;
 O listen! for the vale profound
 Is overflowing with the sound.

No nightingale did ever chant
 So sweetly to reposing bands
Of travellers in some shady haunt
 Among Arabian sands:

A voice so thrilling ne'er was heard
In spring-time from the cuckoo-bird,
   Breaking the silence of the seas
   Among the farthest Hebrides.

Will no one tell me what she sings?
   Perhaps the plaintive numbers flow
For old, unhappy, far-off things,
   And battles long ago;
Or is it some more humble lay,
Familiar matter of to-day?
   Some natural sorrow, loss, or pain,
   That has been, and may be again?

Whate'er the theme, the maiden sang
   As if her song could have no ending;
I saw her singing at her work
   And o'er the sickle bending;—
I listened till I had my fill,
And, when I mounted up the hill,
   The music in my heart I bore
   Long after it was heard no more.

From Wordsworth's *Michael.*

Upon the forest-side in Grasmere Vale
There dwelt a shepherd, Michael was his name,
An old man, stout of heart and strong of limb.
His bodily frame had been from youth to age
Of an unusual strength; his mind was keen,
Intense, and frugal, apt for all affairs,
And in his shepherd's calling he was prompt
And watchful more than ordinary men.
Hence had he learned the meaning of all winds,
Of blasts of every tone; and, oftentimes,
When others heeded not, he heard the South
Make subterraneous music, like the noise
Of bagpipers on distant Highland hills.
The shepherd, at such warning, of his flock
Bethought him, and he to himself would say,
" The winds are now devising work for me."
And, truly, at all times, the storm, that drives

The traveller to a shelter, summoned him
Up to the mountains: he had been alone
Amid the heart of many thousand mists,
That came to him and left him on the heights.
So lived he till his eightieth year was past.
And grossly that man errs who should suppose
That the green valleys and the streams and rocks
Were things indifferent to the shepherd's thoughts.
Fields, where with cheerful spirits he had breathed
The common air; the hills, which he so oft
Had climbed with vigorous steps; which had impressed
So many incidents upon his mind
Of hardship, skill or courage, joy or fear;
Which, like a book, preserved the memory
Of the dumb animals, whom he had saved,
Had fed or sheltered, linking to such acts
The certainty of honorable gain;—
Those fields, those hills—what could they less? had laid
Strong hold on his affections, were to him
A pleasurable feeling of blind love,
The pleasure which there is in life itself.
    His days had not been passed in singleness.
His helpmate was a comely matron, old—
Though younger than himself full twenty years
She was a woman of a stirring life,
Whose heart was in her house: two wheels she had
Of antique form, this large for spinning wool,
That small for flax; and, if one wheel had rest
It was because the other was at work.
The pair had but one inmate in their house,
An only child, who had been born to them
When Michael, telling o'er his years, began
To deem that he was old,—in shepherd's phrase
With one foot in the grave. This only son,
With two brave sheep-dogs, tried in many a storm,
The one of an inestimable worth,
Made all their household. I may truly say
That they were as a proverb in the vale
For endless industry. When day was gone,
And from their occupations out of doors
The son and father were come home, even then

Their labor did not cease; unless when all
Turned to their cleanly supper-board, and there,
Each with a mess of pottage and skimmed milk,
Sat round their basket piled with oaten cakes,
And their plain home-made cheese. Yet when their meal
Was ended, Luke (for so the son was named)
And his old father both betook themselves
To such convenient work as might employ
Their hands by the fireside; perhaps to card
Wool for the housewife's spindle, or repair
Some injury done to sickle, flail, or scythe,
Or other implement of house or field.
    Down from the ceiling, by the chimney's edge,
That in our ancient, uncouth, country style
Did with a huge projection overbrow
Large space beneath, as duly as the light
Of day grew dim, the housewife hung a lamp
An aged utensil, which had performed
Service beyond all others of its kind.
Early at evening did it burn and late,
Surviving comrade of uncounted hours,
Which, going by from year to year, had found
And left the couple neither gay, perhaps,
Nor cheerful, yet with objects and with hopes,
Living a life of eager industry.
And now, when Luke had reached his eighteenth year,
There by the light of this old lamp they sat,
Father and son, while late into the night
The housewife plied her own peculiar work,
Making the cottage through the silent hours
Murmur as with the sound of summer flies.
This light was famous in its neighborhood,
And was a public symbol of the life
That thrifty pair had lived. For, as it chanced,
Their cottage on a plot of rising ground
Stood single, with large prospect, north and south,
High into Easedale, up to Dunmail-Raise,
And westward to the village near the Lake;
And from this constant light, so regular
And so far seen, the house itself, by all
Who dwelt within the limits of the vale,

Both old and young, was named THE EVENING STAR.
　　Thus living on through such a length of years,
The shepherd, if he loved himself, must needs
Have loved his helpmate; but to Michael's heart
This son of his old age was yet more dear,
Less from instinctive tenderness, the same
Blind spirit which is in the blood of all,
Than that a child, more than all other gifts,
Brings hope with it and forward-looking thoughts
And stirrings of inquietude, when they
By tendency of nature needs must fail.
Exceeding was the love he bare to him,
His heart and his heart's joy! For oftentimes
Old Michael, while he was a babe in arms,
Had done him female service, not alone
For pastime and delight, as is the use
Of fathers, but with patient mind enforced
To acts of tenderness; and he had rocked
His cradle with a woman's gentle hand.
　　And, in a later time, ere yet the boy
Had put on boy's attire, did Michael love,
Albeit of a stern, unbending mind,
To have the young one in his sight, when he
Had work by his own door, or when, he sat
With sheep before him on his shepherd's stool
Beneath that large old oak, which near their door
Stood,—and, from its enormous breadth of shade
Chosen for the shearer's covert from the sun,
Thence in our rustic dialect was called
The CLIPPING TREE, a name which yet it bears.
There, while they two were sitting in the shade,
With others round them, earnest all and blithe,
Would Michael exercise his heart with looks
Of fond correction and reproof bestowed
Upon the child, if he disturbed the sheep
By catching at their legs, or with his shouts
Scared them, while they lay still beneath the shears.
　　And, when by Heaven's good grace the boy grew up
A healthy lad, and carried in his cheek
Two steady roses that were five years old,
Then Michael from a winter coppice cut

With his own hand a sapling, which he hooped
With iron, making it throughout in all
Due requisites a perfect shepherd's staff,
And gave it to the boy; wherewith equipt,
He as a watchman oftentimes was placed
At gate or gap, to stem or turn the flock;
And, to his office prematurely called,
There stood the urchin, as you will divine,
Something between a hindrance and a help;
And for this cause not always, I believe,
Receiving from his father hire of praise;
Though naught was left undone which staff or voice
Or looks or threatening gestures could perform.

But soon as Luke, full ten years old, could stand
Against the mountain blasts, and to the heights,
Not fearing toil, nor length of weary days,
He with his father daily went, and they
Were as companions, why should I relate
That objects which the shepherd loved before
Were dearer now? that from the boy there came
Feelings and emanations—things which were
Light to the sun and music to the wind;
And that the old man's heart seemed born again?
Thus in his father's sight the boy grew up:
And now, when he had reached his eighteenth year,
He was his comfort and his daily hope.

While in this sort the simple household lived
From day to day, to Michael's ear there came
Distressful tidings. Long before the time
Of which I speak, the shepherd had been bound
In surety for his brother's son, a man
Of an industrious life and ample means,—
But unforeseen misfortunes suddenly
Had prest upon him, and old Michael now
Was summoned to discharge the forfeiture,
A grievous penalty, but little less
Than half his substance. This unlooked-for claim,
At the first hearing, for a moment took
More hope out of his life than he supposed
That any old man ever could have lost.
As soon as he had gathered so much strength

That he could look his trouble in the face,
It seemed that his sole refuge was to sell
A portion of his patrimonial fields.
Such was his first resolve; he thought again,
And his heart failed him. " Isabel," said he,
Two evenings after he had heard the news,
"I have been toiling more than seventy years,
And in the open sunshine of God's love
Have we all lived; yet, if these fields of ours
Should pass into a stranger's hand, I think
That I could not lie quiet in my grave.
Our lot is a hard lot; the sun himself
Has scarcely been more diligent than I;
And I have lived to be a fool at last
To my own family. An evil man
That was, and made an evil choice, if he
Were false to us; and if he were not false,
There are ten thousand to whom loss like this
Had been no sorrow. I forgive him—but
'Twere better to be dumb than to talk thus.

     When I began, my purpose was to speak
Of remedies and of a cheerful hope.
Our Luke shall leave us, Isabel; the land
Shall not go from us, and it shall be free;
He shall possess it, free as is the wind
That passes over it. We have, thou know'st,
Another kinsman, he will be our friend
In this distress. He is a prosperous man,
Thriving in trade, and Luke to him shall go,
And, with his kinsman's help and his own thrift,
He quickly will repair this loss, and then
May come again to us. If here he stay,
What can be done? Where every one is poor,
What can be gained?"

     .   .   .   .

     Near the tumultuous brook of Green-head Ghyll,
In that deep valley, Michael had designed
To build a sheep-fold; and, before he heard
The tidings of his melancholy loss,
For this same purpose he had gathered up
A heap of stones, which by the streamlet's edge

Lay thrown together, ready for the work.
With Luke that evening thitherward he walked;
And soon as they had reached the place he stopped,
And thus the old man spake to him:—"My son,
To-morrow thou wilt leave me: with full heart
I look upon thee, for thou art the same
That wert a promise to me ere thy birth,
And all thy life hast been my daily joy.
I will relate to thee some little part
Of our two histories; 'twill do thee good
When thou art from me, even if I should speak
Of things thou canst not know of.   After thou
First camest into the world—as oft befalls
To new-born infants—thou didst sleep away
Two days, and blessings from thy father's tongue
Then fell upon thee.   Day by day passed on,
And still I loved thee with increasing love.
Never to living ear came sweeter sounds
Than when I heard thee by our own fireside
First uttering, without words, a natural tune;
When thou, a feeding babe, didst in thy joy
Sing at thy mother's breast.   Month followed month,
And in the open fields my life was passed
And on the mountains; else I think that thou
Hadst been brought up upon thy father's knees.
But we were playmates, Luke; among these hills,
As well thou knowest, in us the old and young
Have played together, nor with me didst thou
Lack any pleasure which a boy can know."
Luke had a manly heart, but at these words
He sobbed aloud.   The old man grasped his hand,
And said, "Nay, do not take it so—I see
That these are things of which I need not speak.
Even to the utmost I have been to thee
A kind and a good father; and herein
I but repay a gift which I myself
Received at others' hands; for, though now old
Beyond the common life of man, I still
Remember them who loved me in my youth.
Both of them sleep together: here they lived,
As all their forefathers had done; and when

At length their time was come, they were not loth
To give their bodies to the family mould.
I wished that thou shouldst live the life they lived.
But, 'tis a long time to look back, my son,
And see so little gain from threescore years,
These fields were burthened when they came to me;
Till I was forty years of age, not more
Than half of my inheritance was mine.
I toiled and toiled; God blessed me in my work,
And till these three weeks past the land was free.
It looks as if it never could endure
Another master.   Heaven forgive me, Luke,
If I judge ill for thee, but it seems good
That thou shouldst go."   At this the old man paused;
Then, pointing to the stones near which they stood,
Thus, after a short silence, he resumed:—
" This was a work for us, and now, my son,
It is a work for me.   But, lay one stone—
Here, lay it for me, Luke, with thine own hands,
Nay, boy, be of good hope, we both may live
To see a better day.   At eighty-four
I still am strong and hale;—do thou thy part,
I will do mine.   I will begin again
With many tasks that were resigned to thee:
Up to the heights, and in among the storms,
Will I without thee go again, and do
All works which I was wont to do alone,
Before I knew thy face.   Heaven bless thee, boy!
Thy heart these two weeks has been beating fast
With many hopes.   It should be so—yes—yes—
I knew that thou couldst never have a wish
To leave me, Luke; thou hast been bound to me
Only by links of love: when thou art gone
What will be left to us!—But, I forget
My purposes.   Lay now the corner-stone,
As I requested; and hereafter, Luke,
When thou art gone away, should evil men
Be thy companions, think of me, my son,
And of this moment; hither turn thy thoughts
And God will strengthen thee: amid all fear
And all temptation, Luke, I pray that thou
Mayst bear in mind the life thy fathers lived

Who, being innocent, did for that cause
Bestir them in good deeds.   Now, fare thee well—
When thou returnest, thou in this place wilt see
A work which is not here: a covenant
'Twill be between us——But, whatever fate
Befall thee, I shall love thee to the last,
And bear thy memory with me to the grave."
   The shepherd ended here; and Luke stooped down,
And, as his father had requested, laid
The first stone of the sheep-fold.   At the sight
The old man's grief broke from him: to his heart
He pressed his son, he kissèd him and wept;
And to the housè together they returned.
Hushed was that house in peace, or seeming peace,
Ere the night fell:—with morrow's dawn the boy
Began his journey, and when he had reached
The public way, he put on a bold face;
And all the neighbors, as he passed their doors,
Came forth with wishes and with farewell prayers,
That followed him till he was out of sight.
   A good report did from their kinsman come,
Of Luke and his well-doing: and the boy
Wrote loving letters, full of wondrous news,
Which, as the housewife phrased it, were throughout
"The prettiest letters that were ever seen."
Both parents read them with rejoicing hearts.
So, many months passed on, and once again
The shepherd went about his daily work
With confident and cheerful thoughts; and now
Sometimes, when he could find a leisure hour,
He to that valley took his way, and there
Wrought at the sheep-fold.   Meantime Luke began
To slacken in his duty; and, at length,
He in the dissolute city gave himself
To evil courses: ignominy and shame
Fell on him, so that he was driven at last
To seek a hiding-place beyond the seas.
   There is a comfort in the strength of love;
'Twill make a thing endurable, which else
Would overset the brain, or break the heart.
I have conversed with more than one who well
Remember the old man, and what he was

Years after he had heard this heavy news.
His bodily frame had been from youth to age
Of an unusual strength.   Among the rocks
He went, and still looked up towards the sun,
And listened to the wind; and, as before,
Performed all kinds of labor for his sheep,
And for the land, his small inheritance.
And to that hollow dell from time to time
Did he repair to build the fold of which
His flock had need.   'Tis not forgotten yet
The pity which was then in every heart
For the old man, and 'tis believed by all
That many and many a day he thither went,
And never lifted up a single stone.
　　There, by the sheep-fold, sometimes was he seen
Sitting alone, with that his faithful dog,
Then old, beside him, lying at his feet.
The length of full seven years, from time to time,
He at the building of this sheep-fold wrought,
And left the work unfinished when he died.
Three years or little more did Isabel
Survive her husband; at her death the estate
Was sold and went into a stranger's hand.
The cottage which was named the EVENING STAR
Is gone, the ploughshare has been through the ground
On which it stood; great changes have been wrought
In all the neighborhood:—yet the oak is left
That grew beside their door; and the remains
Of the unfinished sheep-fold may be seen
Beside the boisterous brook of Green-head Ghyll.

FURTHER READING.—*Intimations of Immortality* in the Rhetoric; and *The Excursion*, Bk. I., in pamphlet, by Clark & Maynard.

LESSON 61.

SIR WALTER SCOTT.—"Scott was Wordsworth's dear friend, and his career as a poet began, 1805, when Wordsworth first came to Grasmere, with the *Lay of the Last Minstrel*. *Marmion* followed in 1808, and the *Lady of the Lake* in 1810. These were his best poems; the others, with the exception of some lyrics which touch the sadness and the brightness of life with equal power, do not count in our estimate of him. He perfected the narrative poem. In *Marmion* and the *Lady of the Lake,* his wonderful inventiveness in narration is at its height, and it is matched by the vividness of his natural description. No poet, and in this he carries on the old Scotch quality, is a finer colorist. His landscapes are painted in color, and the color is always true. Nearly all his natural description is Scotch, and he was the first who opened to the delight of the world the wild scenery of the Highlands and the Lowland moorland. He touched it all with a pencil so light, graceful, and true that the very names are made for ever romantic."

"Looking to the poetic side of his character, the trumpet certainly would have been the instrument that would have best symbolized the spirit both of Scott's thought and of his verses. His is almost the only poetry in the English language that heats the head in which it runs, by the mere force of its hurried frankness of style, to use Scott's own terms, or by that of its strong and pithy eloquence, as Campbell phrased it. Scott prefers action itself for his subject to any feeling however active in its bent. There is no rich music in his verse, it is its rapid onset, its hurrying strength which fixes it in the mind. *Marmion* was composed, in great part, in the saddle, and the stir of a charge of cavalry seems to be at the very core of it. The hurried tramp of his somewhat monotonous metre is apt to weary the ears of men who do not find their sufficient happiness, as he did, in dreaming of the wild and daring enterprises of his loved Border-land."—*Richard H. Hutton.*

CAMPBELL.—"Scotland produced another poet in THOMAS CAMPBELL. His earliest poem, the *Pleasures of Hope,* 1799, belonged, in its formal rhythm and rhetoric and in its artificial feeling for Nature, to the time of Thomson and Gray rather than to the newer time. His later poems, such as *Gertrude of Wyoming* and *O'Connor's Child,* were far more natural, but they lost the superb rhetoric so remarkable in the *Pleasures of Hope.* Campbell will chiefly live by his lyrics. *Hohenlinden,* the *Battle of the Baltic,* the *Mariners of England* are

splendid specimens of the war poetry of England; and the
Song to the Evening Star and *Lord Ullin's Daughter* are full
of tender feeling, and mark the influence of the more natural
style that Wordsworth had brought to perfection.

ROGERS AND MOORE.—SAMUEL ROGERS is another poet
whose work is apart from the great movement of the Revolution.   In his long life of ninety years he produced two octavo
volumes.   The *Pleasures of Memory*, 1792, his first poem,
links him to the past generation and has its characters.   The
later poems, added to it in 1812, and the *Italy*, 1822, are the
work of a slow and cultivated mind, and contain some labored
but fine descriptions.   The curious thing is, that, living apart
in a courtly region of culture, there is not a trace in all his
work that Europe and England and society had passed during
his life through a convulsion of change.

To that convulsion the best work of THOMAS MOORE, an
Irishman, may be referred.   Ireland during Moore's youth
endeavored to exist under the dreadful and wicked weight of
its Penal Code.   The excitement of the French Revolution
kindled the anger of Ireland into the rebellion of 1798, and
Moore's genius, such as it was, into writing songs to the Irish
airs collected in 1796.   The best of these have for their
hidden subject the struggle of Ireland against England.   They
went everywhere with him into society, and it is not too much
to say that they helped by the interest they stirred to further
Catholic Emancipation.   Moore's Oriental tales in *Lalla Rookh*
are chiefly flash and glitter, but they are pleasant reading.
He had a slight, pretty, rarely true, lyrical power, and all the
songs have this one excellence, they are truly things to be
sung."

BIBLIOGRAPHY.   CAMPBELL.—Redding's *Lit. Reminis.* and *Memoirs* of; Chambers'
Papers for the People; Hazlitt's *Spirit of the Age;* W. Irving's *Spanish Papers and
other Miscel.;* Ward's *Anthology;* Ecl. Mag., March and May, 1849; July, 1851.
   MOORE.—Russell's *Memoirs, Journal and Cor.* of; Ward's *Anthology;* Bent.
Miscel., Apr., 1852; Black. Mag., vs. 71 and 72, 1852; Ed. Rev., v. 99; Ecl. Mag., v. 26,
1852, and 28, 1853; N. A. Rev., v. 76, 1853; Quar. Rev. v. 93, 1853; West. Rev. v. 60,
1853, and 67, 1857.

Campbell's *Ye Mariners of England.*

Ye Mariners of England,
That guard our native seas;
Whose flag has braved, a thousand years,
The battle and the breeze!
Your glorious standard launch again
To match another foe!
And sweep through the deep,
While the stormy winds do blow;
While the battle rages loud and long,
And the stormy winds do blow.

The spirits of your fathers
Shall start from every wave!—
For the deck it was their field of fame,
And Ocean was their grave:
Where Blake and mighty Nelson fell,
Your manly hearts shall glow,
As ye sweep through the deep,
While the stormy winds do blow;
While the battle rages loud and long,
And the stormy winds do blow.

Britannia needs no bulwark,
No towers along the steep;
Her march is o'er the mountain-waves,
Her home is on the deep.
With thunders from her native oak,
She quells the floods below,—
As they roar on the shore,
When the stormy winds do blow;
When the battle rages loud and long,
And the stormy winds do blow.

The meteor flag of England
Shall yet terrific burn;
Till danger's troubled night depart,
And the star of peace return.
Then, then, ye ocean-warriors!
Our song and feast shall flow

To the fame of your name,
When the storm has ceased to blow;
When the fiery fight is heard no more,
And the storm has ceased to blow.

Campbell's *Lord Ullin's Daughter.*

A chieftain, to the Highlands bound, cries, "Boatman, do not tarry!
And I'll give thee a silver pound to row us o'er the ferry."
"Now, who be ye would cross Lochgyle, this dark and stormy
    water?"
"Oh, I'm the chief of Ulva's isle, and this, Lord Ullin's daughter;
And fast before her father's men three days we've fled together;
For, should he find us in the glen, my blood would stain the heather.
His horsemen hard behind us ride; should they our steps discover,
Then who will cheer my bonny bride when they have slain her lover?"

Out spoke the hardy Highland wight, "I'll go, my chief—I'm ready;
It is not for your silver bright, but for your winsome lady;
And, by my word, the bonny bird in danger shall not tarry;
So, though the waves are raging white, I'll row you o'er the ferry."
By this the storm grew loud apace, the water-wraith was shrieking,
And in the scowl of Heaven each face grew dark as they were speak-
    ing.
But still, as wilder blew the wind, and as the night grew drearer,
Adown the glen rode armèd men, their trampling sounded nearer.
"Oh! haste thee, haste!" the lady cries, "though tempests round us
    gather;
I'll meet the raging of the skies, but not an angry father."

The boat has left a stormy land, a stormy sea before her,
When, oh! too strong for human hand, the tempest gathered o'er her.
And still they rowed amid the roar of waters fast prevailing:
Lord Ullin reached that fatal shore, his wrath was changed to wailing.
For sore dismayed, through storm and shade, his child he did dis-
    cover;
One lovely hand she stretched for aid, and one was round her lover.
"Come back! come back!" he cried in grief, "across this stormy
    water,
And I'll forgive your Highland chief, my daughter—O my daughter!"
'Twas vain: the loud waves lashed the shore, return or aid preventing;
The waters wild went o'er his child, and he was left lamenting.

Moore's *The Meeting of the Waters.*

There is not in the wide world a valley so sweet
As that vale in whose bosom the bright waters meet;
Oh! the last rays of feeling and life must depart
Ere the bloom of that valley shall fade from my heart.

Yet it was not that nature had shed o'er the scene
Her purest of crystal and brightest of green;
'Twas not her soft magic of streamlet or hill—
Oh no! it was something more exquisite still.

'Twas that friends, the beloved of my bosom, were near,
Who made every dear scene of enchantment more dear,
And who felt how the best charms of nature improve
When we see them reflected from looks that we love.

Sweet vale of Avoca! how calm could I rest
In thy bosom of shade, with the friends I love best!
Where the storms that we feel in this cold world should cease,
And our hearts, like thy waters, be mingled in peace!

FURTHER READING.—Canto I. of *The Lay of the Last Minstrel*, selections from Canto VI. of *Marmion* and from Parts I. and II. of *The Fire-Worshippers*, and abridgment of *Pleasures of Hope*, in pamphlet, by Clark & Maynard.

LESSON 62.

BYRON.—" We turn to very different types of men when we come to Lord Byron, Shelley, and Keats. *Childe Harold*, cantos i. and ii., Byron's first true poem, appeared in 1812, Shelley's *Queen Mab* in 1813, Keats' first volume in 1817.

Of the three, LORD BYRON had most of the quality we may call force. Born in 1788, his *Hours of Idleness*, a collection of short poems, in 1807, was mercilessly lashed in the *Edinburgh Review*. The attack only served to awaken his genius, and he replied with astonishing vigor in the satire of *English Bards and Scotch Reviewers*, in 1809. Eastern travel gave birth to the first two cantos of *Childe Harold*, to the *Giaour* and the *Bride of Abydos* in 1813, to the *Corsair* and *Lara* in 1814. The *Siege of Corinth*, *Parisina*, the *Prisoner of Chil-*

lon, Manfred, and *Childe Harold* were finished before 1819. In 1818 he began a new style in *Beppo,* which he developed fully in the successive issues of *Don Juan,* 1819–1823.   During this time a number of dramas came from him, partly historical, as his *Marino Faliero,* partly imaginative, as the *Cain.* His life had been wild and useless, but he died in trying to redeem it for the sake of the freedom of Greece.   At Missolonghi he was seized with fever, and passed away in April, 1824.

The position of Byron as a poet is a curious one.   He is partly of the past and partly of the present.   Something of the school of Pope clings to him; in *Childe Harold* he imitates Spenser, yet no one more completely broke away from old measures and old manners to make his poetry individual, not imitative.   At first, he has no interest whatever in the human questions which were so strongly felt by Wordsworth and Shelley.   His early work is chiefly narrative poetry, written that he might talk of himself and not of mankind.   Nor has he any philosophy except that which centres round the problem of his own being.   *Cain,* the most thoughtful of his productions, is in reality nothing more than the representation of the way in which the doctrines of original sin and final reprobation affected his own soul.

We feel naturally great interest in this strong personality, put before us with such obstinate power, but it wearies at last.   Finally it wearied himself.   As he grew in thought, he escaped from his morbid self, and ran into the opposite extreme in *Don Juan.*   It is chiefly in it that he shows the influence of the revolutionary spirit.   It is written in bold revolt against all the conventionality of social morality and religion and politics.   It claimed for himself and for others absolute freedom of individual act and thought in opposition to that force of society which tends to make all men after one pattern.   This was the best result of his work, though the way in which it was done can scarcely be approved.   He es-

caped still more from his diseased self when, fully seized on
by the new spirit of setting men free from oppression, he sacrificed his life for the deliverance of Greece.

As *the poet of Nature* he belongs also to the old and to the
new school. We have mentioned those poets before Cowper
who had less a sympathy with Nature than a sympathy with
themselves as they forced her to reflect them, men who followed the vein of Rousseau. Byron's poetry of natural description is often of this class. But he also escapes from this
position of the 18th century poets, and with those of the 19th
looks on Nature as she is, apart from himself; and this escape is made, as in the case of his poetry of Man, in his later
poems. Lastly, it is his colossal power and the ease that
comes from it, in which he resembles Dryden, that marks him
specially. But it is always power of the intellect rather than
that of the imagination."

"Scarce a page of Byron's verse even aspires to perfection; hardly a
stanza will bear the minute word-by-word dissection which only brings
into clearer view the delicate touches of Keats or Tennyson; his pictures with a big brush were never meant for the microscope. 'I can
never recast anything. I am like the tiger; if I miss the first spring,
I go grumbling back to my jungle.' No one else—except, perhaps,
Wordsworth—who could write so well, could also write so ill. His best
inspirations are spoilt by the interruption of incongruous commonplace.
He had none of the guardian delicacy of taste, or the thirst after com-
pleteness which marks the consummate artist.

Southern critics have maintained that he had a southern nature, and
was in his true element on the Lido or under an Andalusian night.
Others dwell on the English pride that went along with his Italian habits and Greek sympathies. The truth is, he had the power of making
himself poetically everywhere at home; and this, along with the fact of
all his writings being perfectly intelligible, is the secret of his European
influence.

This scion of a long line of lawless bloods—a Scandinavian Berserker,
if there ever was one—the literary heir of the Eddas—was specially created to smite the conventionality which is the tyrant of England with
the hammer of Thor, and to sear with the sarcasm of Mephistopheles
the hollow hypocrisy—sham taste, sham morals, sham religion—of

the society by which he was surrounded and infected, and which all
but succeeded in seducing him. His greatness, as well as his weakness,
lay in the fact that from boyhood battle was the breath of his being.
To tell him not to fight was like telling Wordsworth not to reflect, or
Shelley not to sing. His instrument is a trumpet of challenge; and he
lived, as he appropriately died, in the progress of an unaccomplished
campaign."—*John Nichol.*

"His personality inspires no love like that which makes the devotees
of Shelley as faithful to the man as they are loyal to the poet. His intellect, though robust and masculine, is not of the kind to which we
willingly submit. As a man, as a thinker, as an artist, he is out of harmony with us. Nevertheless, nothing can be more certain than Byron's
commanding place in English literature. He is the only British poet of
the nineteenth century who is also European; nor will the lapse of time
fail to make his greatness clearer to his fellow-countrymen, when a just
critical judgment finally dominates the fluctuations of fashion to which
he has been subject."—*J. A. Symonds.*

BIBLIOGRAPHY. BYRON.—T. Moore's *Letters and Journals* of; H. Giles' *Lectures and Essays;* Macaulay's *Essays; Eng. Men of Let.* Series ; Ward's *Anthology;* Whipple's *Charac. of Men of Genius,* and *Essays and Reviews;* Howitt's *Homes and Haunts of Brit. Poets;* J. Morley's *Crit. Miscel.;* J. Paget's *Paradoxes;* Fras. Mag., v. 80, 1869; Quar. Rev., v. 127, 1869; West. Rev., v. 69, 1858; Ecl. Mag., Jan. and Oct., 1872; and Nov., 1880.

Byron's *Napoleon's Farewell.*

Farewell to the Land where the gloom of my Glory
  Arose and o'ershadow'd the earth with her name—
She abandons me now, but the page of her story,   .
  The brightest or blackest, is filled with my fame.
I have warr'd with a world which vanquish'd me only
  When the meteor of conquest allured me too far;
I have coped with the nations which dread me thus lonely—
  The last single captive to millions in war.

Farewell to thee, France! when thy diadem crown'd me,
  I made thee the gem and the wonder of earth,—
But thy weakness decrees I should leave as I found thee,
  Decay'd in thy glory, and sunk in thy worth.
Oh! for the veteran hearts that were wasted
  In strife with the storm, when their battles were won—
Then the eagle, whose gaze in that moment was blasted,
  Had still soar'd with eyes fix'd on victory's sun!

Farewell to thee, France!—but when Liberty rallies
    Once more in thy regions, remember me then.
The violet still grows in the depth of thy valleys;
    Though wither'd, thy tear will unfold it again.
Yet, yet, I may baffle the hosts that surround us,
    And yet may thy heart leap awake to my voice—
There are links which must break in the chain that has bound us,
    Then turn thee, and call on the Chief of thy choice!

From *Childe Harold—An August Evening in Italy.*

The moon is up, and yet it is not night—
    Sunset divides the sky with her,—a sea
Of glory streams along the Alpine height
    Of blue Friuli's mountains; Heaven is free
    From clouds, but of all colors seems to be
Melted to one vast Iris of the West,
    Where the Day joins the past Eternity;
While, on the other hand, meek Dian's crest
Floats through the azure air—an island of the blest!

A single star is at her side, and reigns
    With her o'er half the lovely heaven: but still
Yon sunny sea heaves brightly, and remains
    Roll'd o'er the peak of the far Rhætian hill,
    As Day and Night contending were, until
Nature reclaim'd her order:—gently flows
    The deep-dyed Brenta, where their hues instil
The odorous purple of a new-born rose,
Which streams upon her stream, and glassed within it glows,

Filled with the face of heaven, which, from afar,
    Comes down upon the waters; all its hues,
From the rich sunset to the rising star,
    Their magical variety diffuse:
    And now they change; a paler shadow strews
Its mantle o'er the mountains; parting day
    Dies like the dolphin, whom each pang imbues
With a new color as it gasps away,
The last still loveliest, till—'tis gone—and all is gray.

From *Parisina.*

It is the hour when from the boughs
  The nightingale's high note is heard;
It is the hour when lovers' vows
  Seem sweet in every whisper'd word;
And gentle winds and waters near
Make music to the lonely ear.
Each flower the dews have lightly wet,
And in the sky the stars are met,
And on the wave is deeper blue,
And on the leaf a browner hue,
And in the heaven that clear obscure,
So softly dark, and darkly pure,
Which follows the decline of day,
As twilight melts beneath the moon away.

But it is not to list to the waterfall
That Parisina leaves her hall,
And it is not to gaze on the heavenly light
That the lady walks in the shadow of night;
And, if she sits in Este's bower,
'Tis not for the sake of its full-blown flower.
She listens, but not for the nightingale,
Though her ear expects as soft a tale.
There glides a step through the foliage thick,
And her cheek grows pale, and her heart beats quick.
There whispers a voice through the rustling leaves,
And her blush returns, and her bosom heaves;
A moment more, and they shall meet,
'Tis past—her lover's at her feet.

From *The Siege of Corinth.*

Lightly and brightly breaks away
The Morning from her mantle gray,
And the Noon will look on a sultry day.
Hark to the trump and the drum
And the mournful sound of the barbarous horn
And the flap of the banners, that flit as they're borne,
And the neigh of the steed and the multitude's hum
And the clash and the shout, "They come! they come!"

The horsetails are pluck'd from the ground, and the sword
From its sheath; and they form, and but wait for the word.
Tartar and Spahi and Turcoman,
Strike your tents, and throng to the van;
Mount ye, spur ye, skirr the plain
That the fugitive may flee in vain
When he breaks from the town; and none escape,
Agèd or young, in the Christian shape;
While your fellows on foot, in a fiery mass,
Bloodstain the breach through which they pass.
The steeds are all bridled, and snort to the rein;
Curved is each neck, and flowing each mane;
White is the foam of their champ on the bit:
The spears are uplifted; the matches are lit;
The cannon are pointed, and ready to roar,
And crush the wall they have crumbled before.
Forms in his phalanx each Janizar,
Alp at their head; his right arm is bare,
So is the blade of his scimitar;
The khan and the pachas are all at their post;
The vizier himself at the head of the host.
When the culverin's signal is fired, then on;
Leave not in Corinth a living one—
A priest at her altars, a chief in her halls,
A hearth in her mansions, a stone on her walls.
God and the prophet—Alla Hu!
Up to the skies with that wild halloo!
"There the breach lies for passage, the ladder to scale;
And your hands on your sabres, and how should ye fail?
He who first downs with the red cross may crave
His heart's dearest wish; let him ask it, and have!"
Thus uttered Coumourgi, the dauntless vizier;
The reply was the brandish of sabre and spear,
And the shout of fierce thousands in joyous ire:—
Silence—hark to the signal—fire!

.   .   .   .

The rampart is won and the spoil begun
And all but the after carnage done.
But here and there, where 'vantage ground
Against the foe may still be found,

Desperate groups of twelve or ten
Make a pause, and turn again—
With banded backs against the wall
Fiercely stand, or, fighting, fall.

There stood an old man—his hairs were white,
But his veteran arm was full of might:
So gallantly bore he the brunt of the fray
The dead before him, on that day,
In a semicircle lay;
Still he combated unwounded,
Though retreating, unsurrounded.
Many a scar of former fight
Lurk'd beneath his corslet bright;
But of every wound his body bore,
Each and all had been ta'en before:
Though aged, he was so iron of limb
Few of our youth could cope with him.
Still the old man stood erect,
And Alp's career a moment check'd.
"Yield thee, Minotti; quarter take,
For thine own, thy daughter's sake."
"Never, renegado, never!
Though the life of thy gift would last forever."

"Francesca! Oh, my promised bride!
Must she too perish by thy pride?"
"She is safe."—"Where? where?"—"In heaven;
From whence thy traitor soul is driven—
Far from thee, and undefiled."
Grimly then Minotti smiled,
As he saw Alp staggering bow
Before his words, as with a blow.
"Oh God! when died she?"—"Yesternight—
Nor weep I for her spirit's flight:
None of my pure race shall be
Slaves to Mahomet and thee.
Come on!"   That challenge is in vain—
Alp's already with the slain!
While Minotti's words were wreaking
More revenge in bitter speaking

Than his falchion's point had found
Had the time allowed to wound,
From within the neighboring porch
Of a long-defended church,
Where the last and desperate few
Would the failing fight renew,
The sharp shot dash'd Alp to the ground.
Ere an eye could view the wound
That crash'd through the brain of the infidel,
Round he spun, and down he fell.

The Destruction of Sennacherib.

The Assyrian came down like the wolf on the fold,
And his cohorts were gleaming in purple and gold;
And the sheen of their spears was like stars on the sea,
When the blue wave rolls nightly on deep Galilee.

Like the leaves of the forest when Summer is green,
That host with their banners at sunset were seen;
Like the leaves of the forest when Autumn hath blown,
That host on the morrow lay withered and strown.

For the Angel of Death spread his wings on the blast,
And breathed in the face of the foe as he passed;
And the eyes of the sleepers waxed deadly and chill,
And their hearts but once heaved, and forever grew still!

And there lay the steed with his nostril all wide,
But through it there rolled not the breath of his pride;
And the foam of his gasping lay white on the turf,
And cold as the spray of the rock-beating surf.

And there lay the rider distorted and pale,
With the dew on his brow and the rust on his mail;
And the tents were all silent, the banners alone,
The lances unlifted, the trumpet unblown.

And the widows of Ashur are loud in their wail,
And their idols are broke in the temple of Baal,
And the might of the Gentile, unsmote by the sword,
Hath melted like snow in the glance of the Lord!

From *Don Juan.*

The isles of Greece! the isles of Greece!
  Where burning Sappho loved and sung,
Where grew the arts of war and peace,
  Where Delos rose, and Phœbus sprung!
Eternal summer gilds them yet,
But all, except their sun, is set.

The Scian and the Teian muse,
  The hero's harp, the lover's lute
Have found the fame your shores refuse;
  Their place of birth alone is mute
To sounds which echo farther west
Than your sires' "Islands of the Blest."

The mountains look on Marathon—
  And Marathon looks on the sea;
And musing there an hour alone,
  I dream'd that Greece might still be free;
For, standing on the Persians' grave,
I could not deem myself a slave.

A king sate on the rocky brow
  Which looks o'er sea-born Salamis;
And ships, by thousands, lay below,
  · And men in nations;—all were his!
He counted them at break of day—
And, when the sun set, where were they?

And where are they? and where art thou,
  My country? On thy voiceless shore
The heroic lay is tuneless now—
  The heroic bosom beats no more!
And must thy lyre, so long divine,
Degenerate into hands like mine?

'Tis something, in the dearth of fame,
  Though link'd among a fetter'd race,
To feel at least a patriot's shame,
  Even as I sing, suffuse my face;
For what is left the poet here?
For Greeks a blush—for Greece a tear.

Must *we* but weep o'er days more blest?
   Must *we* but blush?—Our fathers bled.
Earth! render back from out thy breast
   A remnant of our Spartan dead!
Of the three hundred grant but three,
To make a new Thermopylæ!

What, silent still? and silent all?
   Ah! no;—the voices of the dead
Sound like a distant torrent's fall,
   And answer, "Let one living head,
But one arise,—we come, we come!"
'Tis but the living who are dumb.

OTHER READING.—Cantos I and II of *Prophecy of Dante* and the *Prisoner of Chillon*, in pamphlet, by Clark & Maynard.

LESSON 63.

PERCY BYSSHE SHELLEY.—" In Shelley, 1792–1822, the imagination is supreme and the intellect its servant. He produced, while yet a boy, some utterly worthless tales, but soon showed in *Queen Mab*, 1813, the influence of the revolutionary era combined in him with a violent attack on the existing forms of religion. The poem is a poor one, but its poverty prophesies greatness. Its chief idea was the new one that had come into literature—the idea of the destined perfection of mankind in a future golden age. The whole heart of Shelley was absorbed in this conception, in its faith, and in the hopes it stirred. To help the world towards it and to denounce and overthrow all that stood in its way was the object of half of Shelley's poetry. The other half was personal, an outpouring of himself in his seeking after the perfect ideal he could not find, and, sadder still, could not even conceive. *Queen Mab* is an example of the first, *Alastor* of the second.

The hopes for man with which *Queen Mab* was written grew cold; he himself fell ill and looked for death; the world seemed chilled to all the ideas he loved, and he turned from writing about mankind to describe in *Alastor* the life and

wandering and death of a lonely poet. It was himself he described, but Shelley was too stern a moralist to allow that a
life lived apart from human interests was a noble one, and the
title of the poem expresses this. It is *Alastor*—'a spirit of
evil, a spirit of solitude.'

How wrong he felt such a life to be is seen in his next poem,
the *Revolt of Islam*, 1817. He wrote it with the hope that
men were beginning to recover from the apathy and despair
into which the failure of the revolutionary ideas had thrown
them, and to show them what they should strive and hope for
and destroy. But it is still only a martyr's hope that the poet
possesses. The two chief characters of the poem, Laon and
Cythna, are both slain in their struggle against tyranny, but
their sacrifice is to bring forth hereafter the fruit of freedom.
The poem itself has finer passages in it than *Alastor*, but as a
whole it is inferior to it. It is quite formless. The same year
Shelley went to Italy, and renewed health and the climate
gave him renewed power. *Rosalind and Helen* appeared, and,
in 1818, *Julian and Maddalo* was written. The first tale circles round a social subject that interested him, the second is a
familiar conversation on the story of a madman in San Lazzaro
at Venice. In it his poetry becomes more masculine, and he
has for the first time won mastery over his art.

The new life and joy he had now gained brought back his
enthusiasm for mankind, and he broke out into the splendid
lyric drama of *Prometheus Unbound*. Prometheus bound on
his rock represents Humanity suffering under the reign of
Evil impersonated in Jupiter. Asia, at the beginning of the
drama separated from Prometheus, is the all-pervading Love
which in loving makes the universe of nature. The time
comes when Evil is overthrown. Prometheus is then delivered and united to Asia; that is, Man is wedded to the spirit
in Nature, and Good is all in all. The fourth act is the choral
song of the regenerated universe. It is the finest example we
have of the working out in poetry of that idea of a glorious

destiny for the whole of Man which Cowper introduced into
English poetry. The marriage of Asia and Prometheus, of
Nature and Humanity, the distinct existence of each for that
purpose, is the same idea as Wordsworth's, differently expressed; and Shelley and he are the only two poets who have
touched it philosophically, Wordsworth with most contemplation, Shelley with most imagination. Shelley's poetry
of Man reached its height in *Prometheus Unbound,* and he
turned now to try his matured power upon other subjects.
Two of these were neither personal nor for the sake of man.

The first was the drama of the *Cenci,* the gravest and noblest tragedy since Webster wrote, which we possess. It is as
restrained in expression as the previous poem is exuberant; yet
there is no other poem of Shelley's in which passion and thought
and imagery are so wrought together. The second was the
Adonais, a lament for the death of John Keats. It is a poem
written by one who seems a spirit about a spirit, belonging in
expression, thought, and feeling to that world above the senses
in which Shelley habitually lived. Of all this class of poems,
to which many of his lyrics belong, *Epipsychidion* is the most
impalpable, but, to those who care for Shelley's ethereal world,
the finest, poem he ever wrote. No critic can ever comprehend it; it is the artist's poem, and all Shelley's philosophy of
life is contained in it. Of the same class is the *Witch of Atlas,*
the poem in which he has personified divine Imagination in
her work in poetry and all her attendants and all her doings
among men.

As a lyric poet, Shelley, on his own ground, is easily great.
Some of the lyrics are purely personal; some, as in the very
finest, the *Ode to the West Wind,* mingle together personal
feelings and prophetic hopes for Man. Some are lyrics of
Nature; some are dedicated to the rebuke of tyranny and the
cause of liberty; others belong to the passion of love, and
others are written on the shadows of dim dreams of thought.
They form together the most sensitive, the most imaginative,

and the most musical, but the least tangible, lyrical poetry we possess.

As the poet of Nature, he had the same idea as Wordsworth, that Nature was alive; but while Wordsworth made the active principle which filled and made Nature to be Thought, Shelley made it Love. As each distinct thing in Nature had to Wordsworth a thinking spirit in it, so each thing had to Shelley a loving spirit in it; even the invisible spheres of vapor sucked by the sun from the forest pool had each its indwelling spirit. We feel, then, that Shelley as well as Wordsworth, and for a similar reason, could give a special love to, and therefore describe vividly, each thing he saw. He wants the closeness of grasp of nature which Wordsworth and Keats had, but he had the power in a far greater degree than they of describing a vast landscape melting into indefinite distance. In this he stands first among English poets, and is in poetry what Turner was in landscape painting.

Towards the end of his life, his poetry became overloaded with mystical metaphysics. What he might have been we cannot tell, for at the age of thirty he left us, drowned in the sea he loved, washed up and burned on the sandy spits near Pisa. His ashes lie beneath the walls of Rome, and *Cor cordium*, 'Heart of hearts,' written on his tomb, well says what all who love poetry feel when they think of him."

"As a poet, Shelley contributed a new quality to English literature—a quality of ideality, freedom, and spiritual audacity which severe critics of other nations think we lack. Whether we consider his minor songs, his odes, or his more complicated choral dramas, we acknowledge that he was the loftiest and the most spontaneous singer of our language. In range of power also he was conspicuous above the rest. Not only did he write the best lyrics but the best tragedy, the best translations, and the best familiar poems of his century.

While his genius was so varied and its flight so unapproached in swiftness, it would be vain to deny that Shelley, as an artist, had faults. The most prominent of these are haste, incoherence, verbal carelessness, incompleteness, a want of narrative force, and a weak hold on objective realities. In his eager self-abandonment to inspiration, he produced much that is unsatisfactory simply because it is not ripe. There was no defect of power in him, but a defect of patience; and the final word to be pronounced in estimating the larger bulk of his poetry is the word *immature.* Not only was the poet young but the fruit of his young mind had been plucked before it had been duly mellowed by reflection. He did not care enough for common things to present them with artistic fulness. He was intolerant of detail, and thus failed to model with the roundness that we find in Goethe's work. He flew at the grand, the spacious, the sublime, and did 'not always succeed in realizing for his readers what he had imagined. A certain want of faith in his own powers prevented him from finishing what he began.

Some of these defects · were in a great measure the correlative of his chief quality—ideality. He composed with all his faculties, mental, emotional, and physical, at the utmost strain, at a white heat of intense fervor, striving to attain one object—the truest and most passionate investiture for the thoughts which had inflamed his ever-quick imagination. The result is, that his finest work has more the stamp of something natural and elemental—the wind, the sea, the depth of air—than of a mere artistic product. Plato would have said the Muses filled this man with sacred madness, and when he wrote, he was no longer in his own control. There was, moreover, ever-present in his nature an effort, an aspiration after a better than the best this world can show which prompted him to blend the choicest products of his thought and fancy with the fairest images borrowed from the earth on which he lived. This persistent upward striving, this earnestness, this passionate intensity, this piety of soul, and purity of inspiration, give a quite unique spirituality to his poems."—*John A. Symonds.*

BIBLIOGRAPHY. SHELLEY.—W. M. Rossetti's *Memoir* of; *Eng. Men of Let.* Series; W. Bagehot's *Estimates,* etc.; De Quincey's *Essays on the Poets;* Howitt's *Homes of Brit. Poets;* Ward's *Anthology;* L. Hunt's *Memoirs* of; J. L. Peacock's *Works;* At. Mo., v. 6, 1860; and 11, 1863; Macmillan, Nov., 1860; Black. Mag., v. 111, 1812; Dub. U. Mag., v. 67, 1866; Harper's Mo., v. 38; Nat. Rev., v. 16, 1863; N. Br. Rev., v. 34, 1861; Quar. Rev., v. 110, 1861; West Rev., v. 69, 1858; New Mo. Mag., vs. 34, 35, and 38; Ecl. Mag., May, 1879, and Aug., 1880.

Shelley's *The Cloud.*

I bring fresh showers for the thirsting flowers,
    From the seas and the streams;
I bear light shade for the leaves when laid
    In their noonday dreams.

From my wings are shaken the dews that waken
   The sweet buds every one,
When rocked to rest on their Mother's breast,
   As she dances about the sun.
I wield the flail of the lashing hail,
   And whiten the green plains under;
And then again I dissolve it in rain,
   And laugh as I pass in thunder.

I sift the snow on the mountains below,
   And their great pines groan aghast;
And all the night 'tis my pillow white,
   While I sleep in the arms of the Blast.
Sublime on the towers of my skyey bowers
   Lightning, my pilot, sits;
In a cavern under is fettered the Thunder,
   It struggles and howls at fits;
Over earth and ocean, with gentle motion
   This pilot is guiding me,
Lured by the love of the genii that move
   In the depths of the purple sea;
Over the rills and the crags and the hills,
   Over the lakes and the plains,
Wherever he dream under mountain or stream
   The Spirit he loves remains;
And I all the while bask in heaven's blue smile,
   Whilst he is dissolving in rains.

The sanguine Sunrise, with his meteor eyes,
   And his burning plumes outspread,
Leaps on the back of my sailing rack
   When the morning-star shines dead,
As on the jag of a mountain-crag,
   Which an earthquake rocks and swings,
An eagle alit one moment may sit
   In the light of its golden wings.
And, when Sunset may breathe from the lit sea beneath
   Its ardors of rest and of love,
And the crimson pall of eve may fall
   From the depth of heaven above,
With wings folded I rest on mine airy nest,
   As still as a brooding dove.

That orbèd maiden with white fire laden,
  Whom mortals call the Moon,
Glides glimmering o'er my fleece-like floor,
  By the midnight breezes strewn;
And, wherever the beat of her unseen feet,
  Which only the angels hear,
May have broken the woof of my tent's thin roof,
  The Stars peep behind her and peer.
And I laugh to see them whirl and flee
  Like a swarm of golden bees,
When I widen the rent in my wind-built tent,—
  Till the calm rivers, lakes, and seas,
Like strips of the sky fallen through me on high,
  Are each paved with the moon and these.

I bind the Sun's throne with a burning zone,
  And the Moon's with a girdle of pearl;
The volcanoes are dim, and the Stars reel and swim,
  When the whirlwinds my banner unfurl.
From cape to cape, with a bridge-like shape,
  Over a torrent sea,
Sunbeam-proof, I hang like a roof;
  The mountains its columns be.
The triumphal arch through which I march
  With hurricane, fire, and snow,
When the powers of the air are chained to my chair,
  Is the million-colored bow;
The sphere-fire above its soft colors wove,
  While the moist Earth was laughing below.

I am the daughter of the Earth and Water,
  And the nursling of the Sky;
I pass through the pores of the ocean and shores;
  I change, but I cannot die.
For after the rain, when, with never a stain
  The pavilion of heaven is bare,
And the winds and sunbeams with their convex gleams
  Build up the blue dome of air,
I silently laugh at my own cenotaph,
  And out of the caverns of rain,
Like a child from the womb, like a ghost from the tomb,
  I arise, and unbuild it again.

LESSON 64.

JOHN KEATS. — "Keats lies near Shelley, cut off like him ere his genius ripened; not so great, but possessing perhaps greater possibilities of greatness; not so ideal, but for that very reason closer in his grasp of nature than Shelley. In one thing he was entirely different from Shelley—he had no care whatever for the great human questions which stirred Shelley; the present was entirely without interest to him. He marks the close of that poetic movement which the ideas of the Revolution in France had started in England, as Shelley marks the attempt to revive it.   Keats, finding nothing to move him in an age which had now sunk into apathy on these points, went back to Greek and mediæval life to find his subjects, and established, in doing so, that which has been called the *literary poetry* of England.

His first subject, after some minor poems in 1817, was *Endymion*, 1818, his last *Hyperion*, 1820.   These, along with *Lamia*, were poems of Greek life.   *Endymion* has all the faults and all the promise of a great poet's early work, and no one knew its faults better than Keats, whose preface is a model of just self-judgment.   *Hyperion*, a fragment of a tale of the overthrow of the Titans, is itself like a Titanic torso, and in it the faults of *Endymion* are repaired and its promise fulfilled.   Both are filled with that which was deepest in the mind of Keats, the love of loveliness for its own sake, the sense of its rightful and pre-eminent power; and, in the singleness of worship which he gave to Beauty, Keats is especially the artist, and the true father of the latest modern school of poetry.

Not content with carrying us into Greek life, he took us back into mediæval romance, and in this also he started a new type of poetry.   There are two poems which mark this revival—*Isabella*, and the *Eve of St. Agnes*. *Isabella* is a

version of Boccaccio's tale of the *Pot of Basil; St. Agnes' Eve*
is, as far as I know, original; the former is purely mediæval,
the latter is tinged with the conventional mediævalism of
Spenser. Both poems are however modern and individual.
The overwrought daintiness of style, the pure sensuousness,
the subtle flavor of feeling belong to no one but Keats.
Their originality has caused much imitation of them, but
they are too original for imitation.

In smaller poems, such as the *Ode to a Grecian Urn*, the
poem to *Autumn*, and some sonnets, he is perhaps at his very
best. In these and in all, his painting of Nature is as close
and as direct as Wordsworth's; less full of the imagination that
links human thought to Nature, but more full of the imagination which broods upon enjoyment of beauty. His career
was short; he had scarcely begun to write when death took
him away from the loveliness he loved so keenly. Consump-
tion drove him to Rome, and there he died almost alone. He
lies not far from Shelley, near the pyramid of Caius Cestius."

"Poetry, according to Milton's famous saying, should be 'simple,
sensuous, impassioned.' Keats, as a poet, is abundantly and enchantingly
sensuous; the question with some people will be, whether he is anything else. 'The yearning passion for the Beautiful,' which was with
Keats, as he himself truly says, the master-passion, is not a passion of
the sensuous or sentimental man, is not a passion of the sensuous or
sentimental poet. It is an intellectual and spiritual passion. In his
last days Keats wrote, 'I have loved the principle of beauty in all
things; and, if I had had time, I would have made myself remembered.'
He *has* made himself remembered, and remembered as no merely sensuous poet could be; and he has done it by having 'loved the principle
of beauty in all things.' For to see things in their beauty is to see
things in their truth, and Keats knew it. And with beauty goes not
only truth, joy goes with her also; and this too Keats saw and said. It
is no small thing to have so loved the principle of beauty as to perceive
the necessary relation of beauty with truth, and of both with joy.

Let and hindered as he was, and with a short time and imperfect experience, by virtue of his feeling for beauty and of his perception of
the vital connection of beauty with truth, Keats accomplished so much

in poetry that in one of the two great modes by which poetry interprets, in the faculty of naturalistic interpretation, he ranks with Shakespeare. No one else in English poetry, save Shakespeare, has in expression quite the fascinating felicity of Keats, his perfection of loveliness. For the second great half of poetic interpretation, for that faculty of moral interpretation which is in Shakespeare, and is informed by him with the same power of beauty as his naturalistic interpretation, Keats was not ripe."—*Matthew Arnold.*

BIBLIOGRAPHY. KEATS.—Milnes' *Life, Letters, and Lit. Remains* of; De Quincey's *Essays;* Howitt's *Homes and Haunts of Brit. Poets;* Ward's *Anthology;* Lowell's *Among My Books,* 2d Ser.; S. Phillips' *Essays from the Times;* Macmillan, Nov., 1860; At. Mo., v. 7, 1861; and 11, 1863; Temple Bar, July, 1873; Ecl. Mag., Feb., 1849; Gent's. Mag., Feb., 1873.

Keats's *Ode to a Nightingale.*

My heart aches, and a drowsy numbness pains
  My sense, as though of hemlock I had drunk,
Or emptied some dull opiate to the drains
  One minute past, and Lethe-wards had sunk.
'Tis not through envy of thy happy lot,
  But being too happy in thy happiness,—
That thou, light-wingèd Dryad of the trees,
    In some melodious plot
Of beechen green, and shadows numberless,
Singest of summer in full-throated ease.

Oh for a draught of vintage that hath been
  Cooled a long age in the deep-delved earth,
Tasting of Flora and the country-green,
  Dance, and Provençal song, and sun-burnt mirth!
Oh for a beaker full of the warm South,
  Full of the true, the blushful Hippocrene,
With beaded bubbles winking at the brim,
    And purple-stainèd mouth;
That I might drink, and leave the world unseen,
And with thee fade away into the forest dim!

Fade far away, dissolve, and quite forget
  What thou among the leaves hast never known,
The weariness, the fever, and the fret
  Here, where men sit and hear each other groan;

Where palsy shakes a few, sad, last, grey hairs,
　Where youth grows pale, and spectre-thin, and dies;
Where but to think is to be full of sorrow
　　　And leaden-eyed despairs;
　Where Beauty cannot keep her lustrous eyes,
Or new Love pine at them beyond to-morrow.

Away! away! for I will fly to thee,
　Not charioted by Bacchus and his pards,
But on the viewless wings of Poesy,
　Though the dull brain perplexes and retards.
Already with thee! tender is the night,
　And haply the Queen-Moon is on her throne,
Clustered around by all her starry fays;
　　　But here there is no light,
　Save what from heaven is with the breezes blown
Through verdurous glooms and winding, mossy ways.

I cannot see what flowers are at my feet,
　Nor what soft incense hangs upon the boughs,
But, in embalmèd darkness, guess each sweet
　Wherewith the seasonable month endows
The grass, the thicket, and the fruit-tree wild;
　White hawthorn, and the pastoral eglantine,
Fast-fading violets covered up in leaves;
　　　And mid-May's eldest child,
　The coming musk-rose, full of dewy wine,
The murmurous haunt of flies on summer eves.

Darkling I listen, and for many a time
　I have been half in love with easeful Death,
Called him soft names in many a musèd rhyme,
　To take into the air my quiet breath.
Now more than ever seems it rich to die,
　To cease upon the midnight with no pain,
While thou art pouring forth thy soul abroad
　　　In such an ecstasy!
　Still wouldst thou sing, and I have ears in vain—
To thy high requiem become a sod.

Thou wast not born for death, immortal Bird!
No hungry generations tread thee down;
The voice I hear this passing night was heard
In ancient days by emperor and clown:
Perhaps the self-same song that found a path
    Through the sad heart of Ruth, when, sick for home,
She stood in tears amid the alien corn;
        The same that oft-times hath
    Charmed magic casements, opening on the foam
Of perilous seas, in faery lands forlorn.

Forlorn! the very word is like a bell
    To toll me back from thee to my sole self!
Adieu! the fancy cannot cheat so well
    As she is famed to do, deceiving elf.
Adieu! adieu! thy plaintive anthem fades
    Past the near meadows, over the still stream,
Up the hill-side; and now 'tis buried deep
        In the next valley-glades.
    Was it a vision, or a waking dream?
Fled is that music; do I wake or sleep?

LESSON 65.

TENNYSON.—"Keats marks the exhaustion of the impulse which began with Burns and Cowper. There was no longer now in England any large wave of public thought or feeling such as could awaken poetry. But with the Reform agitation, and the new religious agitation at Oxford, which was of the same date, a new excitement or a new form of the old, came on England, and with it a new tribe of poets arose, among whom we live. The elements of their poetry were also new, though their germs were sown in the previous poetry. It took up the theological, sceptical, social, and political questions which disturbed England. It gave itself to metaphysics and to analysis of human character. It carried the love of natural scenery into almost every county in England, and described the whole land. Some of its best writers are ROBERT

BROWNING, MRS. BROWNING, MATTHEW ARNOLD, and A. H. CLOUGH.

One of them, ALFRED TENNYSON, has for forty years remained the first. All the great subjects of his time he has touched poetically, and enlightened. His feeling for Nature is accurate, loving, and of a wide range.' His human sympathy fills as wide a field. The large interests of mankind and of his own time, the lives of simple people, and the subtler phases of thought and feeling which arise in our overwrought society are wisely and tenderly written of in his poems. His drawing of distinct human characters is the best we have in pure poetry since Chaucer wrote. He writes true songs, and he has excelled all English writers in the pure Idyll. The Idylls of the King are a kind of epic, and he has lately tried the drama. In lyrical measures, as in the form of his blank verse, he is as inventive as original. It is by the breadth of his range that he most conclusively takes the first place among the modern poets."

" If I may take my own experience as an indication of the nature of Tennyson's influence generally, I should say that he is pre-eminently distinguished by the quality of *charm*. The element of sweetness pervades his poetry; sweetness too subtle to define, sweetness never permitted to cloy the reader, sweetness cunningly allied with, or relieved by, what the poet calls 'the bitter of the sweet.' I accept the ancient canon of criticism—that poetry ought to be not only beautiful but sweet, and I think that it is in the exceeding beauty of Tennyson's that one chief secret of its sweetness lies.

Not only do these poems display no vulgar smartness but no fun, no humor, no caricature. A Greek severity of style is everywhere apparent; a reverence as of one for whom song has in very truth the sacredness of worship. And even if we decide that in the work of Tennyson as a whole there is too much of rule and measure, too marked an absence of humor, too little of the wild witching graces of freedom, we are, I think, safe in regarding the classic purity, the chastened enthusiasm—in one word, the moderation, of his first poems as a good omen. The earnestness noted by Hallam was the best proof of capacity to take pains, the best guarantee of staying power.

To describe his command of language by any ordinary terms expressive of fluency or force would be to convey an idea both inadequate and erroneous. It is not only that he knows every word in the language suited to express his every idea; he can select with the ease of magic the word that above all others is best for his purpose: nor is it that he can at once summon to his aid the best word the language affords; with an art which Shakespeare never scrupled to apply, though in our day it is apt to be counted mere Germanism, and pronounced contrary to the genius of the language, he combines old words into new epithets, he daringly mingles all colors to bring out tints that never were on sea or shore. His words gleam like pearls and opals, like rubies and emeralds. He yokes the stern vocables of the English tongue to the chariot of his imagination, and they become gracefully brilliant as the leopards of Bacchus, soft and glowing as the Cytherean doves. He must have been born with an ear for verbal sounds, an instinctive appreciation of the beautiful and delicate in words, hardly ever equalled. Though his later works speak less of the blossom-time—show less of the efflorescence and iridescence, and mere glance and gleam of colored words—they display no falling off, but rather an advance, in the mightier elements of rhythmic speech."—*Peter Bayne.*

BIBLIOGRAPHY. TENNYSON.—P. Bayne's *Lessons from my Masters;* Bromley's *Essays;* Stedman's *Victorian Poets;* Taine's *Hist. Eng. Lit.;* J. Sterling's *Essays and Tales;* Howitt's *Homes and Haunts of Brit. Poets;* Black. Mag , v. 79, 1856; 88, 1860; and 96, 1864; Fras. Mag., v. 52, 1855; 53, 1856; and 60, 1859; N. Br. Rev., v. 31, 1849; 41, 1864; and 53, 1871; Ed. Rev., vs. 102 and 131; Quar. Rev., v. 106, 1859; 119, 1866; 128, 1870; and 131, 1871; West. Rev., v. 72, 1859; and 82, 1864; Nat. Quar. Rev., v. 5, 1862; and 19, 1869; Contem. Rev., v. 7, 1867; New Englander, v. 18, 1860; and 22, 1868.

MRS. BROWNING.—Black. Mag., v. 81, 1857: and 87, 1860; Nat. Quar. Rev., v. 1, 1860; and 5, 1862; N. Br. Rev., v. 26, 1856; 36, 1862; and 51, 1870; N. A. Rev., v. 85 1857.

MR. BROWNING.—Ed. Rev., v. 120, 1864; 130, 1869; and 135, 1872; Fort. Rev., v. 11, 1869; and 16, 1871; Macmillan, Jan. and Apr., 1869; Contem. Rev., Jan. and Feb. 1867; and May, 1874; N. Br. Rev., v. 34, 1861; and 49, 1868.

From Tennyson's *Maud.*

Come into the garden, Maud,
　For the black bat, night, has flown,
Come into the garden, Maud,
　I am here at the gate alone;
And the woodbine spices are wafted abroad,
　And the musk of the roses blown.

For a breeze of morning moves,
  And the planet of Love is on high,
Beginning to faint in the light that she loves
  On a bed of daffodil sky,
To faint in the light of the sun that she loves,
  To faint in his light, and to die.

All night have the roses heard
  The flute, violin, bassoon;
All night has the casement jessamine stirr'd
  To the dancers dancing in tune;
Till a silence fell with the waking bird,
  And a hush with the setting moon.

I said to the lily, " There is but one
  With whom she has heart to be gay.
When will the dancers leave her alone?
  She is weary of dance and play."
Now half to the setting moon are gone,
  And half to the rising day;
Low on the sand and loud on the stone
  The last wheel echoes away.

I said to the rose, " The brief night goes
  In babble and revel and wine.
O young lord-lover, what sighs are those
  For one that will never be thine?
But mine, but mine," so I sware to the rose,
" For ever and ever, mine."

And the soul of the rose went into my blood,
  As the music clash'd in the hall;
And long by the garden lake I stood,
  For I heard your rivulet fall
From the lake to the meadow and on to the wood.
  Our wood, that is dearer than all;

From the meadow your walks have left so sweet
  That, whenever a March-wind sighs,
He sets the jewel-print of your feet
  In violets blue as your eyes,
To the woody hollows in which we meet
  And the valleys of Paradise.

The slender acacia would not shake
  One long milk-bloom on the tree;
The white lake-blossom fell into the lake
  As the pimpernel dozed on the lee;
But the rose was awake all night for your sake,
  Knowing your promise to me;
The lilies and roses were all awake,
  They sigh'd for the dawn and thee.

Queen rose of the rosebud garden of girls,
  Come hither, the dances are done,
In gloss of satin and glimmer of pearls,
  Queen lily and rose in one;
Shine out, little head, sunning over with curls,
  To the flowers, and be their sun.

There has fallen a splendid tear
  From the passion-flower at the gate.
She is coming, my dove, my dear;
  She is coming, my life, my fate;
The red rose cries, "She is near, she is near;"
  And the white rose weeps, "She is late;"
The larkspur listens, "I hear, I hear;"
  And the lily whispers, "I wait."

She is coming, my own, my sweet;
  Were it ever so airy a tread,
My heart would hear her and beat,
  Were it earth in an earthy bed;
My dust would hear her and beat,
  Had I lain for a century dead;
Would start and tremble under her feet,
  And blossom in purple and red.

The Defence of Lucknow.

Banner of England, not for a season, O banner of Britain, hast thou
Floated in conquering battle or flapt to the battle-cry!
Never with mightier glory than when we had rear'd thee on high
Flying at top of the roofs in the ghastly siege of Lucknow—
Shot thro' the staff or the halyard, but ever we raised thee anew,
And ever upon the topmost roof our banner of England blew.

Frail were the works that defended the hold that we held with our lives—
Women and children among us, God help them, our children and wives!
Hold it we might—and for fifteen days or for twenty at most.
"Never surrender, I charge you, but every man die at his post!"
Voice of the dead whom we loved, our Lawrence the best of the brave:
Cold were his brows when we kiss'd him—we laid him that night in his
    grave.
"Every man die at his post!" and there hail'd on our houses and halls
Death from their rifle-bullets, and death from their cannon-balls,
Death in our innermost chamber, and death at our slight barricade,
Death while we stood with the musket, and death while we stoopt to
    the spade,
Death to the dying, and wounds to the wounded, for often there fell
Striking the hospital wall, crashing thro' it, their shot and their shell,
Death—for their spies were among us, their marksmen were told of our
    best,
So that the brute bullet broke thro' the brain that could think for the
    rest;
Bullets would sing by our foreheads, and bullets would rain at our feet—
Fire from ten thousand at once of the rebels that girdled us round—
Death at the glimpse of a finger from over the breadth of a street,
Death from the heights of the mosque and the palace, and death in the
    ground!
Mine? Yes, a mine! Countermine! down, down! and creep thro' the
    hole!
Keep the revolver in hand! you can hear him—the murderous mole!
Quiet, ah! quiet—wait till the point of the pick axe be thro'!
Click with the pick, coming nearer and nearer again than before—
Now let it speak, and you fire, and the dark pioneer is no more;
And ever upon the topmost roof our banner of England blew!

Ay, but the foe sprung his mine many times, and it chanced on a day
Soon as the blast of that underground thunderclap echo'd away,
Dark thro' the smoke and the sulphur like so many fiends in their hell—
Cannon-shot, musket-shot, volley on volley, and yell upon yell—
Fiercely on all the defences our myriad enemy fell.
What have they done? where is it? Out yonder. Guard the Redan!
Storm at the water-gate! storm at the Bailey-gate! storm, and it ran
Surging and swaying all round us, as ocean on every side
Plunges and heaves at a bank that is daily drown'd by the tide—
So many thousands that, if they be bold enough, who shall escape?

Kill or be kill'd, live or die, they shall know we are soldiers and men!
Ready! take aim at their leaders—their masses are gapp'd with our
grape—
Backward they reel like the wave, like the wave flinging forward again,
Flying and foil'd at the last by the handful they could not subdue;
And ever upon the topmost roof our banner of England blew.

Handful of men as we were, we were English in heart and limb,
Strong with the strength of the race to command, to obey, to endure,
Each of us fought as if hope for the garrison hung but on him;
Still—could we watch at all points? we were every day fewer and fewer.
There was a whisper among us, but only a whisper that past:
"Children and wives—if the tigers leap into the fold unawares—
Every man die at his post—and the foe may outlive us at last—
Better to fall by the hands that they love than to fall into theirs!"
Roar upon roar, in a moment two mines, by the enemy sprung,
Clove into perilous chasms our walls and our poor palisades.
Rifleman, true is your heart, but be sure that your hand be as true!
Sharp is the fire of assault, better aimed are your flank fusillades—
Twice do we hurl them to earth from the ladders to which they had
clung,
Twice from the ditch where they shelter we drive them with hand-
grenades;
And ever upon the topmost roof our banner of England blew.

Then on another wild morning another wild earthquake out-tore
Clean from our lines of defence ten or twelve good paces or more.
Rifleman, high on the roof, hidden there from the light of the sun—
One has leapt up on the breach, crying out, "Follow me, follow me!"
Mark him—he falls! then another, and *him* too, and down goes he.
Had they been bold enough then, who can tell but the traitors had won?
Boardings and rafters and doors—an embrasure! make way for the gun!
Now double-charge it with grape! It is charged and we fire, and they
run.
Praise to our Indian brothers, and let the dark face have his due!
Thanks to the kindly dark faces who fought with us, faithful and few,
Fought with the bravest among us, and drove them, and smote them and
slew,
That ever upon the topmost roof our banner in India blew.

Men will forget what we suffer and not what we do. We can fight!
But to be soldier all day and be sentinel all thro' the night—

Ever the mine and assault, our sallies, their lying alarms.
Bugles and drums in the darkness, and shoutings and soundings to arme,
Ever the labor of fifty, that had to be done by five,
Ever the marvel among us that one should be left alive,
Ever the day with its traitorous death from the loopholes around,
Ever the night with its coffinless corpse to be laid in the ground,
Heat like the mouth of hell, or a deluge of cataract skies,
Stench of old offal decaying, and infinite torment of flies,
Thoughts of the breezes of May blowing over an English field,
Cholera, scurvy, and fever, the wound that *would not* be heal'd,
Lopping away of the limb by the pitiful-pitiless knife,—
Torture and trouble in vain,—for it never could save us a life.
Valor of delicate women who tended the hospital bed,
Horror of women in travail among the dying and dead,
Grief for our perishing children, and never a moment for grief,
Toil and ineffable weariness, faltering hopes of relief,
Havelock baffled or beaten, or butchered for all that we knew—
Then day and night, day and night, coming down on the still shatter'd
    walls,
Millions of musket-bullets, and thousands of cannon-balls—
But ever upon the topmost roof our banner of England blew.

Hark! Cannonade, fusillade! is it true what was told by the scout,
Outram and Havelock breaking their way through the fell mutineers?
Surely the pibroch of Europe is ringing again in our ears!
All on a sudden the garrison utter a jubilant shout,
Havelock's glorious Highlanders answer with conquering cheers,
Sick from the hospital echo them, women and children come out,
Blessing the wholesome white faces of Havelock's good fusileers,
Kissing the war-harden'd hand of the Highlander wet with their tears!
Dance to the pibroch!—saved! we are saved!—is it you? is it you?
Saved by the valor of Havelock, saved by the blessing of Heaven!
"Hold it for fifteen days!" we have held it for eighty-seven!
And ever aloft on the palace-roof the old banner of England blew.

From *Locksley Hall.*

Comrades, leave me here a little, while as yet 'tis early morn;
Leave me here, and when you want me, sound upon the bugle horn.
'Tis the place, and all around it, as of old, the curlews call,
Dreary gleams about the moorland flying over Locksley Hall;

Locksley Hall, that in the distance overlooks the sandy tracts,
And the hollow ocean-ridges roaring into cataracts.
Many a night from yonder ivied casement, ere I went to rest,
Did I look on great Orion sloping slowly to the west.
Many a night I saw the Pleiads, rising thro' the mellow shade,
Glitter like a swarm of fire-flies tangled in a silver braid.
Here about the beach I wander'd, nourishing a youth sublime
With the fairy tales of science, and the long result of time;
When the centuries behind me like a fruitful land reposed;
When I clung to all the present for the promise that it closed;
When I dipt into the future far as human eye could see;
Saw the vision of the world, and all the wonder that would be.

In the spring a fuller crimson comes upon the robin's breast;
In·the spring the wanton lapwing gets himself another crest;
In the spring a livelier iris changes on the burnish'd dove;
In the spring a young man's fancy lightly turns to thoughts of love.
Then her cheek was pale and thinner than should be for one so young,
And her eyes on all my motions with a mute observance hung.
And I said, " My cousin Amy, speak, and speak the truth to me,
Trust me, cousin, all the current of my being sets to thee."
On her pallid cheek and forehead came a color and a light,
As I have seen the rosy red flushing in the northern night.
And she turn'd—her bosom shaken with a sudden storm of sighs—
All the spirit deeply dawning in the dark of hazel eyes—
Saying, " I have hid my feelings, fearing they should do me wrong;"
Saying, " Dost thou love me, cousin?" weeping, "I have loved thee
     long."
Love took up the glass of time, and turn'd it in his glowing hands;
Every moment, lightly shaken, ran itself in golden sands.
Love took up the harp of life, and smote on all the chords with might;
Smote the chord of self, that, trembling, pass'd in music out of sight.
Many a morning on the moorland did we hear the copses ring,
And her whisper throng'd my pulses with the fulness of the spring.
Many an evening by the waters did we watch the stately ships,
And our spirits rush'd together at the touching of the lips.

O my cousin, shallow-hearted!   O my Amy, mine no more!
O the dreary, dreary moorland!   O the barren, barren shore!
Falser than all fancy fathoms, falser than all songs have sung,
Puppet to a father's threat, and servile to a shrewish tongue!
Is it well to wish thee happy?—having known me—to decline
On a range of lower feelings and a narrower heart than mine!

Yet it shall be: thou shalt lower to his level day by day,
What is fine within thee growing coarse to sympathize with clay.
As the husband is, the wife is: thou art mated with a clown,
And the grossness of his nature will have weight to drag thee down.
He will hold thee, when his passion shall have spent its novel force,
Something better than his dog, a little dearer than his horse.
What is this? his eyes are heavy: think not they are glazed with wine,
Go to him, it is thy duty; kiss him, take his hand in thine.
It may be my lord is weary, that his brain is overwrought;
Soothe him with thy finer fancies, touch him with thy lighter thought.
He will answer to the purpose easy things to understand—
Better thou wert dead before me, tho' I slew thee with my hand!
Cursed be the social wants that sin against the strength of youth!
Cursed be the social lies that warp us from the living truth!
Cursed be the sickly forms that err from honest nature's rule!
Cursed be the gold that gilds the straiten'd forehead of the fool!

.   .   .   .

What is that which I should turn to, lighting upon days like these?
Every door is barr'd with gold, and opens but to golden keys.
Every gate is throng'd with suitors, all the markets overflow.
I have but an angry fancy: what is that which I should do?
I had been content to perish, falling on the foeman's ground,
When the ranks are roll'd in vapor, and the winds are laid with sound.
But the jingling of the guinea helps the hurt that honor feels,
And the nations do but murmur, snarling at each other's heels.
Can I but relive in sadness? I will turn that earlier page.
Hide me from my deep emotion, O thou wondrous Mother-Age!
Make me feel the wild pulsation that I felt before the strife,
When I heard my days before me, and the tumult of my life;
Yearning for the large excitement that the coming years would yield,
Eager-hearted as a boy when first he leaves his father's field,
And at night along the dusky highway, near and nearer drawn,
Sees in heaven the light of London flaring like a dreary dawn;
And his spirit leaps within him to be gone before him then,
Underneath the light he looks at, in among the throngs of men;
Men, my brothers, men the workers, ever reaping something new:
That which they have done but earnest of the things that they shall do.
For I dipt into the future, far as human eye could see,
Saw the vision of the world, and all the wonder that would be;
Saw the heavens fill with commerce, argosies of magic sails,
Pilots of the purple twilight, dropping down with costly bales;

Heard the heavens fill with shouting, and there rain'd a ghastly dew
From the nations' airy navies grappling in the central blue;
Far along the world-wide whisper of the south-wind rushing warm,
With the standards of the peoples plunging thro' the thunder-storm;
Till the war-drum throbb'd no longer, and the battle-flags were furl'd
In the Parliament of man, the Federation of the world.
There the common sense of most shall hold a fretful realm in awe,
And the kindly earth shall slumber, lapt in universal law.
So I triumphed, ere my passion sweeping thro' me left me dry,
Left me with a palsied heart, and left me with the jaundiced eye;
Eye to which all order festers, all things here are out of joint,
Science moves, but slowly, slowly, creeping on from point to point;
Slowly comes a hungry people, as a lion, creeping nigher,
Glares at one that nods and winks behind a slowly-dying fire.
Yet I doubt not thro' the ages one increasing purpose runs,
And the thoughts of men are widen'd with the process of the suns.
What is that to him that reaps not harvest of his youthful joys,
Tho' the deep heart of existence beat forever like a boy's?
Knowledge comes, but wisdom lingers, and I linger on the shore,
And the individual withers, and the world is more and more.
Knowledge comes, but wisdom lingers, and he bears a laden breast,
Full of sad experience, moving toward the stillness of his rest.
Hark, my merry comrades call me, sounding on the bugle-horn,
They to whom my foolish passion were a target for their scorn:
Shall it not be scorn to me to harp on such a moulder'd string?
I am shamed thro' all my nature to have loved so slight a thing.

. . . .

Not in vain the distance beacons. Forward, forward, let us range.
Let the great world spin forever down the ringing grooves of change.
Thro' the shadow of the globe we sweep into the younger day:
Better fifty years of Europe than a cycle of Cathay.
Mother-Age, (for mine I know not) help me as when life begun:
Rift the hills, and roll the waters, flash the lightnings, weigh the sun—
Oh, I see the crescent promise of my spirit hath not set.
Ancient founts of inspiration well thro' all my fancy yet.
Howsoever these things be, a long farewell to Locksley Hall!
Now for me the woods may wither, now for me the roof-tree fall.
Comes a vapor from the margin, blackening over heath and holt,
Cramming all the blast before it, in its breast a thunderbolt.
Let it fall on Locksley Hall, with rain or hail or fire or snow;
For the mighty wind arises, roaring seaward, and I go.

LESSON 66.

MORRIS AND OTHERS.—" Within the last ten years, the impulse given in '32 has died away. The vital interest in theological and social questions, in human questions of the present has decayed; and the same thing which we find in the case of Keats has again taken place. A new class of literary poets has arisen, who have no care for a present they think dull, for religious questions to which they see no end. They too have gone back to Greek and mediæval and old Norse life for their subjects. They find much of their inspiration in Italy and in Chaucer; but they continue to love poetry and the poetry of natural description. No English poetry exceeds SWINBURNE'S in varied melody; and the poems of ROSSETTI, within their limited range, are instinct with passion at once subtle and intense.

Of them all WILLIAM MORRIS is the greatest, and of him much more is to be expected. At present he is our most delightful story-teller. He loses much by being too long, but we pardon the length for the ideal charm. The *Death of Jason* and the stories told month by month in the *Earthly Paradise*, a Greek and mediæval story alternately, will long live to give pleasure to the holiday times of men. It is some pity that it is foreign and not English story, but we can bear to hear alien tales, for Tennyson has always kept us close to the scenery, the traditions, the daily life, and the history of England; and his last poem, the drama of *Queen Mary*, 1875, is written almost exactly twelve hundred years since the date of our first poem, Cædmon's *Paraphrase*. To think of one and then of the other, and of the great and continuous stream of literature that has flowed between them, is more than enough to make us all proud of the name of Englishmen."

BIBLIOGRAPHY. ROSSETTI.—Stedman's *Vic. Poets;* Cath. World, May, 1874; Fras. Mag., May, 1870; Fort. Rev., v. 13, 1870; West. Rev., v. 95, 1871; Contem. Rev., v. 18, 1871.

MORRIS.—Ed. Rev., v. 133, 1871; Fort. Rev., July, 1867; Contem. Rev., Dec., 1874; Fras. Mag., v. 79, 1869; New Englander, v. 30, 1871; Scrib. Mo., Feb., 1875; West. Rev., v. 90, 1868

SWINBURNE.—Lowell's *My Study Windows;* Stedman's *Vic. Poets;* Lond. Quar. Rev., Jan., 1869; Cath. World, Dec., 1874; Fras. Mag., v. 71, 1865; and 74, 1868; Galaxy, Dec., 1866; Nat. Quar. Rev., v. 14, 1867; West. Rev., v. 87, 1867.

From Morris's *Life and Death of Jason.**

But when they reached the precinct of the God,
And on the hallowed turf their feet now trod,
Medea turned to Jason, and she said,—
" O love, turn round, and note the goodlihead
My father's palace shows beneath the stars.
Bethink thee of the men grown old in wars,
Who do my bidding; what delights I have,
How many ladies lie in wait to save
My life from toil and carefulness, and think
How sweet a cup I have been used to drink,
And how I cast it to the ground for thee.
Upon the day thou weariest of me,
I wish that thou mayst somewhat think of this,
And 'twixt thy new-found kisses, and the bliss
Of something sweeter than thine old delight,
Remember thee a little of this night
Of marvels, and this starlit, silent place,
And these two lovers, standing face to face."
    "O love," he said, "by what thing shall I swear
That while I live thou shalt not be less dear
Than thou art now?"
                    "Nay, sweet," she said, "let be;
Wert thou more fickle than the restless sea,
Still should I love thee, knowing thee for such;
Whom I know not, indeed, but fear the touch

* Pelias dethroned his brother Æson, King of Iolchos, and sought the life of Jason, Æson's son. The boy was concealed, and, reaching maturity, demanded the crown. Pelias promised it to him if he would fetch him a famous golden fleece—that of a ram sacrificed to Jupiter and given to Æëtes, King of Colchis. Jason organized an expedition, and set sail in the ship Argo. Arriving at Colchis, Jason wins the love of Medea, daughter of Æëtes, and is helped by her to perform the hard tasks imposed by her father as a condition of receiving the fleece. The tasks performed, Æëtes refuses the reward. The going of Jason and Medea to the temple where the treasure was kept, the charming of the monster that guarded it, the capture of the fleece, and their escape are described in the passage quoted.

Of Fortune's hand when she beholds our bliss,
And knows that nought is good to me but this,
  But now be ready, for I long full sore
To hear the merry dashing of the oar,
And feel the freshness of the following breeze
That sets me free, and sniff the rough salt seas.
Look! yonder thou mayst see armed shadows steal
Down to the quays, the guiders of thy keel;
Now follow me, though little shalt thou do
To gain this thing, if Hecate be true
Unto her servant. Nay, draw not thy sword,
And, for thy life, speak not a single word
Until I bid thee, else may all be lost,
And of this game our lives yet pay the cost."
  Then toward the brazen temple-door she went,
Wherefrom, half-open, a faint gleam was sent;
For little need of lock it had forsooth,
Because its sleepless guardian knew no ruth,
And had no lust for precious things or gold.
Whom, drawing near, Jason could now behold,
As back Medea thrust the heavy door,
For prone he lay upon the gleaming floor,
Not moving, though his restless, glittering eyes
Gave unto them no least hope of surprise.
Hideous he was, where all things else were fair;
Dull-skinned, foul-spotted, with lank, rusty hair
About his neck; and hookèd yellow claws
Just showed from 'neath his belly and huge jaws,
Closed in the hideous semblance of a smile.
Then Jason shuddered, wondering with what wile
That fair king's daughter such a beast could tame,
And of his sheathed sword had but little shame.
  But being within the doors, both mantle grey
And heavy gown Medea cast away,
And in thin clinging silk alone was clad,
And round her neck a golden chain she had,
Whereto was hung a harp of silver white.
Then the great dragon, at that glittering sight,
Raised himself up upon his loathly feet,
As if to meet her, while her fingers sweet
Already moved amongst the golden strings,

Preluding nameless and delicious things.
But now she beckoned Jason to her side,
For slowly towards them 'gan the beast to glide,
And when close to his love the hero came,
She whispered breathlessly, "On me the blame
If here we perish; if I give the word,
Then know that all is lost, and draw thy sword,
And manlike die in battle with the beast;
So dying shalt thou fail to see at least
This body thou desiredst so to see,
In thy despite here mangled wretchedly.
Peace, for he cometh.   O thou Goddess bright,
What help wilt thou be unto me this night?"
  So murmured she, while ceaselessly she drew
Her fingers through the strings, and fuller grew
The tinkling music; but the beast, drawn nigh,
Went slower still, and, turning, presently
Began to move around them in a ring.
And as he went, there fell a strange rattling
Of his dry scales; but, as he turned, she turned,
Nor failed to meet the eyes that on her burned,
With steadfast eyes, and, lastly, clear and strong
Her voice broke forth in sweet melodious song:—

     " O evil thing, what brought thee here
    To be a wonder and a fear
    Unto the river-haunting folk?
    Was it the God of Day that broke
    The shadow of thy windless trees,
    Gleaming from golden palaces,
    And shod with light, and armed with light,
    Made thy slime stone, and day thy night,
    And drove thee forth unwillingly
    Within his golden house to lie?
     Or rather, thy dull, waveless lake
    Didst thou not leave for her dread sake
    Who, passing swift from glade to glade,
    The forest-dwellers makes afraid
    With shimmering of her silver bow
    And dreadful arrows? Even so
    I bid thee now to yield to me,
    Her maid, who overmastered thee,

The three-formed dreadful one who reigns
In heaven and the fiery plains,
But on the green earth best of all.
  Lo, now thine upraised crest let fall,
Relax thy limbs, let both thine eyes
Be closed, and bestial fantasies
Fill thy dull head till dawn of day
And we are far upon our way."

  As thus she sung, the beast seemed not to hear
Her words at first, but ever drew anear,
Circling about them, and Medea's face
Grew pale unto the lips, though still the place
Rung with the piercing sweetness of her song.   .
But slower soon he dragged his length along,
And on his limbs he tottered, till at last
All feebly by the wondering prince he passed,
And whining to Medea's feet he crept,
With eyes half closed, as though well-nigh he slept,
And there before her laid his head adown;
Who, shuddering, on his wrinkled neck and brown
Set her white foot, and whispered, "Haste, O love!
Behold the keys; haste! while the Gods above
Are friendly to us; there behold the shrine
Where thou canst see the lamp of silver shine.
Nay, draw not death upon both thee and me
With fearless kisses; fear, until the sea
Shall fold green arms about us lovingly,
And kindly Venus to thy keel be nigh."
  Then lightly from her soft side Jason stept,
While still upon the beast her foot she kept,
Still murmuring softly many an unknown word,
As when through half-shut casements the brown bird
We hearken, when the night is come in June,
And thick-leaved woods are 'twixt us and his tune.
  .   .   .   .   .   .

  Therewith he threw the last door open wide,
Whose hammered iron did the marvel hide,
And shut his dazzled eyes, and stretched his hands
Out towards the sea-born wonder of all lands,
And buried them deep in the locks of gold,
Grasping the fleece within his mighty hold.

Which when Medea saw, her gown of grey
She caught up from the ground, and drew away
Her'wearied foot from off the rugged beast,
And, while from her soft strain she never ceased,
In the dull folds she hid her silk from sight,
And then, as bending 'neath the burden bright,
Jason drew nigh, joyful, yet still afraid,
She met him, and her wide grey mantle laid
Over the fleece, whispering, "Make no delay;
He sleeps who never slept by night or day
Till now; nor will his charmèd sleep be long.
Light-foot am I, and sure thine arms are strong;
Haste, then! no word! nor turn about to gaze
At me, as he who in the shadowy ways
Turned round to see once more the twice-lost face."
   Then swiftly did they leave the dreadful place,
Turning no look behind, and reached the street,
That with familiar look and kind did greet
Those wanderers, mazed with marvels and with fear.
And so, unchallenged, did they draw anear
The long white quays, and at the street's end now
Beheld the ships' masts standing row by row
Stark black against the stars.   Then cautiously
Peered Jason forth, ere they took heart to try
The open starlit place; but nought he saw
Except the night-wind twitching the loose straw
From half-unloaded keels, and nought he heard
But the strange twittering of a caged green bird
Within an Indian ship, and from the hill
A distant baying; yea, all was so still,
Somewhat they doubted, natheless forth they passed,
And Argo's painted sides they reached at last.
   Then saw Medea men like shadows grey
Rise from the darksome decks, who took straightway
With murmured joy, from Jason's outstretched hands,
The conquered fleece, the wonder of all lands,
While with strong arms he took the royal maid,
And in their hold the precious burthen laid;
And scarce her dainty feet could touch the deck,
Ere down he leapt, and little now did reck
That loudly clanged his armor therewithal.

But, turning townward, did Medea call,—
" O noble Jason, and ye heroes strong,
To sea! to sea! nor pray ye loiter long;
For surely shall ye see the beacons flare
Ere in mid stream ye are, and running fair
On toward the sea with tide and oar and sail.
My father wakes, nor bides he to bewail
His loss and me; I see his turret gleam
As he goes toward the beacon, and down stream
Absyrtus lurks before the sandy bar
In mighty keel well-manned and dight for war."

Now swift beneath the oar-strokes Argo flew,
While the sun rose behind them, and they drew
Unto the river's mouth, nor failed to see
Absyrtus' galley waiting watchfully
Betwixt them and the white-topped turbid bar.
Therefore they gat them ready now for war,
With joyful hearts, for sharp they sniffed the sea,
And saw the great waves tumbling green and free
Outside the bar upon the way to Greece,
The rough green way to glory and sweet peace.

Then to the prow gat Jason, and the maid
Must needs be with him, though right sore afraid,
As nearing now the Colchian ship, they hung
On balanced oars; but the wild Arcas strung
His deadly bow, and clomb into the top.

Then Jason cried, " Absyrtus, will ye stop
Our peaceful keel, or let us take the sea?
Soothly, have we no will to fight with thee
If we may pass unfoughten; therefore say
What is it thou wilt have this dawn of day?"

Now on the other prow Absyrtus stood,
His visage red with eager, wrathful blood,
And in his right hand shook a mighty spear,
And said, " O seafarers, ye pass not here,
For gifts or prayers, but, if it must be so,
Over our sunken bulwarks shall ye go."

Then Jason wrathfully threw up his head,
But ere the shout came, fair Medea said,
In trembling whisper thrilling through his ear
" Haste, quick upon them! if before is fear

Behind is death." Then Jason, turning, saw
A tall ship staggering with the gusty flaw,
Just entering the long reach where they were,
And heard her horns through the fresh morning air.
     Then lifted he his hand, and with a cry
Back flew the balanced oars full orderly,
And toward the doomed ship mighty Argo passed;
Thereon Absyrtus shouted loud, and cast
His spear at Jason, that before his feet
Stuck in the deck; then out the arrows fleet   ·
Burst from the Colchians; and scarce did they spare
Medea's trembling side and bosom fair;
But Jason, roaring as the lioness
When round her helpless whelps the hunters press,
Whirled round his head his mighty brass-bound spear,
That, flying, smote the prince beneath the ear,
As Arcas' arrow sunk into his side.
Then, falling, scarce he met the rushing tide,
Ere Argo's mighty prow had thrust apart
The huddled oars, and through the fair ship's heart
Had thrust her iron beak, then the green wave
Rushed in as rush the waters through a cave
That tunnels half a sea-girt, lonely rock.
Then drawing swiftly backward from the shock,
And heeding not the cries of fear and woe,
They left the waters dealing with their foe;
Then at the following ship threw back a shout,
And seaward o'er the bar drave Argo out.
     Then joyful felt all men as now at last
From hill to green hill of the sea they passed;
But chiefly joyed Medea, as now grew
The Colchian hills behind them faint and blue,
And like a white speck showed the following ship.
There 'neath the canopy, lip pressed to lip,
They sat and told their love, till scarce he thought
What precious burden back to Greece he brought
Besides the maid, nor for his kingdom cared,
As on her beauty with wet eyes he stared,
And heard her sweet voice soft as in a dream,
Where all seems gained, and trouble dead does seem.

LESSON 67.

AMERICAN POETRY.—WILLIAM CULLEN BRYANT was born at Cummington, Mass., 1794; entered Williams College, 1810; admitted to the bar, 1815; became connected with the Evening Post, 1826, and afterwards was its editor-in-chief. Wrote *Thanatopsis* at the age of eighteen; published his first volume of poems, 1821; the first complete collection, 1832; and an additional volume, 1864. His translation of the *Iliad* appeared 1870; and of the *Odyssey*, 1871. He died in 1878.

"The poetry of Bryant is not great in amount, but it represents a great deal of work, as few men are more finished artists than he, or more patient in shaping and polishing their productions. No piece of verse ever left his hands till it had received the last touch demanded by the most correct judgment and the most fastidious taste. Thus the style of his poetry is always admirable. Nowhere can one find in what he has written a careless or slovenly expression, an awkward phrase, or an ill-chosen word. He never puts in an epithet to fill out a line, and never uses one which could be improved by substituting another.

The range within which he moves is not wide. He has not written narrative or dramatic poems; he has not painted poetical portraits; he has not aspired to the honors of satire, of wit, or of humor; he has made no contributions to the poetry of passion. His poems may be divided into two great classes—those which express the moral aspect of humanity, and those which interpret the language of Nature; though it may be added that in not a few of his productions these two elements are combined.

Those of the former class are not so remarkable for originality of treatment as for the beauty and truth with which they express the reflections of the general mind and the emotions of the general heart. In these poems we see our own experience returned to us, touched with the lights and colored with the hues of the most exquisite poetry.

In his study of Nature he combines the faculty and the vision, the eye of the naturalist and the imagination of the poet. No man observes the outward shows of earth and sky more accurately; no man feels them more vividly; no man describes them more beautifully."—*G. S. Hillard.*

Bryant's *The Snow Shower.*

Stand here by my side and turn, I pray,
　　On the lake below thy gentle eyes;
The clouds hang over it, heavy and gray,
　　And dark and silent the water lies;
And out of that frozen mist the snow
In wavering flakes begins to flow;
　　　　Flake after flake
They sink in the dark and silent lake.

See how in a living swarm they come
　　From the chambers beyond that misty veil;
Some hover awhile in air, and some
　　Rush prone from the sky like summer hail.
All, dropping swiftly or settling slow,
Meet, and are still in the depths below;
　　　　Flake after flake
Dissolved in the dark and silent lake.

Here delicate snow-stars, out of the cloud,
　　Come floating downward in airy play,
Like spangles dropped from the glistening crowd
　　That whiten by night the Milky Way;
There broader and burlier masses fall;
The sullen water buries them all—
　　　　Flake after flake—
All drowned in the dark and silent lake.

And some, as on tender wings they glide
　　From their chilly birth-cloud, dim and gray,
Are joined in their fall, and, side by side,
　　Come clinging along their unsteady way;
As friend with friend, or husband with wife
Makes hand in hand the passage of life;
　　　　Each mated flake
Soon sinks in the dark and silent lake.

Lo! while we are gazing, in swifter haste
　　Stream down the snows, till the air is white,
As, myriads by myriads madly chased,
　　They fling themselves from their shadowy height.

The fair, frail creatures of middle sky,
What speed they make, with their grave so nigh,
    Flake after flake,
To lie in the dark and silent lake!

I see in thy gentle eyes a tear;
   They turn to me in sorrowful thought;
Thou thinkest of friends, the good and dear,
   Who were for a time and now are not;
Like these fair children of cloud and frost
That glisten a moment and then are lost,
    Flake after flake—
All lost in the dark and silent lake.

Yet look again, for the clouds divide;
   A gleam of blue on the water lies;
And, far away, on the mountain-side,
   A sunbeam falls from the opening skies.
But the hurrying host that flew between
The cloud and the water no more is seen;
    Flake after flake
At rest in the dark and silent lake.

June.

I gazed upon the glorious sky
   And the green mountains round;
And thought that, when I came to lie
   Within the silent ground,
'Twere pleasant, that in flowery June,
When brooks send up a cheerful tune,
   And groves a joyous sound,
The sexton's hand, my grave to make,
The rich, green mountain turf should break.

A cell within the frozen mould,
   A coffin borne through sleet,
And icy clouds above it rolled,
   While fierce the tempests beat—
Away! I will not think of these—
Blue be the sky, and soft the breeze,
   Earth green beneath the feet,
And be the damp mould gently pressed
Into my narrow place of rest.

There, through the long, long summer hours,
  The golden light should lie,
And thick young herbs and groups of flowers
  Stand in their beauty by.
The oriole should build and tell
His love-tale close beside my cell;
  The idle butterfly
Should rest him there, and there be heard
The housewife bee and humming-bird.

And what if cheerful shouts at noon
  Come, from the village sent,
Or songs of maids, beneath the moon
  With fairy laughter blent?
And what if, in the evening light,
Betrothèd lovers walk in sight
  Of my low monument?
I would the lovely scene around
Might know no sadder sight nor sound.

I know, I know I should not see
  The season's glorious show,
Nor would its brightness shine for me,
  Nor its wild music flow;
But if, around my place of sleep,
The friends I love should come to weep,
  They might not haste to go.
Soft airs and song and light and bloom
Should keep them lingering by my tomb.

These to their softened hearts should bear
  The thought of what has been,
And speak of one who cannot share
  The gladness of the scene;
Whose part, in all the pomp that fills
The circuit of the summer hills,
  Is—that his grave is green;
And deeply would their hearts rejoice
To hear again his living voice.

Robert of Lincoln.

Merrily swinging on briar and weed,
  Near to the nest of his little dame,
Over the mountain-side or mead,
  Robert of Lincoln is telling his name:
      Bob-o'-link, bob-o'-link,
      Spink, spank, spink;
Snug and safe is that nest of ours,
Hidden among the summer flowers.
                Chee, chee, chee.

Robert of Lincoln is gaily drest,
  Wearing a bright black wedding-coat;
White are his shoulders and white his crest,
  Hear him call in his merry note:
      Bob-o'-link, bob-o'-link,
      Spink, spank, spink;
Look, what a nice new coat is mine,
Sure there was never a bird so fine.
                Chee, chee, chee.

Robert of Lincoln's Quaker wife,
  Pretty and quiet, with plain brown wings,
Passing at home a patient life,
  Broods in the grass while her husband sings:
      Bob-o'-link, bob-o'-link,
      Spink, spank, spink;
Brood, kind creature; you need not fear
Thieves and robbers while I am here.
                Chee, chee, chee.

Modest and shy as a nun is she;
  One weak chirp is her only note.
Braggart and prince of braggarts is he,
  Pouring boasts from his little throat:
      Bob-o'-link, bob-o'-link,
      Spink, spank, spink;
Never was I afraid of man;
Catch me, cowardly knaves, if you can.
                Chee, chee, chee.

Six white eggs on a bed of hay,
  Flecked with purple, a pretty sight!
There as the mother sits all day,
  Robert is singing with all his might:
    Bob-o'-link, bob-o'-link,
    Spink, spank, spink;
Nice, good wife, that never goes out,
Keeping house while I frolic about.
                    Chee, chee, chee.

Soon as the little ones chip the shell,
  Six wide mouths are open for food;
Robert of Lincoln bestirs him well,
  Gathering seeds for the hungry brood.
    Bob-o'-link, bob-o'-link,
    Spink, spank, spink;
This new life is likely to be
Hard for a gay young fellow like me.
                    Chee, chee, chee.

Robert of Lincoln at length is made
  Sober with work, and silent with care;
Off is his holiday garment laid,
  Half forgotten that merry air,
    Bob-o'-link, bob-o'-link,
    Spink, spank, spink;
Nobody knows but my mate and I
Where our nest and our nestlings lie.
                    Chee, chee, chee.

Summer wanes; the children are grown;
  Fun and frolic no more he knows;
Robert of Lincoln 's a humdrum crone;
  Off he flies, and we sing as he goes:
    Bob-o'-link, bob-o'-link,
    Spink, spank, spink;
When you can pipe that merry old strain,
Robert of Lincoln, come back again.
                    Chee, chee, chee.

Translation from the *Odyssey*.

They took their rest.   But, when the child of dawn,
Aurora, rosy-fingered, looked abroad,
Ulysses put his vest and mantle on;
The nymph, too, in a robe of silver white,
Ample and delicate and beautiful,
Arrayed herself, and round about her loins
Wound a fair golden girdle, drew a veil
Over her head, and planned to send away
Magnanimous Ulysses.   She bestowed
A heavy axe of steel and double-edged,
Well fitted to the hand, the handle wrought
Of olive wood, firm set and beautiful.
A polished adze she gave him next, and led
The way to a far corner of the isle
Where lofty trees, alders and poplars, stood,
And firs that reached the clouds, sapless and dry
Long since, and fitter thus to ride the waves.
Then, having shown where grew the tallest trees,
Calypso, glorious goddess, sought her home.
    Trees then he felled, and soon the task was done.
Twenty in all he brought to earth, and squared
Their trunks with the sharp steel, and carefully
He smoothed their sides, and wrought them by a line.
Calypso, gracious goddess, having brought
Wimbles, he bored the beams, and, fitting them
Together, made them fast with nails and clamps.
As when some builder, skilful in his art,
Frames, for a ship of burden, the broad keel,
Such ample breadth Ulysses gave the raft.
Upon the massy beams he reared a deck,
And floored it with long planks from end to end.
On this a mast he raised, and to the mast
Fitted a yard; he shaped a rudder neat
To guide the raft along her course, and round
With woven work of willow boughs he fenced
Her sides against the dashings of the sea.
Calypso, gracious goddess, brought him store
Of canvas, which he fitly shaped to sails,
And, rigging her with cords and ropes and stays,

Heaved her with levers into the great deep.
'Twas the fourth day; his labors now were done,
And, on the fifth, the goddess from her isle
Dismissed him, newly from the bath, arrayed
In garments given by her, that shed perfumes.
A skin of dark red wine she put on board,
A larger one of water, and for food
A basket, stored with viands such as please
The appetite. A friendly wind and soft
She sent before. The great Ulysses spread
His canvas joyfully to catch the breeze,
And sat and guided with nice care the helm,
Gazing with fixed eye on the Pleiades,
Boötes setting late, and the Great Bear,
By others called the Wain, which, wheeling round,
Looks ever toward Orion, and alone
Dips not into the waters of the deep.
For so Calypso, glorious goddess, bade
That, on his ocean journey, he should keep
That constellation ever on his left.
Now seventeen days were in the voyage past,
And on the eighteenth shadowy heights appeared,
The nearest point of the Pheacian land,
Lying on the dark ocean like a shield.

To a Waterfowl.

Whither, midst falling dew,
While glow the heavens with the last steps of day,
Far, through their rosy depths, dost thou pursue
    Thy solitary way?

Vainly the fowler's eye
Might mark thy distant flight to do thee wrong,
As, darkly painted on the crimson sky,
    Thy figure floats along.

Seek'st thou the plashy brink
Of weedy lake or marge of river wide
Or where the rocking billows rise and sink
    On the chafed ocean side?

There is a Power whose care
Teaches thy way along that pathless coast,—
The desert and illimitable air,—
 Lone wandering, but not lost.

All day thy wings have fanned,
At that far height, the cold, thin atmosphere,
Yet stoop not, weary, to the welcome land,
 Though the dark night is near.

And soon that toil shall end;
Soon shalt thou find a summer home, and rest,
And scream among thy fellows; reeds shall bend
 Soon o'er thy sheltered nest.

Thou'rt gone, the abyss of heaven
Hath swallowed up thy form; yet, on my heart
Deeply hath sunk the lesson thou hast given,
 And shall not soon depart.

He who, from zone to zone,
Guides through the boundless sky thy certain flight
In the long way that I must tread alone
 Will lead my steps aright.

The Future Life.

How shall I know thee in the sphere which keeps
 The disembodied spirits of the dead,
When all of thee that time could wither sleeps,
 And perishes among the dust we tread?

For I shall feel the sting of ceaseless pain
 If there I meet thy gentle presence not;
Nor hear the voice I love, nor read again
 In thy serenest eyes the tender thought.

Will not thy own meek heart demand me there?
 That heart whose fondest throbs to me were given
My name on earth was ever in thy prayer,
 Shall it be banished from thy tongue in heaven?

In meadows fanned by heaven's life-breathing wind,
  In the resplendence of that glorious sphere,
And larger movements of the unfettered mind,
  Wilt thou forget the love that joined us here?

The love that lived through all the stormy past,
  And meekly with my harsher nature bore,
And deeper grew, and tenderer to the last,
  Shall it expire with life and be no more?

A happier lot than mine and larger light
  Await thee there; for thou hast bowed thy will
In cheerful homage to the rule of right,
  And lovest all, and renderest good for ill.

For me—the sordid cares in which I dwell
  Shrink and consume my heart, as heat the scroll;
And wrath has left its scar—that fire of hell
  Has left its frightful scar upon my soul.

Yet, though thou wear'st the glory of the sky,
  Wilt thou not keep the same beloved name,
The same fair thoughtful brow, and gentle eye,
  Lovelier in heaven's sweet climate, yet the same?

Shalt thou not teach me, in that calmer home,
  The wisdom that I learned so ill in this—
The wisdom which is love—till I become
  Thy fit companion in that land of bliss?

LESSON 68.

AMERICAN POETRY.—HENRY WADSWORTH LONGFELLOW was born at Portland, Me., in 1807; was graduated at Bowdoin College in 1825; and, after studying in France, Spain, Italy, and Germany, entered, in 1828, upon the professorship of modern languages at Bowdoin, to which he had been elected in 1826. In 1835 he was elected to the chair of modern languages and literature at Harvard College. In 1836 he entered upon his new professorship, occupying Cragie House, Washington's headquarters, which he afterwards bought and made his home. Published *Hyperion* and *Voices in the Night* in 1839; *The Spanish Student,* a drama, in 1843; *Evangeline* in 1847; *Kavanagh,* a tale, in 1849; *The Song of Hiawatha* in 1855; *The Courtship of Miles Standish* in 1858; *The Tales of a Wayside Inn* (of which *The Birds of Killingworth* is one) in 1863; a *Translation of Dante* in 1867–70; and other poems during these years and since. He resigned his Chair at Harvard in 1854, and in 1874 received a large complimentary vote for the lord rectorship of the University of Edinburgh. He died March 24, 1882.

"In Longfellow's latest books we are aware of the same magic that charmed us of yore. The poet keeps throughout the grace and subtile power of the past; he keeps all that was ever his own, even to the love of profuse simile, and the quaint doubt of his reader implied by the elaborated meaning; and he loses only the tints and flavors not thoroughly assimilated or not native in him. Throughout is the same habit of recondite and scholarly allusion, the same quick sympathy with the beautiful in simple and common things, the same universality, the same tenderness for country and for home. Over all presides individuality superior to accidents of resemblance, and distinguishing each poem with traits unmistakably and only the author's; and the equality in the long procession of his beautiful thoughts never wearies, but is like that of some fine bass-relief in which the varying allegory reveals one manner and many inspirations.

Together with this peculiar artistic quality in the poems of Mr. Longfellow is a spiritual maturity, which the reader cannot fail to notice. As there never has been anything unripe or decrepit in this master's art, so there never has been anything crude or faltering in his devotion to greatness and purity in life. His work is not the record of a career beginning in generous and impossible dreams, and ending in sordid doubt and pitiful despite; nor the history of a soul born to spiritual poverty, and working at last into tardy hopes and sympathies which scarcely suffice to discharge the errors of the past. His books tell of a soul clothed at once in human affections and divine aspirations, of a poetic nature filled with conscious and instinctive reverence for the supreme office of poetry in the world. They form, indeed, so perfect a biography of the author that, if one knew nothing of his literary life, here one might read more than could otherwise be told of its usefulness and beauty.

It is, of course, not the poet's merely literary life that is recorded in his books. He who touches the hearts of others must write from his own, and doubtless the songs of a true poet preserve the memory, not only of all the events but of all the moods of his life. But the hospitality that invites the whole world home is exquisitely proud and shy, and its house is built like those old palaces in which a secret gallery was made for the musicians, and gay or plaintive music from an invisible source delighted the banqueting guests."—*N. A. Review.*

Longfellow's *The Birds of Killingworth.*

It was the season when, through all the land,
    The merle and mavis build, and, building, sing
Those lovely lyrics, written by His hand
    Whom Saxon Cædmon calls the Blithe-heart King;
When on the boughs the purple buds expand,
    The banners of the vanguard of the Spring,
And rivulets, rejoicing, rush and leap
And wave their fluttering signals from the steep.

The robin and the blue-bird, piping loud,
    Filled all the blossoming orchards with their glee;
The sparrows chirped as if they still were proud
    Their race in Holy Writ should mentioned be;
And hungry crows, assembled in a crowd,
    Clamored their piteous prayer incessantly,
Knowing who hears the ravens cry, and said,
"Give us, O Lord, this day our daily bread!"

Across the Sound the birds of passage sailed,
    Speaking some unknown language strange and sweet
Of tropic isle remote, and, passing, hailed
    The village with the cheers of all their fleet;
Or, quarrelling together, laughed and railed
    Like foreign sailors landed in the street
Of seaport town, and with outlandish noise
Of oaths and gibberish frightening girls and boys.

Thus came the jocund Spring in Killingworth,
    In fabulous days, some hundred years ago;
And thrifty farmers, as they tilled the earth,
    Heard with alarm the cawing of the crow,

That mingled with the universal mirth,
  Cassandra-like, prognosticating woe;
They shook their heads, and doomed with dreadful words
To swift destruction the whole race of birds.

And a town-meeting was convened straightway
  To set a price upon the guilty heads
Of these marauders, who, in lieu of pay,
  Levied blackmail upon the garden beds
And corn-fields, and beheld without dismay
  The awful scarecrow, with his fluttering shreds,
The skeleton that waited at their feast,
Whereby their sinful pleasure was increased.

Then from his house, a temple painted white,
  With fluted columns, and a roof of red,
The Squire came forth, august and splendid sight!
  Slowly descending, with majestic tread,
Three flights of steps, nor looking left nor right,
  Down the long street he walked, as one who said,
" A town that boasts inhabitants like me
Can have no lack of good society!"

From the Academy, whose belfry crowned
  The hill of Science with its vane of brass,
Came the Preceptor, gazing idly round
  Now at the clouds and now at the green grass,
And all absorbed in reveries profound
  Of fair Almira in the upper class,
Who was, as in a sonnet he had said,
As pure as water and as good as bread.

And next the Deacon issued from his door,
  In his voluminous neck-cloth white as snow;
A suit of sable bombazine he wore;
  His form was ponderous, and his step was slow;
There never was so wise a man before;
  He seemed the incarnate "Well, I told you so!"
And to perpetuate his great renown
There was a street named after him in town.

These came together in the new town-hall,
  With sundry farmers from the region round.
The Squire presided, dignified and tall,
  His air impressive, and his reasoning sound;
Ill fared it with the birds, both great and small,
  Hardly a friend in all that crowd they found,
But enemies enough, who every one
Charged them with all the crimes beneath the sun.

When they had ended, from his place apart
  Rose the Preceptor to redress the wrong,
And, trembling like a steed before the start,
  Looked round bewildered on the expectant throng;
Then thought of fair Almira, and took heart
  To speak out what was in him, clear and strong,
Alike regardless of their smile or frown,   '
And quite determined not to be laughed down.

"Plato, anticipating the Reviewers,
  From his Republic banished without pity
The Poets; in this little town of yours
  You put to death, by means of a Committee,
The ballad-singers and the Troubadours,
  The street-musicians of the heavenly city,
The birds, who make sweet music for us all
In our dark hours, as David did for Saul.

The thrush that carols at the dawn of day
  From the green steeples of the piny wood;
The oriole in the elm; the noisy jay,
  Jargoning like a foreigner at his food;
The blue-bird balanced on some topmost spray,
  Flooding with melody the neighborhood;
Linnet and meadow-lark and all the throng
That dwell in nests and have the gift of song.

You slay them all! and wherefore? for the gain
  Of a scant handful, more or less, of wheat
Or rye or barley or some other grain,
  Scratched up at random by industrious feet,

Searching for worm or weevil after rain!
  Or a few cherries that are not so sweet
As are the songs these uninvited guests
Sing at their feast with comfortable breasts.

Do you ne'er think what wondrous beings these?
  Do you ne'er think who made them, and who taught
The dialect they speak, where melodies
  Alone are the interpreters of thought?
Whose household words are songs in many keys,
  Sweeter than instrument of man e'er caught.
Whose habitations in the tree-tops even
Are half-way houses on the road to heaven.

Think, every morning when the sun peeps through
  The dim, leaf-latticed windows of the grove,
How jubilant the happy birds renew
  Their old, melodious madrigals of love!
And when you think of this, remember, too,
  'Tis always morning somewhere, and above
The awakening continents, from shore to shore,
Somewhere the birds are singing evermore.

Think of your woods and orchards without birds!
  Of empty nests that cling to boughs and beams,
As in an idiot's brain remembered words
  Hang empty 'mid the cobwebs of his dreams!
Will bleat of flocks or bellowing of herds
  Make up for the lost music, when your teams
Drag home the stingy harvest, and no more
The feathered gleaners follow to your door?

What! would you rather see the incessant stir
  Of insects in the windrows of the hay,
And hear the locust and the grasshopper
  Their melancholy hurdy-gurdies play?
Is this more pleasant to you than the whirr
  Of meadow-lark, and its sweet roundelay,
Or twitter of little field-fares, as you take
Your nooning in the shade of bush and brake?

You call them thieves and pillagers; but know
   They are the winged wardens of your farms,
Who from the cornfields drive the insidious foe,
   And from your harvests keep a hundred harms;
Even the blackest of them all, the crow,
   Renders good service as your man-at-arms,
Crushing the beetle in his coat of mail,
And crying havoc on the slug and snail.

How can I teach your children gentleness
   And mercy to the weak and reverence
For Life, which, in its weakness or excess,
   Is still a gleam of God's omnipotence,
Or Death, which, seeming darkness, is no less
   The self-same light, although averted hence,
When, by your laws, your actions, and your speech,
You contradict the very things I teach?"

With this he closed; and through the audience went
   A murmur, like the rustle of dead leaves;
The farmers laughed and nodded, and some bent
   Their yellow heads together like their sheaves;
Men have no faith in fine-spun sentiment
   Who put their trust in bullocks and in beeves.
The birds were doomed; and, as the record shows,
A bounty offered for the heads of crows.

There was another audience out of reach,
   Who had no voice nor vote in making laws,
But in the papers read his little speech,
   And crowned his modest temples with applause.
They made him conscious, each one more than each,
   He still was victor, vanquished in their cause.
Sweetest of all the applause he won from thee,
O fair Almira at the Academy!

And so the dreadful massacre began;
   O'er fields and orchards and o'er woodland crests,
The ceaseless fusillade of terror ran.
   Dead fell the birds, with blood-stains on their breasts,

Or wounded crept away from sight of man,
　While the young died of famine in their nests;
A slaughter to be told in groans, not words,
The very St. Bartholomew of Birds!

The summer came, and all the birds were dead;
　The days were like hot coals; the very ground
Was burned to ashes; in the orchards fed
　Myriads of caterpillars, and around
The cultivated fields and garden beds
　Hosts of devouring insects crawled, and found
No foe to check their march till they had made
The land a desert, without leaf or shade.

Devoured by worms, like Herod, was the town,
　Because, like Herod, it had ruthlessly
Slaughtered the Innocents.　From the trees spun down
　The canker-worms upon the passers-by,
Upon each woman's bonnet, shawl, and gown,
　Who shook them off with just a little cry;
They were the terror of each favorite walk,
The endless theme of all the village talk.

The farmers grew impatient, but a few
　Confessed their error, and would not complain,
For, after all, the best thing one can do
　When it is raining, is to let it rain.
Then they repealed the law, although they knew
　It would not call the dead to life again;
As school-boys, finding their mistake too late,
Draw a wet sponge across the accusing slate.

That year in Killingworth the Autumn came
　Without the light of his majestic look,
The wonder of the falling tongues of flame,
　The illumined pages of his Doom's-Day book.
A few lost leaves blushed crimson with their shame,
　And drowned themselves despairing in the brook,
While the wild wind went moaning everywhere,
Lamenting the dead children of the air.

But the next spring a stranger sight was seen,
  A sight that never yet by bard was sung,
As great a wonder as it would have been
  If some dumb animal had found a tongue!
A wagon, overarched with evergreen,
  Upon whose boughs were wicker cages hung,
All full of singing-birds, came down the street,
Filling the air with music wild and sweet.

From all the country round these birds were brought,
  By order of the town, with anxious quest,
And, loosened from their wicker prisons, sought
  In woods and fields the places they loved best,
Singing loud canticles, which many thought
  Were satires to the authorities addressed,
While others, listening in green lanes, averred
Such lovely music never had been heard!

But blither still and louder carolled they
  Upon the morrow, for they seemed to know
It was the fair Almira's wedding-day,
  And everywhere, around, above, below,
When the Preceptor bore his bride away,
  Their songs burst forth in joyous overflow,
And a new heaven bent over a new earth
Amid the sunny farms of Killingworth.

LESSON 69.

AMERICAN POETRY.—JOHN GREENLEAF WHITTIER was born at Haverhill, Mass., 1807. Spent two years at the Haverhill Academy; became Editor of the *American Manufacturer*, 1829; of the *New England Weekly Review*, 1830; of the *Pennsylvania Freeman*, 1838; and Corresponding Editor of the *National Era*, 1847. Has lived for many years in literary retirement. Several editions of his poems have been printed, among the best of which is the Centennial Edition of 1876. His prose writings are numerous.

JAMES RUSSELL LOWELL was born at Cambridge, Mass.,

1819; was graduated at Harvard College, 1838, and at Harvard Law School, 1840; published a small volume of poems, *A Year's Life*, 1841; another volume, 1844; and in 1848 another, containing *The Vision of Sir Launfal, A Fable for Critics*, and *The Biglow Papers*, first series. He succeeded Longfellow as Professor of modern languages and literature at Harvard, 1855; was editor of the *Atlantic Monthly*, 1857–62; and of the *North American Review*, 1863–72. Published a new series of *Biglow Papers*, 1867; and two volumes of essays, *My Study Windows* and *Among My Books*, 1870. A second series of the latter followed soon after. In 1880 Lowell became U. S. Minister to England.

" The leading articles in Mr. Lowell's volumes, notably those on Dryden, Shakespeare, Lessing, Wordsworth, and Milton, exhibit, with some difference of degree, perhaps, the same conscientious thoroughness, the same minutest accuracy of observation, the same elegance and force of language, the same mastery of æsthetic principles, and, what is equally essential to all good criticism, a healthful moral tone such as is born only of sound principles and genuine conviction. Instead of the one-sidedness of the partisan and special pleader, one finds in all the fairness and candor which spring naturally from largeness of mind and a simple love of truth It is worthy of special notice, too, that in estimating the merit of literary work, Mr. Lowell, although himself a university professor, finds his standard and test of excellence rather in direct appeal to the consciousness, the intuitions, and the common judgments and sensibilities of men, than in any conventional canons or dicta of the schools. His criticisms carry conviction to the mind of the average reader—who knows little and cares less about the prescribed rules of composition—not because of their recognized accord with received authorities, but because they command the sanction of his reason and his heart."—*Ray Palmer*.

" The poems of Mr. Lowell have a peculiar and specific value, derived partly from their intrinsic merits, and partly from the time and circumstances of their composition. He began to write at a time when the reformatory agitations of New England had developed among the refined and enlightened classes an unwonted activity and independence of thought. Theories of metaphysics and religion, previously unknown on this side of the Atlantic, and a more fervent appreciation of the scope of that sentiment of 'humanity,' underlying and prompting the recent movements of social amelioration, had initiated a convulsion with which our political and religious world still shakes from side to side. Of course, literature could not withstand the contagion, and of all our young poets no one more distinctly received and embodied the new spirit of the age than Mr. Lowell. This, we think, furnishes the key-note and explanation of his poems. An acquaintance with the contemporary events which suggested or affected their composition is as essential to the full enjoyment of them as a knowledge of the life and times of Wordsworth is to the full understanding of the philosophy of ' The Excursion,' which grew out of them; and the want of this among ordinary readers may account for the limited popularity of a large portion of the more elaborate efforts of the New England poet. This peculiarity it is which has limited the circle of Mr. Lowell's readers—in some degree he has been obliged to create the taste he would gratify.

In what other modern poet shall we find a more manly and robust mould of imagination and thought, a more subtile insight, a more intense sympathy with nature in all her forms, or a soul more alive to those moods and impressions which a close and loving intimacy with nature and humanity can alone create? What poet has expressed with more homely beauty and directness those sweet and precious, but almost voiceless, sentiments and emotions which have their hiding-place in the innermost chambers of every human heart?"—*N. A. Review.*

Lowell's *The Changeling.**

I had a little daughter,
  And she was given to me
To lead me gently backward
  To the Heavenly Father's knee,
That I, by the force of nature,
  Might in some dim wise divine
The depth of his infinite patience
  To this wayward soul of mine.

I know not how others saw her,
  But to me she was wholly fair,
And the light of the heaven she came from
  Still lingered and gleamed in her hair;

---

* For illustrations of Lowell's prose, see his criticisms on various authors throughout this work.

For it was as wavy and golden,
  And as many changes took,
As the shadows of sun-gilt ripples
  On the yellow bed of a brook.

.To what can I liken her smiling
  Upon me, her kneeling lover?
How it leaped from her lips to her eyelids,
  And dimpled her wholly over,
Till her outstretched hands smiled also,
  And I almost seemed to see
The very heart of her mother
  Sending sun through her veins to me!

She had been with us scarce a twelvemonth,
  And it hardly seemed a day,
When a troop of wandering angels
  Stole my little daughter away;
Or perhaps those heavenly Zincali
  But loosed the hampering strings,
And, when they had opened her cage-door,
  My little bird used her wings.

But they left in her stead a changeling,
  A little angel child,
That seems like her bud in full blossom,
  And smiles as she never smiled.
When I wake in the morning, I see it
  Where she always used to lie,
And I feel as weak as a violet
  ·Alone 'neath the awful sky;

As weak, yet as trustful also;
  For the whole year long I see
All the wonders of faithful nature
  Still worked for the love of me.
Winds wander, and dews drip earthward,
  Rain falls, suns rise and set,
Earth whirls, and all but to prosper
  A poor little violet.

This child is not mine as the first was,
    I cannot sing it to rest,
I cannot lift it up fatherly
    And bliss it upon my breast;
Yet it lies in my little one's cradle,
    And it sits in my little one's chair,
And the light of the heaven she's gone to
    Transfigures its golden hair.

The Courtin'.*

God makes sech nights, all white an' still
    Fur'z you can look or listen,
Moonshine an' snow on field an' hill,
    All silence an' all glisten.

Zekle crep' up quite unbeknown
    An' peeked in thru' the winder,
An' there sot Huldy all alone,
    'Ith no one nigh to hender.

A fireplace filled the room's one side
    With half a cord o' wood in—
There warn't no stoves (tell comfort died)
    To bake ye to a puddin'.

The wa'nut logs shot sparkles out
    Towards the pootiest, bless her,
An' leetle flames danced all about
    The chiny on the dresser.

Agin the chimbley crook-necks hung,
    An' in amongst 'em rusted
The ole queen's-arm thet gran'ther Young
    Fetched back from Concord, busted.

The very room, coz she was in,
    Seemed warm from floor to ceilin',
An' she looked full ez rosy agin
    Ez the apples she was peelin'.

---

* This poem and the two series of *The Biglow Papers* are written in the Yankee
dialect.

'T was kin' o' kingdom-come to look
  On sech a blessed cretur,
A dogrose blushin' to a brook
  Ain't modester nor sweeter.

He was six foot o' man A 1,
  Clean grit an' human natur';
None couldn't quicker pitch a ton
  Nor dror a furrer straighter.

He'd sparked it with full twenty gals,
  He'd squired 'em, danced 'em, druv 'em,
Fust this one, an' then thet, by spells—
  All is, he couldn't love 'em.

But long o' her his veins 'ould run
  All crinkly like curled maple,
The side she breshed felt full o' sun
  Ez a south slope in Ap'il.

She thought no v'ice hed sech a swing
  Ez hisn in the choir;
My! when he made Ole Hunderd ring,
  She *knowed* the Lord was nigher.

An' she'd blush scarlit, right in prayer,
  When her new meetin'-bunnet
Felt somehow thru' its crown a pair
  O' blue eyes sot upon it.

Thet night, I tell ye, she looked *some!*
  She seemed to 've got a new soul,
For she felt sartin-sure he'd come,
  Down to her very shoe-sole.

She heered a foot, an' knowed it tu,
  A-raspin' on the scraper.—
All ways to once her feelins flew
  Like sparks in burnt-up paper.

He kin' o' l'itered on the mat,
  Some doubtfle o' the sekle,
His heart kep' goin' p.ty-pat,
  But hern went pity Zekle.

An' yit she giu her cheer a jerk
   Ez though she wished him furder,
An' on her apples kep' to work,
   Parin' away like murder.

" You wan't to see my Pa, I s'pose?"
   " Wal . . . . no . . . I come dasignin' "—
" To see my Ma?   She's sprinklin' clo'es
   Agin to-morrer's i'nin'."

To say why gals acts so or so,
   Or don't, 'ould be presumin';
Mebby to mean *yes* an' say *no*
   Comes natoral to women.

He stood a spell on one foot fust,
   Then stood a spell on t'other,
An' ou which one he felt the wust
   He couldn't ha' told ye nuther.

Says he, " I'd better call agin;"
   Says she, " Think likely, Mister;"
Thet last word pricked him like a pin,
   An' . . . . wal, he up an' kist her.

When ma bimeby upon 'em slips,
   Huldy sot pale ez ashes,
All kin' o' smily roun' the lips
   An' teary roun' the lashes.

For she was jis' the quiet kind
   Whose natures never vary,
Like streams that keep a summer mind
   Snowhid in Jenooary.

The blood clost roun' her heart felt glued
   Too tight for all expressin',
Tell mother see how metters stood,
   An' gin 'em both her blessin'.

Then her red come back like the tide
   Down to the Bay o' Fundy,
An' all I know is, they was cried
   In meetin' come nex' Sunday.

Vision of Sir Launfal.*

Prelude to Part Second.

Down swept the chill wind from the mountain peak,
　From the snow five thousand summers old;
On open wold and hill-top bleak
　It had gathered all the cold,
And whirled it like sleet on the wanderer's cheek;
It carried a shiver everywhere
From the unleafed boughs and pastures bare.
The little brook heard it and built a roof
'Neath which he could house him, winter-proof;
All night by the white stars' frosty gleams
He groined his arches and matched his beams;
Slender and clear were his crystal spars
As the lashes of light that trim the stars;
He sculptured every summer delight
In his halls and chambers out of sight.
Sometimes his tinkling waters slipt
Down through a frost-leaved forest-crypt,
Long, sparkling aisles of steel-stemmed trees
Bending to counterfeit a breeze;
Sometimes the roof no fretwork knew
But silvery mosses that downward grew;
Sometimes it was carved in sharp relief
With quaint arabesques of ice-fern leaf;

---

* The story ran that the Holy Grail, the Cup out of which Jesus partook of the last supper with his disciples, was brought into England by Joseph of Arimathea, and remained many years in the keeping of his descendants. It was incumbent on those having charge of it to be chaste in thought, word, and deed. One of these violating this condition, the Holy Grail disappeared. To go in search of it was said to have been a favorite enterprise with the knights of the mythic Arthur's Court.

In this poem of Lowell's, Sir Launfal is represented as having a vision as he lay asleep on the rushes through the night before he is to start out in search of the Holy Cup. The first of the vision, in which the knight sees himself, young, strong, haughty, and splendidly arrayed, set forth in the spring-time is described in Part First of the poem.

The last of the vision in which the knight sees himself, old, bent, in rags, and humbled in spirit, return in the winter-time, unsuccessful in his search, is described in Part Second, which we quote. This Part is preceded by a Prelude descriptive of winter, as Part First is by a Prelude descriptive of spring.

Sometimes it was simply smooth and clear
For the gladness of heaven to shine through, and here
He had caught the nodding bulrush-tops
And hung them thickly with diamond drops,
That crystalled the beams of moon and sun,
And made a star of every one.
No mortal builder's most rare device
Could match this winter-palace of ice;
'Twas as if every image that mirrored lay
In his depths serene through the summer day,
Each fleeting shadow of earth and sky,
　Lest the happy model should be lost,
Had been mimicked in fairy masonry
　By the elfin builders of the frost.

Within the hall are song and laughter,
　The cheeks of Christmas glow red and jolly,
And sprouting is every corbel and rafter
　With the lightsome green of ivy and holly;
Through the deep gulf of the chimney wide
Wallows the Yule-log's roaring tide;
The broad flame-pennons droop and flap
　And belly and tug as a flag in the wind;
Like a locust shrills the imprisoned sap,
　Hunted to death in its galleries blind;
And swift little troops of silent sparks,
　Now pausing, now scattering away as in fear,
Go threading the soot-forest's tangled darks
　Like herds of startled deer.

But the wind without was eager and sharp,
Of Sir Launfal's gray hair it makes a harp,
　　And rattles and wrings
　　The icy strings,
　Singing, in dreary monotone,
　A Christmas carol of its own,
　Whose burden still, as he might guess,
　Was—"Shelterless, shelterless, shelterless!"

The voice of the seneschal flared like a torch
As he shouted the wanderer away from the porch,

And he sat in the gateway and saw all night
　The great hall-fire, so cheery and bold,
　Through the window-slits of the castle old,
Build out its piers of ruddy light
　Against the drift of the cold.

Part Second.

There was never a leaf on bush or tree,
The bare boughs rattled shudderingly;
The river was dumb and could not speak,
　For the weaver Winter its shroud had spun;
A single crow on the tree-top bleak
　From his shining feathers shed off the cold sun;
Again it was morning, but shrunk and cold,
As if her veins were sapless and old,
And she rose up decrepitly
For a last dim look at earth and sea.

Sir Launfal turned from his own hard gate,
For another heir in his earldom sate;
An old, bent man, worn out and frail,
He came back from seeking the Holy Grail;
Little he recked of his earldom's loss,
No more on his surcoat was blazoned the cross,
But deep in his soul the sign he wore,
The badge of the suffering and the poor.

Sir Launfal's raiment, thin and spare,
Was idle mail 'gainst the barbèd air,
For it was just at the Christmas time;
So he mused, as he sat, of a sunnier clime,
And sought for a shelter from cold and snow
In the light and warmth of long ago:
He sees the snake-like caravan crawl
O'er the edge of the desert, black and small,
Then nearer and nearer, till, one by one,
He can count the camels in the sun,
As over the red-hot sands they pass
To where, in its slender necklace of grass,
The little spring laughed and leapt in the shade,
And with its own self like an infant played,
And waved its signal of palms.

"For Christ's sweet sake, I beg an alms;"—
The happy camels may reach the spring,
But Sir Launfal sees only the grewsome thing,
Tht leper, lank as the rain-blanched bone,
That cowers beside him, a thing as lone
And white as the ice-isles of Northern seas
In the desolate horror of his disease.

And Sir Launfal said, "I behold in thee
An image of Him who died on the tree;
Thou also hast had thy crown of thorns—
Thou also hast had the world's buffets and scorns—
And to thy life were not denied
The wounds in the hands and feet and side:
Mild Mary's Son, acknowledge me;
Behold, through him, I give to thee!"

Then the soul of the leper stood up in his eyes
    And looked at Sir Launfal, and straightway he
Remembered in what a haughtier guise
    He had flung an alms to leprosie,
When he girt his young life up in gilded mail
And set forth in search of the Holy Grail.
The heart within him was ashes and dust;
He parted in twain his single crust,
He broke the ice on the streamlet's brink,
And gave the leper to eat and drink,
'Twas a mouldy crust of coarse brown bread,
    'Twas water out of a wooden bowl—
Yet with fine wheaten bread was the leper fed,
    And 'twas red wine he drank with his thirsty soul.

As Sir Launfal mused with a downcast face,
A light shone round about the place;
The leper no longer crouched at his side,
But stood before him glorified,
Shining and tall and fair and straight
As the pillar that stood by the Beautiful Gate—
Himself the Gate whereby men can
Enter the temple of God in Man.

His words were shed softer than leaves from the pine,
And they fell on Sir Launfal as snows on the brine,
Which mingle their softness and quiet in one
With the shaggy unrest they float down upon;
And the voice that was calmer than silence said,
"Lo, it is I, be not afraid!
In many climes, without avail,
Thou hast spent thy life for the Holy Grail;
Behold it is here—this cup which thou
Didst fill at the streamlet for me but now;
This crust is my body broken for thee,
This water His blood that died on the tree;
The Holy Supper is kept, indeed,
In whatso we share with another's need;
Not what we give, but what we share—
For the gift without the giver is bare;
Who gives himself with his alms feeds three—
Himself, his hungering neighbor, and me."
Sir Launfal awoke as from a swound:—
"The Grail in my castle here is found!
Hang my idle armor up on the wall,
Let it be the spider's banquet hall;
He must be fenced with stronger mail
Who would seek and find the Holy Grail."

The castle gate stands open now,
  And the wanderer is welcome to the hall
As the hangbird is to the elm-tree bough;
  No longer scowl the turrets tall,
The Summer's long siege at last is o'er;
When the first poor outcast went in at the door,
She entered with him in disguise,
And mastered the fortress by surprise;
There is no spot she loves so well on ground,
She lingers and smiles there the whole year round;
The meanest serf on Sir Launfal's land
Has hall and bower at his command;
And there's no poor man in the North Countree
But is lord of the earldom as much as he.

Whittier's *The Eternal Goodness.*

O friends! with whom my feet have trod
  The quiet aisles of prayer,
Glad witness to your zeal for God
  And love of man I bear.

I trace your lines of argument;
  Your logic, linked and strong,
I weigh as one who dreads dissent,
  And fears a doubt as wrong.

But still my human hands are weak
  To hold your iron creeds;
Against the words ye bid me speak
  My heart within me pleads.

Who fathoms the Eternal Thought?
  Who talks of scheme and plan?
The Lord is God! He needeth not
  The poor device of man.

I walk with bare, hushed feet the ground
  Ye tread, with boldness shod;
I dare not fix with mete and bound
  The love and power of God.

Ye praise His justice; even such
  His pitying love I deem:
Ye seek a king; I fain would touch
  The robe that hath no seam.

Ye see the curse which overbroods
  A world of pain and loss;
I hear our Lord's beatitudes,
  And prayer upon the cross.

More than your schoolmen teach, within
  Myself, alas! I know;
Too dark ye cannot paint the sin,
  Too small the merit show.

I bow my forehead to the dust,
  I veil mine eyes for shame,
And urge, in trembling self-distrust,
  A prayer without a claim.

I see the wrong that round me lies,
   I feel the guilt within,
I hear, with groan and travail-cries,
   The world confess its sin.

Yet, in the maddening maze of things,
   And tossed by storm and flood,
To one fixed stake my spirit clings;
   I know that God is good!

Not mine to look where cherubim
   And seraphs may not see,
But nothing can be good in Him
   Which evil is in me.

The wrong that pains my soul below
   I dare not throne above ;
I know not of His hate,—I know
   His goodness and His love.

I dimly guess, from blessings known,
   Of greater out of sight;
And, with the chastened Psalmist, own
   His judgments too are right.

I long for household voices gone,
   For vanished smiles I long;
But God hath led my dear ones on,
   And He can do no wrong.

I know not what the future hath
   Of marvel or surprise,
Assured alone that life and death
   His mercy underlies.

And, if my heart and flesh are weak
   To bear an untried pain,
The bruised reed He will not break,
   But strengthen and sustain.

No offering of my own I have,
   Nor works my faith to prove ;
I can but give the gifts He gave,
   And plead His love for love.

And so, beside the Silent Sea,
    I wait the muffled oar;
. No harm from Him can come to me
    On ocean or on shore.

I know not where His islands lift
    Their fronded palms in air;
I only know I cannot drift
    Beyond His love and care.

O brothers! if my faith is vain,
    If hopes like these betray,
Pray for me that my feet may gain
    The sure and safer way.

And Thou, O Lord, by whom are seen
    Thy creatures as they be,
Forgive me if too close I lean
    My human heart on Thee!

SCHEME FOR REVIEW.

INDEX,
BIOGRAPHICAL AND TOPICAL.

www.ingramcontent.com/pod-product-compliance
Lightning Source LLC
Chambersburg PA
CBHW052338110726
47901CB00005B/1277